Brighton's Artists 2014

Created by Alison & Torben Krog

Brighton's Artists 2014

First edition printed 2014 in the United Kingdom.

A catalogue record for this book is available from the British Library.

ISBN 978-0-9928543-0-0

Published by Kemp Street Productions. For more copies of this book, please email: info@artymagazines.com
Tel: 01273 670426

Designed and set by Kemp Street Productions.
www.artymagazines.com
Printed in Great Britain.

Acknowledgements

With thanks to all of the wonderful artists, creators and makers in and around the city of Brighton & Hove who have supported every Arty venture with unerring faith and passion. We are privileged to know you.

Special gratitude to Dominic Vacher at Four Corners Print for his advice and expertise.

Thanks also to Sarah Dyson for her eagle-eyed proof reading and the re-touching skills of Dan Murrell. We really appreciate your input.

And thanks is too small a word for everything Fay and Tom Thomas have done for us since the launch of the first *Brighton's Arty Magazine*.

Cover artwork by Harriet Butler (page 106).

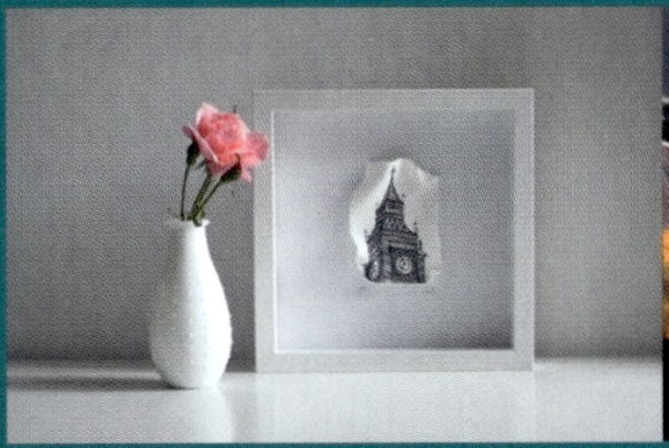
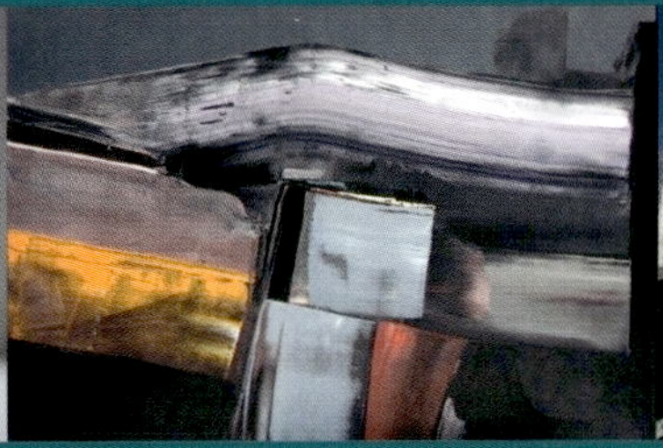
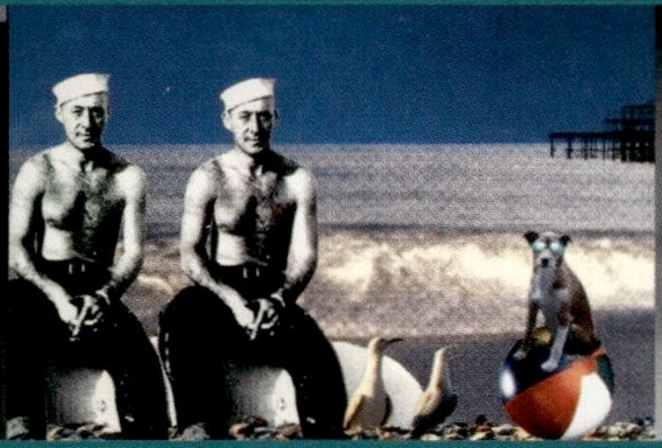
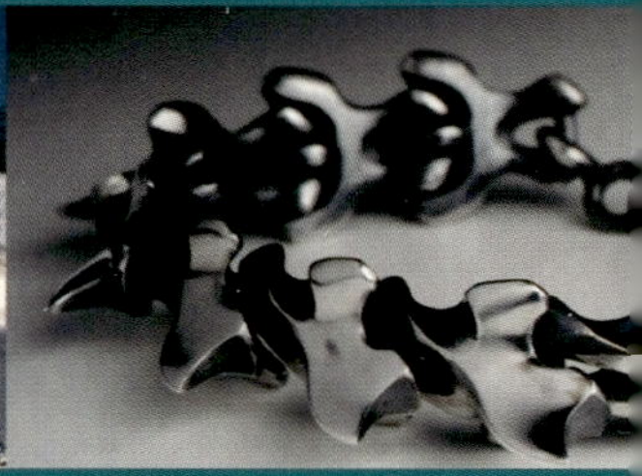
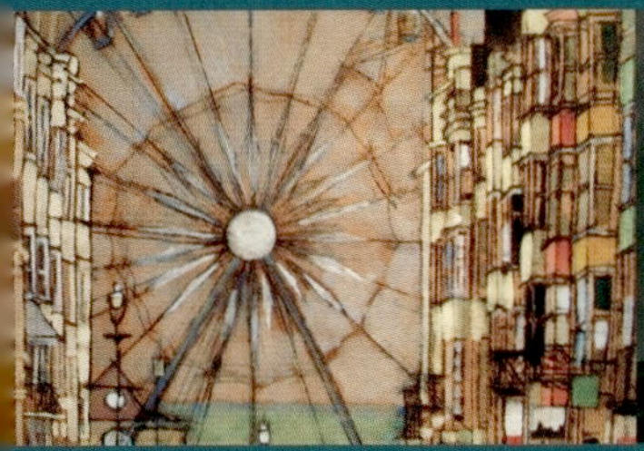
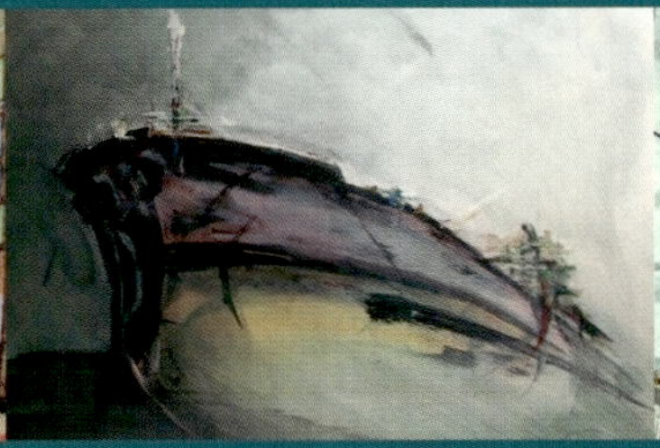
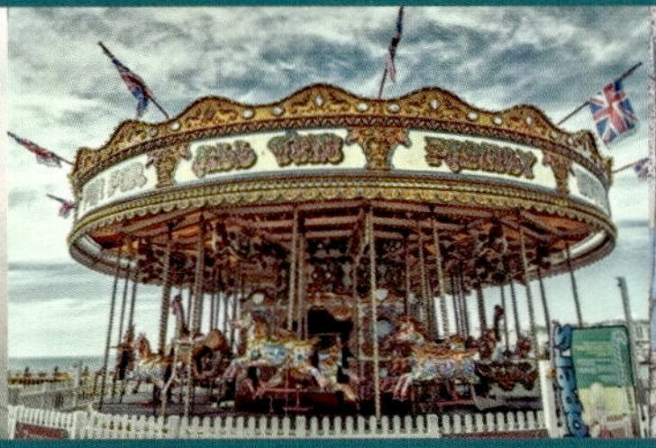
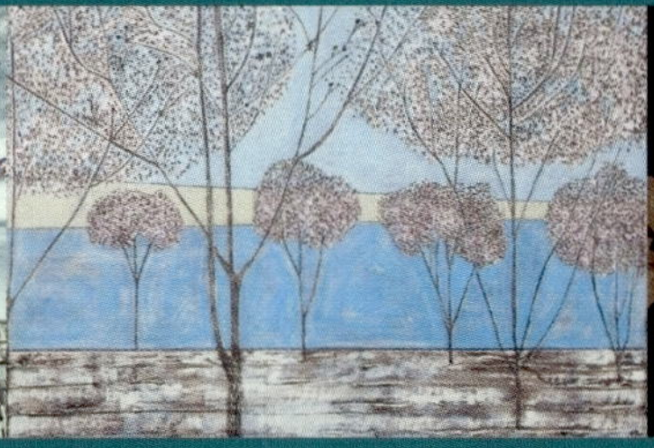
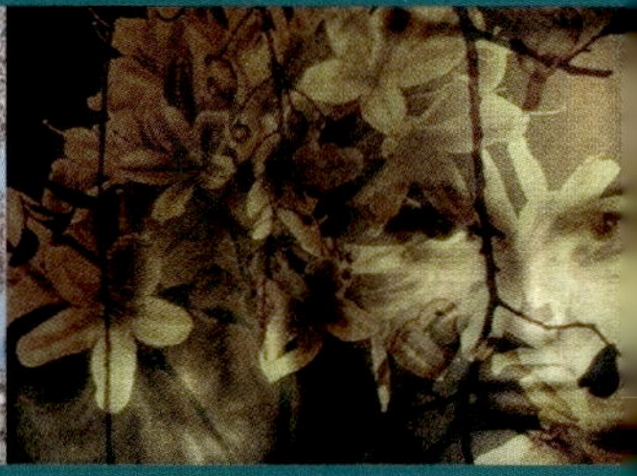

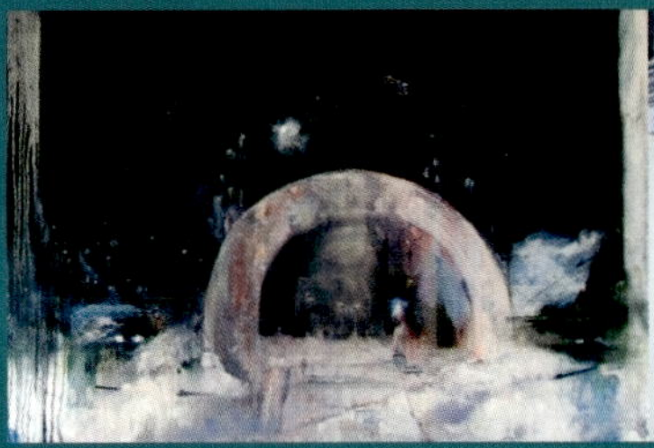
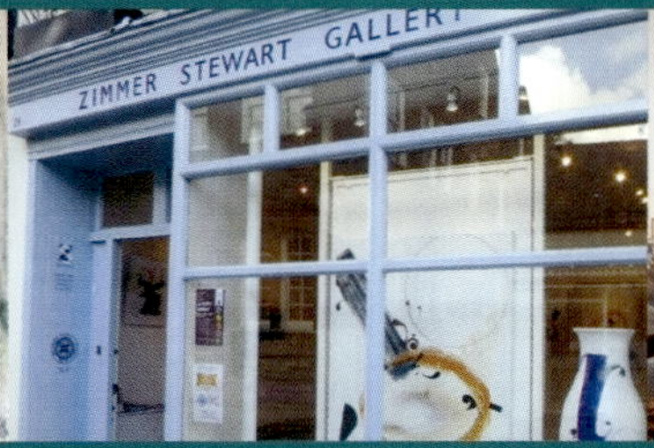

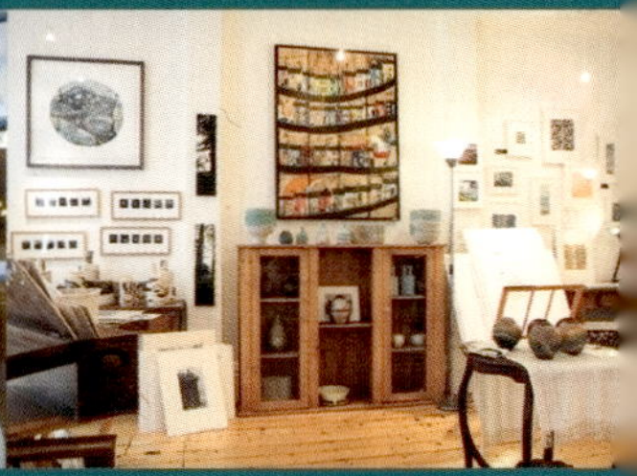

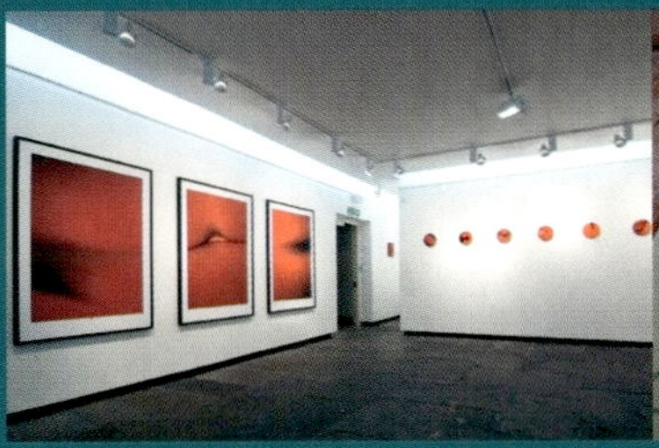
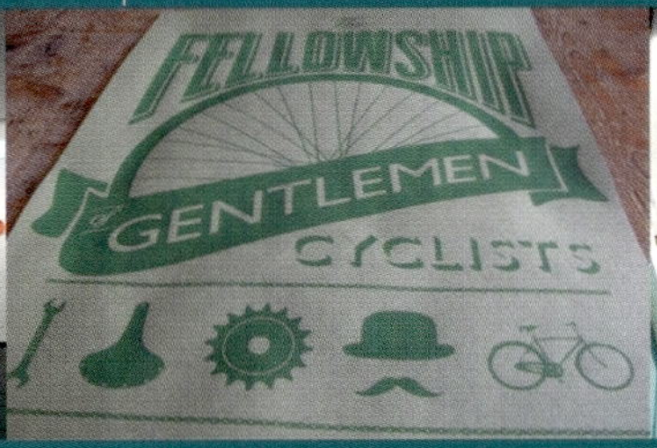

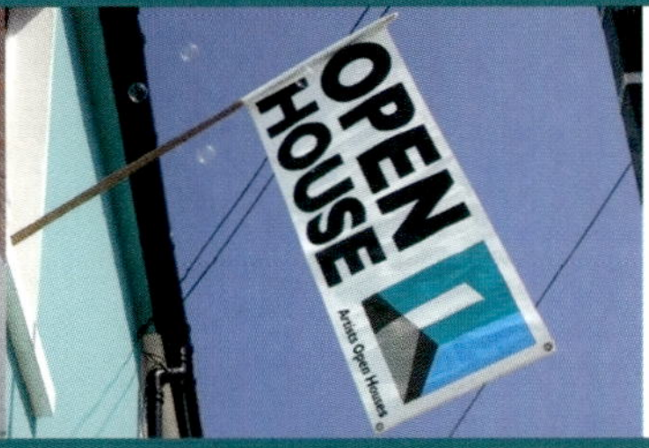

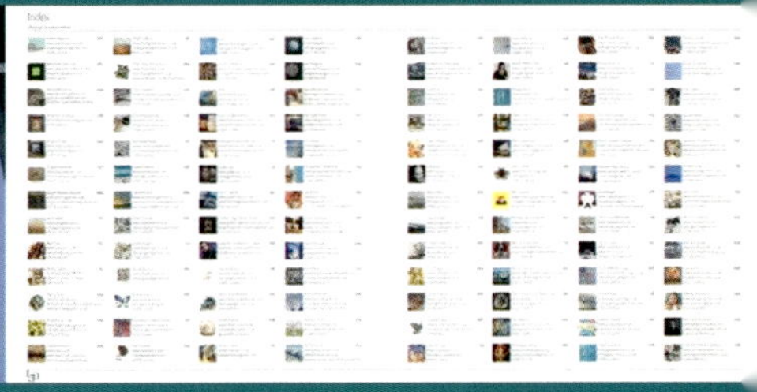

Full contact details of all the people, places and events featured in Brighton's Artists 2014 can be found in the index section at the back of the book.

Artists

We think the cover says it all. This is a book you will return to time and time again – and always find something new to fall in love with – due to Brighton's amazing creative talent.

Luella Martin

Sheila Marlborough

Artist

Clockwise from top left:
Red Landscape;
Yellow Patch; Serenade

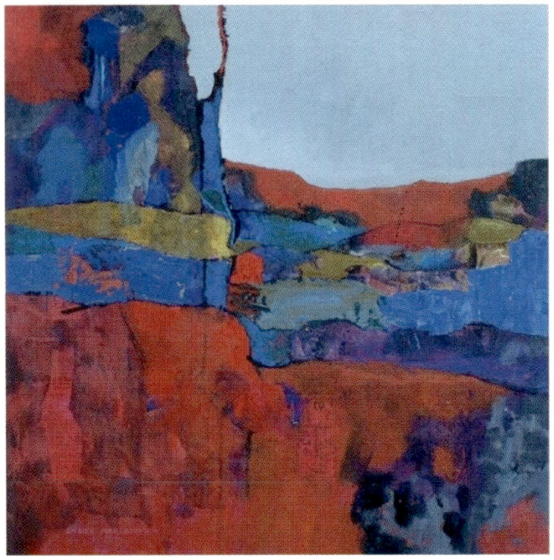

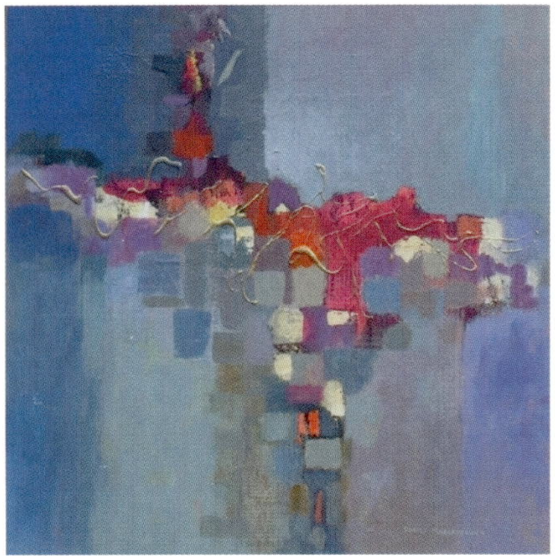

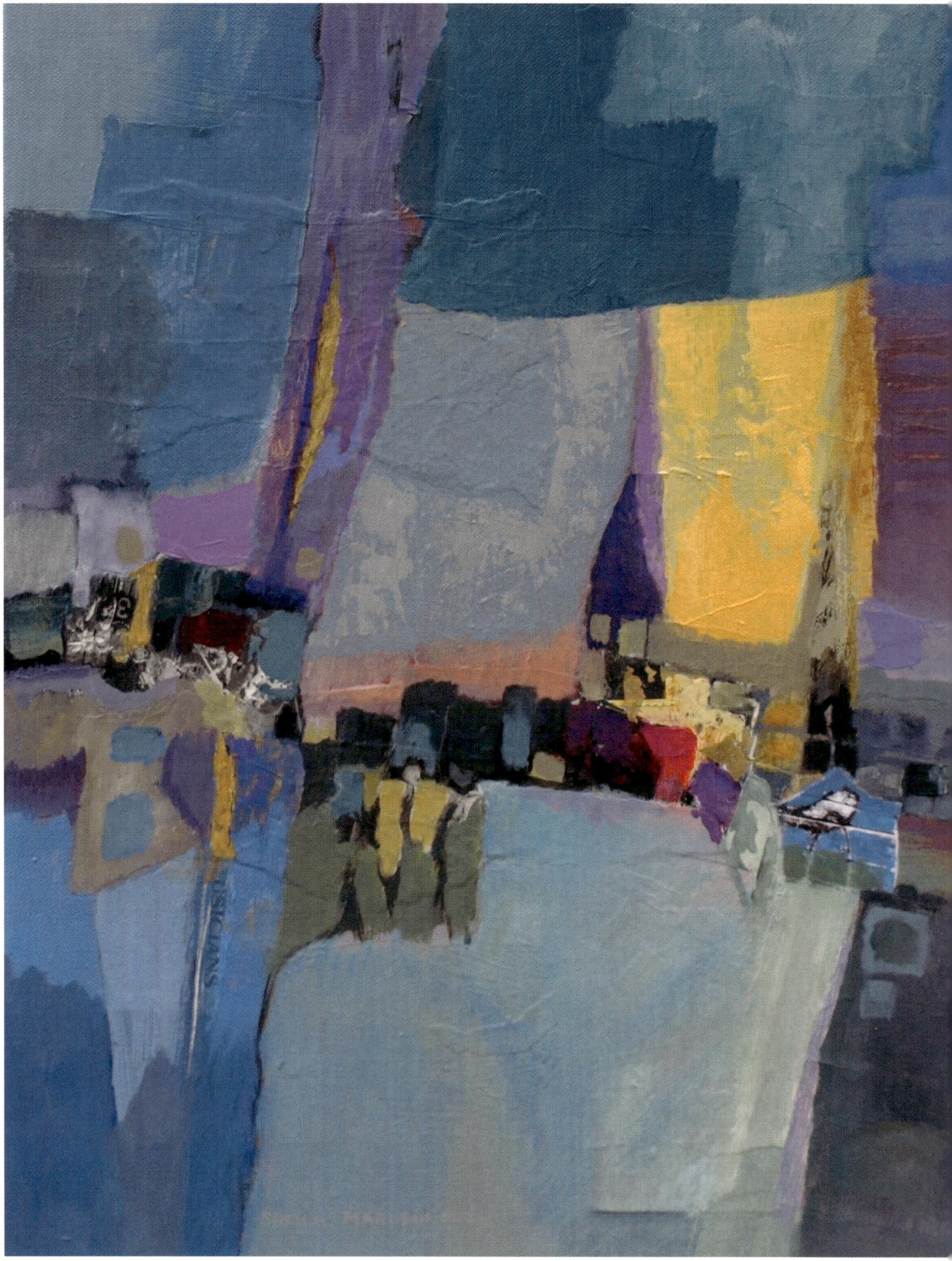

Sheila was born in Sussex and attended courses at Brighton Polytechnic and St Ives School of Painting from 1978-1985. Her work was shown for several years by the RI at the Mall Galleries in London, and in 2002 Sheila won the RWS Open Exhibition Award at the Bankside Gallery. During this time she taught art to adult students for 15 years and exhibited her work throughout Sussex and in St Ives.

In 2005 Sheila was elected President of the Sussex Watercolour Society, and from 2005-2011 was a member of the artist-led Chalk Gallery in Lewes. She has exhibited in the Brighton Open Houses and for the past four years at the Brighton Art Fair.

In March 2012 Sheila and her husband Peter had a joint exhibition in Lewes, and they will be showing at the Hop Gallery again in August 2014, during the Lewes Artwave.

Sheila paints in acrylic or mixed media, often with collage, on deep canvas. She says of her work:

"My aim is to simplify shapes and enhance the colour, either from landscape and still life, or as pure abstraction when listening to music. The colour and movement convey the mood."

Clockwise from top left:
Pet portrait commission; Oxford Rooftops;
Big Ben; Bandstand and West Pier

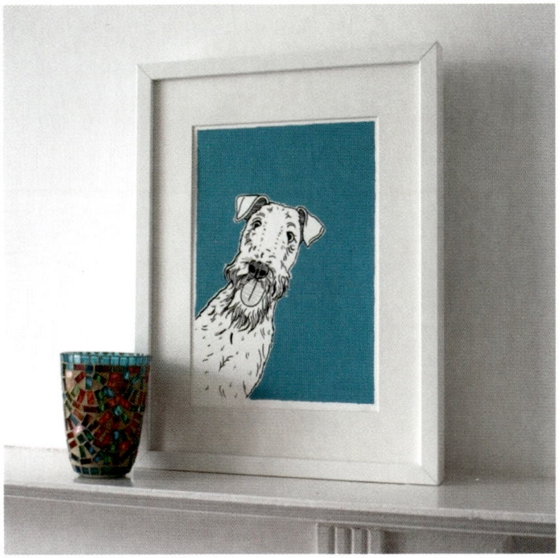

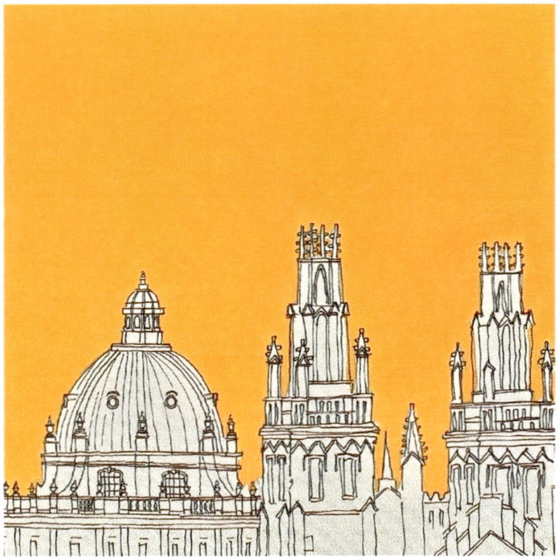

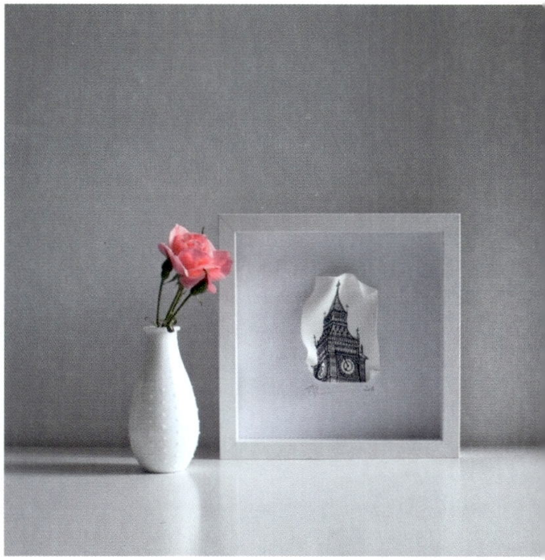

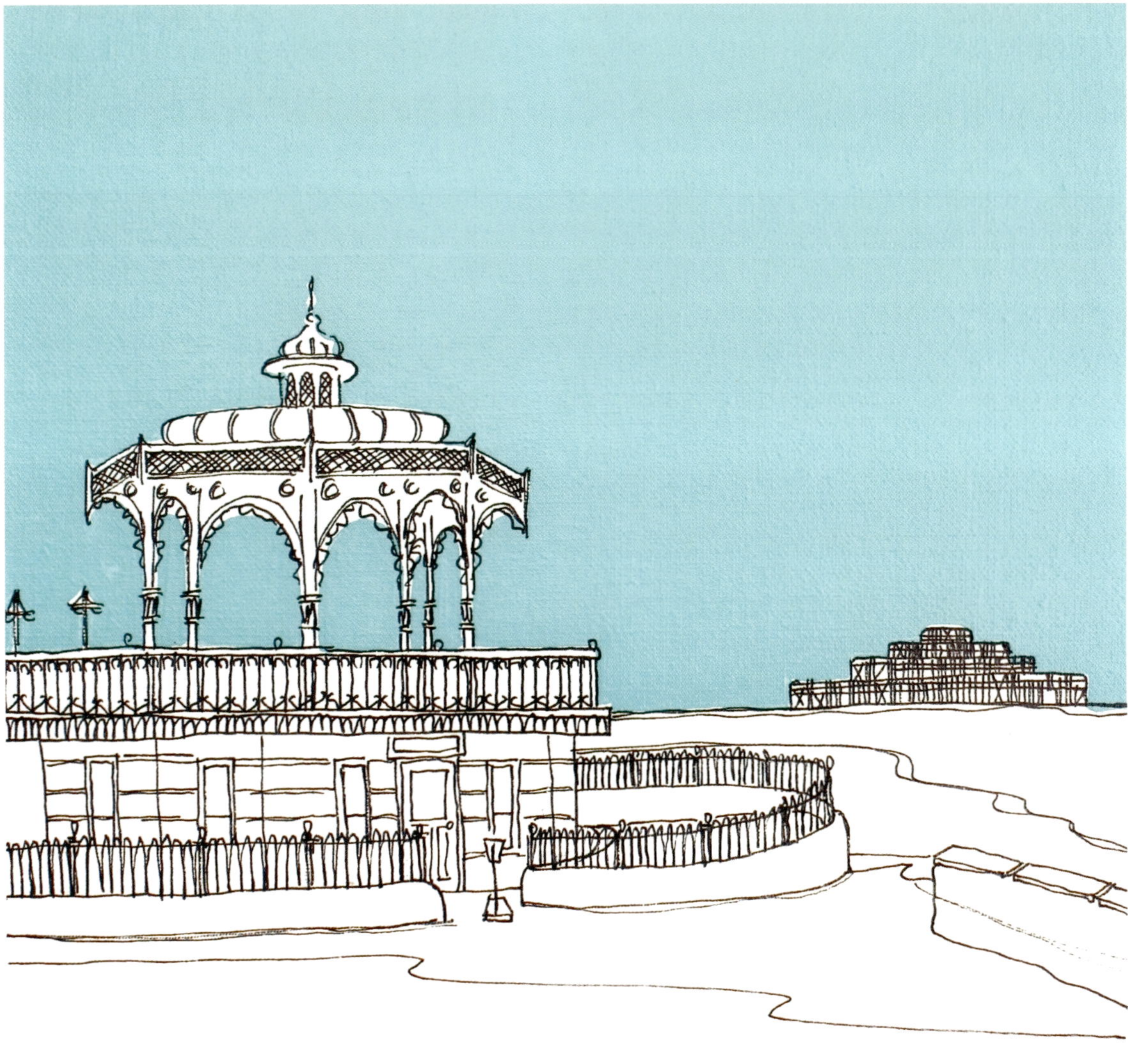

Artist and illustrator Adam Regester studied for an MA at Central Saint Martins College before launching his multifaceted career in art and design.

In the 1980s he started creating an illustrative style based on breaking down complex images into simple and somewhat naive sketchwork with bold block colour accents. This has developed into a style that is both popular and commercial, which translates well not just as original art but also into print.

Adam's brand is inspired by local and iconic architecture, people, animals and objects from everyday life. It includes original canvas art, prints, portraits, homewares, stationery and gifts.

Adam's original artwork and merchandise can be found at various events and on the following websites: notonthehighstreet.com; etsy.com; folksy.com; and redbubble.com.

Mark Charlton

Artist

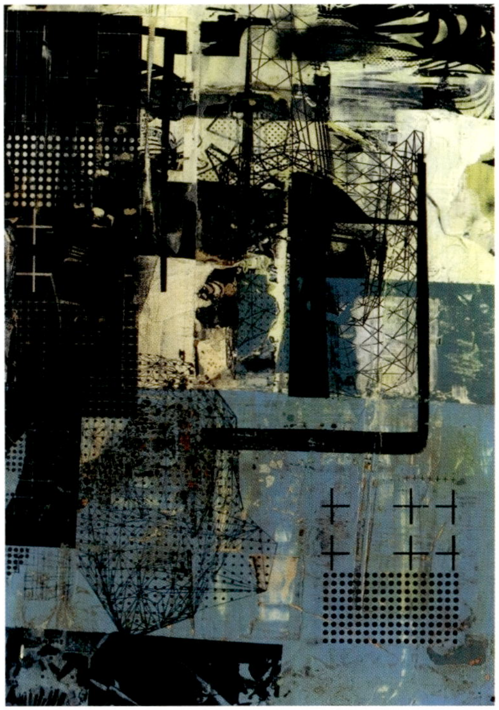

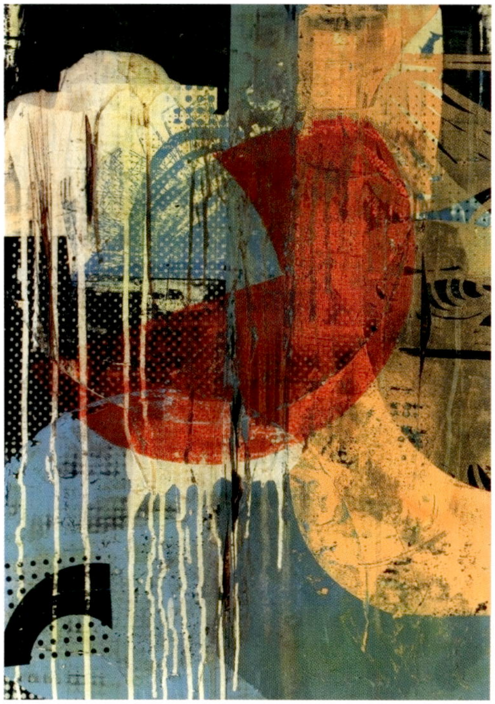

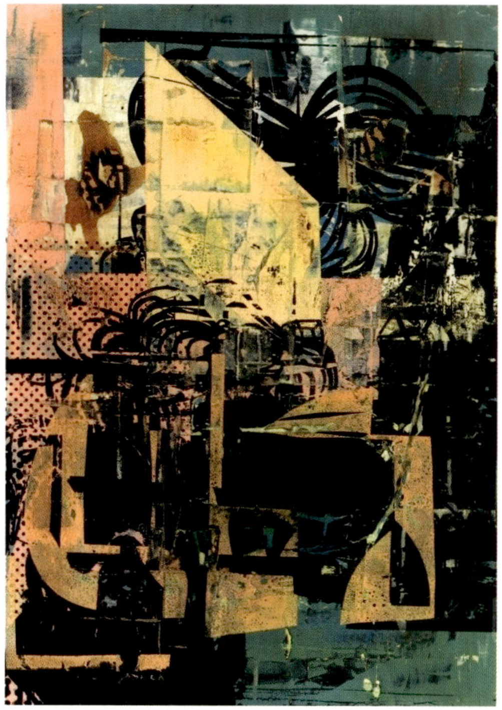

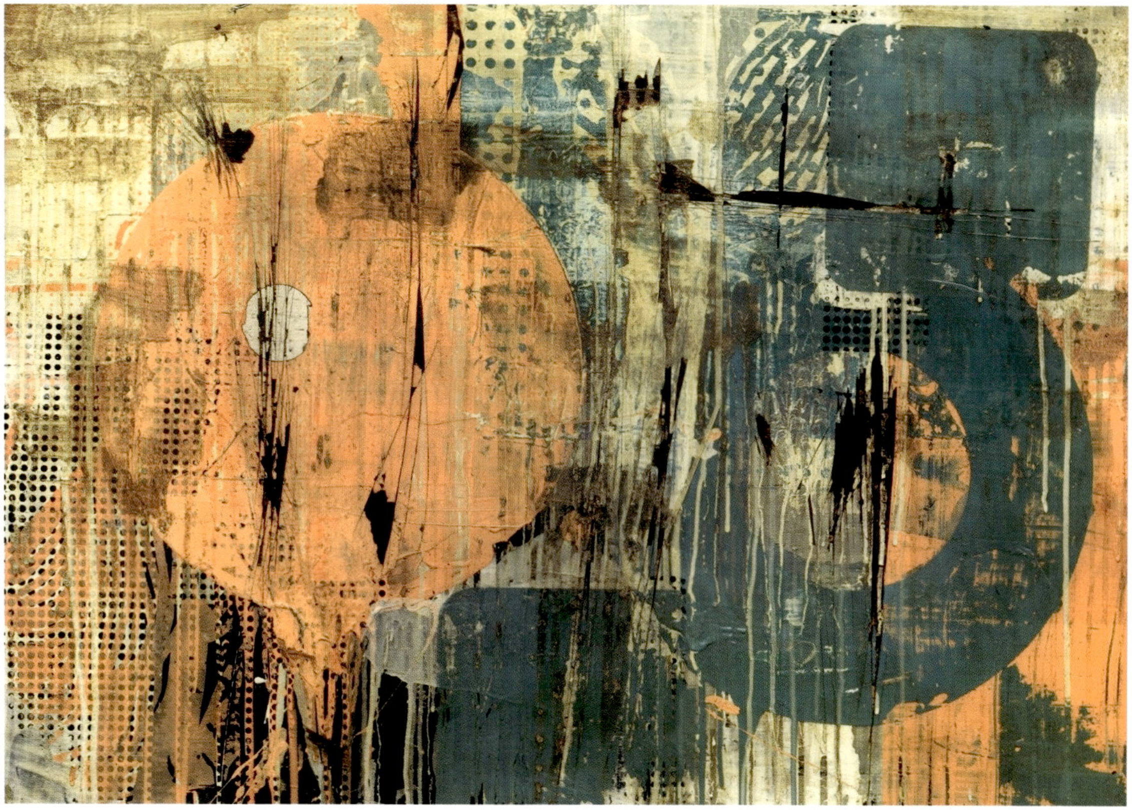

Mark Charlton was born in Margate in 1976. He studied at the North East Wales Institute of Art and Design, gaining a BA Hons in Animation Design in 2001. After spending many productive years working as a freelance animator and motion designer primarily in the music industry, he has devoted his time to developing his own style in 2D mixed media work.

Mark's work is an abstract combination of screenprint, painting and collage technique, which allows the exploration of surface texture and graphical composition. He takes inspiration from science fiction novellas from the 1950s and 1960s, in which he embraces colour and shape and amalgamates with a contemporary gritty urban feel.

Mark's work is energetic and spontaneous, using multiple layers that are built up over a substantial period of time until the final composition is realised and refined. He finds a unique excitement in this layered approach, which sees screenprint forced to react with painted and collaged surfaces. Multiple techniques are used to decay and age the surface, which culminates in a final piece that has a striking first impression and a gentle beauty within its close-up detail.

Mark currently resides in Shoreham-By-Sea and works in his Hove studio.

This page: Space Medicine
Opposite page (clockwise from top left): Automated Engineers; The Deaths of Ben Baxter; Pluribus Unicorn; Hydrogen Song

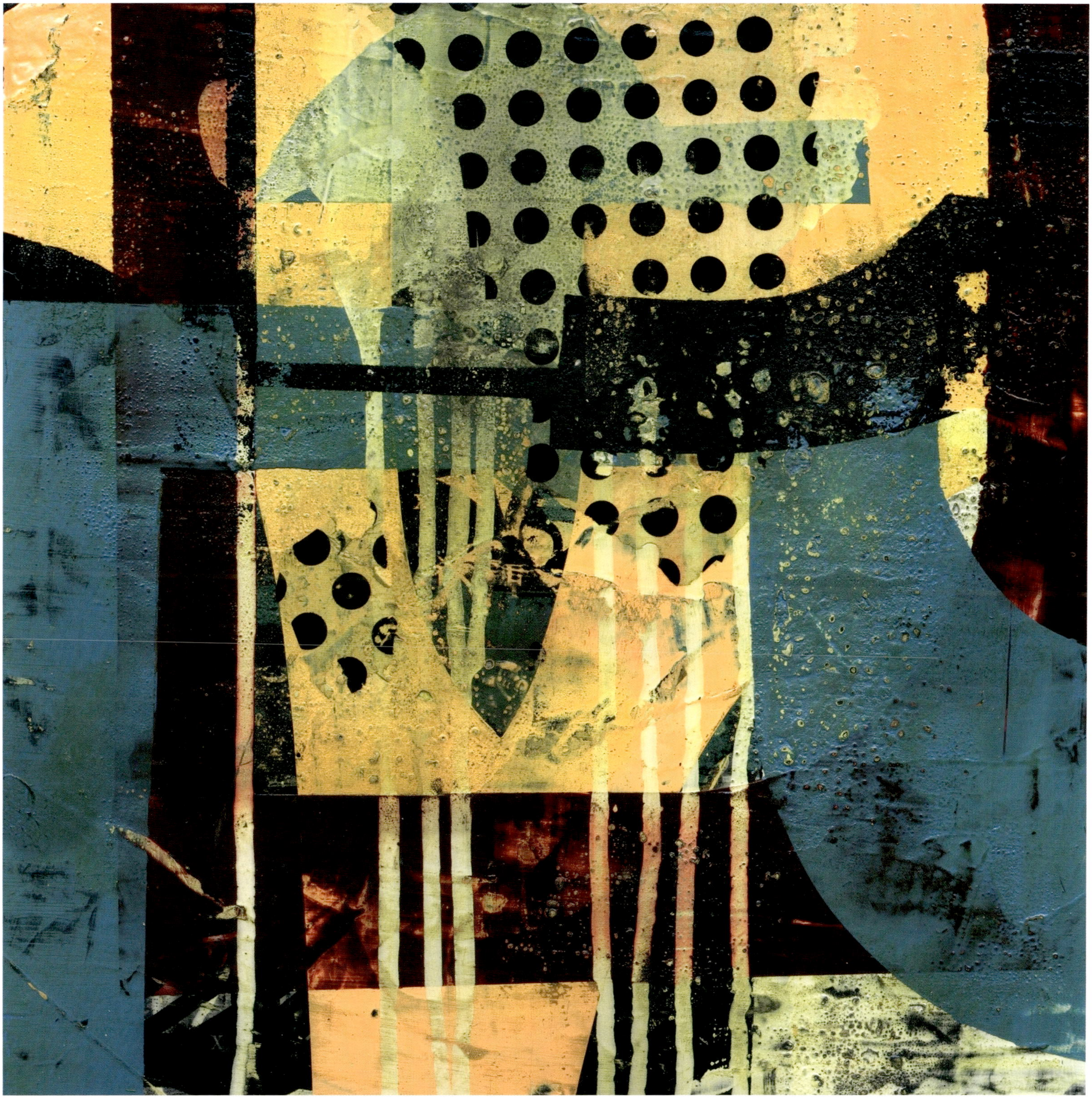

Jo Riddell

Artist

Clockwise from top left:
Silo 3; Small Barn;
Field; Silo 2

Jo Riddell's work is an examination of overlooked and forgotten things. She is drawn to structures found in corners of farmyards and objects in the verges of fields: dead birds, abandoned nests, old barns and corn silos...

As a printmaker, Jo is interested in etchings and woodcuts as an extension of the act of drawing.

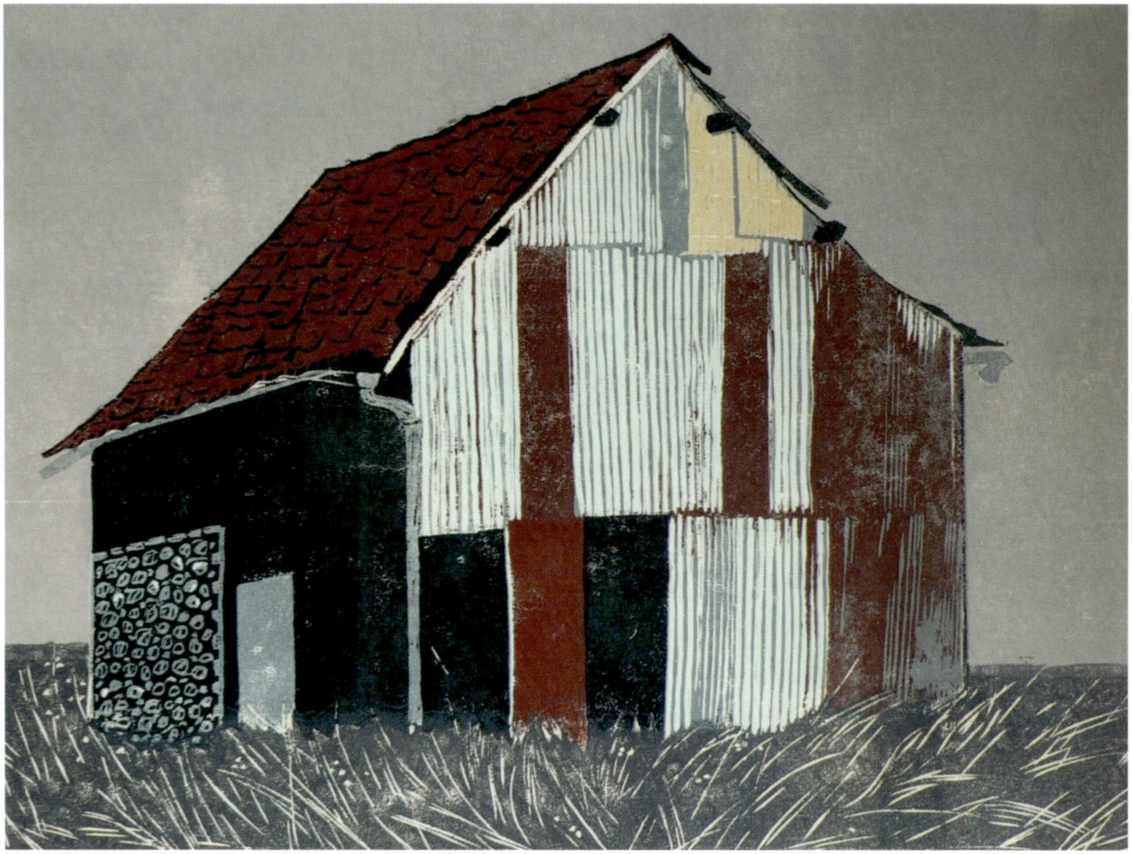

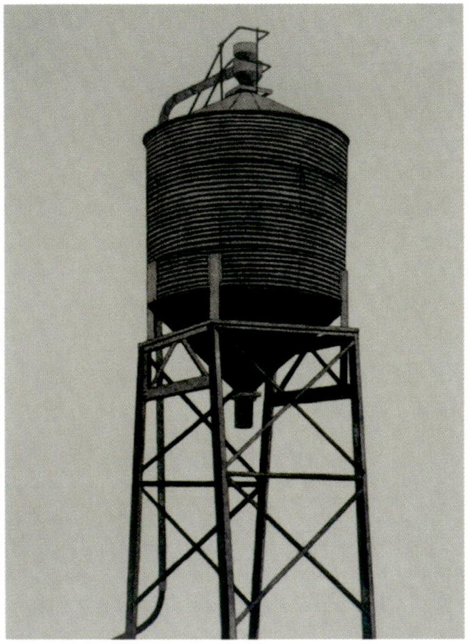

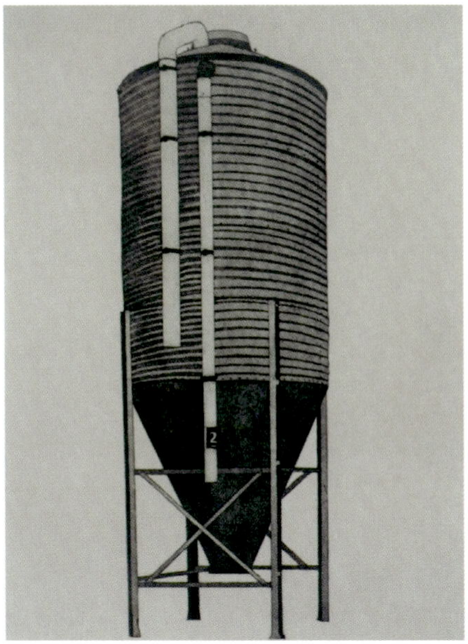

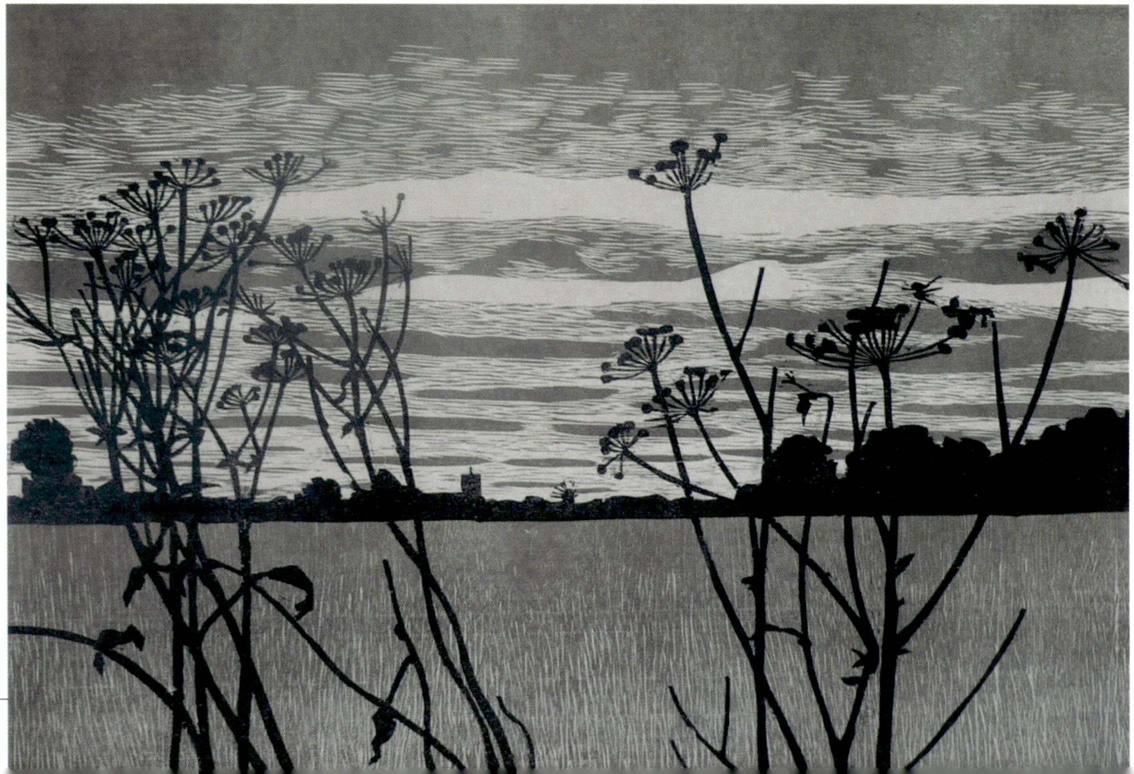

Clockwise from left: The Quiet of the Red, Forest Mist; Profile

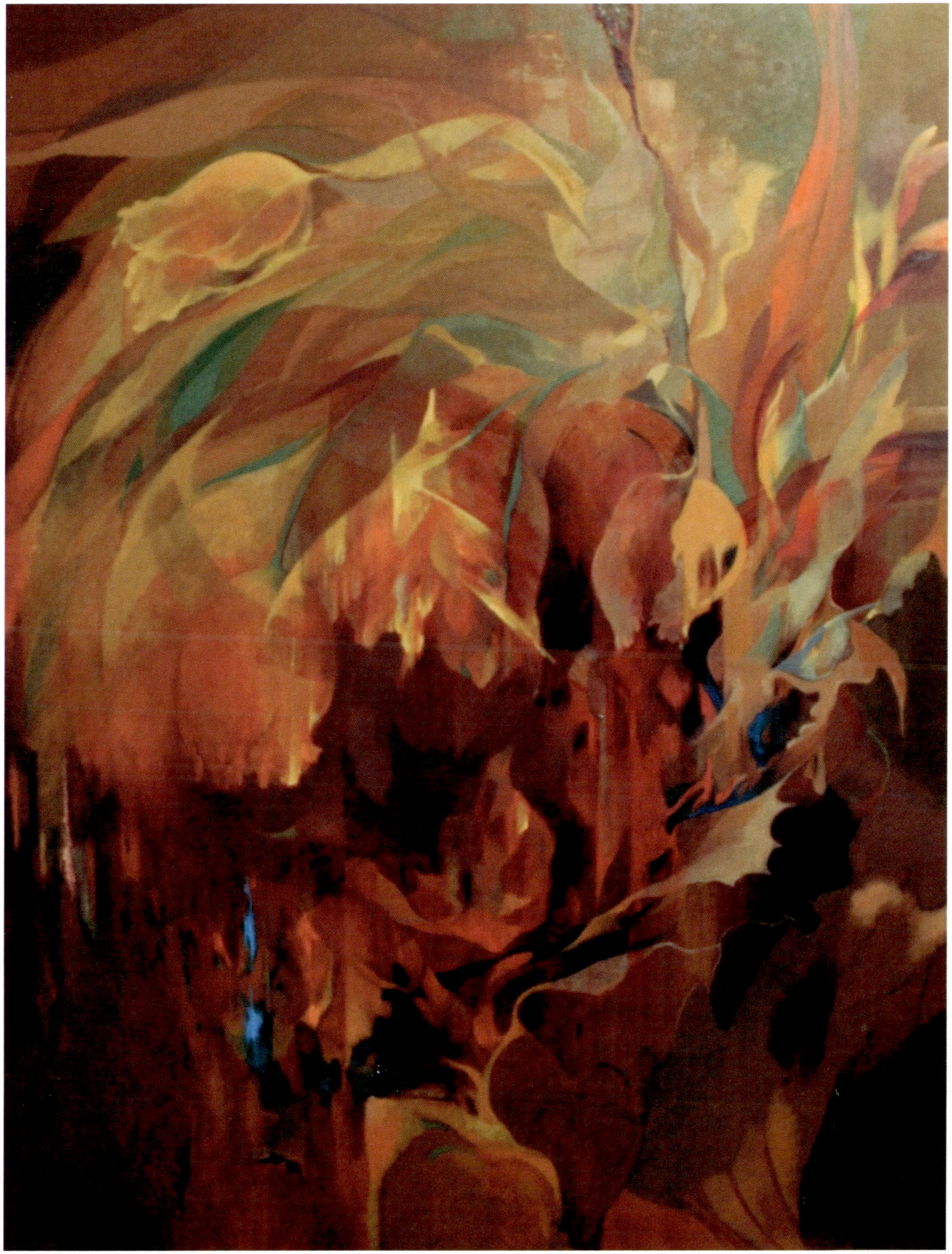

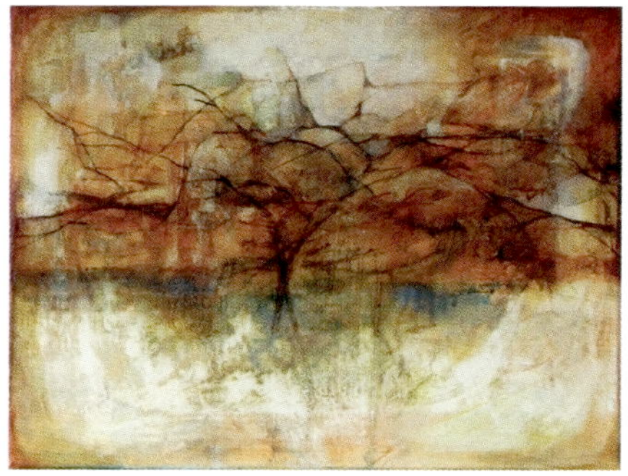

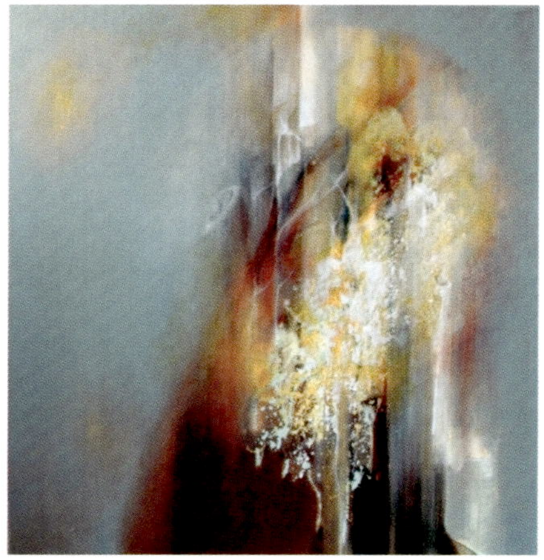

Japanese artist Hiroko Lewis is based in Brighton, where she creates semi-abstract works in oil that draw from and build upon her classical training in tempera. Starting with the hint of something remembered or observed, often derived from nature, her work travels to expand these fragments into a new world using a process of repeated construction, destruction, and reconstruction, in search of another sensory reality.

After graduating with a degree in Fine Art from Kanazawa College of Art, Hiroko pursued a career as an artist and visual designer in Japan. Since moving to Brighton in 2011, she has focused on fine art, aiming to express and adapt to her new-found environment. She will be participating in the Brighton Artists Open Houses Festival in May 2014 at the Chevalier House in Stanmer Park Road near Fiveways.

Rob Ollerenshaw

Artist

Clockwise from top left: Fresh Winds; Hove Beach at Sunset; Devil's Dyke in Winter

The city of Brighton and Hove, and the Sussex shoreline and countryside, provides endless inspiration for local artist Rob Ollerenshaw. Rob uses a range of media including watercolour, gouache, pastel, inks and wax in his works on paper. His paintings are a personal impression of a particular place and time – the fluctuation of light and shadow and the movement of people coming and going across a scene.

Rob is fascinated by changing scenes. As afternoon moves toward evening, or as evening twilight moves toward sunset, he tries to capture the light effects. In this way his paintings are a synthesis of light, colour and texture. A fine art graduate, Rob regularly exhibits in Brighton's Artists Open Houses. He also paints the landscape of Brittany in Northern France and has exhibited in the region several times.

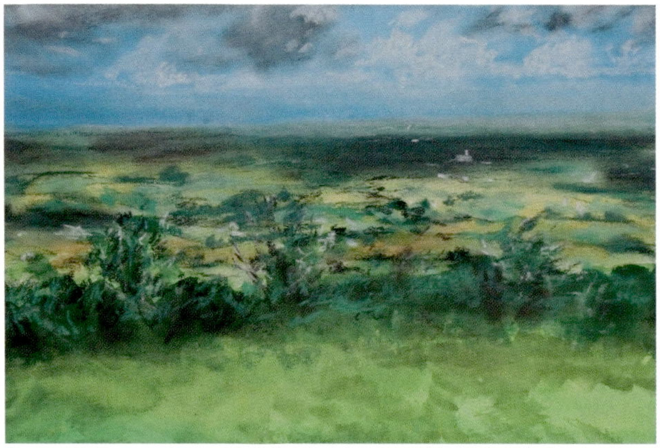

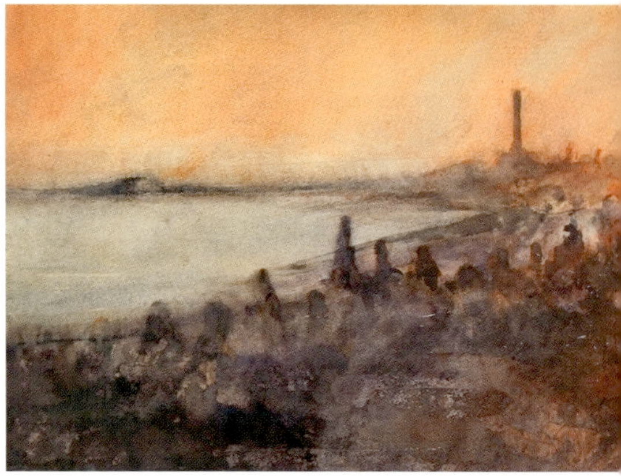

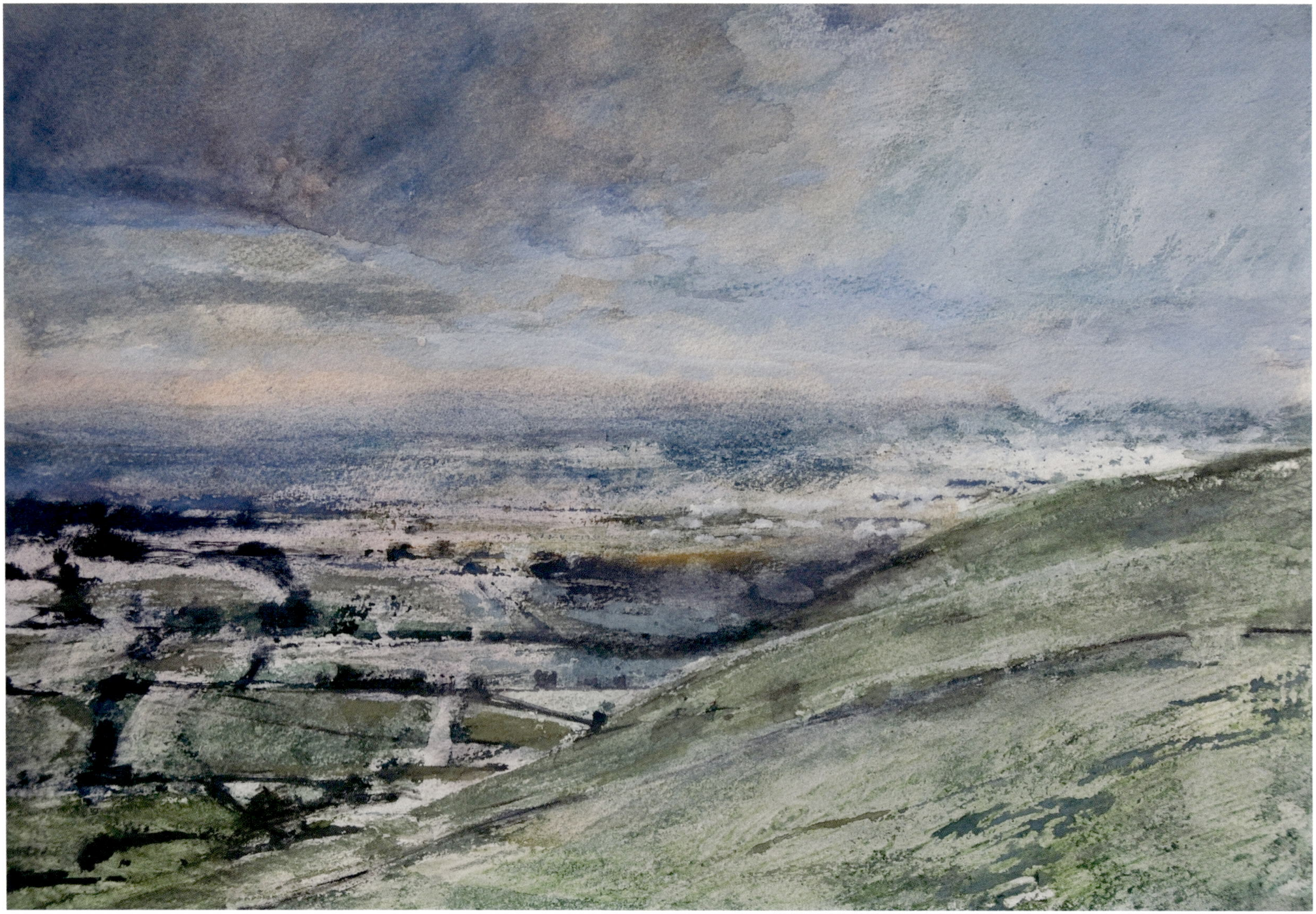

Jacqueline Hammond

Artist

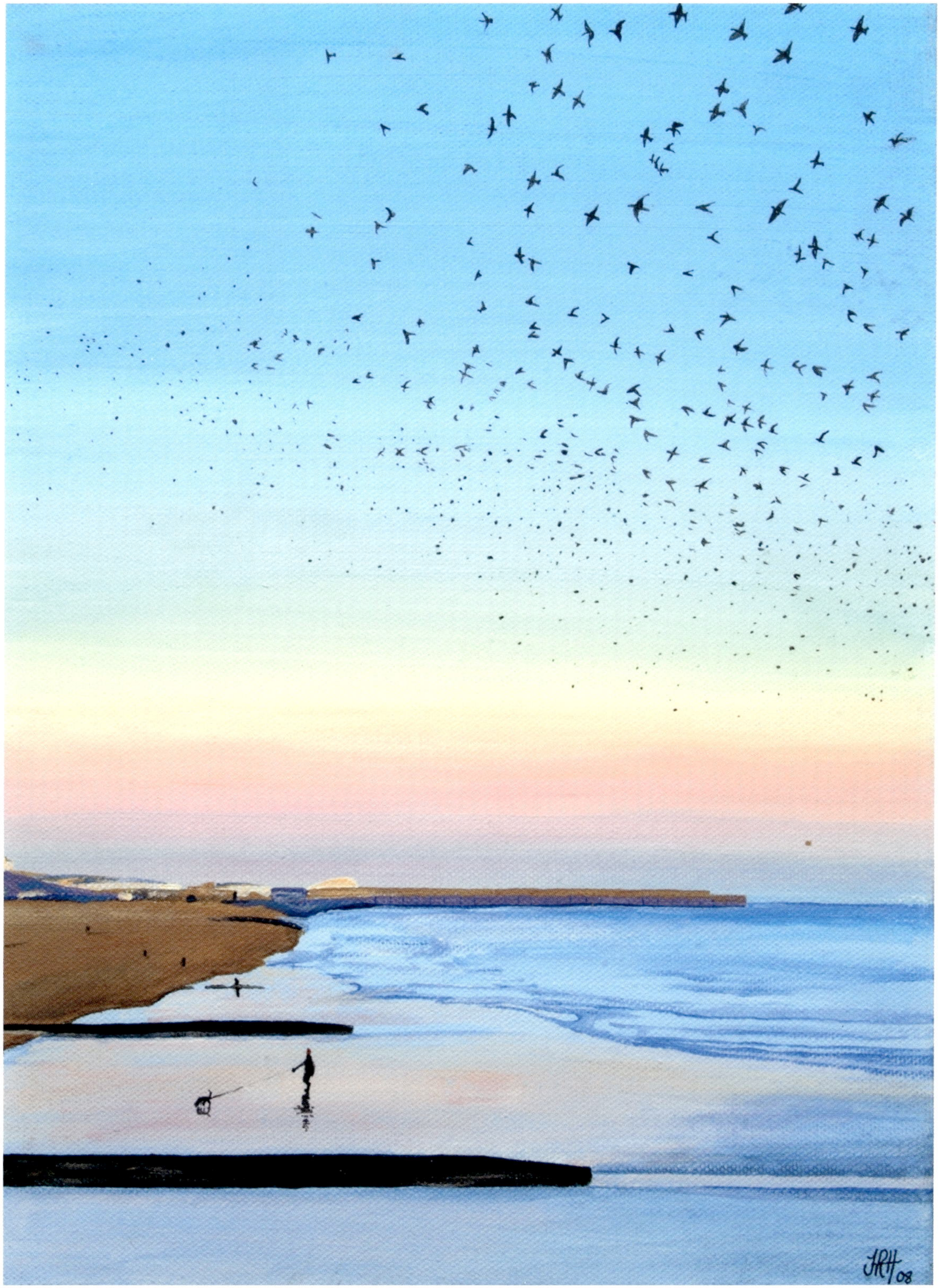

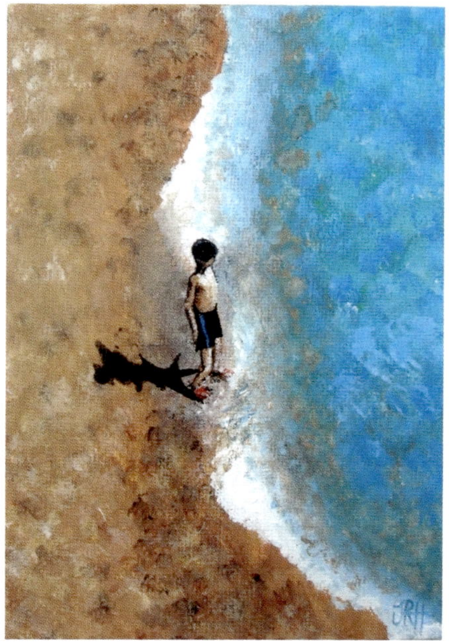

Contemporary British artist Jacqueline Hammond is renowned for producing strong, punchy images that are rich in texture and colour. A prolific painter and multidisciplinary artist, she exhibits widely and is commissioned by individual clients, collectors and high-profile brands. Immediate inspiration comes from direct observation: subject matter is plucked from the world encountered every day. Some ideas evolve, others are reactionary. More thought-provoking themes explore today's society, the media and cultural theory.

Whether inspired by the street or the sea, Jacqueline's work has a consistently striking edge. Her natural disposition is to let the paint dictate the creative process, trusting the medium and her mind's eye to translate the vision. Jacqueline's fresh way of depicting Brighton is popular with residents and visitors alike.

Jacqueline is also well known for her SmartDeco range of contemporary art-inspired home and giftware. You can find her work at her studio on the seafront at JAG Gallery, 283a Madeira Drive, Brighton BN2 1PT.

Jill Tattersall

Artist

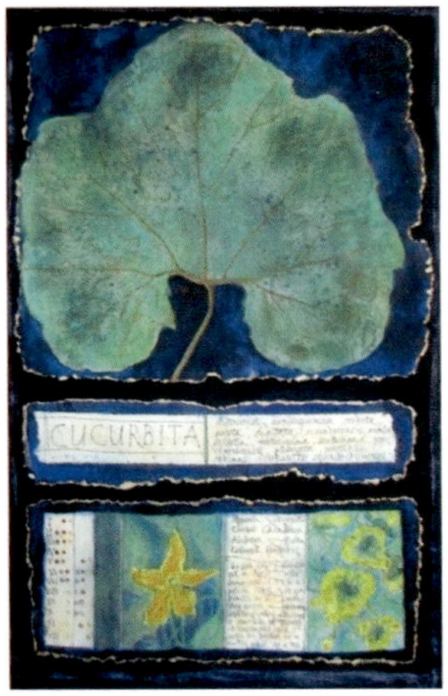

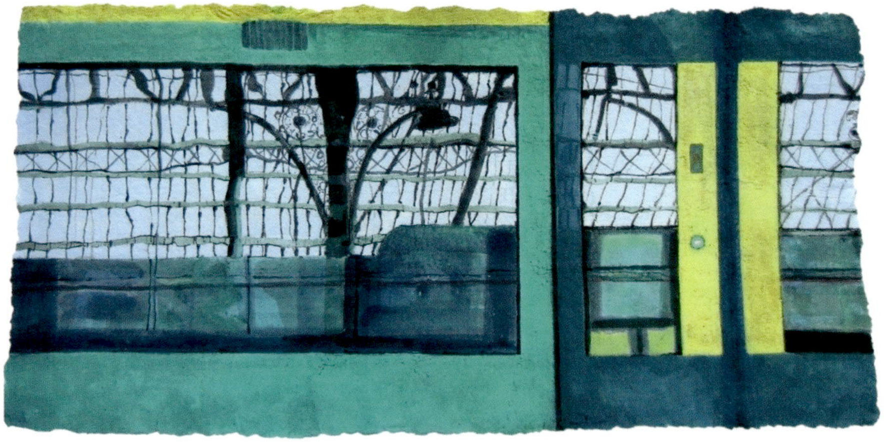

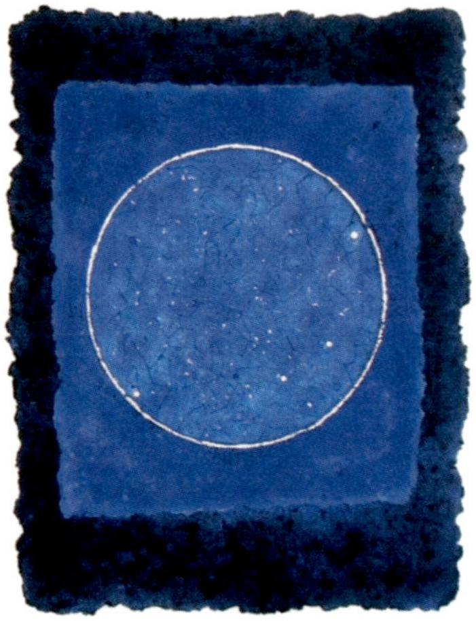

Colour is vital to artist Jill Tattersall. She uses paints, inks, dyes and pigments to build up intense and glowing, but subtle, colours. The process is all a bit risky and time-consuming, involving trial and error, experiment, and a lot of thought and planning. One of Jill's solo shows was called 'Chance or Design?' and that just about sums up her approach.

Jill often uses her own cotton paper to paint on, which offers a seductive, unpredictable surface and can be cast and manipulated. She is constantly experimenting with materials and techniques. Each new piece represents a challenge: a puzzle to solve. Throwaway or reclaimed elements combine with costly ones such as pure pigments and gold and silver leaf. As long as it doesn't rot, fade or rub off, the artist will consider it; she wants people to enjoy the playful, experimental aspect of her work as well as the underlying 'story'.

Jill once taught medieval literature, and her research on maps and travel in early French texts led to a fascination with the ways people have seen and depicted the physical world in different times and cultures. This interest underpins her art. She also loves text as a form of pattern-making as well as a way of conveying meaning.

Jill believes pattern creation and recognition are fundamental to art and music; the rhythms and forces of nature leave traces and create shapes in the physical world. There is a sense of continuity and purpose in knowing that her own urge to mimic them and weave them back into the environment has been felt by people since earliest times. Patterns are everywhere: coastlines, weather systems and blood vessels; maps, mazes and manuscripts; plants, trees and gardens.

Jill has shown work all over the UK with many solo exhibitions in private and public galleries, and done commissions, talks and workshops. She now runs The Wolf at the Door in Hove (Artists Open Studio) and has taken part in the Brighton Arts and Science Festivals.

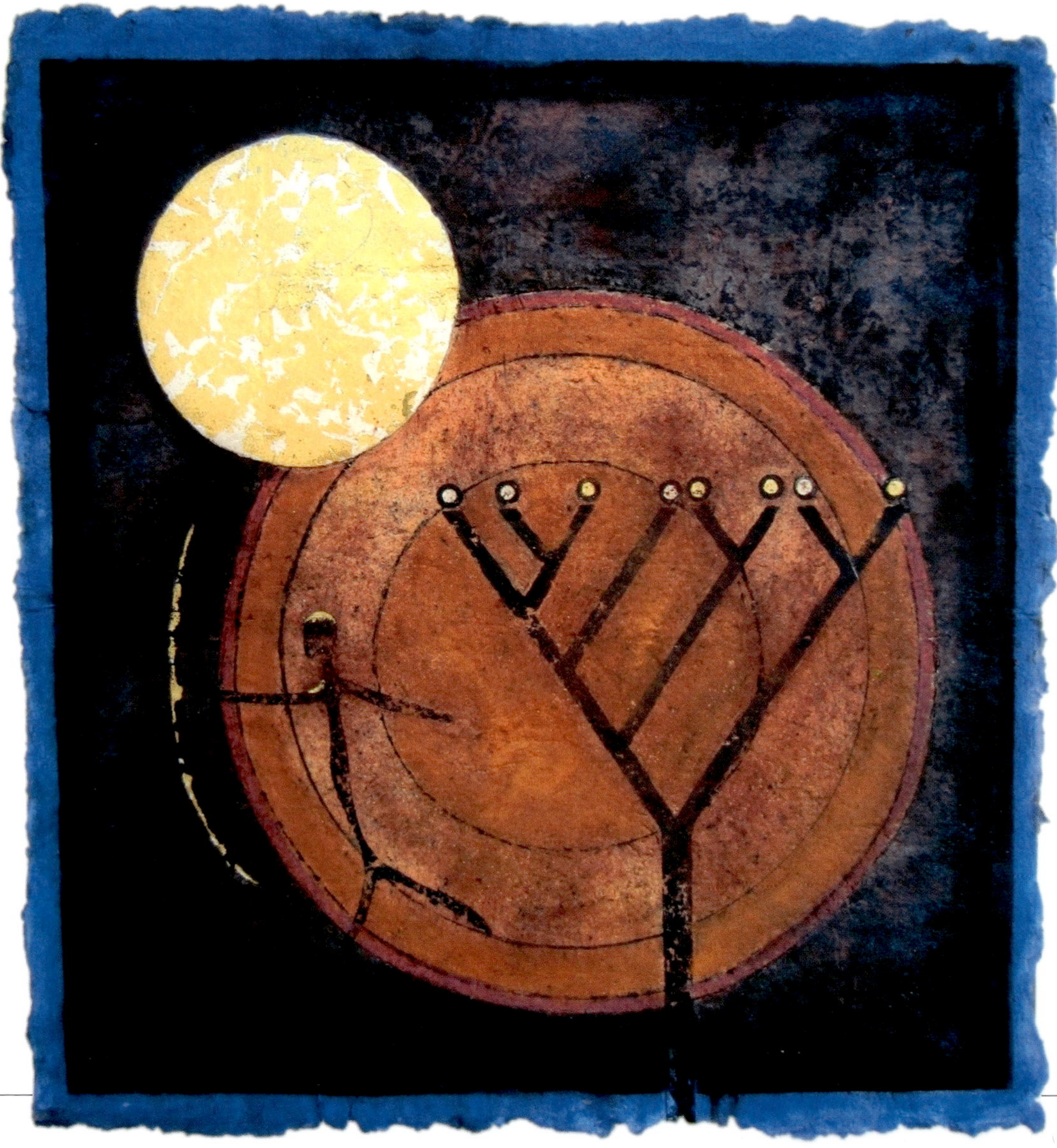

This page: Near 7 Sisters
Opposite page: (clockwise from top left) Giant Squash; Leaving Brighton; Summer Solstice; Who Am I

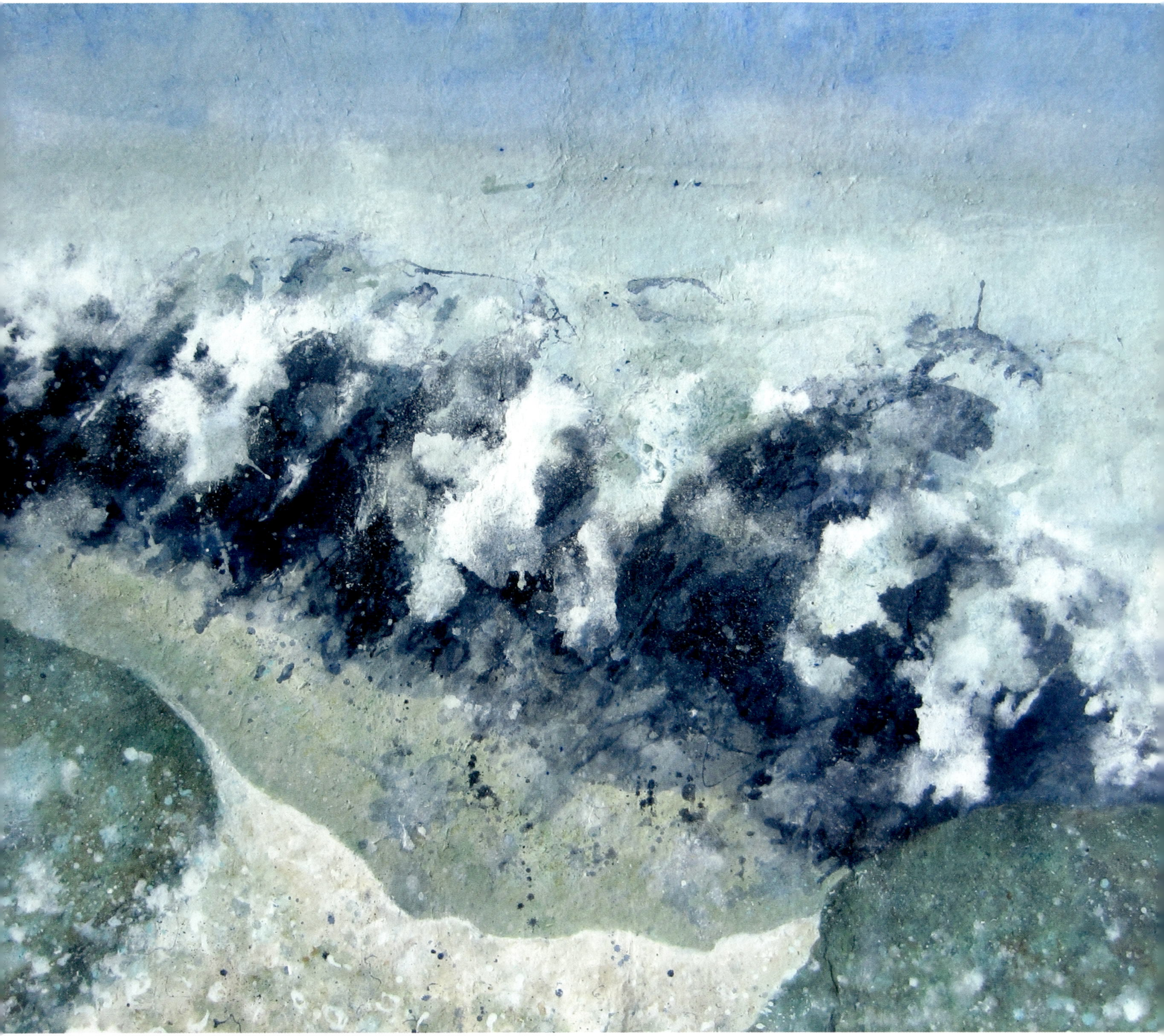

Jane Sampson

Artist & Printmaker

Clockwise from top left: Golden Girl; Blue Girl; Elf

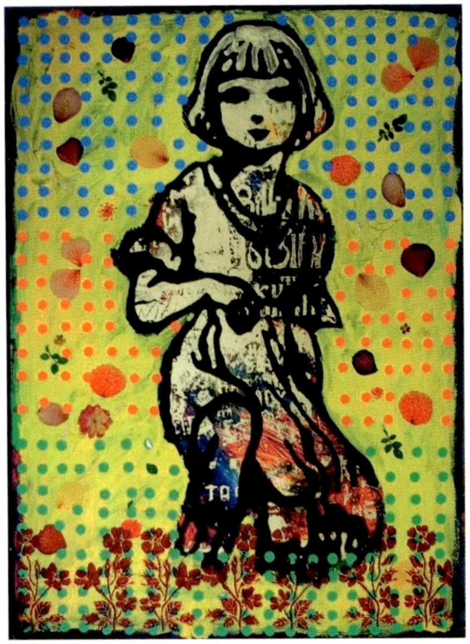

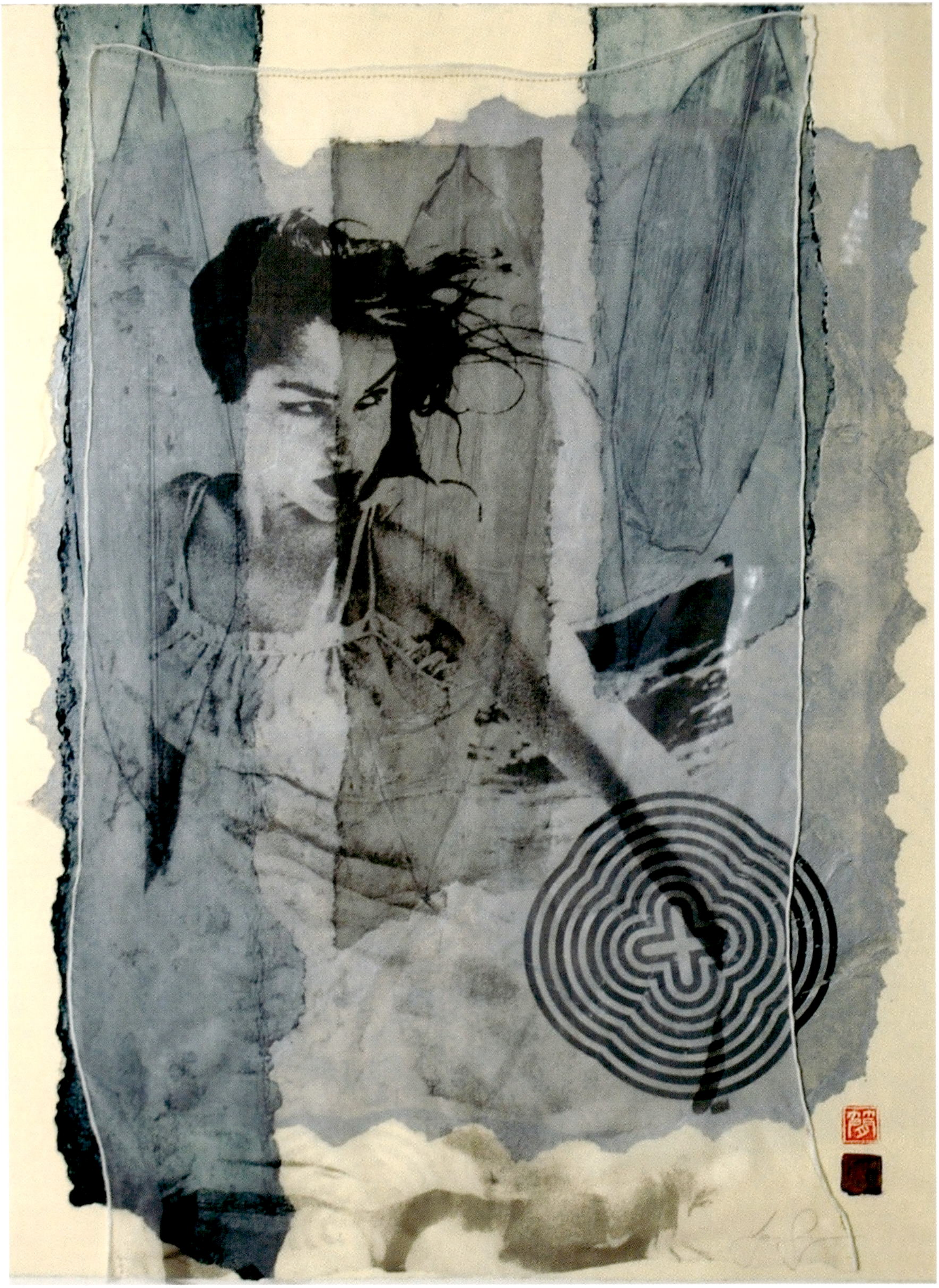

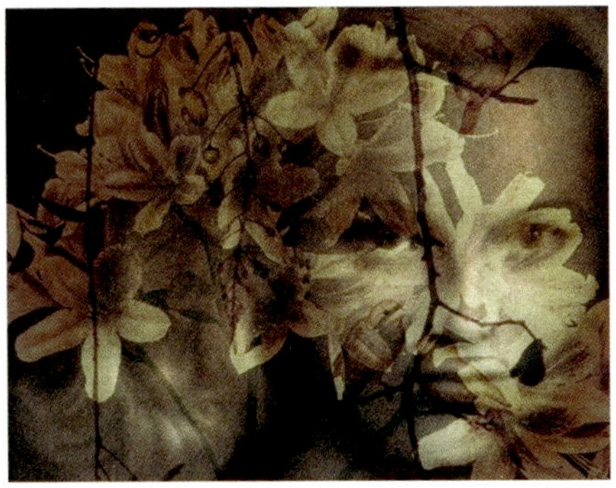

Jane creates works that contain a narrative using a photomontage of images from many different sources. Often these contain a mixture of found and her own photographic or autographic images. This library of iconography is constantly being re-used and manipulated through different media. The use of texture, colour and the layering of imagery is central to her work.

A graduate of Exeter University and the Barber Institute, Birmingham University, Jane moved to Brighton to study printmaking. She did research into photomechanical printmaking techniques for Brighton University and is well known for teaching screen printing both there and at her own studio, Ink Spot Press (see page opposite). She has received several Arts Council awards for her work. Most recently she won the John Purcell prize at the Royal Society of Painter-Printmakers.

Clockwise from top left:
Wood Type, Florence; Screen Print, Letterpress;
Working in the Ink Spot Press Studio

Ink Spot Press

Open Access Fine Art Print Studio

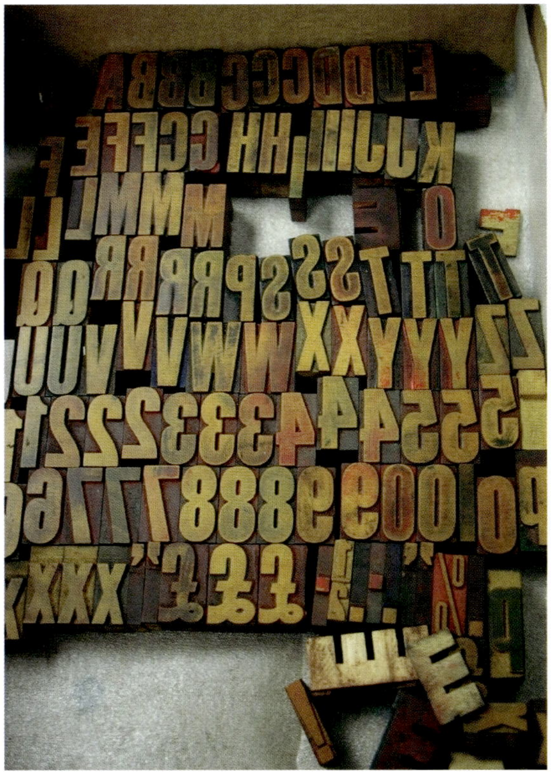

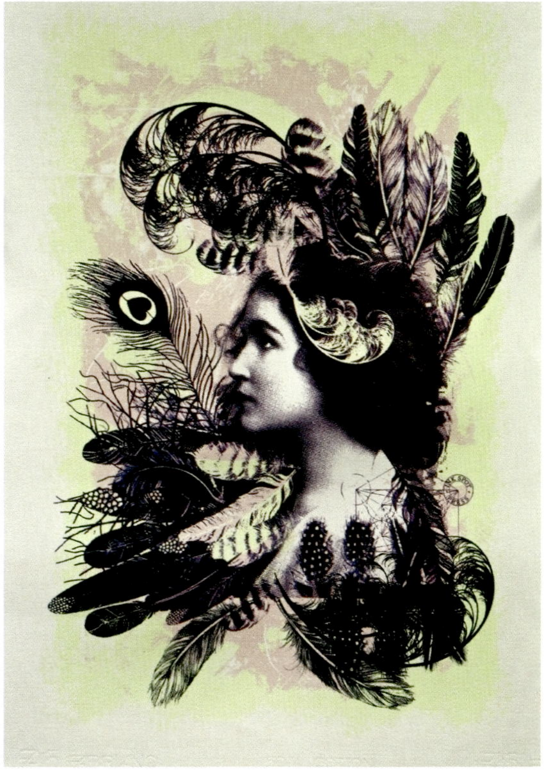

Ink Spot Press is an inspiring and thriving open access facility for artists, which specialises in screen printing, letter press and book binding. The studio offers courses in a friendly and supportive space.

Ink Spot Press facilitates a variety of local and national artists to produce their work. If you're a fan of screen printing or letter press, chances are that some of the work you admire would have been printed here. Ink Spot Press has a great set-up, offering a relaxed atmosphere to learn and print to a professional standard. Whether you're a traditional printmaker or keen to transfer your skills to digital, the team can support your needs from start to finish.

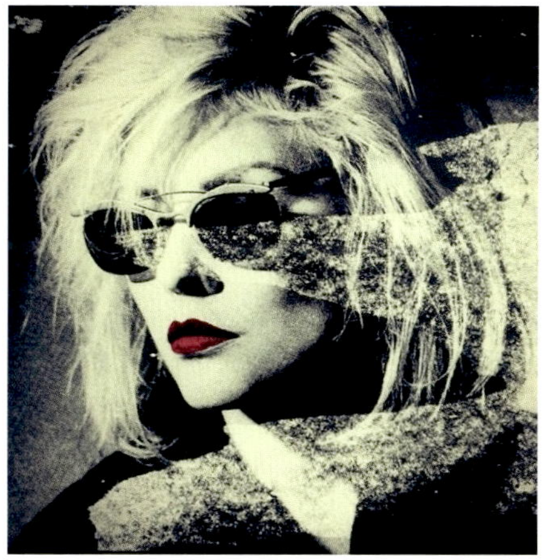

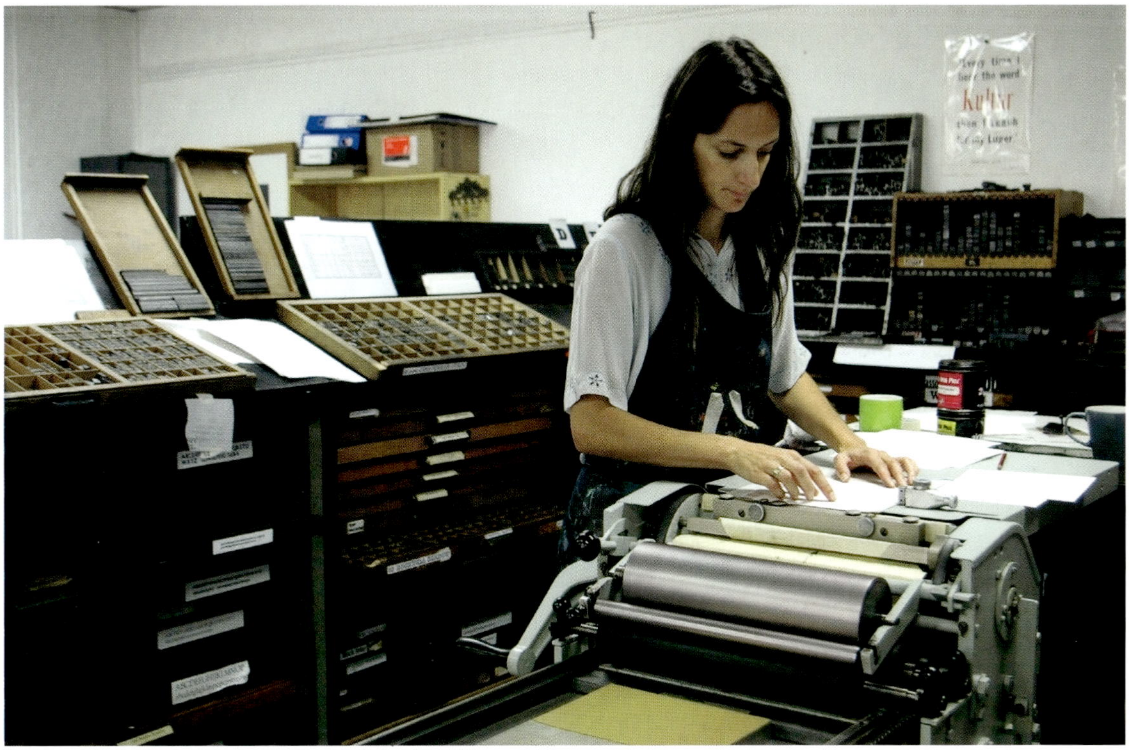

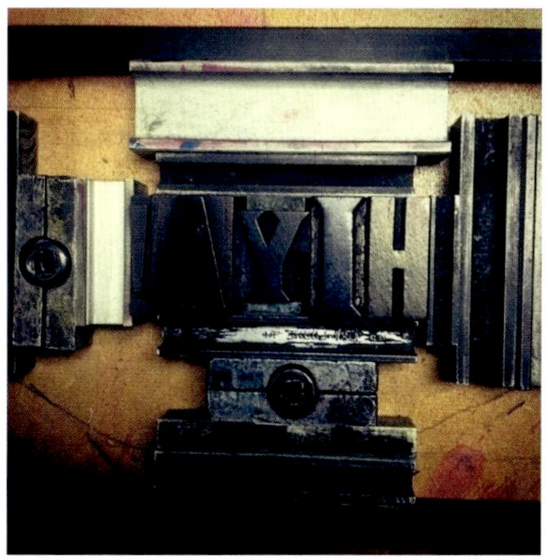

Leila Godden

Artist

Clockwise from left:
Transitions Blue 402; Fragments 401;
Fragments 201; Transitions Blue 601

Leila Godden's seascapes and abstract paintings are exhibited in various galleries in the UK, including Chalk Gallery in Lewes, and were selected for the Cork Street Open Exhibition, London, in August 2013.

Her source of inspiration is her connection with the sea. The vast panorama of changing light, dramatic weather and powerful water, framed by rocks solid with history, yet transient with time and the rhythm of the earth.

Each piece starts with something that resonates, perhaps a glimpse of the play of light as water cascades over a rock, a moody horizon or, less tangible, the feeling of a painting that needs to be expressed.

Mark making and texture are fundamental to her work, as is a limited palette. Her goal is to create paintings that capture the essence of both the subject and the artist, and offer a connection with you, the viewer. Beyond words, but sensed and understood.

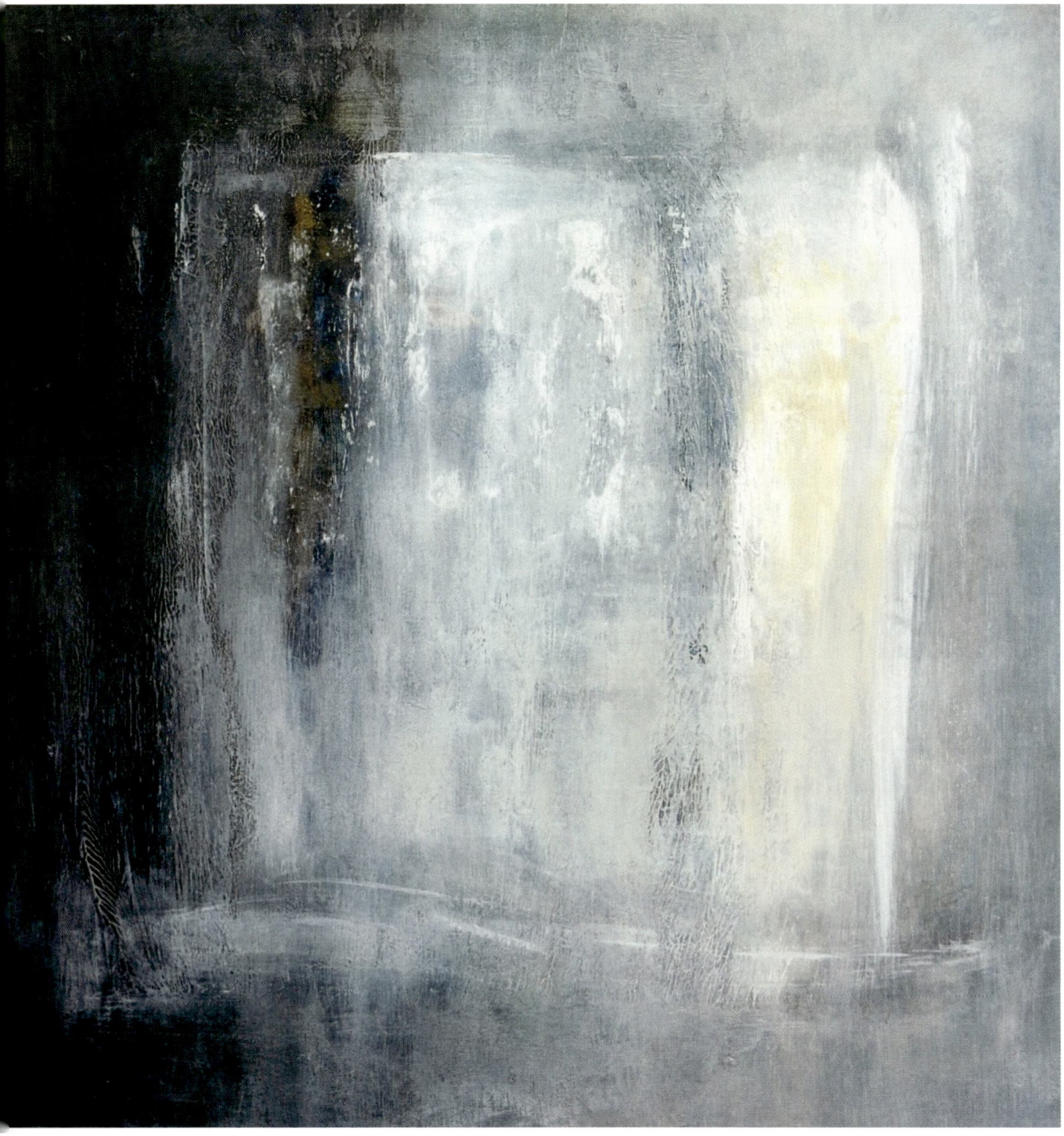

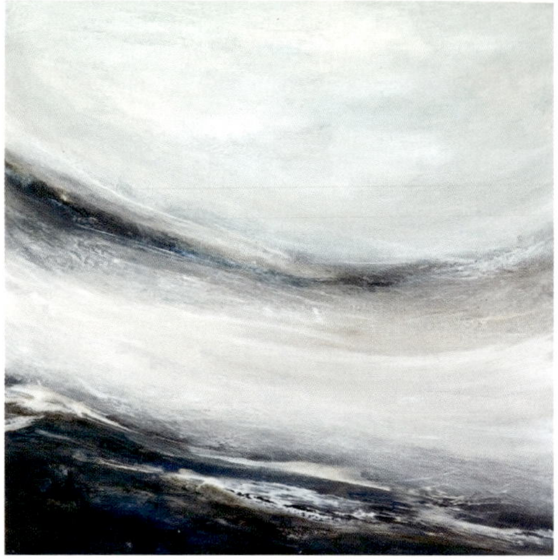

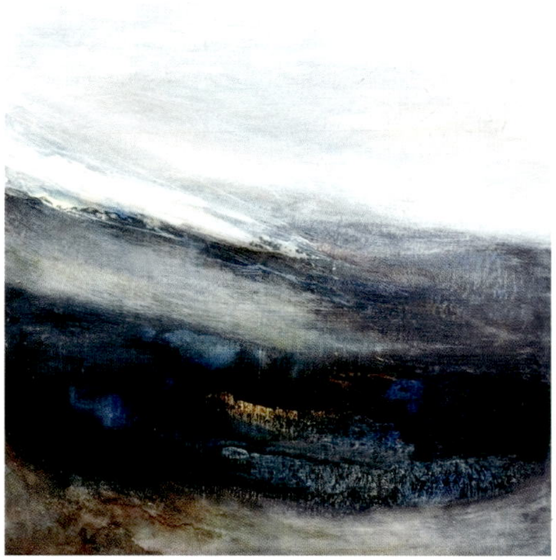

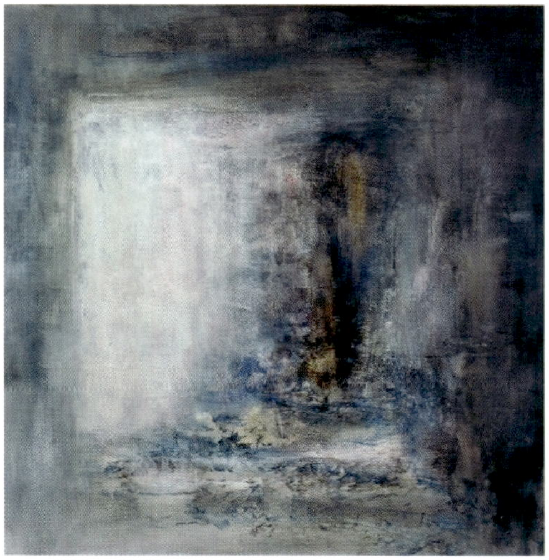

Clockwise from left:
Old Paths; Unlock;
Let's Submerge; Breakthrough

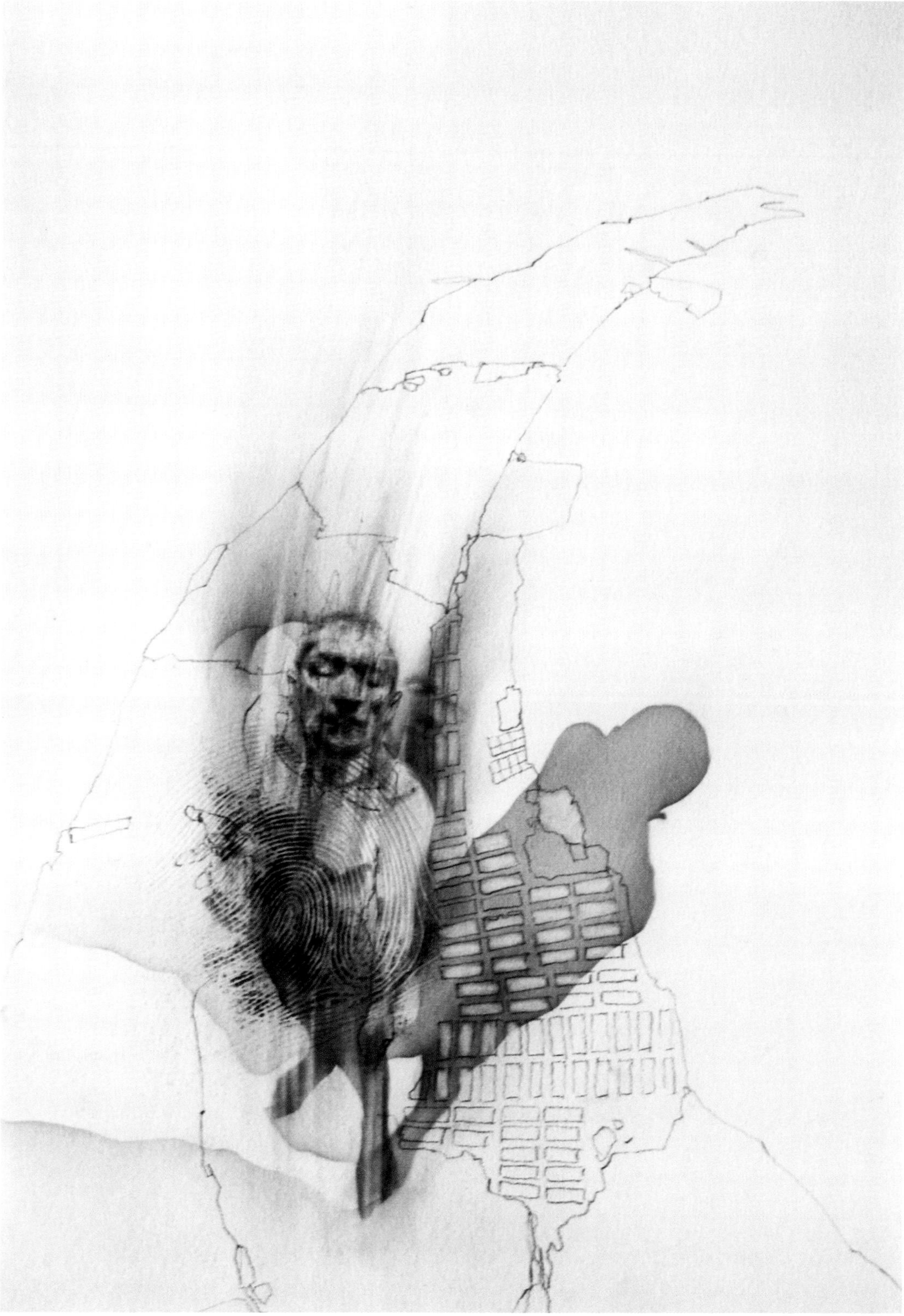

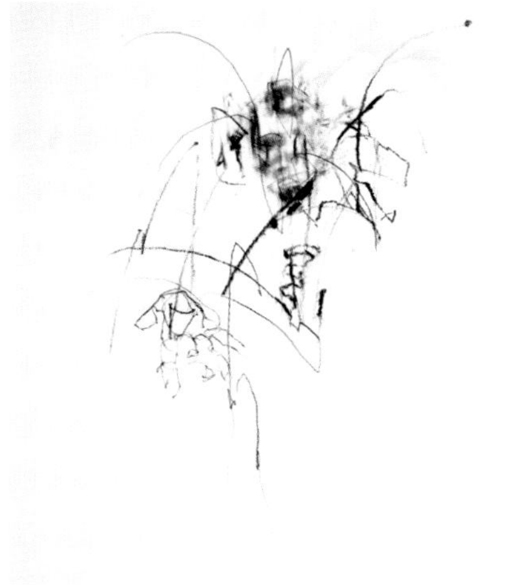

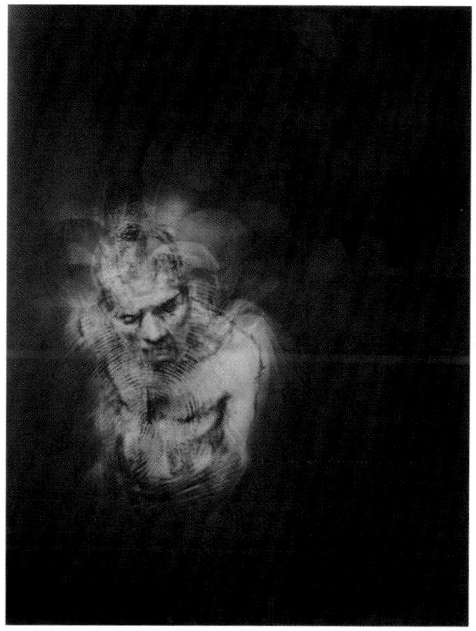

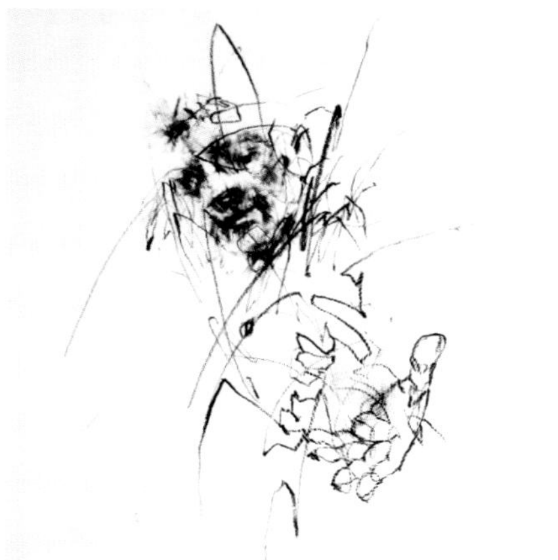

Chris Hawkins

Jeweller

Clockwise from top left: Crow and Bone Cufflinks; Skull and Claw Necklace; Fox and Rabbit cufflinks; Panthera Necklace; Shark Jaw Necklace; Vertebrae Bracelet

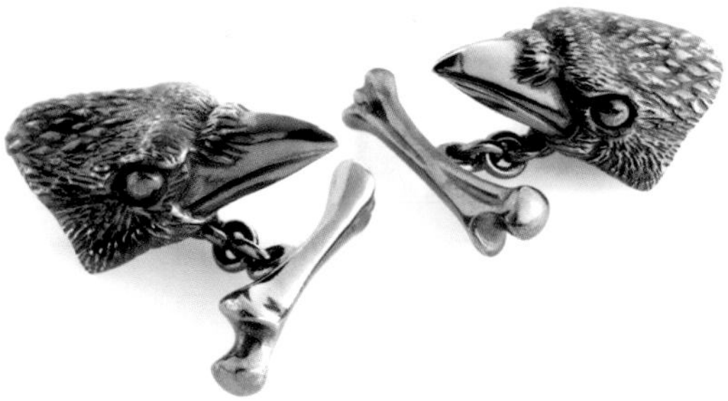

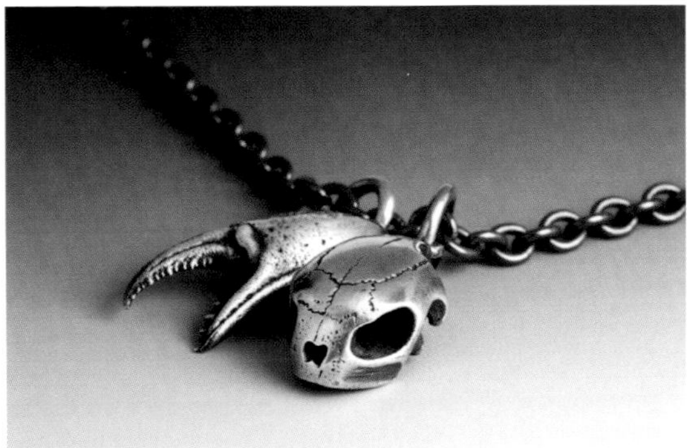

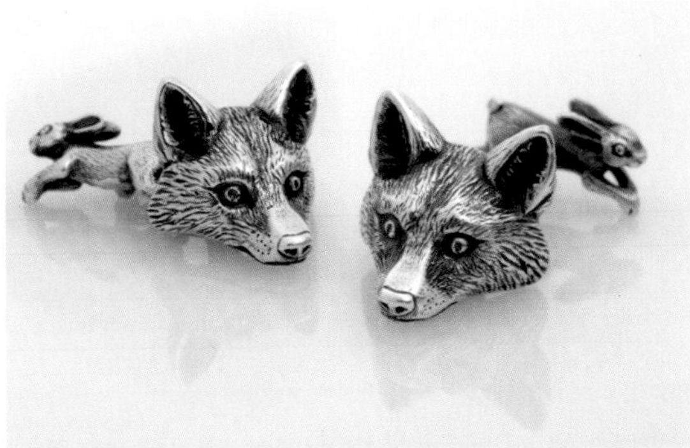

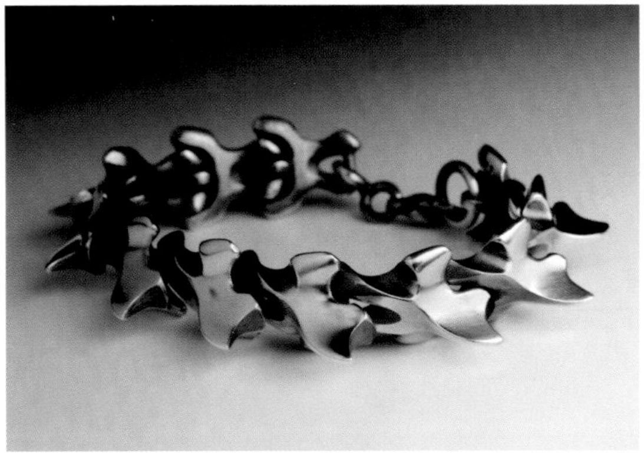

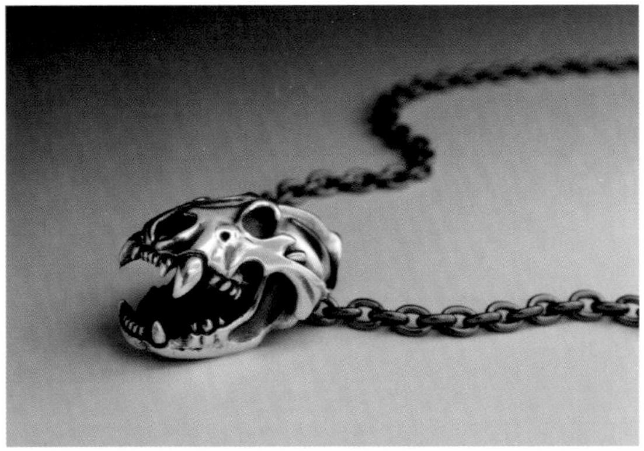

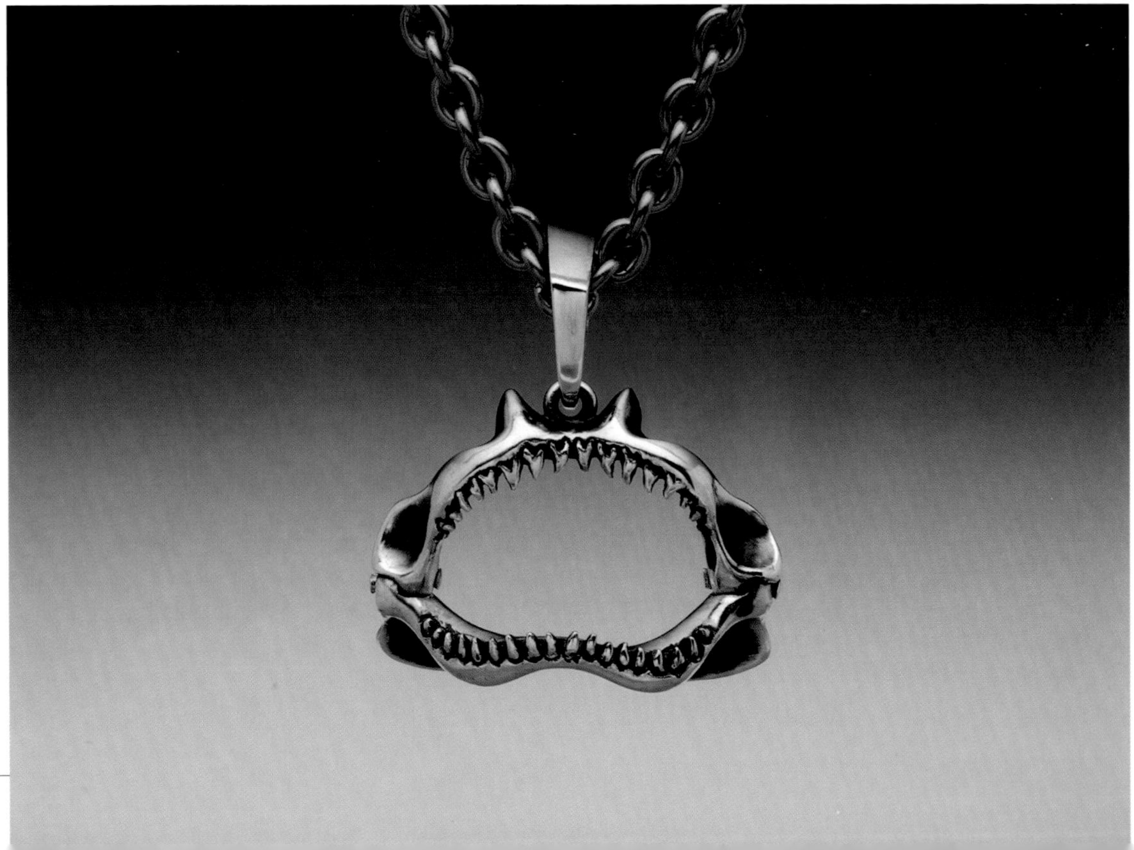

Renowned for his distinctive collections for men, Chris Hawkins brings a unique take on jewellery design inspired by the natural world. Bones, snakes and foxes have all been re-imagined by Chris in his world of precious jewellery and tiny sculptures.

"I work in themes, exploring and developing a natural form and eventually interpreting it into a wearable item of jewellery. I like to work in bold contemporary shapes often combined with intricate detail. Collections are constantly evolving, with recent work more figurative."

After sketching his ideas on paper, Chris forms models from hand-carved wax. It's a process of addition and subtraction that takes many hours before Chris sends the master design off to be cast. This comes back as a rough piece, then it's a question of refinishing and refining the detail. Every piece will be redefined by hand until it's as Chris first conceived it. It's a way of returning his original idea into a piece that can be reproduced.

"It was always my ambition to design, make and market my own collections. Rather than trying to design to the market, I only make designs that interest me, hoping that these will resonate with a certain number people, some of whom will become customers. This approach ensures that I remain excited by jewellery making, and always produce the best work I can."

Chris now supplies shops and galleries all over the UK and beyond, as well as from his own website (see index page 150 for details).

Firefly Studios also runs evening courses that give an introduction to the craft of jewellery making. Students are encouraged to work on their own projects, with expert tutors on hand to advise. Some people have come to make their own wedding rings. Others have progressed to making and selling their own designs at shows and in galleries (see page opposite for details).

Clockwise from top left:
Bird Armour (special commission),
Inside Firefly Studios

Firefly Studios

Jewellery Evening Classes, 79 Beaconsfield Road, Brighton BN1 4QJ

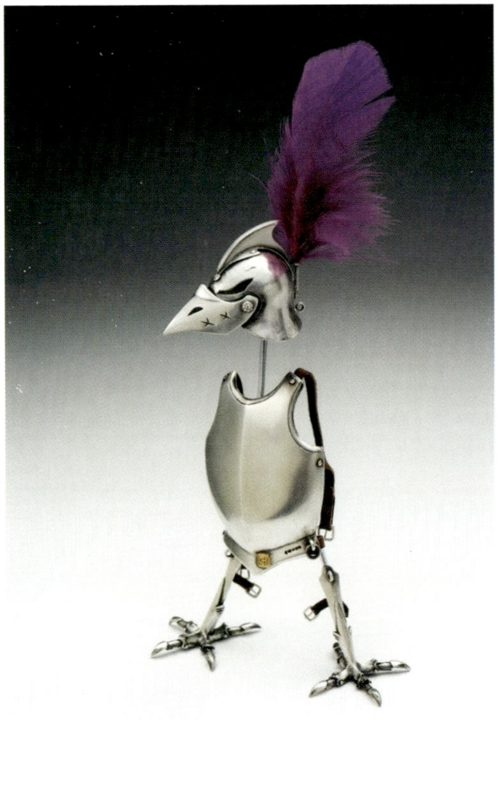

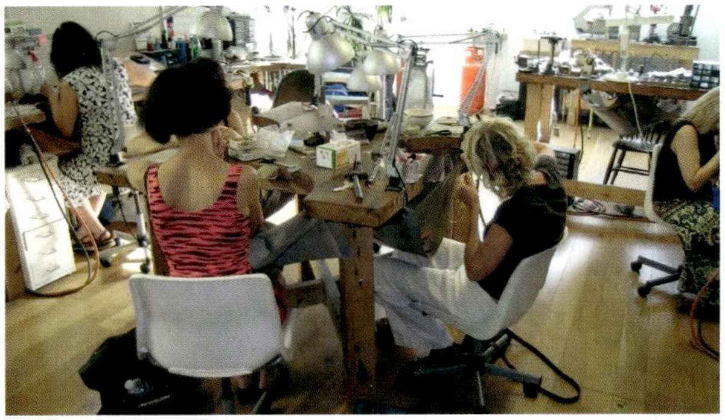

Friendly and informative, the classes at Firefly Studios cover all aspects of jewellery making, and all levels of ability. Whether you are a complete beginner with an interest in jewellery, or someone with some jewellery experience looking to improve and develop their skills. A 10-week course costs £195. Call or email Chris for further information (see index page 150 for contact details).

Workshop space

If you require a fully equipped studio to make jewellery, Firefly Studios has competitive space on a daily, weekly or monthly basis. Rates are: £15/day; £35/weekly; and £118/monthly.

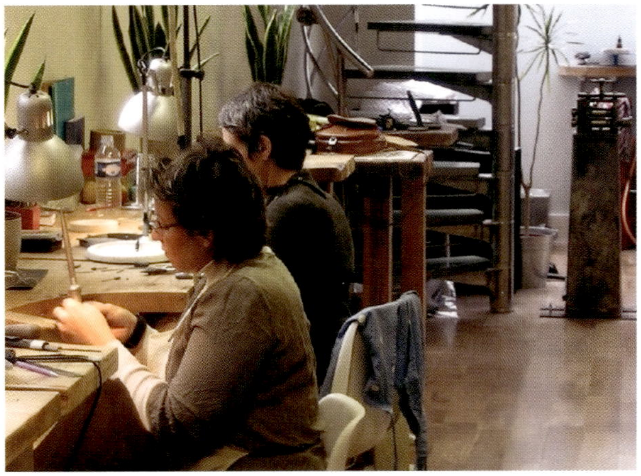

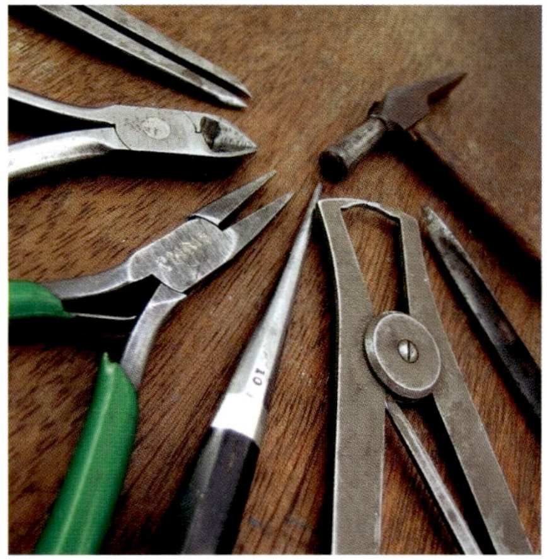

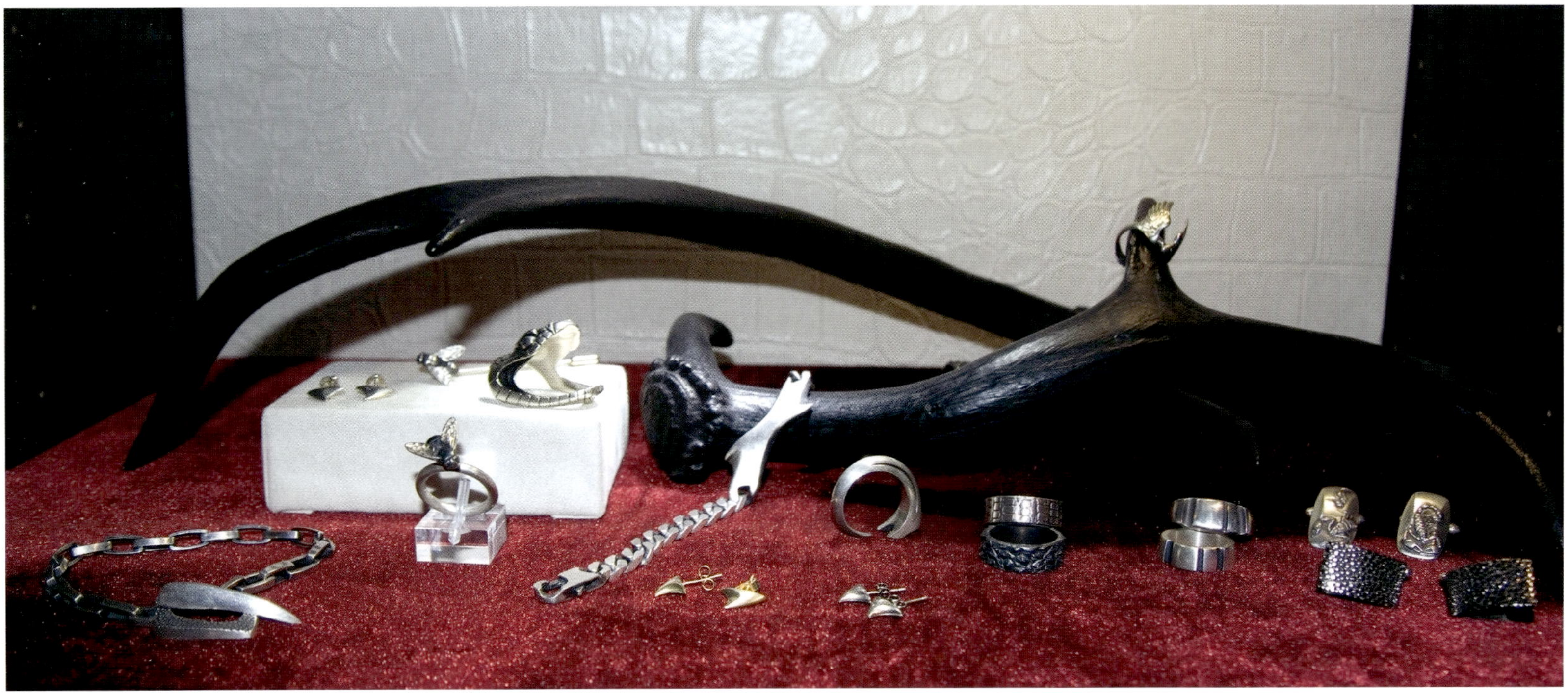

Frances Bloomfield

Artist

Clockwise from top:
Espinoi I; Dialogue Domestique 4;
Dialogue Domestique 14

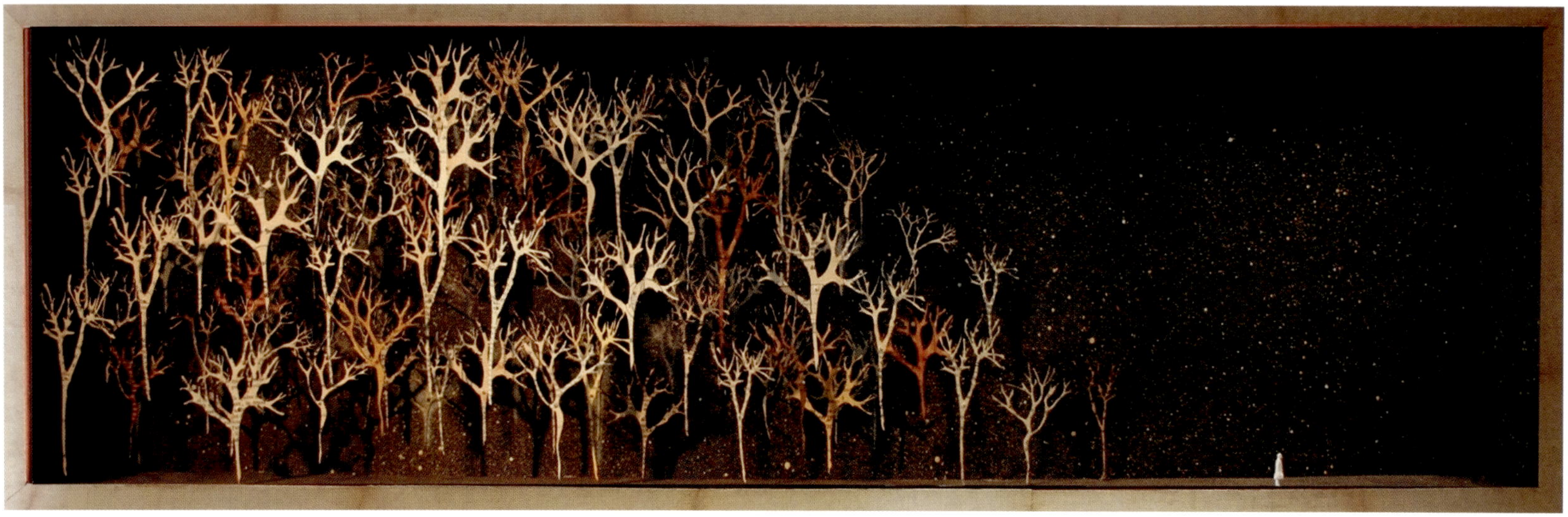

This quote from Paul Auster's novel *Man in the Dark* (2008) clearly expresses the main concerns of the work:

"There's no single reality...there are many realities. There's no single world. There are many worlds, and they all run parallel to one another, worlds and anti-worlds, worlds and shadow-worlds, and each world is dreamed or imagined or written by someone in another world. Each world is the creation of a mind."

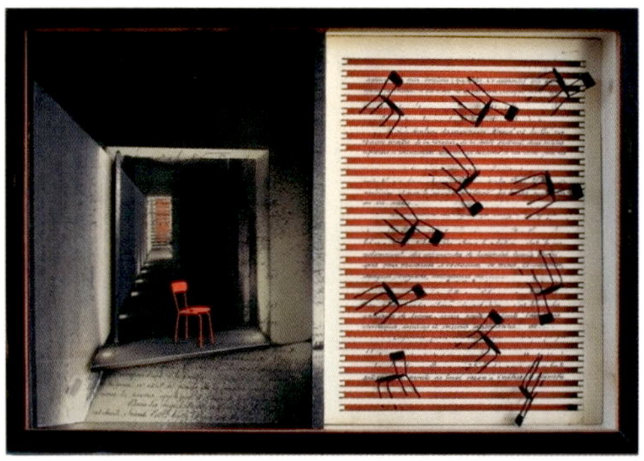

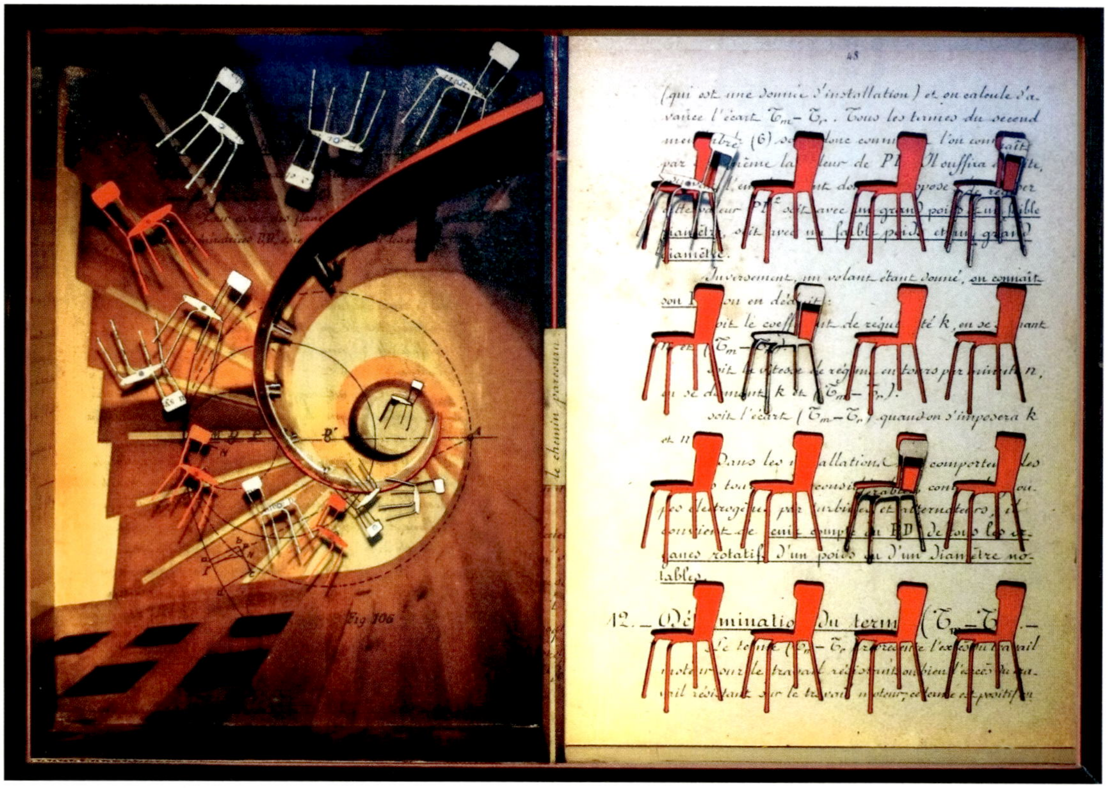

During the past five years, Frances Bloomfield has created a significant body of work, which she has exhibited widely. She is now represented by Saffron Gallery in Battle, Clifton Fine Art in Bristol and Liberty Gallery, who show her work at the major London and regional art fairs.

Her work explores the layered narratives of dreams and the 'improbable' scenarios that we unconsciously construct. The depth and complexity of Frances Bloomfield's dreamboxes offer the viewer a rich landscape for reflection. Curious juxtapositions of elements challenge familiar meanings and open up new dialogues in a variety of settings – rural, industrial and, most recently, 'domestique'.

Clockwise from top left:
The Other Side of London Road; The Fortune of War and Neighbour;
The Great Eastern and Rare Kind; The Web

Jay Collins

Artist

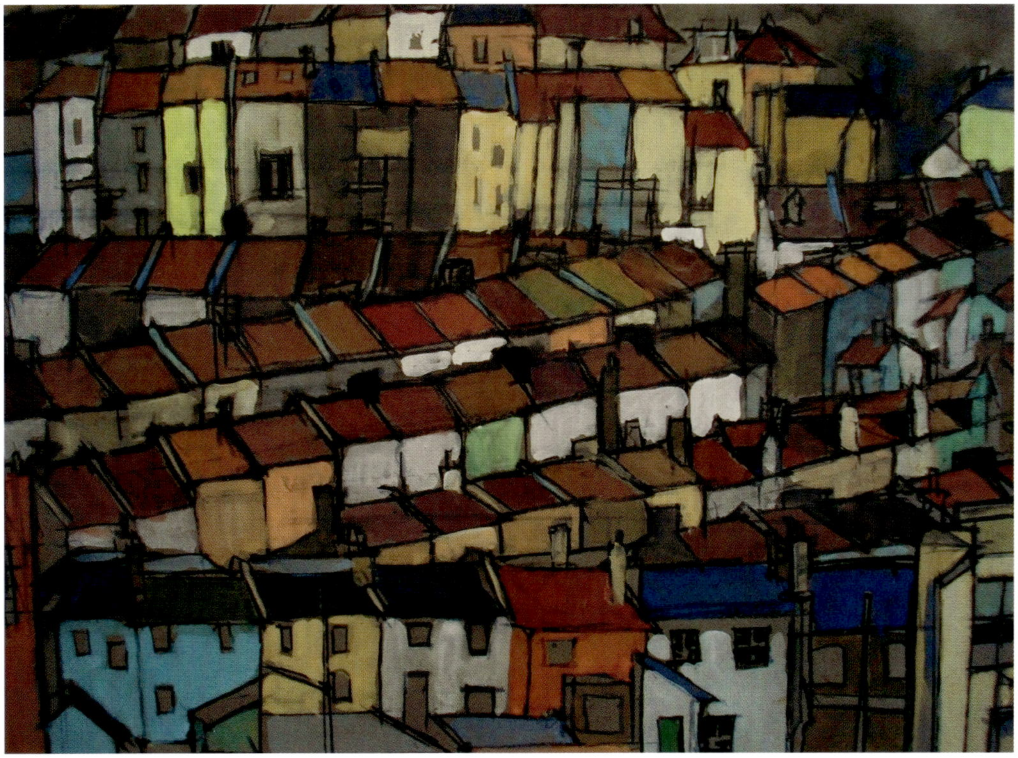

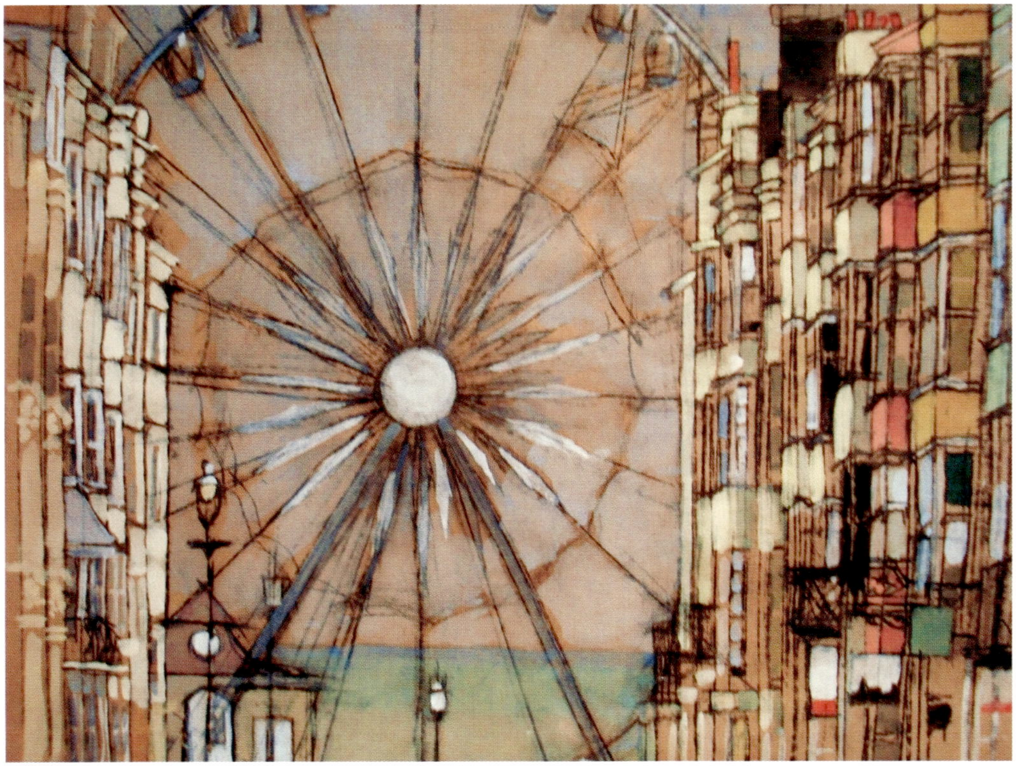

Jay Collins graduated 12 years ago with a BA(Hons) Fine Art degree followed by a Certificate in Printmaking. Her paintings have been selected for prizes and for exhibitions including Sussex, Chichester and Worthing Open exhibitions, and by the BBC *Year of the Artist* programme and Meridian Television. She was short-listed for the national 50 over 50 Exhibition, and in 2012 won the Brighton Fringe Visual Arts Prize. As a local artist, Jay was among the first in Kemptown in 2002 to open her studio to the general public each year during the May Brighton Festival. She contributes colourful illustrations to the pub series in *Viva Brighton* each month.

Being primarily an urban landscape artist, her paintings and prints show Brighton in all its aspects from the sea to the downs, from the back streets to the Georgian facades, in oil, gouache, ink and wash, wood and lino cut.

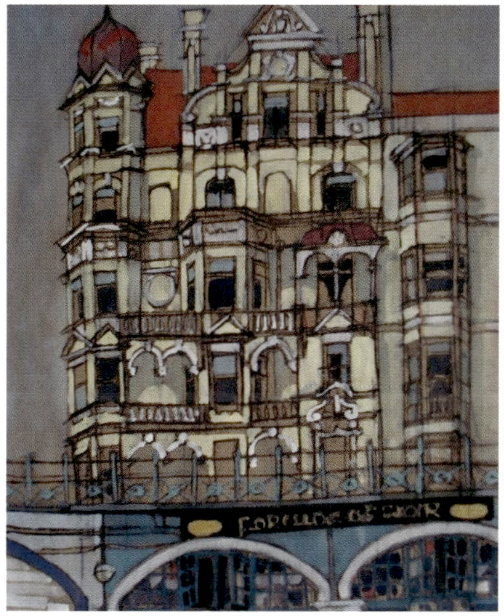

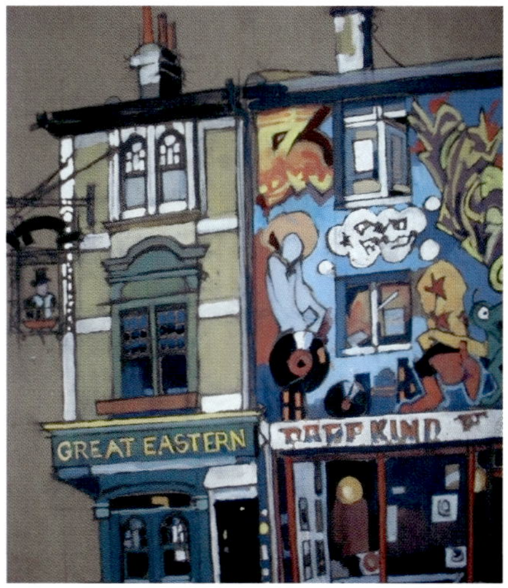

Van Gogh wrote: *"You know... the sunflower is mine in a way."*

Rick Fullwood's modern take on Van Gogh's famous 'Twelve Sunflowers in a Vase' includes modern sunflowers recorded by the relatively modern medium of photography. When the artist painted the original 'Twelve Sunflowers in a Vase' back in 1888 as part of a series, all the flowers were yellow. (Van Gogh loved yellow, and painted his house in Arles yellow.) Rick decided to grow twelve different sunflowers from seed on his allotment garden, including some modern hybrids that were different colours as well as yellow. When they were at their colourful best he photographed each one backed by a section of a Van Gogh painting. Rick used twelve different paintings, one of which was 'Twelve Sunflowers in a Vase'. The resultant 'Twelve of Twelve' were then assembled in a grid-like formation for display. Each image was 20in by 30in and mounted on MDF. The vibrant colours represent those used by Van Gogh in the latter years of his life, and are emphasised by the gloss finish of the final prints.

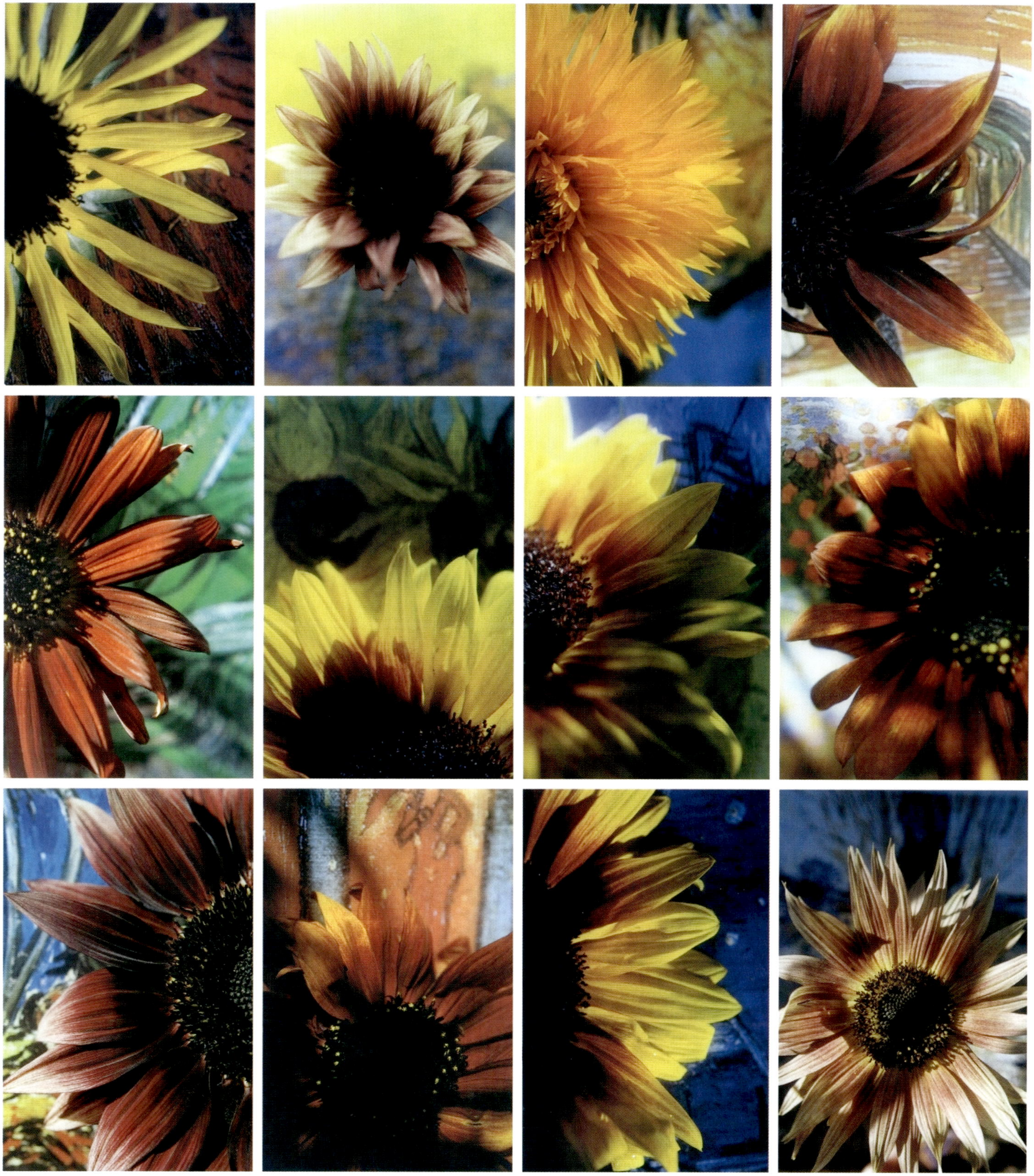

Stephanie Else: Glass in Fusion

Artist

Clockwise from top: White flower dish; Bird Branch (detail); Polar Red II; Floral Scape (detail)

Stephanie Else specialises in making high quality, contemporary glass designs using a variety of kiln-forming techniques. Working with a combination of transparent and opaque glass, she adds metals, foils and lustres to produce a stunning range of both decorative and functional works of art and jewellery.

Inspired by the glass itself, Stephanie combines surface texture, pattern and colour within the glass to create beautifully tactile pieces while exploiting the natural translucent and jewel-like qualities it possesses.

As well as exhibiting her work in galleries, the artist has also completed numerous commission pieces and interior design projects. She offers a bespoke service and is happy to discuss any design ideas you may have.

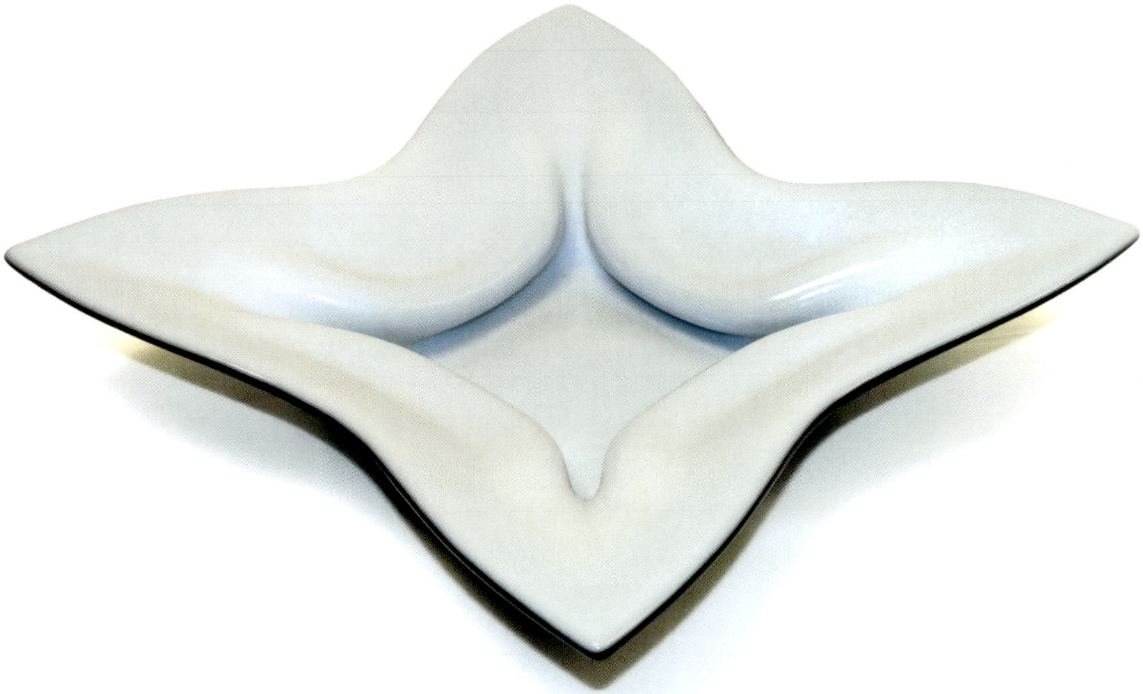

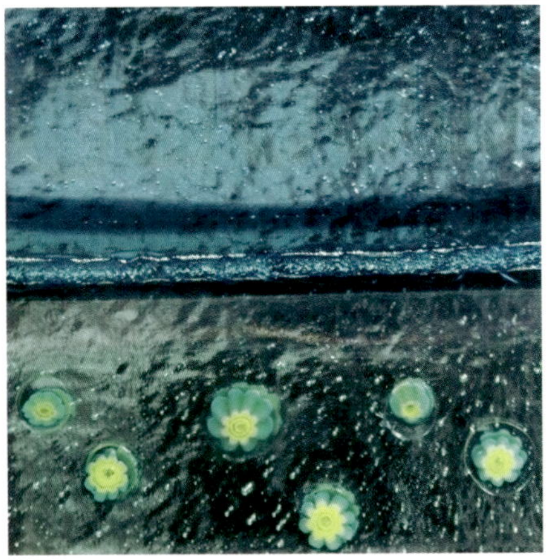

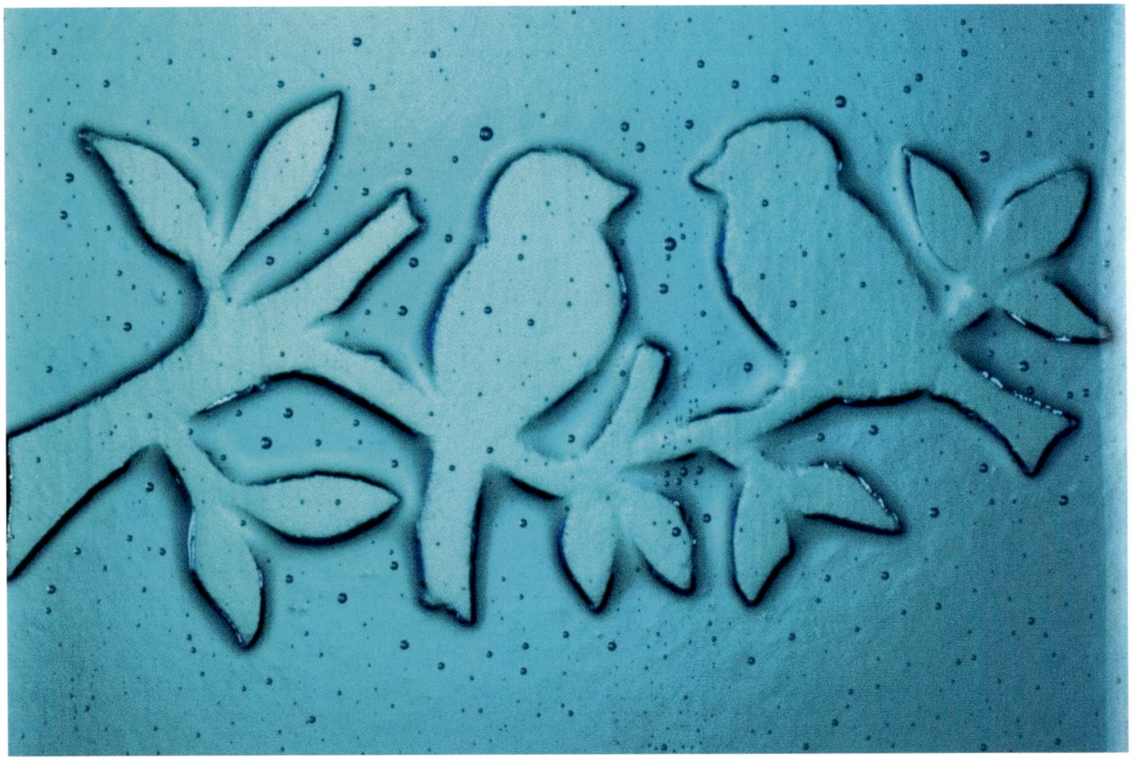

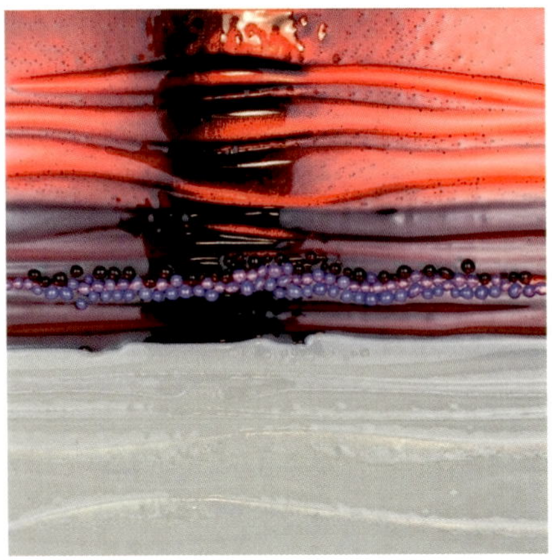

Clockwise from top left:
Yellow Steps; Under Cliff Path;
Indigo Fence

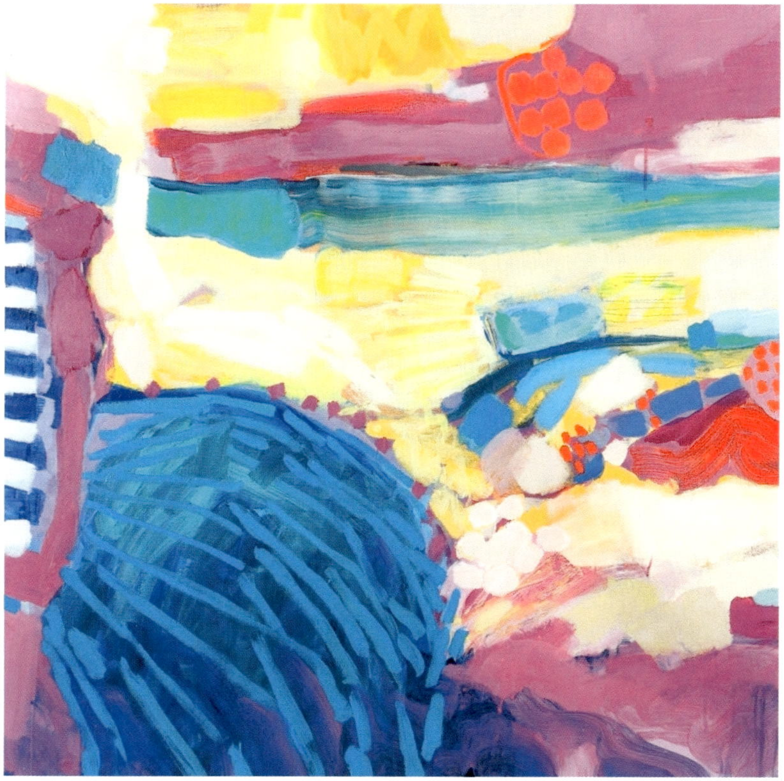

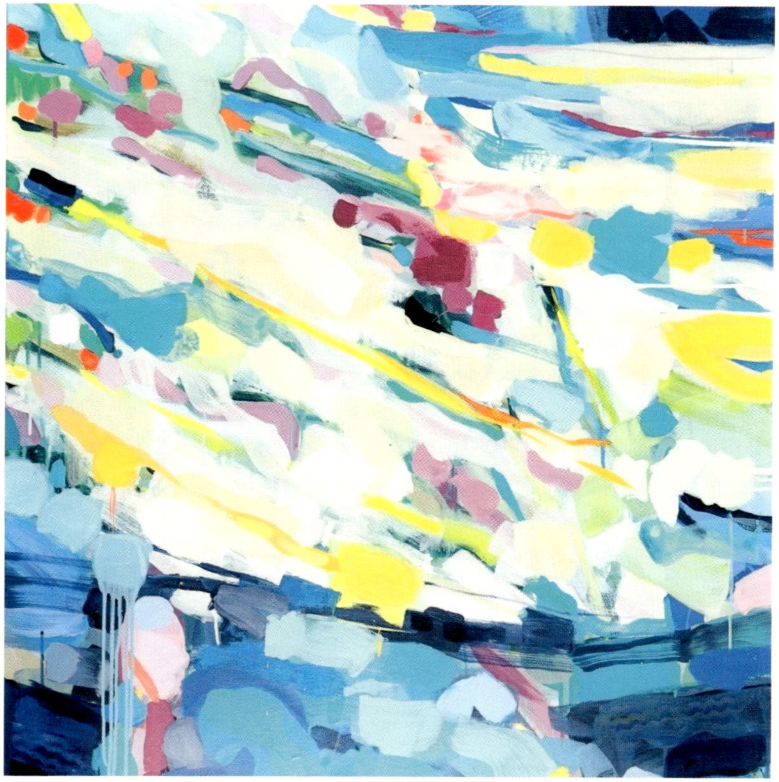

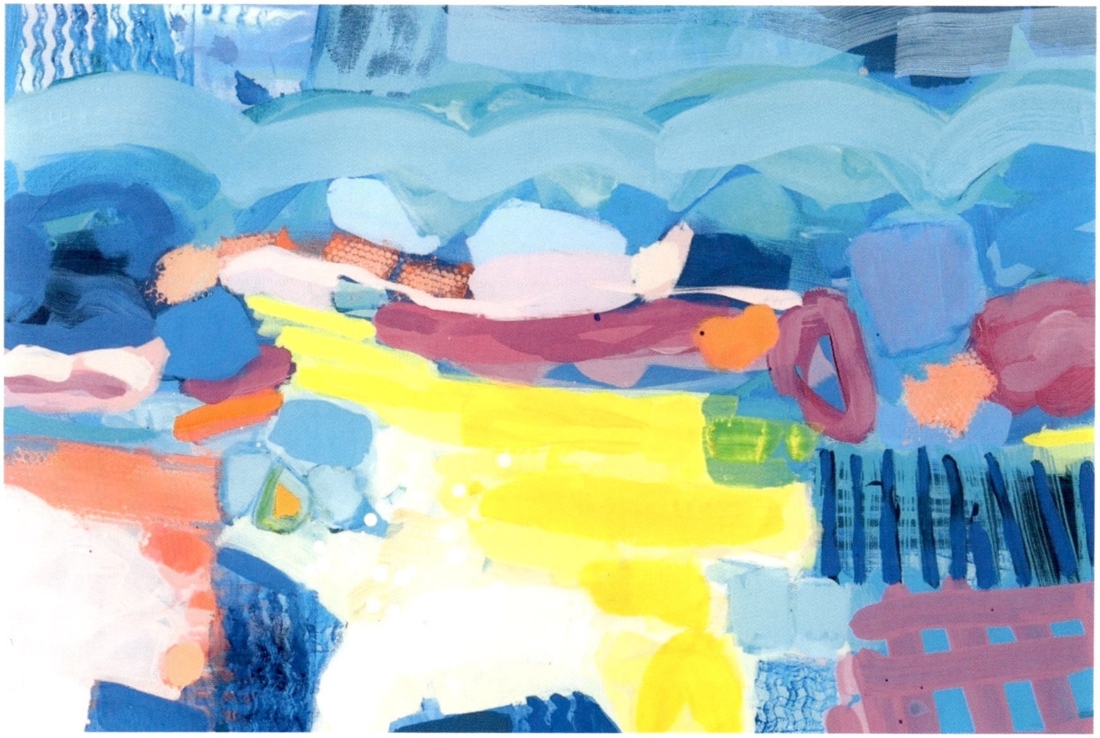

Sophie Abbott's dramatic and colourful paintings are a spontaneous reflection on the world around her: inspired by the beach, an allotment or a flipflop – she paints what she sees in her own unique way. Her style is bold and experimental, and each painting itself evolves through the process of painting.

Sophie lives and works in Brighton. With the sea as her backdrop, she is surrounded by an ever-changing environment that she explores through her fluid, experimental style of painting.

Her aim is to create atmospheric paintings that capture the essence of a place in time. The combination of this visual snapshot and an experimental painting technique creates work that has a playful, luminous and unique quality.

You can see Sophie's paintings at this year's Artists Open Houses event. (See her website for details.)

'Sophie's paintings are incredibly uplifting. Her use of colour and her spontaneous and free mark-making are energising.'

Style of White Magazine

Kate Osborne

Artist

Clockwise from top left:
Still Life with Lemon; Bees and Wildflowers;
Fish; Hippeastrum

Kate Osborne studied textile design in the 1970s and worked in the industry for 20 years, including five years spent in the States, where her paintings sold in galleries in Santa Fe and Los Angeles.

She has lived in Brighton for the past 28 years, moving from illustration and textile design to painting, and now works very freely in watercolour. Whether painting florals, pigs or musicians, she brings a rich sense of colour and energy to the work.

Exhibitions include the Royal Institute of Painters in Watercolour, the Society of Wildlife Artists, Brighton's Artists Open Houses, and galleries across the UK.

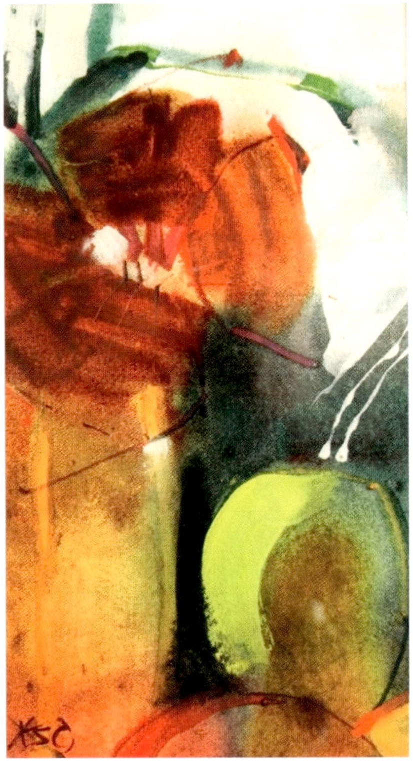

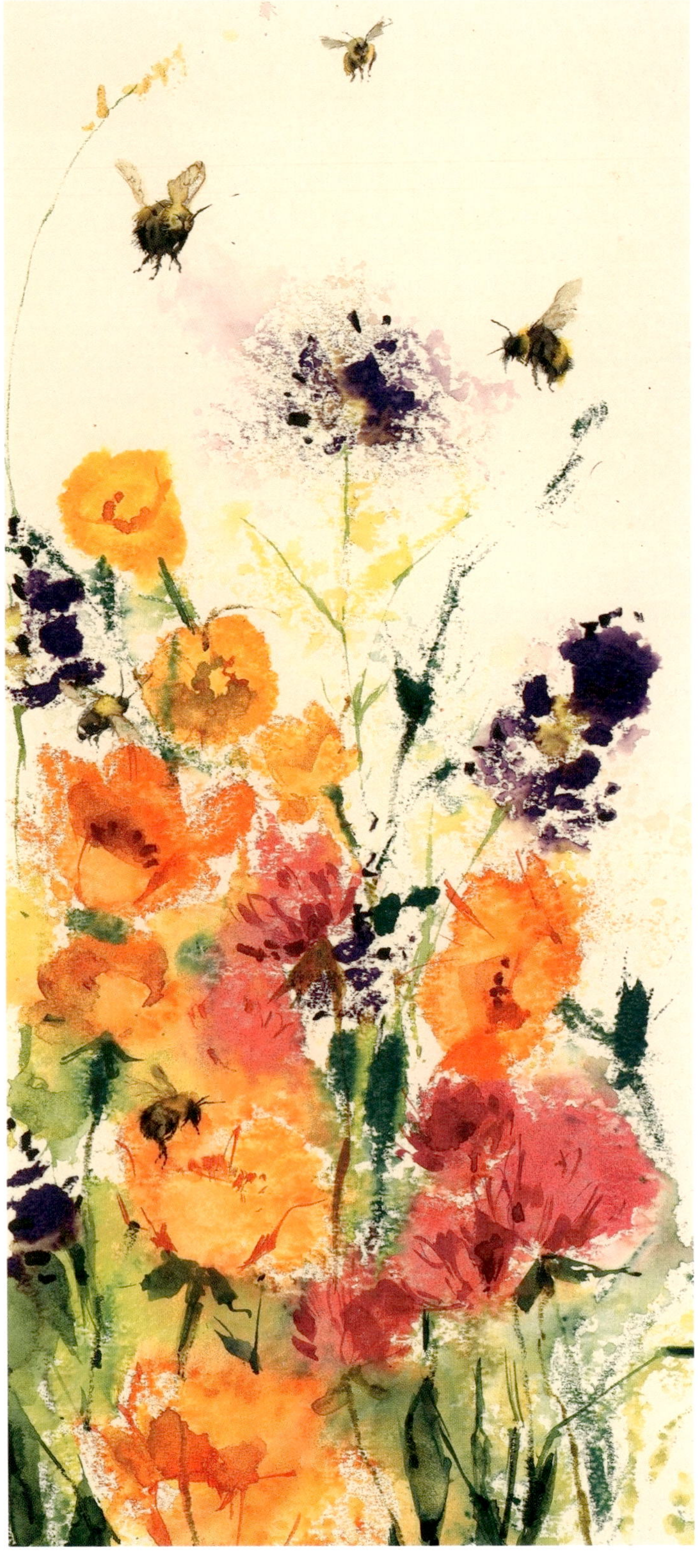

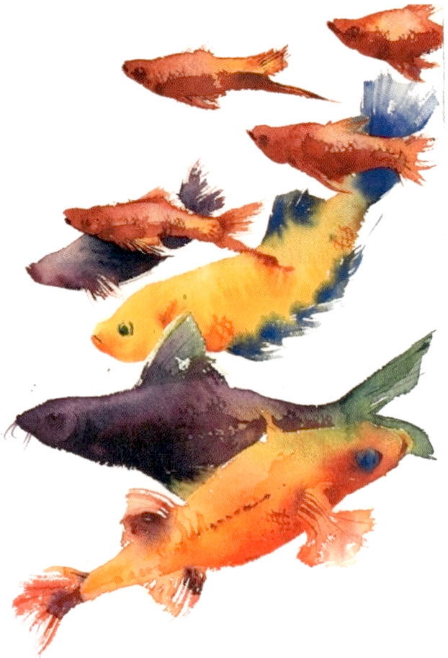

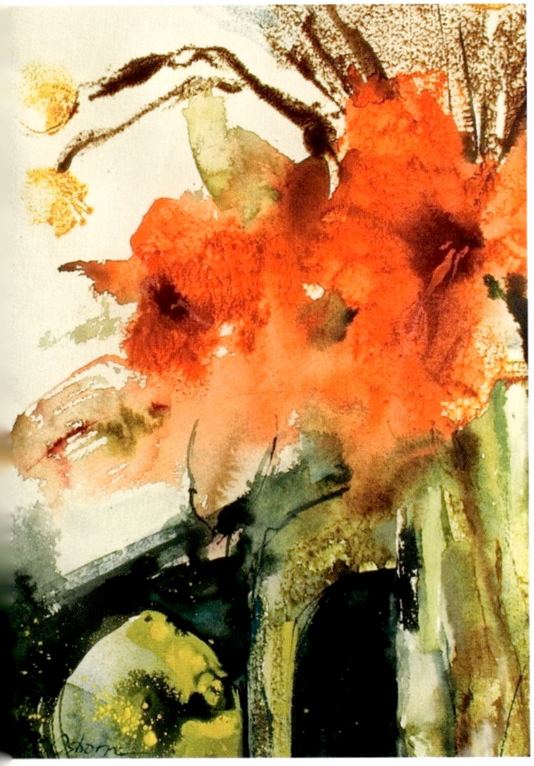

Clockwise from top left:
Charleston – In the eye of the Beholder;
Joy at Turnout V; Joy at Turnout VI

Veronica van Eijk

Artist

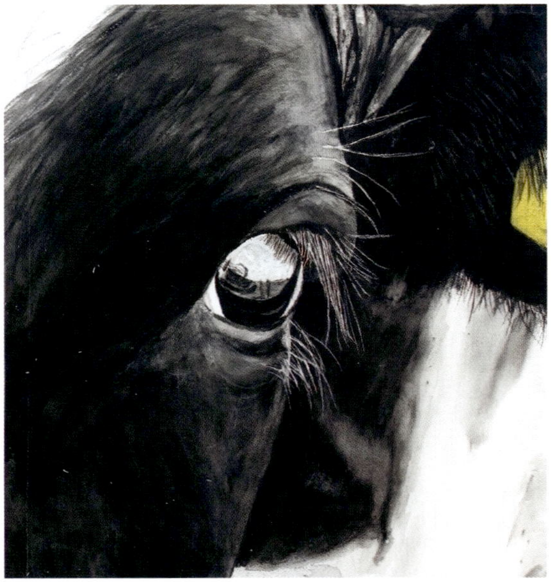

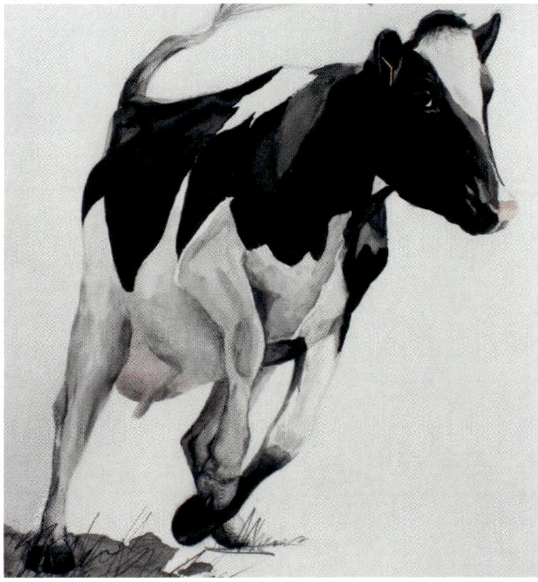

Cows can have such strong expressions in their faces, they have a way of looking at you: curious, interested, haughty, frightened, timid, relaxed; and this is what Veronica likes to capture in paints.

Add a lovely low afternoon light and the cows look very sculptural to her. She loves the way the sun highlights their sometimes quite exaggerated bone structures. When she is painting her subjects – aiming at making them look quite 3D – she takes great joy in adding and taking away the paint, building up the layers of her large watercolours; a process she likens to sculpting with paint.

Veronica is a member of the Chalk Gallery (page 136) in Lewes.

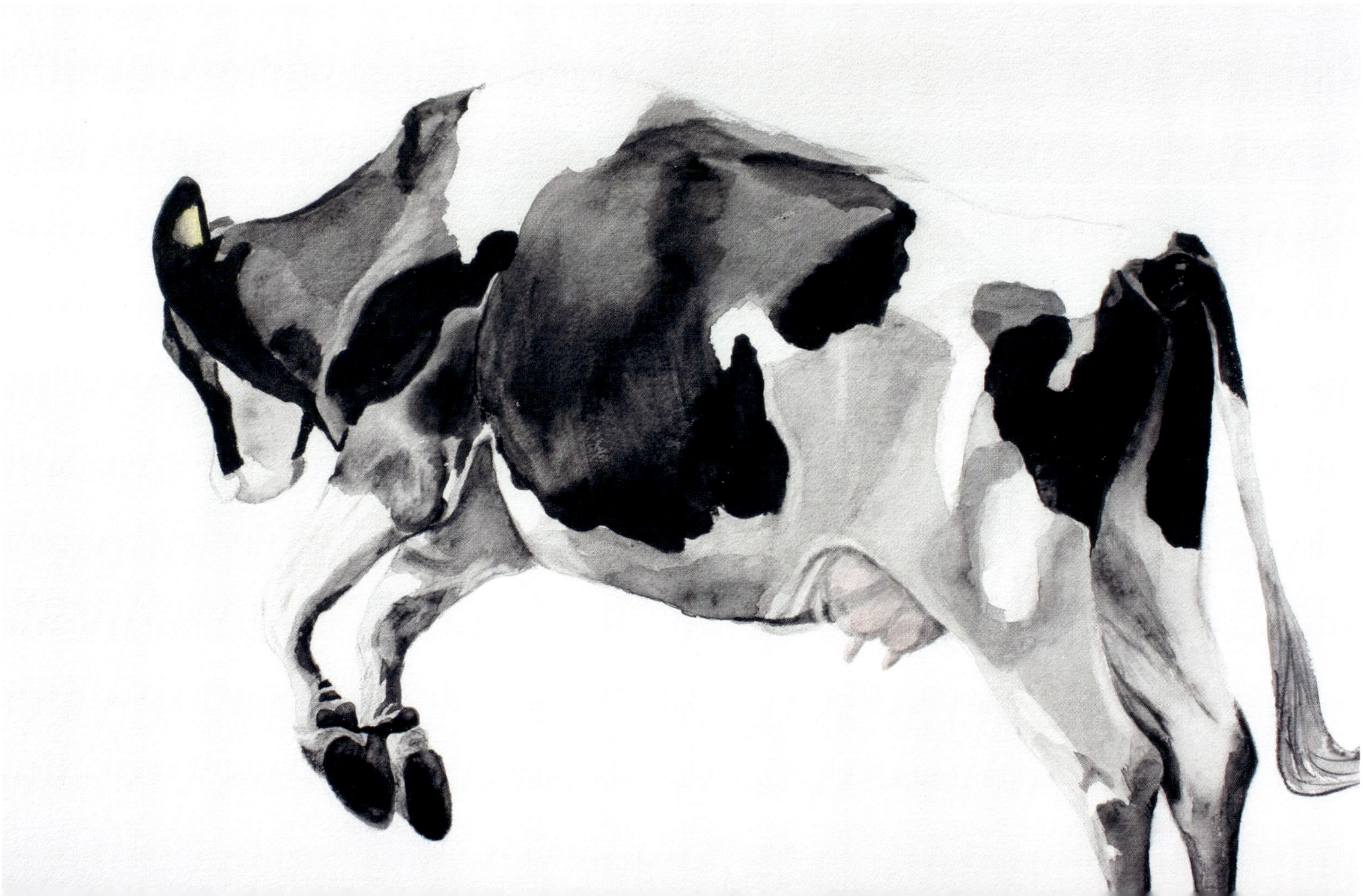

Stuart Dodman

Artist

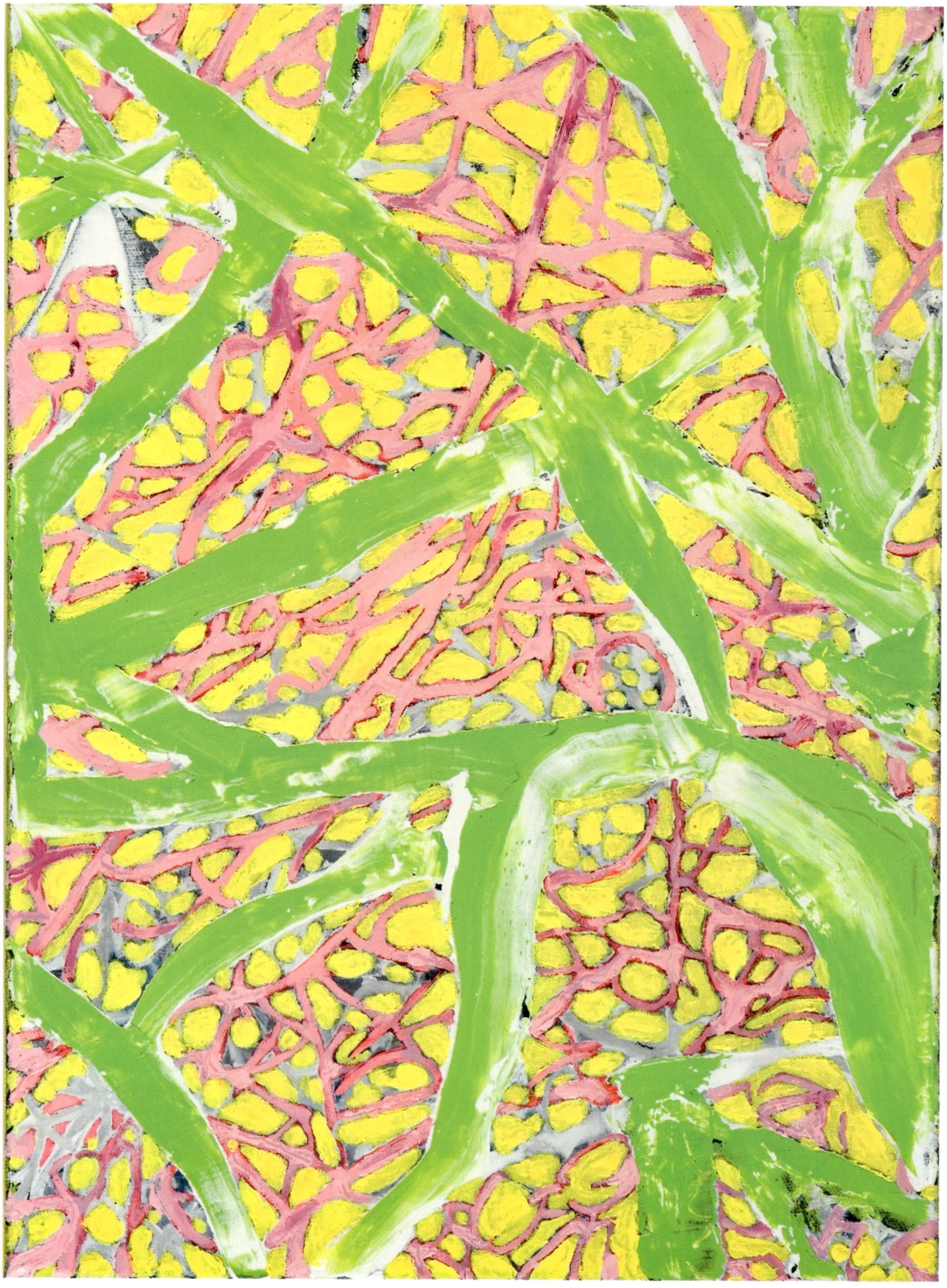

This page: Goliath
Opposite page: Witch

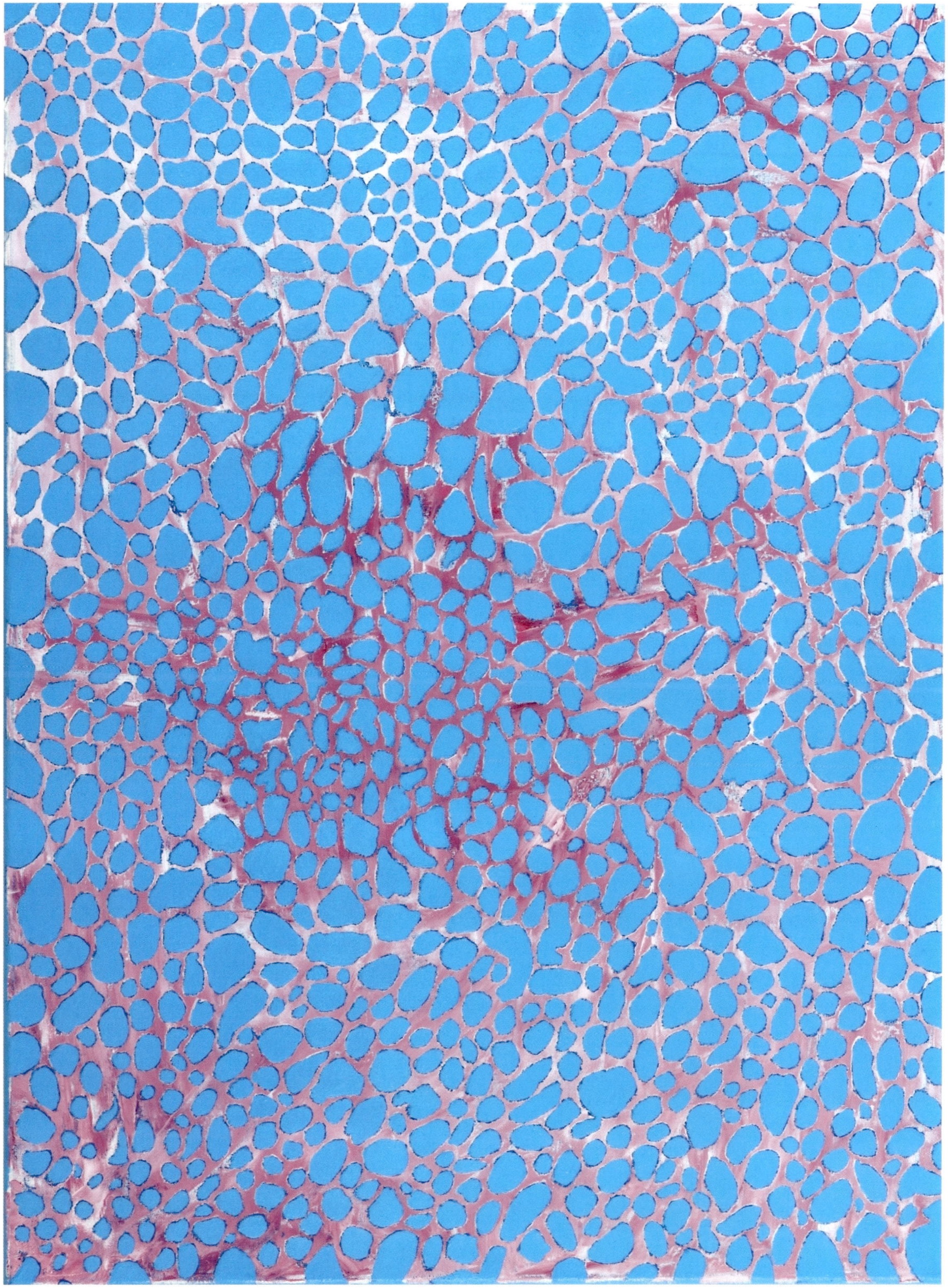

Xavi Dom Buendia

Fine Art Photographer

Clockwise from top left:
Innuendos of HDR; 284;
The Kiss pt II; Self-portrait

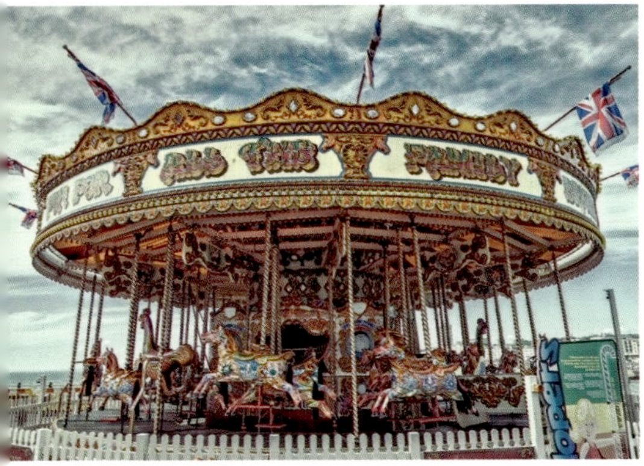

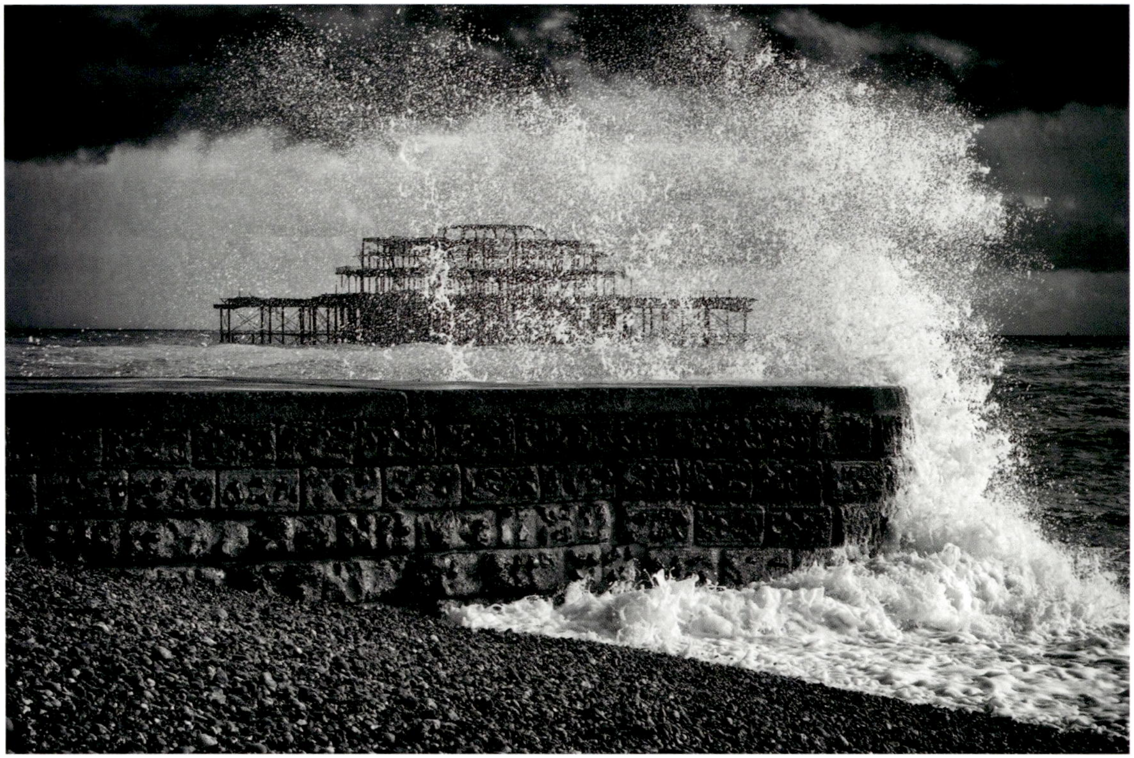

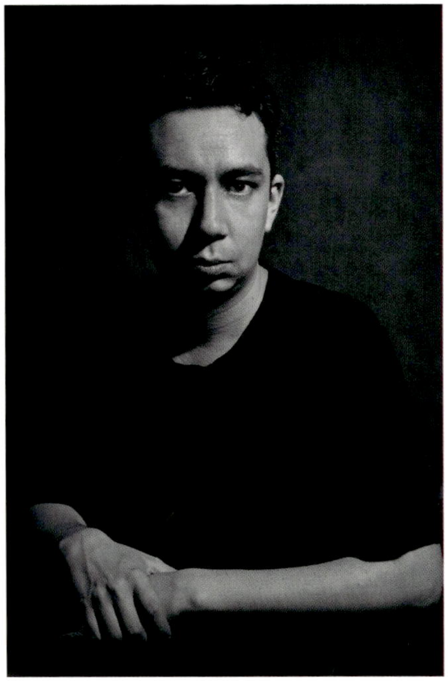

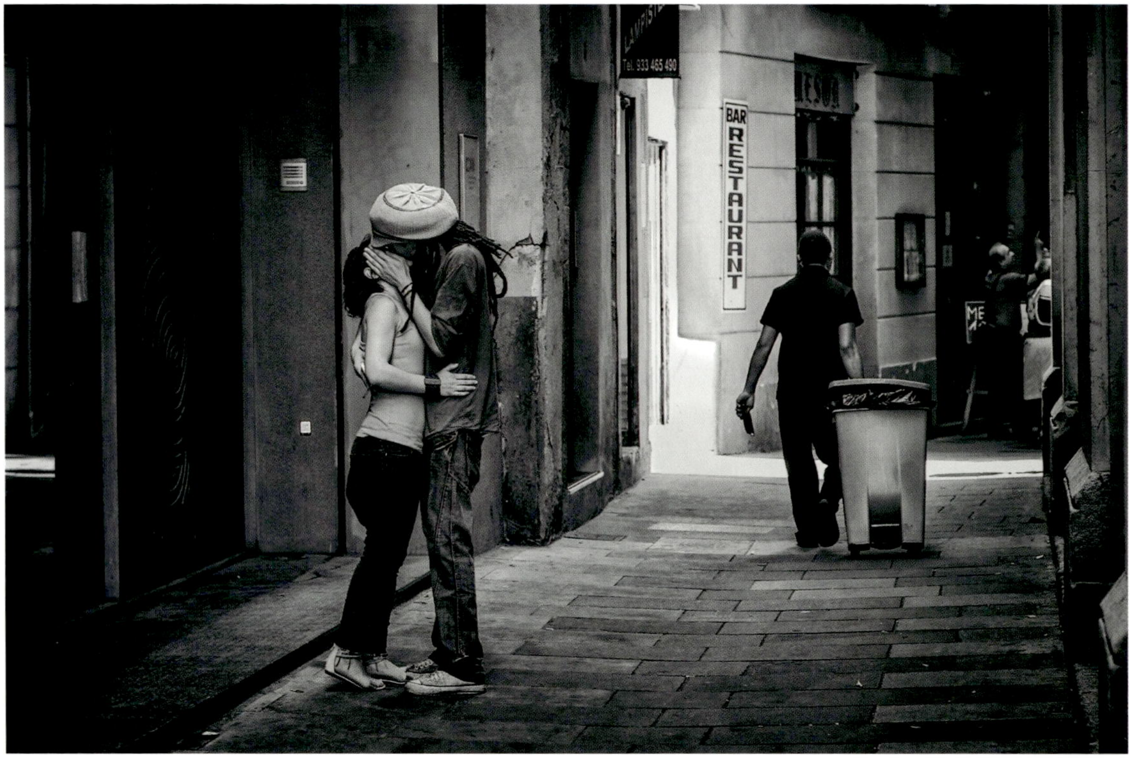

Xavi Dom Buendia is a fine art photographer who works on personal and commissioned projects.

Working mostly in monochrome, he likes to tell stories based on ideas and emotions of everyday situations found on the streets. His use of natural light is a big part of the creative process he follows to achieve such strong images.

Romany Mark Bruce

Artist & Sculptor

Irish-born Romany Mark Bruce is one of Brighton's most highly regarded artists, whose paintings are sought by collectors worldwide.

His unique, sculptural palette strokes have found most recent expression through vibrant canvases: challenging, charged and bold. A successful exhibition in South Australia has led to a number of large-scale commissions, as his reputation grows. Follow Romany on Twitter @romanymarkbruce.

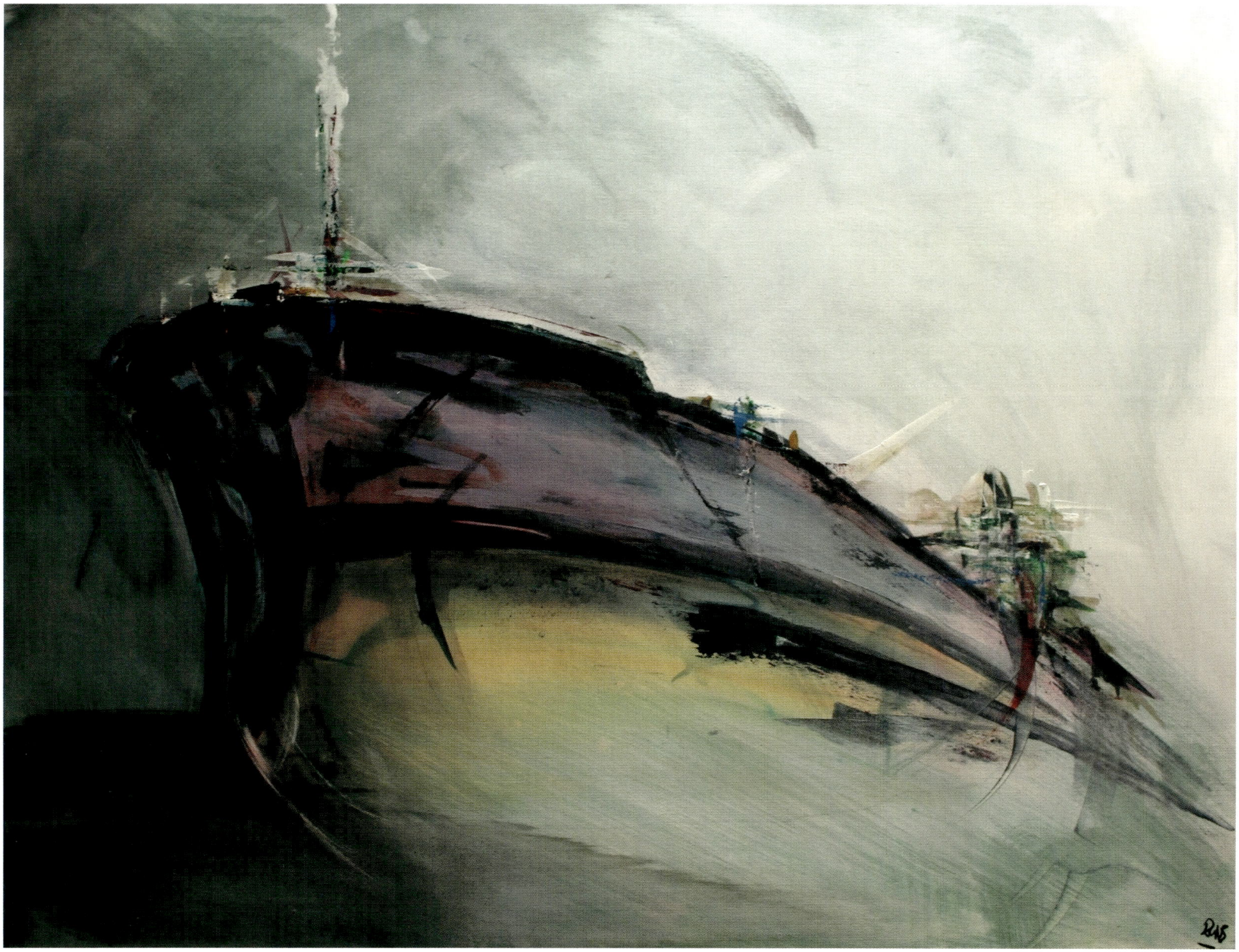

Vincent Donlin

Artist

Clockwise from top:
Wet Day Kensington Place, 2012;
Portrait of Billy Childish, 2013; Amanda, 2011

Vincent Donlin's work spans over three decades, since he started painting in the early seventies.

Vincent is largely self-taught, but was lucky enough to meet and be taught by the late visionary artist Donald Pass at Upbury Manor Secondary School. He later attended Medway College of Design, where he completed a foundation course.

After leaving college, Vincent met artists Stephen and Simon Postgate, Billy Childish, Sexton Ming and Charles Thompson. He also wrote poetry that was published by Charles Thompson, co-founder of the 'Stuckists' group. The poetry was reproduced in Charles's *Cheapo* magazine and was printed on Mr Thompson's own printing press.

During the early eighties, Vincent and his friend and fellow artist-sculptor Stephen Postgate spent time working together in Wales where they shared Stephen's father's cottage in Llandeilo. Here they painted together, sharing ideas, dole cheques, tomato paste, flapjacks, beer and canvas.

Later in London, Vincent and Stephen lived in various squats around Westbourne Park, Latimer Road and Notting Hill Gate. They continued painting large-scale canvases using paint taken from skips, powder paint mixed with washing-up liquid and sized with wallpaper paste on calico. Miraculously, some of this work has survived and is in remarkably good condition.

From 1996 until 2008, Vincent painted pictures of religious subject matter. Since then he has painted numerous paintings of Brighton, which are usually taken from photographs, and portraits in various media including work on an iPad. Most of all he prefers 'the putrefying fecundity of oil paint'. These are painted on canvas or wood using an acrylic underpainting and building up the picture using linseed oil glazes and finished in oil paint.

You can follow Vincent Donlin on Facebook.

Collections
Marino Venturini, Switzerland
Louie Leno, New York
Vivienne Goldman, New York
Bernard and Kirsten, London
The Countess Cowdray, Cowdray Court, West Sussex
Jacqueline and Simon Osborne, Kent
Nick Sharat, Edinburgh, Scotland
Tony Frisby, East Sussex
Les and Helena Heath, Brighton

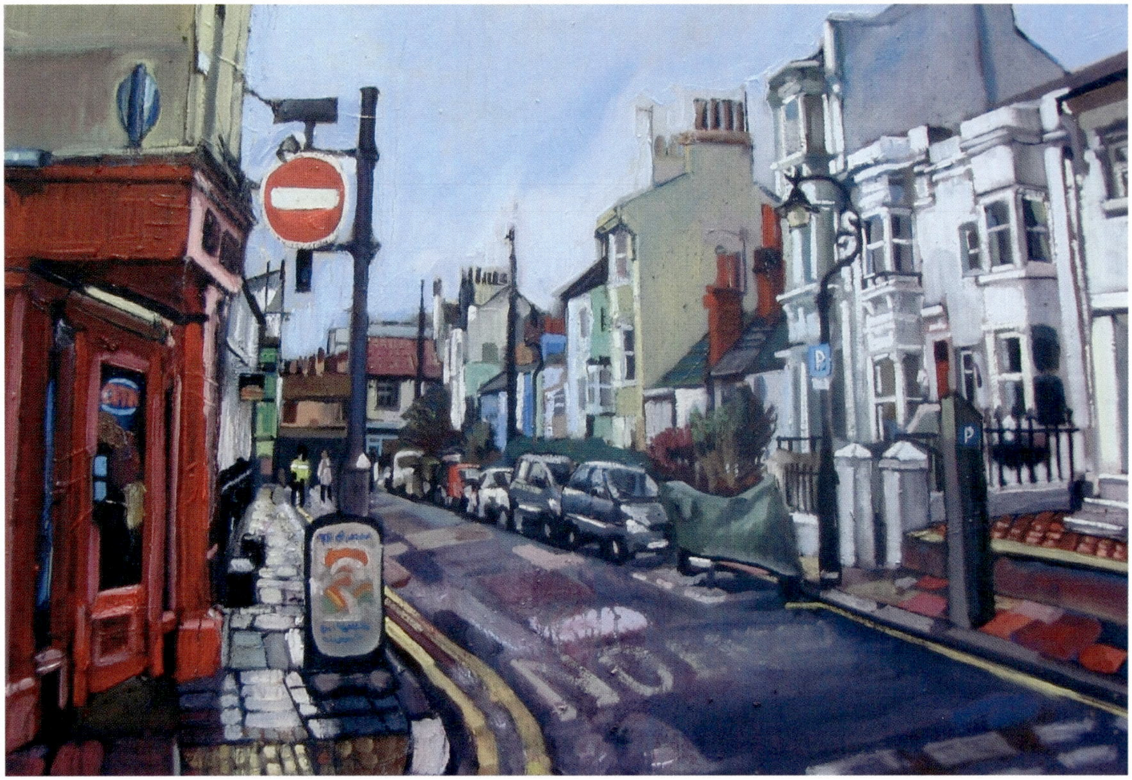

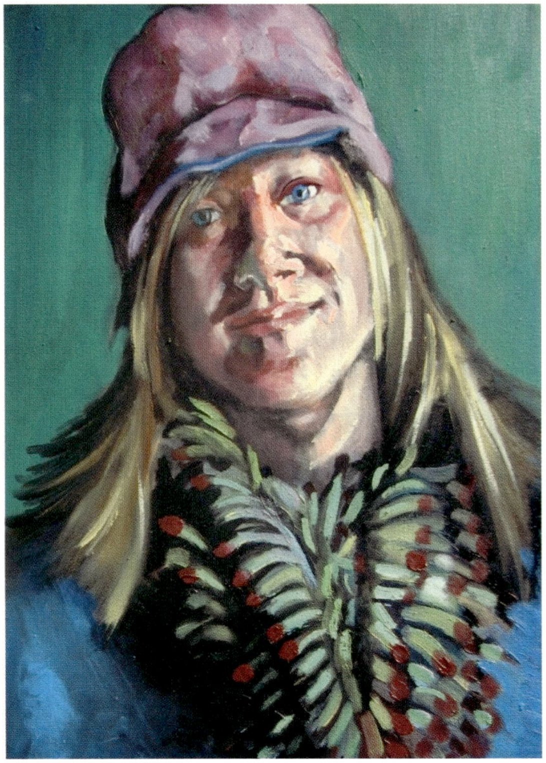

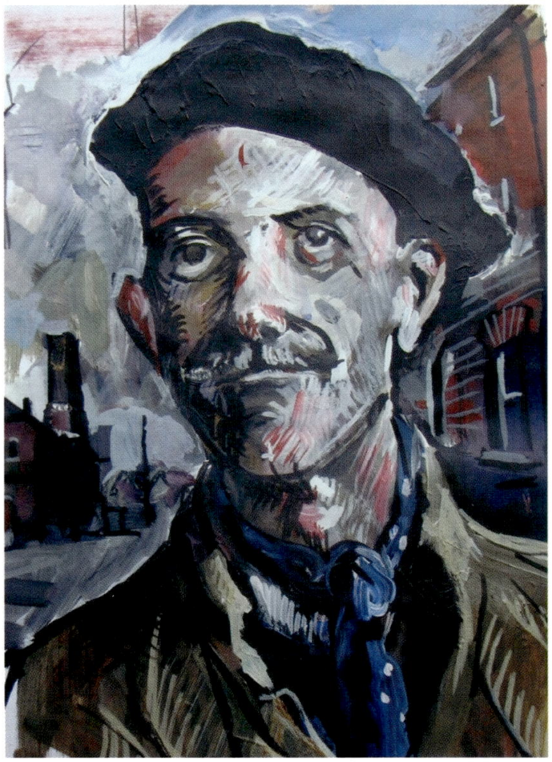

Shops Evening Trafalgar Street, 2012

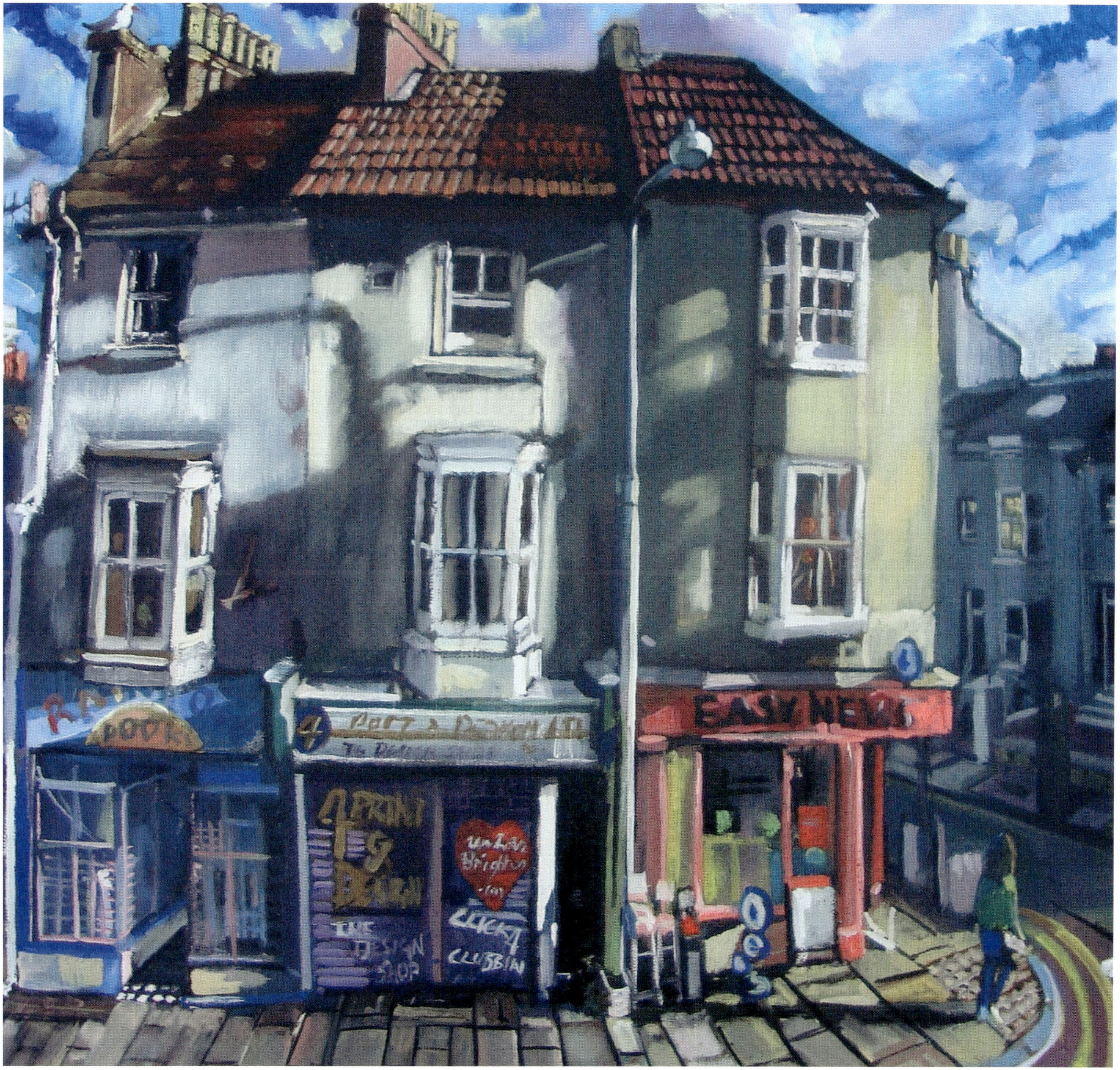

Jessica Barrah

Artist

Clockwise from top left:
E is for Elephant; Feeling Foxy;
Cock Star; Gulls! Gulls! Gulls!

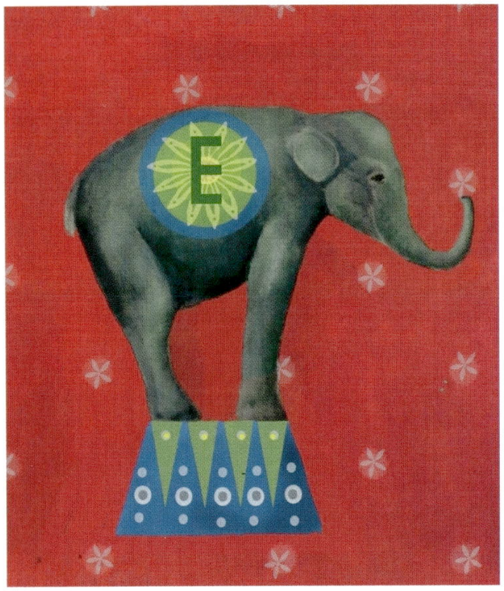

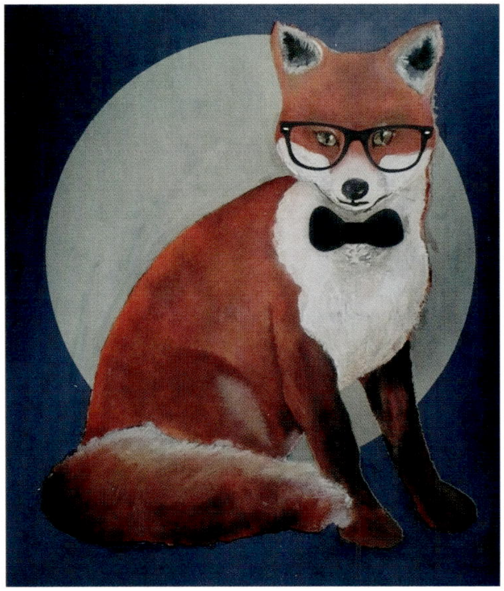

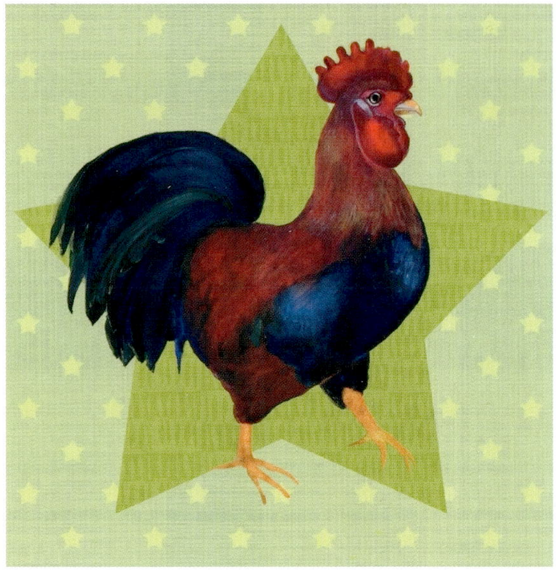

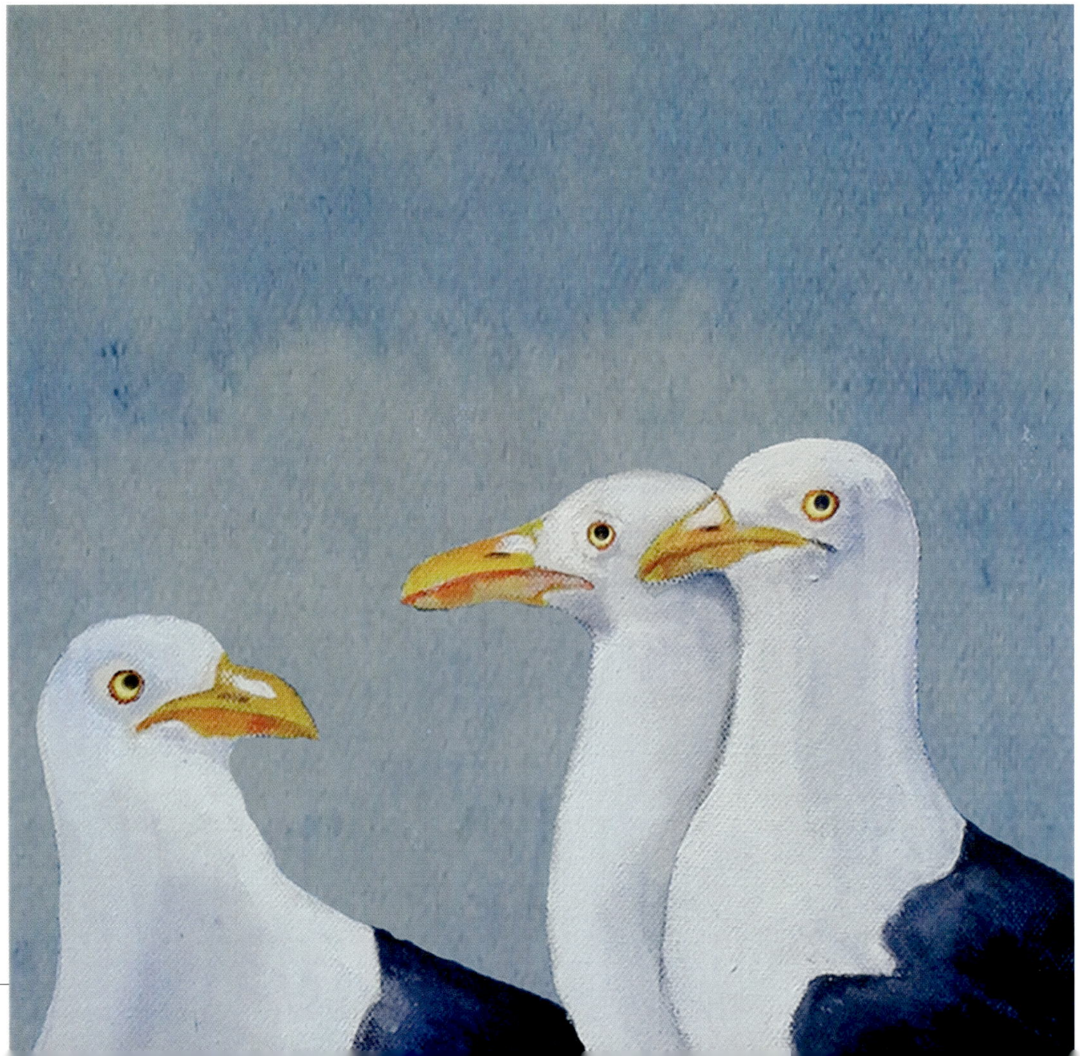

Quirky humour, animals, pattern and a bright but harmonious palette are the hallmarks of Jessica Barrah's designs.

The images shown here form the beginnings of an 'animal alphabet' series. These acrylic paintings and mixed media canvases are a new direction, contrasting with her previous digitally based work.

Jessica is a mainly self-taught artist, having completed a part-time course in Graphic Design at City College Brighton in 2007, and a few evening and weekend classes in illustration, screen printing and linocut.

Since 2011, she has been represented by The Bright Agency, and has featured in a Ladybird nursery rhyme treasury, among other projects. She has also written a children's book to be published in 2014.

For the past few years she has exhibited in various Open Houses and sold her cards, prints and screen-printed textiles at art and craft fairs around Brighton. She also sells online from her website www.birdybrain.com and at www.notonthehighstreet.com/birdybrain.

Jessica is available for commissions – from paintings to personalised prints and invitations – and loves working with clients to bring their ideas to life.

Monika Jakimauskaite

Photographer & Textile Artist

Clockwise from top left
Seven Sisters; Home;
West Pier; Lonely

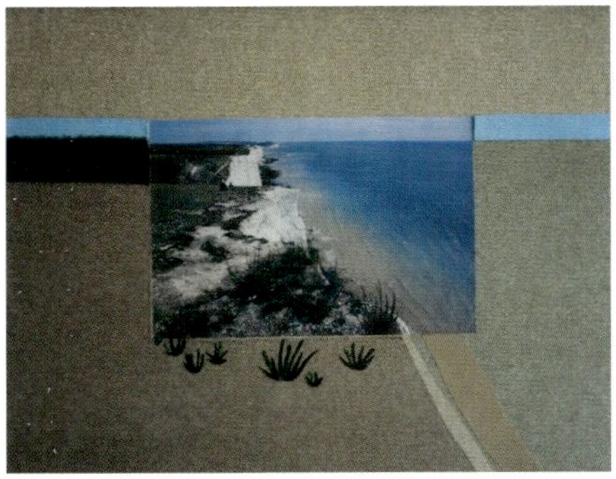

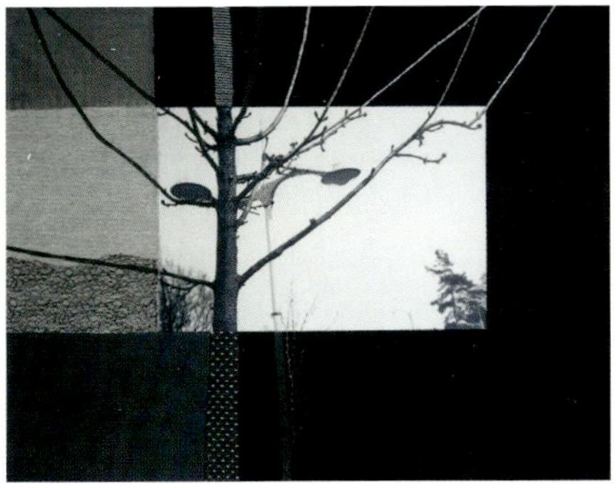

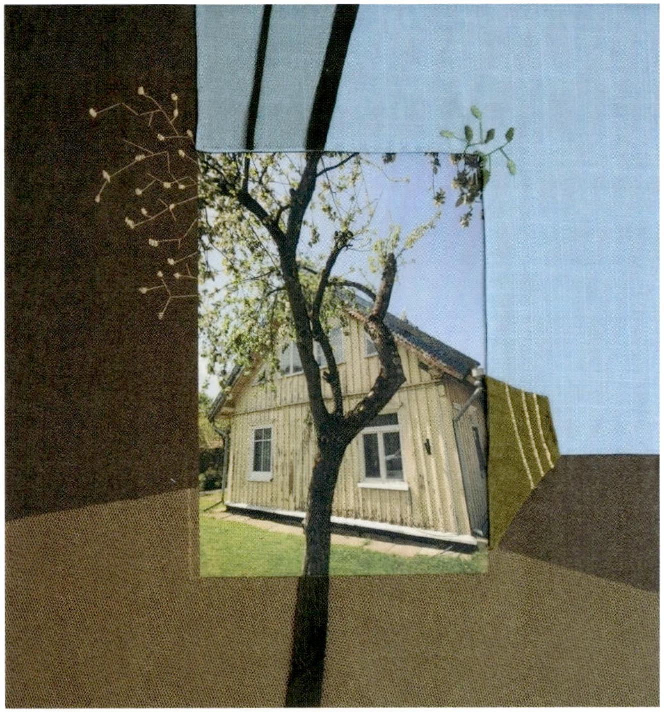

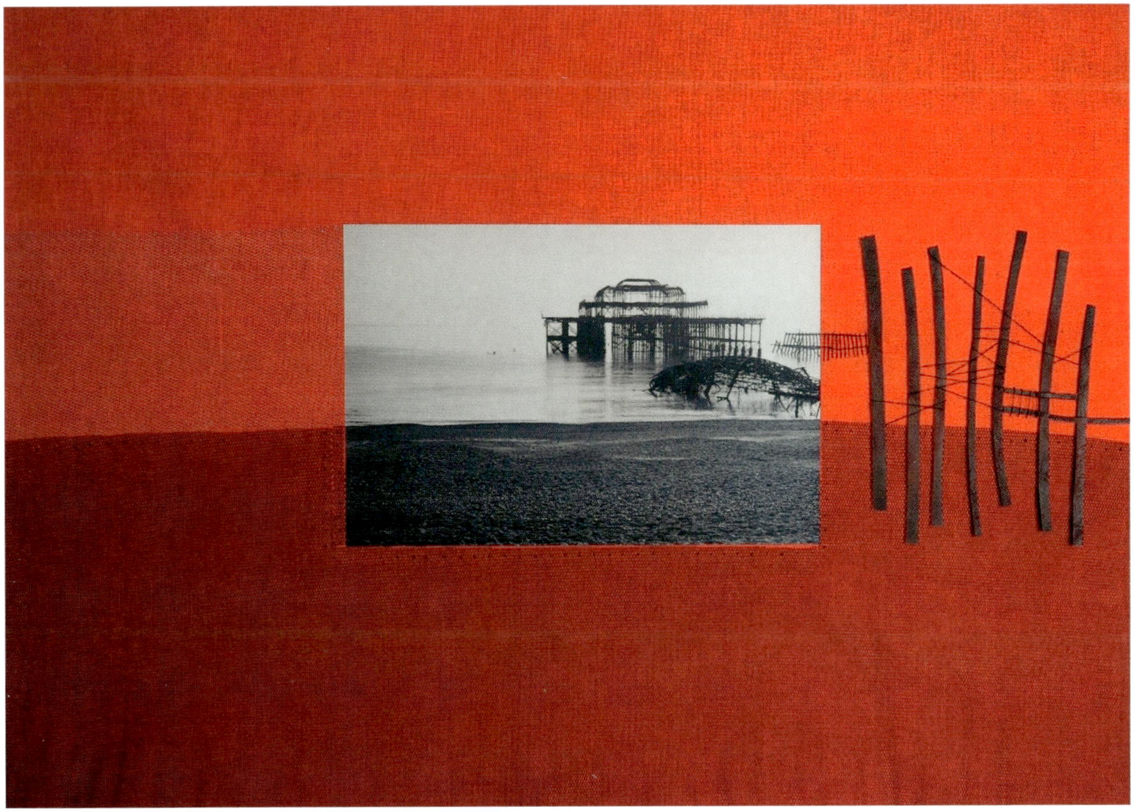

From the moment Monika Jakimauskaite arrived in Brighton she fell in love with the city because it reminded her of her hometown in Lithuania, which is also by the sea. Now, having been selected from thousands of artists based in the UK and internationally, Monika shows her work in the West London-based gallery, Debut Contemporary, as well as exhibiting at other spaces and fairs across the capital, bringing the vibrant Brighton scene and energy to London through her work.

Monika started taking pictures of the city and hoped to show them somewhere one day. After gaining a BA degree in Textile Design & Technology back home at the Lithuania Academy of Arts, she completed a Black & White Photography course at Brighton University and a Printed Textiles course in Brighton and Hove City College. Combining these two techniques created Monika's unexpected and unique mixed media of photography and textile.

Photography is Monika's passion and textile is her craft. The resulting artworks are photographic prints on fabrics, using embroidery and appliqué to extend details. This enables her to capture special sights and moments from every day in a beautiful, totally original combination of mixed media. With landscapes and architecture as her main subjects, Monika uses mostly bright, vibrant colours and intricate details, such as ornaments, to bring her artworks to life. The result is unusual and very intriguing.

With a fashion designer mother, and her father an actor and semi-professional photographer, Monika grew up surrounded and influenced by textiles, photography and culture.

Monika shows her work regularly at exhibitions and art fairs in the UK and back home in Lithuania. She recently had her first solo exhibition in Lithuania, called 'Moments'. Monika has appeared on National TV in Lithuania and has been published in *Aesthetica*, *Brighton's Arty Magazine*, *Laima Magazine*, *West Express*, *Literature & Art* and *Klaipeda Newspapers* in Lithuania.

Heike Roesel

Artist

Clockwise from top left: Spring Gardens ; Up; Magic Mountain 2;

Heike finds the inspiration for her etchings from observing day-to-day life situations. Ordinary objects can be a source she draws on, as much as her surroundings here in Brighton. Heike looks at the shapes, colours, and forms, and mixes these impressions with a large sprinkling of imagination to develop them into visual ideas. The focus in her artistic work is to bring life to these composed 'worlds of their own', that otherwise would not exist.

Since 2010, Heike has been working with acrylic resist etching techniques. This alternative process opened up a wide creative playing field for her ideas. The process has a strong influence as a creative tool in its own right. Down to the printing of each etching, Heike looks for the unexpected: the 'spark' and a surprise at the end of this creative journey. Each of the resulting prints is an original piece of artwork.

With the resulting etchings, Heike hopes to inspire the observer's imagination, so they can discover their own individual 'picture' in her work. Her desire is to send people's minds on a joyful journey, that finds new aspects in the imagery every time they look.

Imagination is what else there might be.

Heike's etchings are on sale in Brighton's iO Gallery (page 124) and Bellis Gallery (page 132); also Cuckoo Cuckoo Gallery, Westhill Arcade, Hastings.

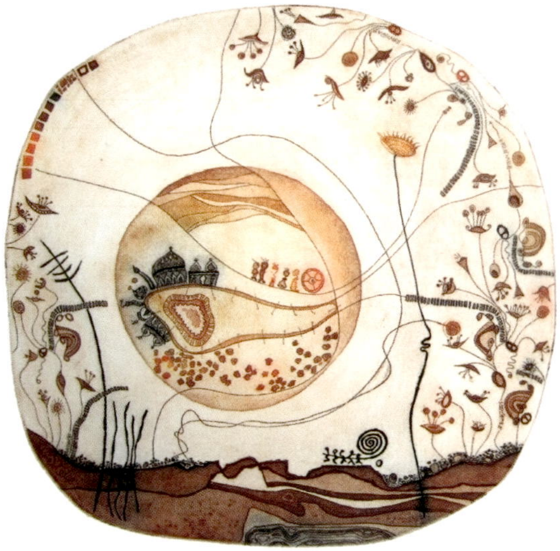

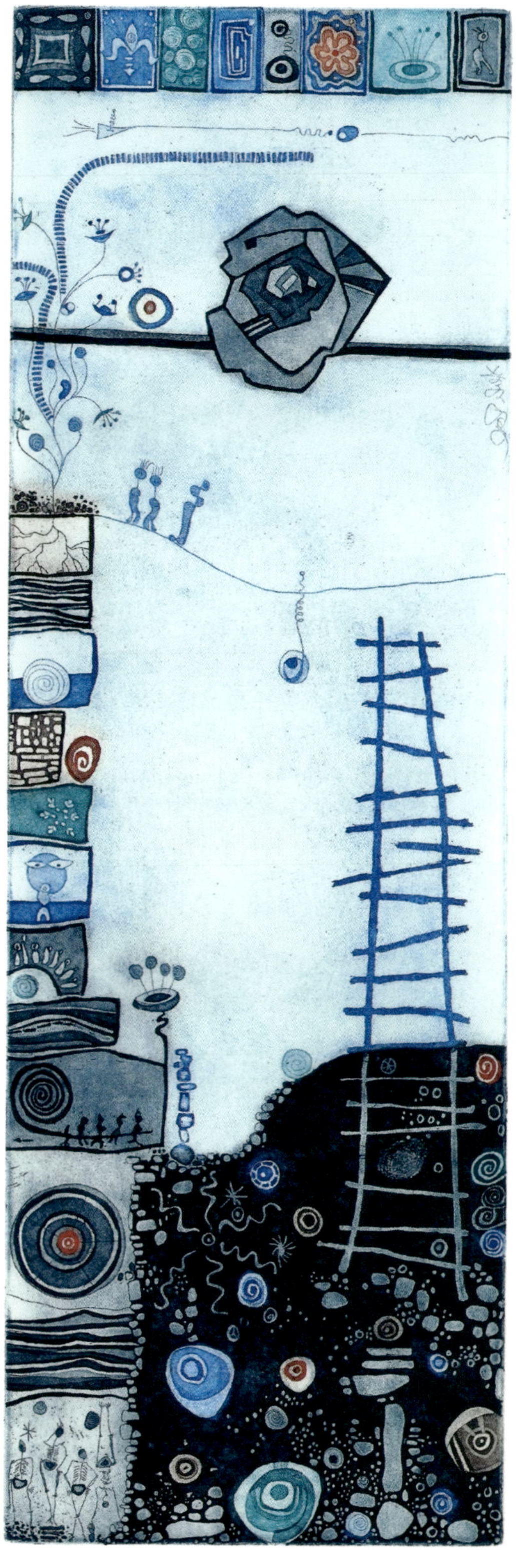

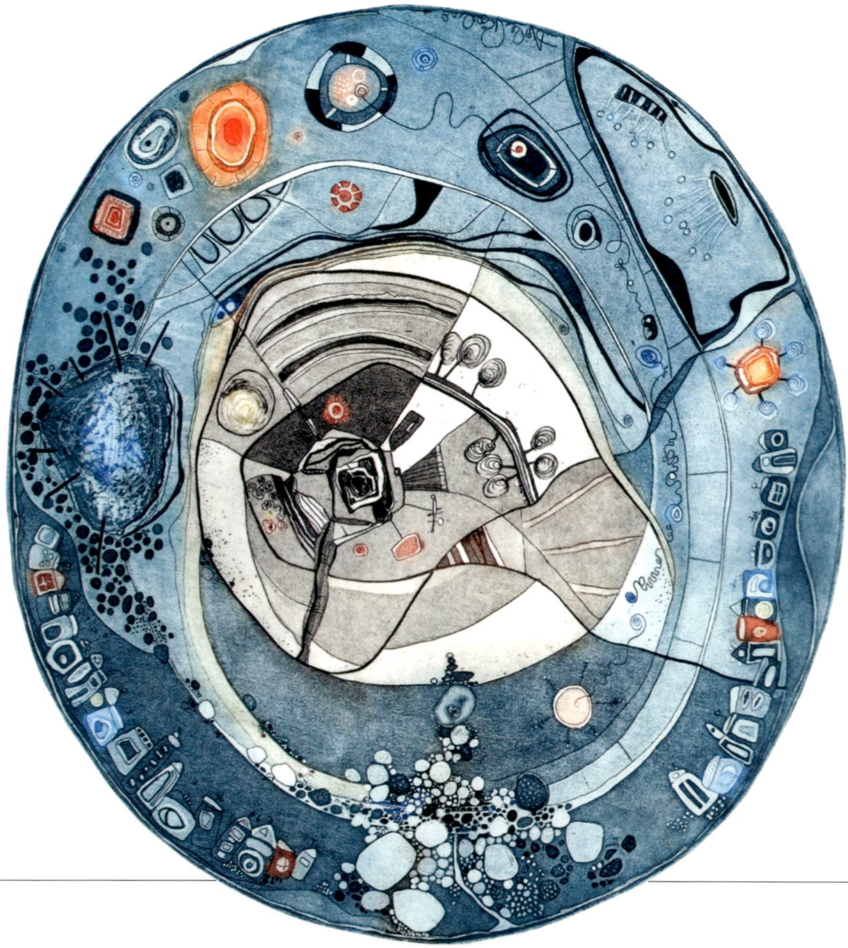

Clockwise from top:
Lost in the Laines; Ticket to Ride;
Up the Hill; Brighton Bits

Janet Brooke

Artist & Printmaker

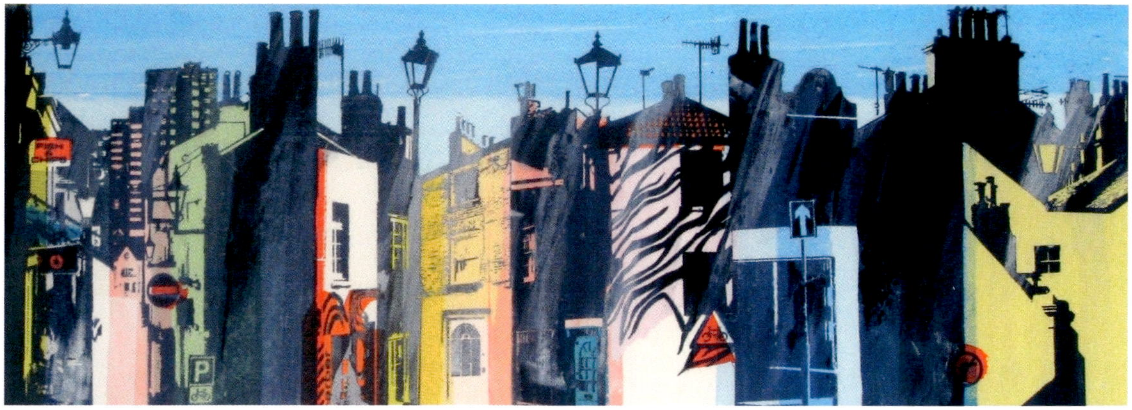

Janet Brooke is a printmaker specialising in the urban landscape. In her linocuts and screen prints she tries to evoke a clear sense of place. During her long career, her eye has been caught by many and varied places from the East End and City of London to cities in the Far East such as Hong Kong and Singapore.

But since her move back here, the place that has fired her imagination most has been Brighton, and in a short period of time she has produced an impressive catalogue of local work. Her prints of this many-faceted city aim to capture something of its essence without resorting to cliché.

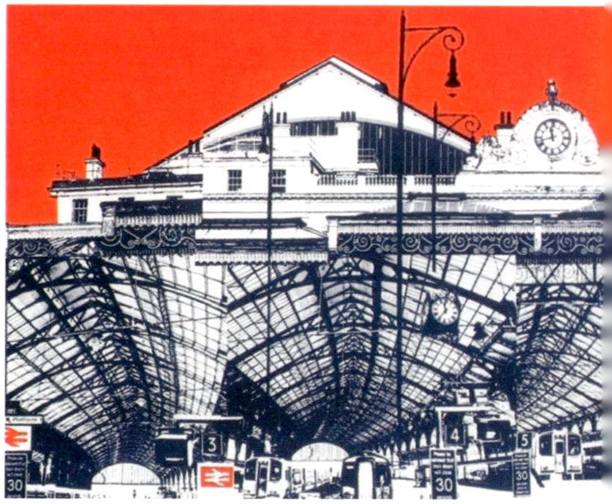

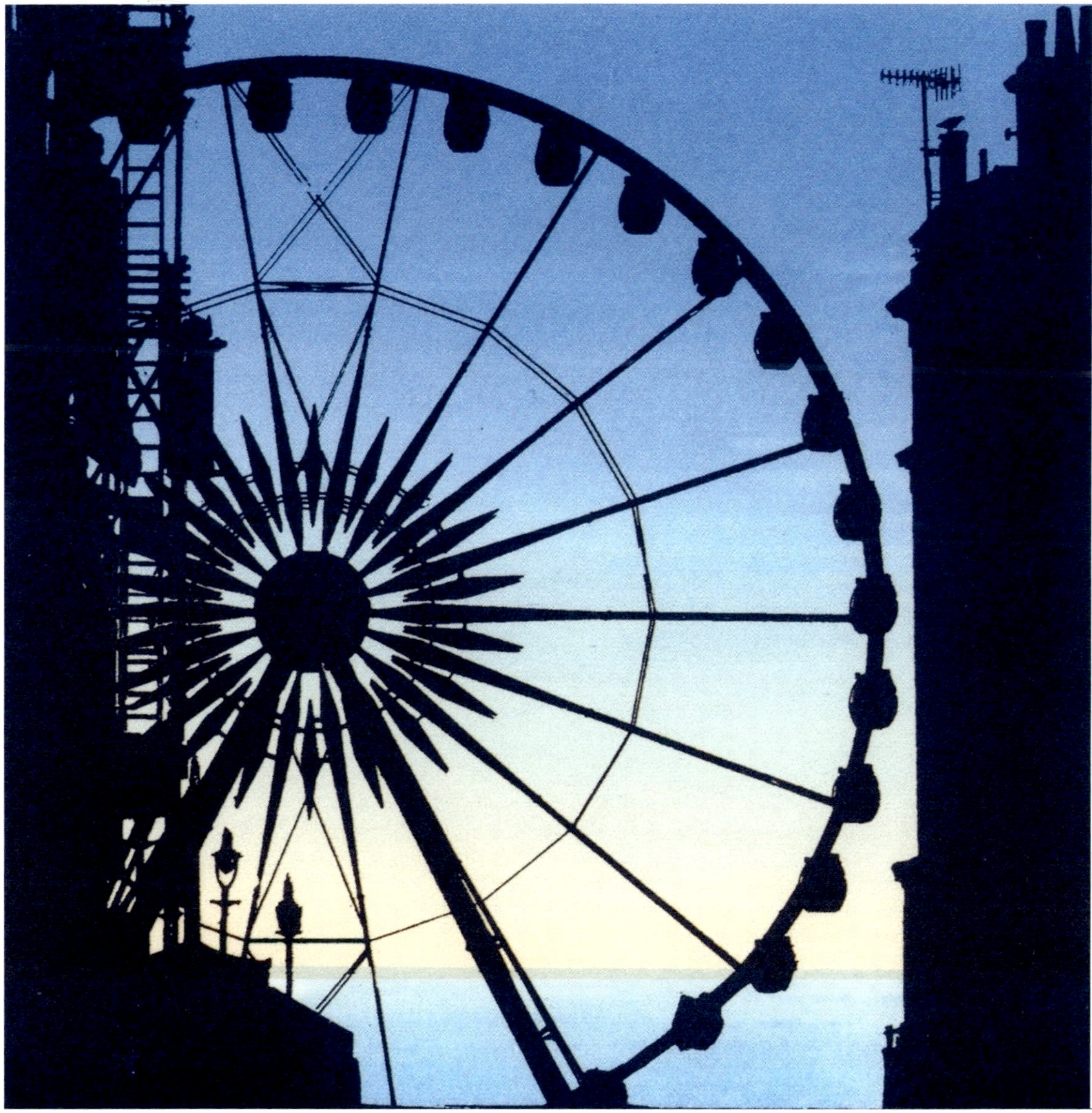

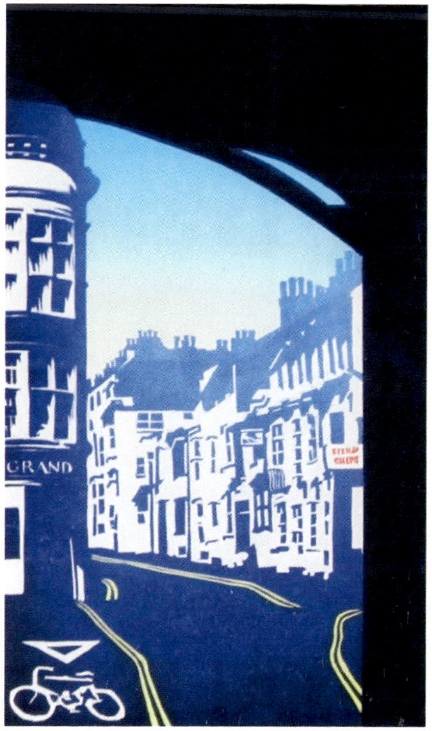

Paul Martin

Artist

Below left: Heavens Above
Below: Er-Lannic

Paul Martin considers the art process a form of dialogue with the world: a way of exploring his relationships to it, and distilling – in visual form – tentative interpretations of things understood and felt. It is a personal process of making meaning, through which the visual manifestations hold potential meaning for others.

His work revolves around a series of long-lived themes. For many years Paul has visited Provence to experience the wildness of the landscape, and his work developed from early realistic studies to the expressive abstraction of wind-blown cherry blossom in 'Provence Spring'. He has an enduring fascination with the ancient standing stones of Brittany and Cornwall, from the healing energy of 'Men-an-tol' to the surging power of the partly submerged 'Er-Lannic' with its sinister black guardian cormorants. Recently he has visited the prehistoric art in the caves of the Dordogne and made a series of paintings responding to the amazing art of our ancestors dating back 30,000 years. 'Falling Horse' from Lascaux combines one of the caves' enigmatic images with its many abstract patterns.

Paul's working process involves intense, on-the-spot research trying to capture a sense of place. In his studio he begins with an idea/feeling/sense of something on the edge of his understanding, then sets off into the work that becomes the focus through which he explores those tentative ideas and feelings. The creative process becomes a strange dance between those original ideas, new insights and the demands that emanate from the work itself. All this is played out through his chosen medium using the elements of formal values such as line, tone, colour, composition, texture etc, and experimentation, to create the desired interpretive effects. It's a voyage of discovery both exhilarating and disturbing as the destination is unknown until he arrives, or not!

Paul trained in Environmental Art & Design at Bournemouth College of Art, and has balanced being a practising artist with a varied education career ranging from Adult Education and co-writing a Painting Degree to being a Senior Lecturer at Brighton University. He gained a PhD in Adults Learning in Art at Surrey University in 1999. Together with his wife Viv, Paul was a founding member of the Fiveways Group in the Brighton Festival and continues to show regularly in Open Studios events.

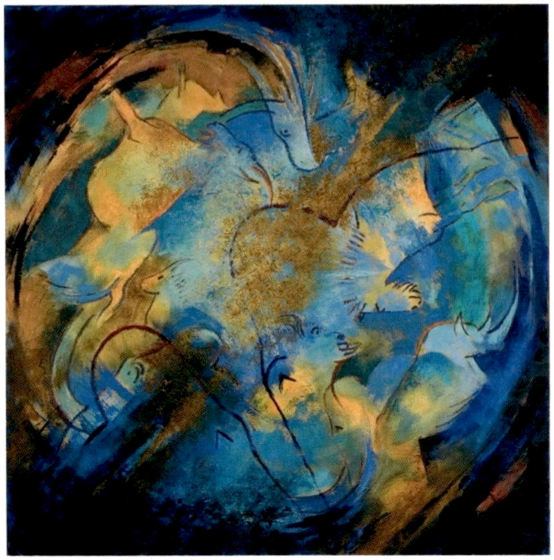

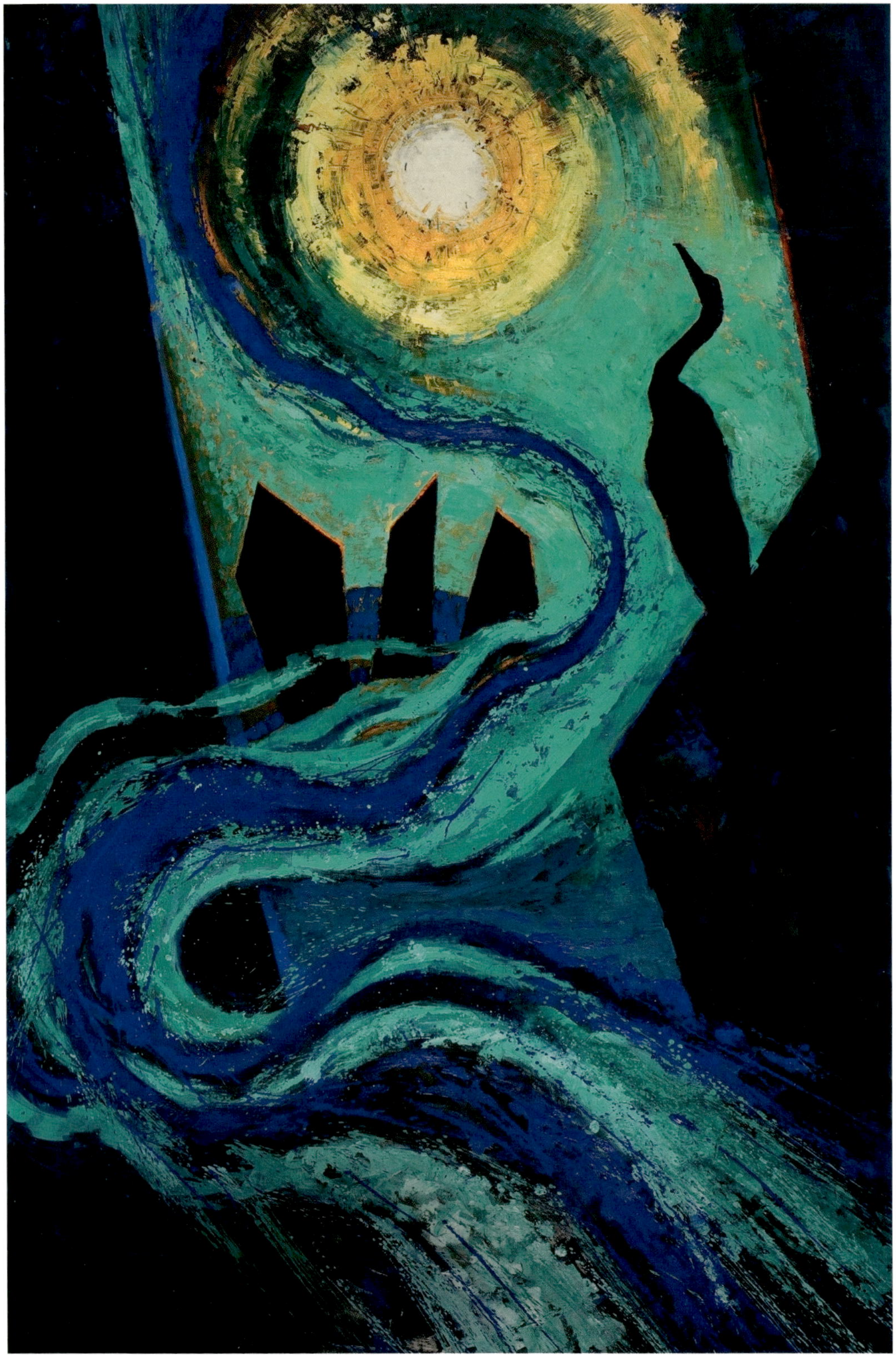

Clockwise from top left
The Cow jumped over the Moon, Falling Horse,
Men-an-tol Portal, Provence Spring

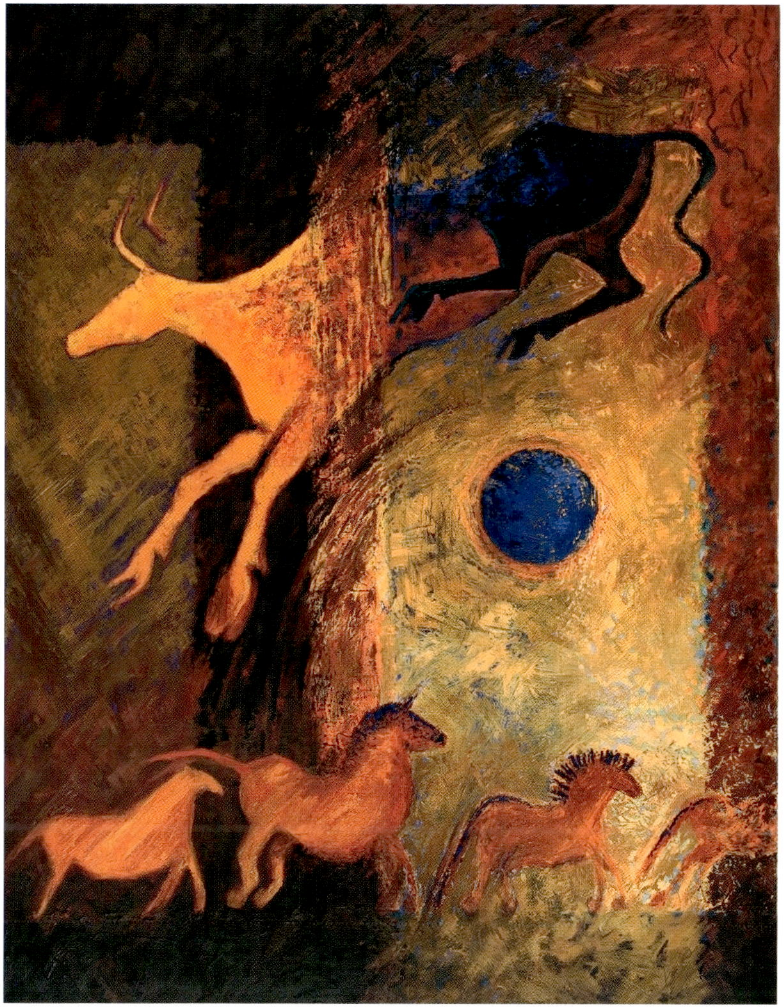

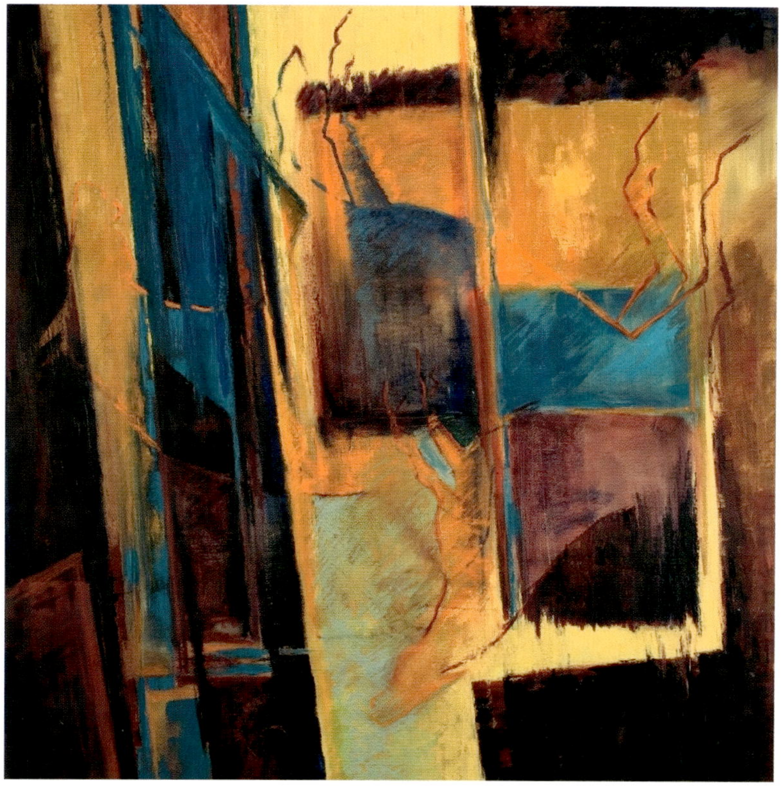

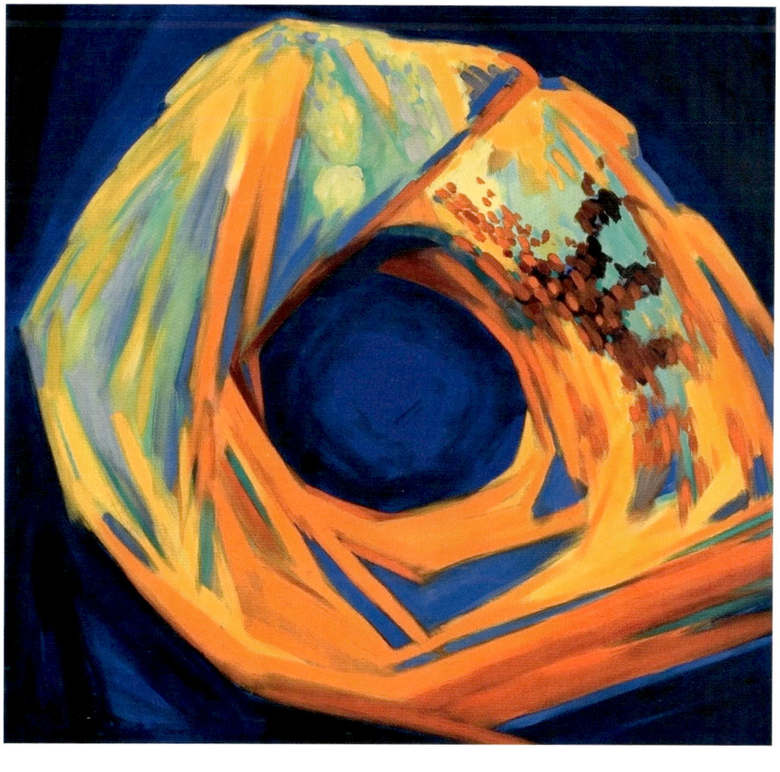

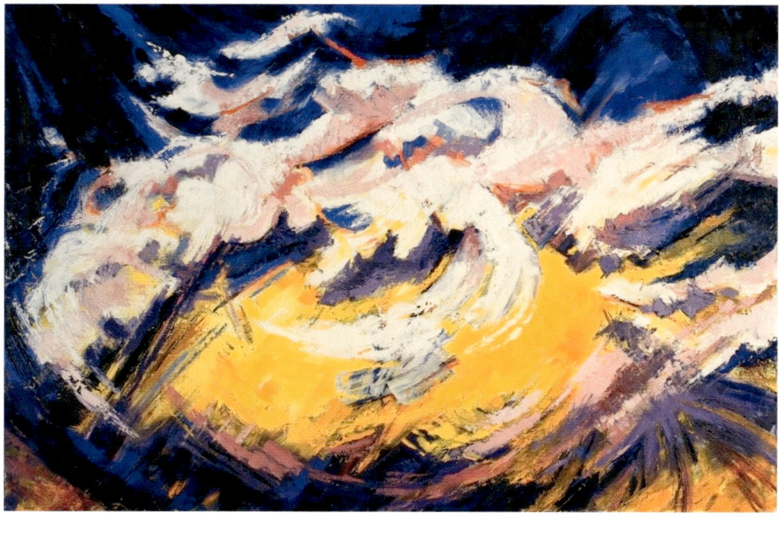

Susan Taylor

Artist

Clockwise from top left:
Black Jaguar;
Bird; Horses; Lion

Artist Susan Taylor gets her inspiration from nature and the environment, painting incredible life-like paintings of animals, flowers and landscapes. She has exhibited here in Brighton, Shoreham and London, and it is her desire to use her art to contribute in some way to protecting endangered species in the wild. With each sale she donates a minimum of 10% to wildlife foundations. Susan also takes commissions for pet portraits.

Follow Susan on Facebook (facebook.com/susantaylor.co.uk) or at Twitter (suzart1).

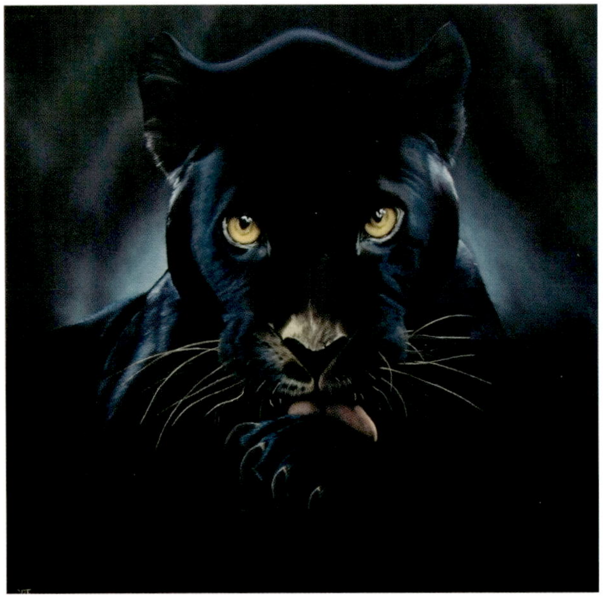

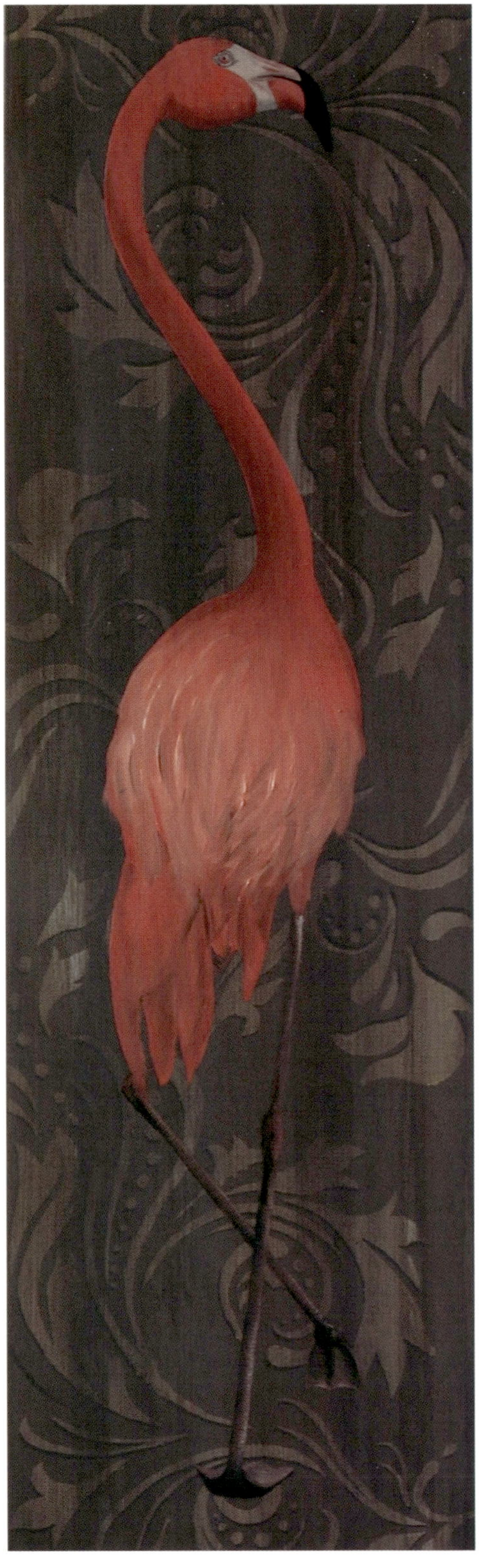

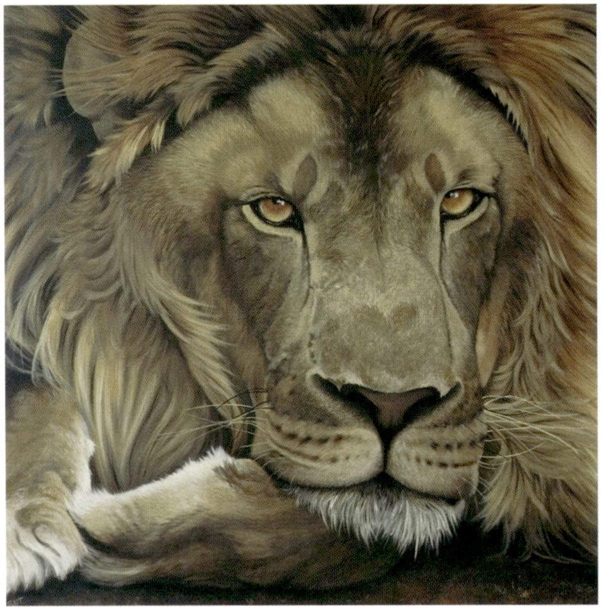

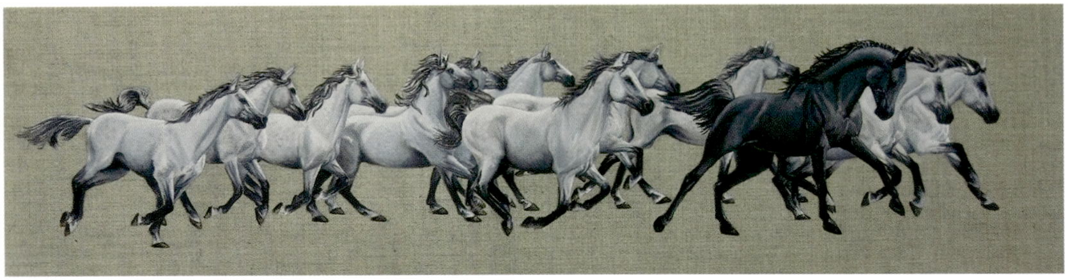

Clockwise from top left:
Layap Lady; The Stones, Glastonbury;
The Proprietor, Tombstone; Summer Rose

Wendy Standen

Artist

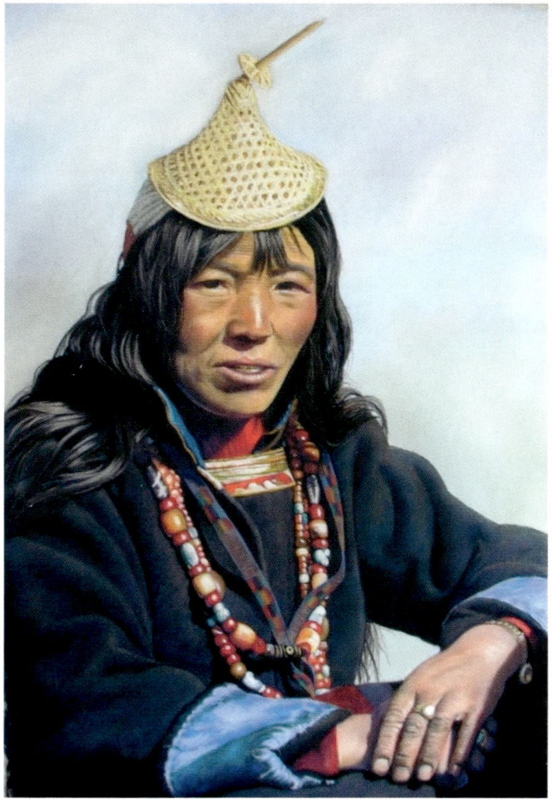

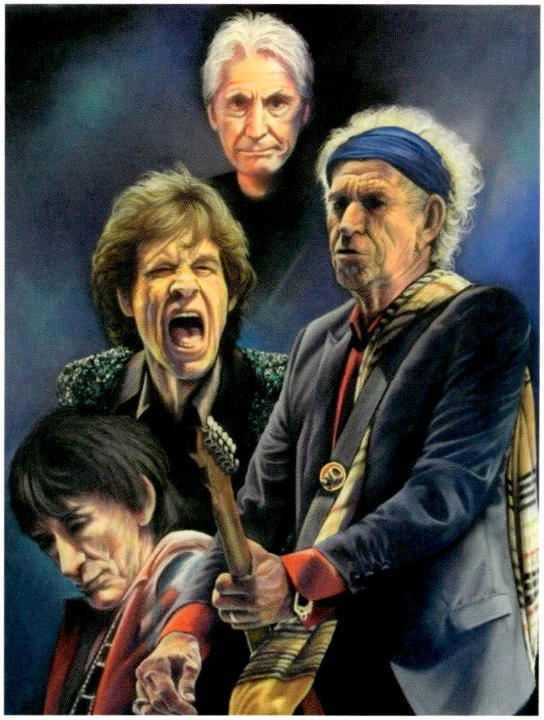

Wendy trained as a teacher specialising in art and design, and taught for the last 20 years of her career in Brighton primary schools. She has recently specialised in painting in pastels, although she also produces work in a range of other media both 2 and 3D.

Wendy has a particular interest in portraiture, both human and animal, working from drawings from life and from photographs. She is a member of several art groups and societies, and is Secretary of the long-established Attic Art Club of Ditchling and has won several awards for her work.

Her work has been published in *Artists & Illustrators Magazine* and shown in the Mall Galleries, London.

Wendy is currently a Director of Shoreham Art Gallery, a collective of more than 20 artists, where some of her work is always on show and for sale. She can be visited by arrangement at her studio in Brighton.

Wendy is available for commissions for portraits in pastel – both human and animal. See her work at Shoreham Gallery, 27 Brunswick Road, Shoreham-by-Sea, BN43 5WA.

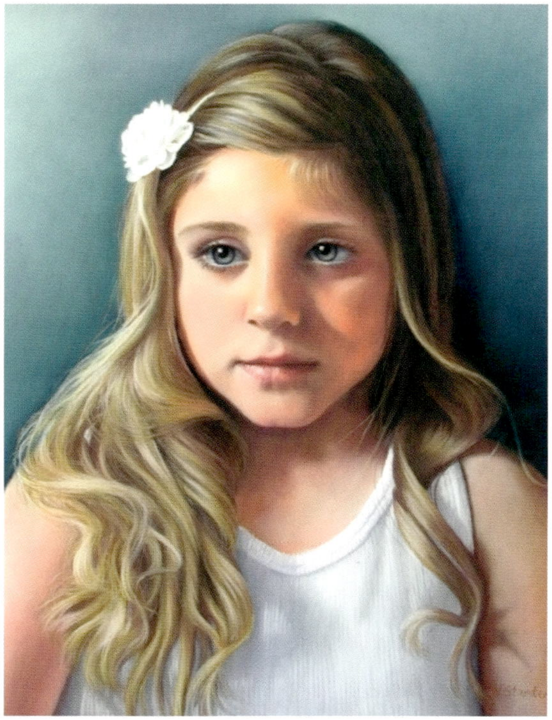

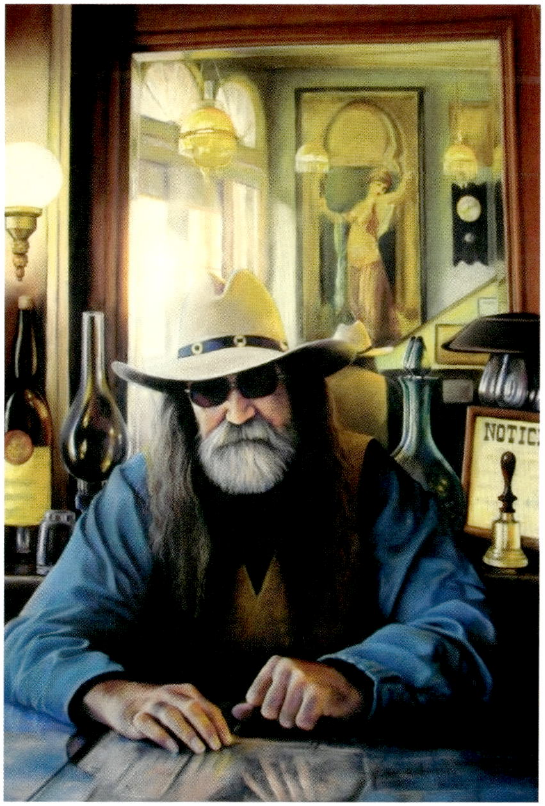

Angela Collier

Photographer

Clockwise from top left: Storm Hercules sunset, on driftwood; Surf Reflection, on textured distressed paper on natural slate; Brighton Abstract Seascapes, on reclaimed wood; Beach Lights, on reclaimed sea groyne

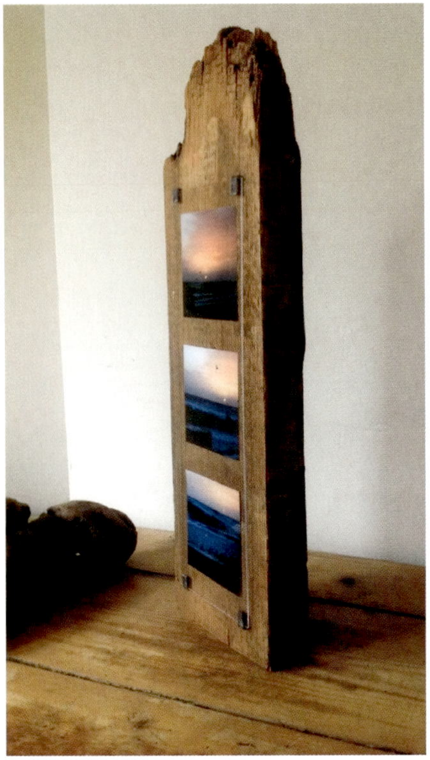

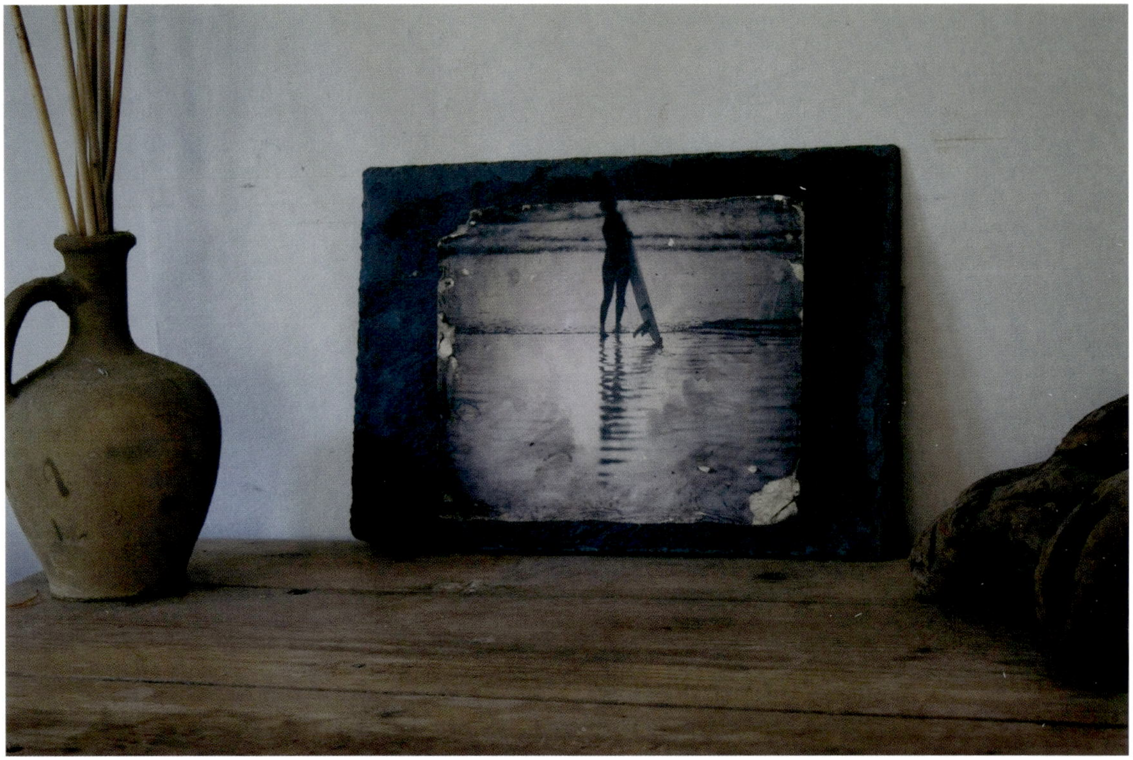

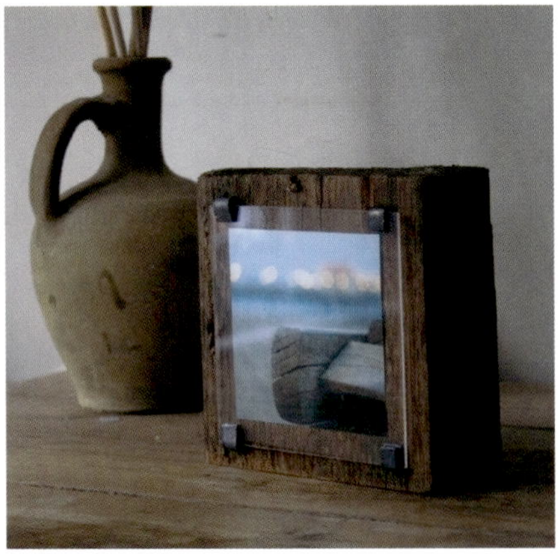

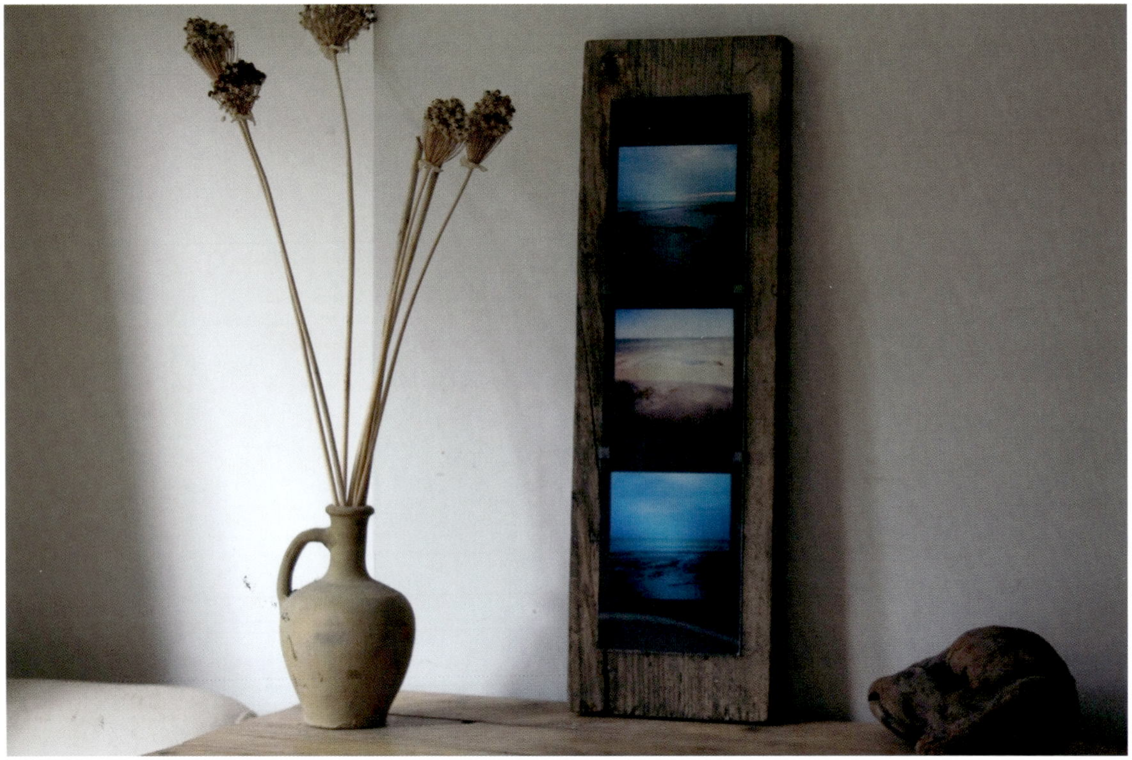

Angela Collier captures ethereal and atmospheric photography featuring moonlight seascapes, and abstract surf and beach photography. These images are complemented by the use of reclaimed wood including sea groynes, driftwood and natural slate.

Each photographic art block is handmade and one of a kind. Commissions for bespoke photographic blocks are welcome.

Below: Monoladybird
Right: Flight of Fancy

Chris MacDonald

Found Object Sculptor

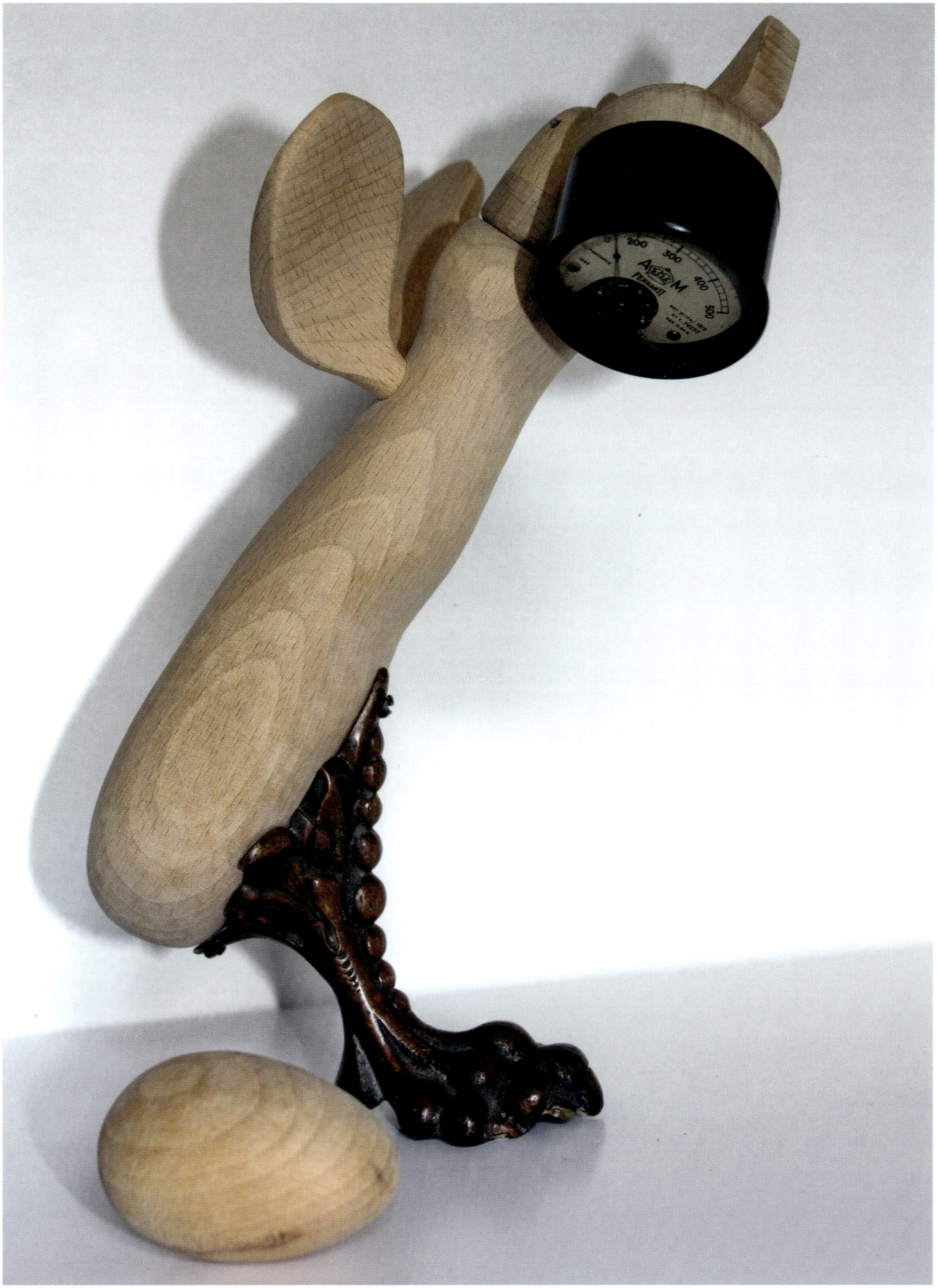

Chris MacDonald's 'Monoladybird' is staring down intently at the perfectly carved egg that's appeared by its perfectly carved bottom. Its perfectly carved wings are raised in surprise. The sculpture is supported by a single brass foot from a long-discarded piece of furniture. "It would have been no use to anyone but me," observes Chris. Which sums up perfectly what this 'found object sculptor' is all about.

His style is suffused with surreal wit. And if you are looking for a truly original piece of 3D artwork, Chris can transform what most regard as 'rubbish' into artworks that amaze with their imagination and skill.

Chris is one of Brighton's most accessible artists, so just give him a call (see index page 150 for contact details).

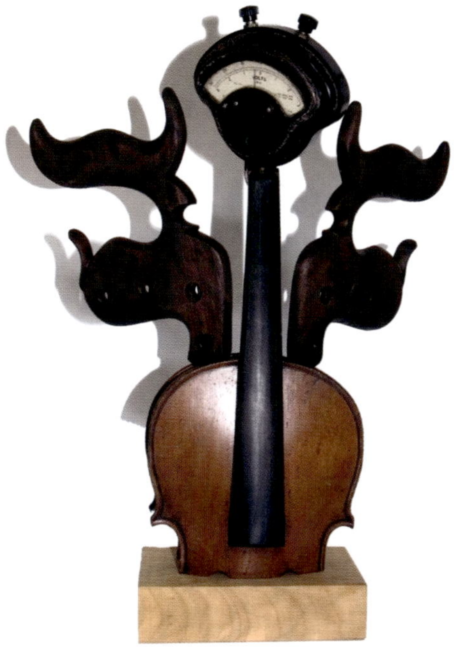

Luella Martin

Artist & Printmaker

Clockwise from top left:
Moon Birds; Floating; Stormy Sunday;
Birds of a Feather; Bird Box; The Fishing Beach

Luella Martin creates paintings and handmade, limited-edition etchings at Phoenix Studios, Brighton.

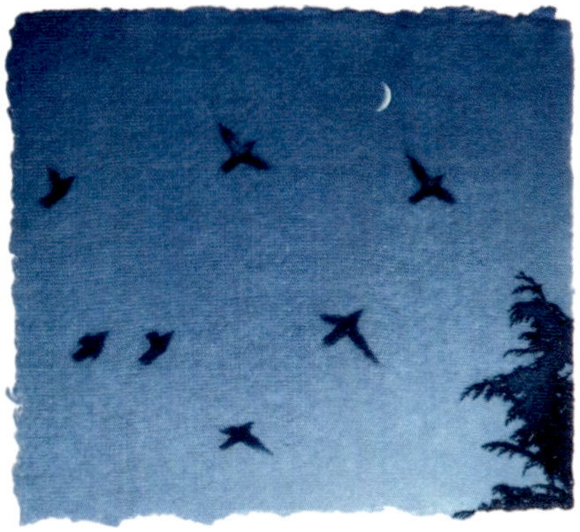

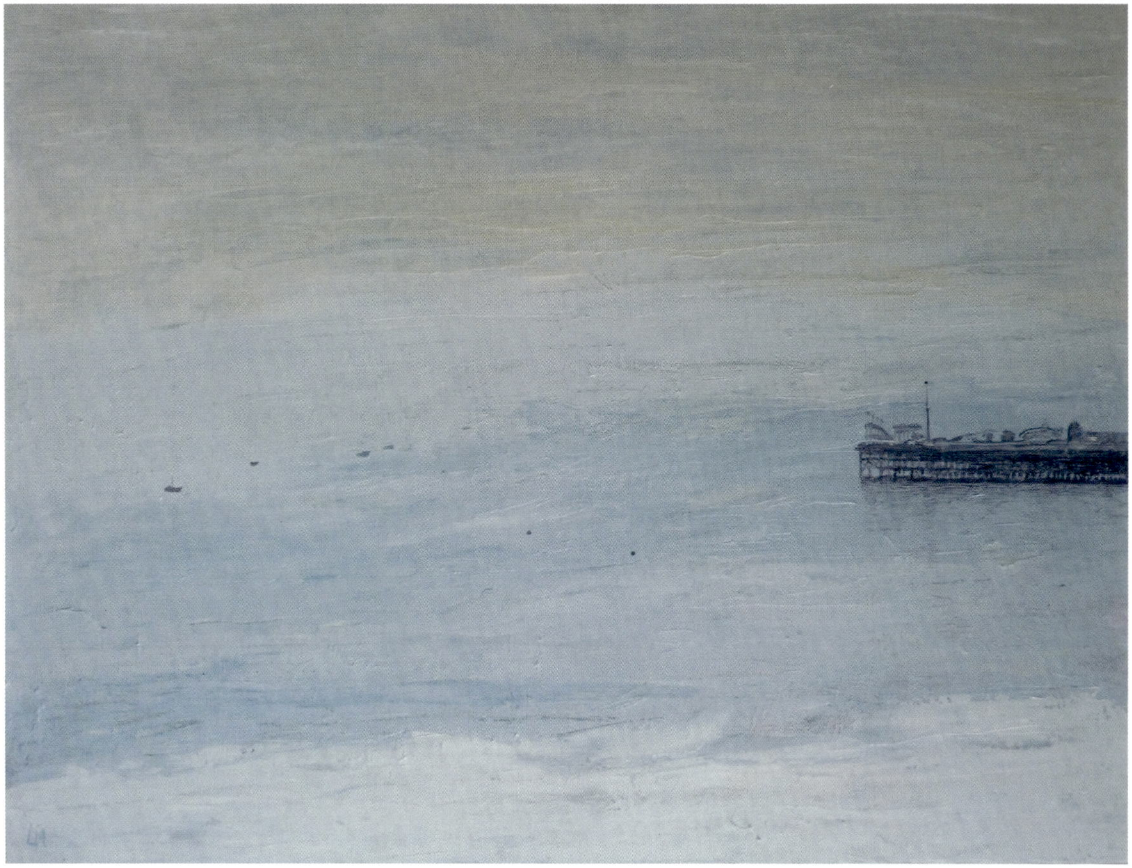

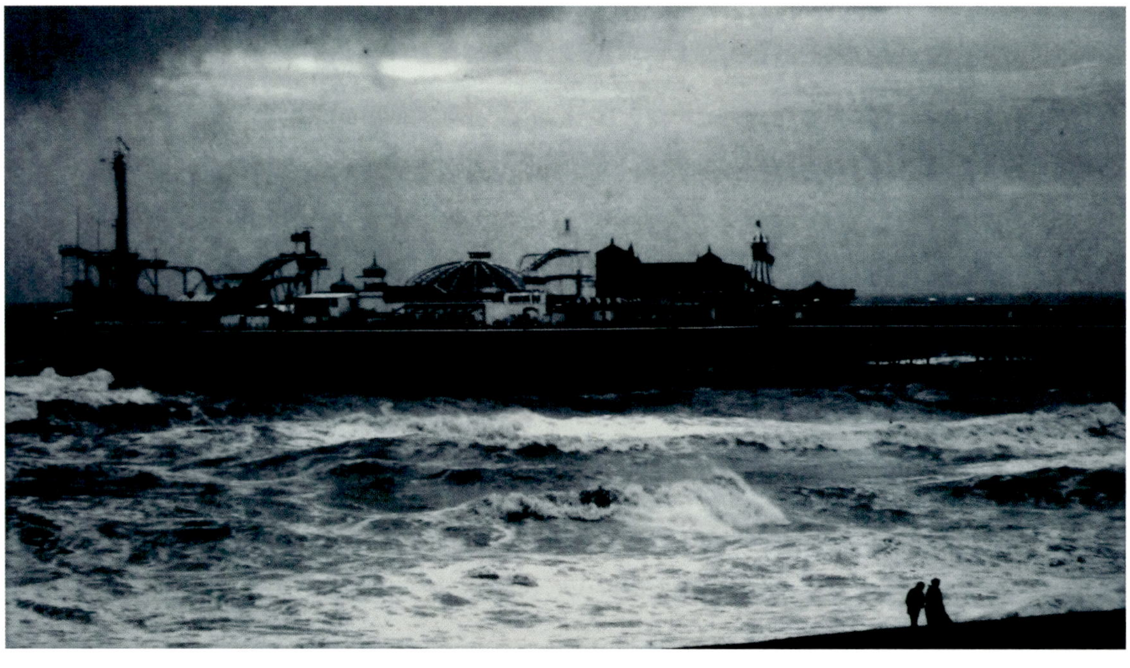

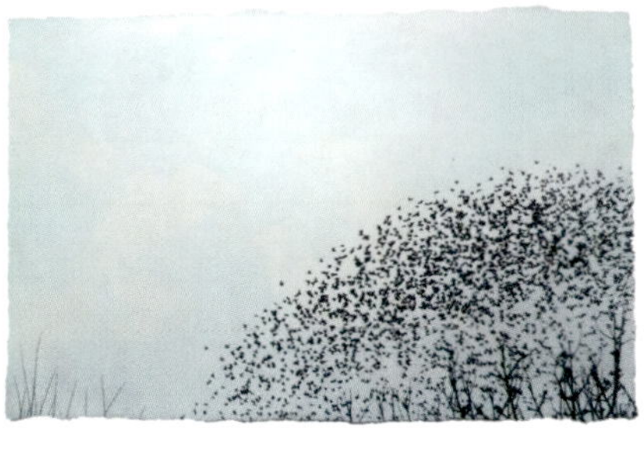

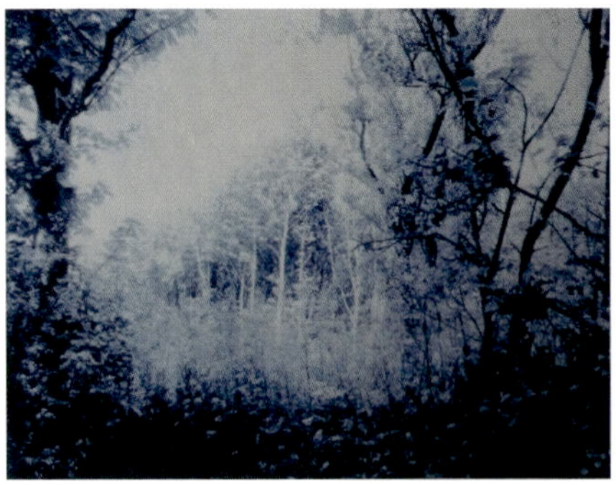

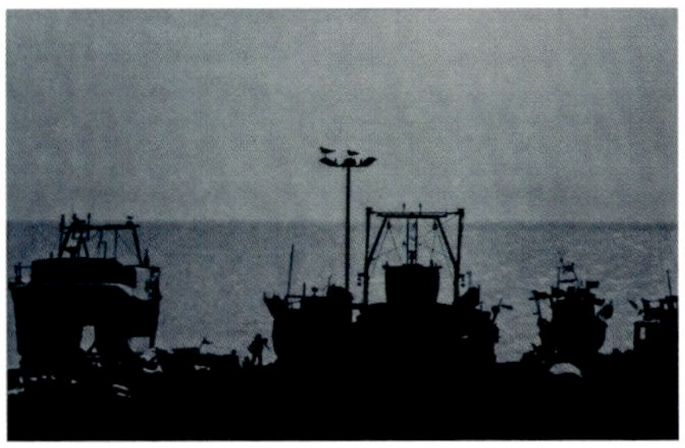

Clockwise from top left:
Nesting; The Great Escape;
Underneath; Whispering Birds

Suzanne Breakwell

Paper Artist & Maker

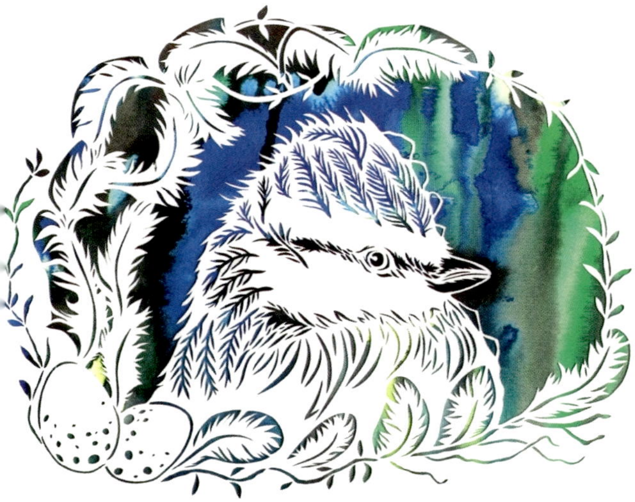

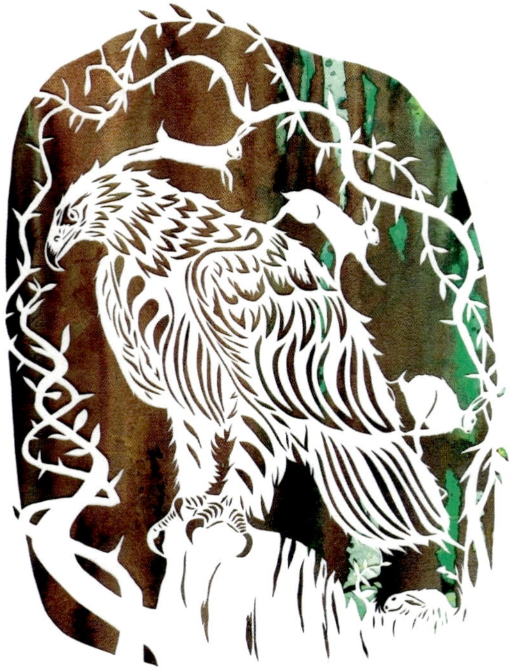

The inspiration for Suzanne Breakwell's artwork comes from her overwhelming love for and fascination with the natural world and all its glorious flora and fauna. She adores paper as a medium, and enjoys the beauty and simplicity of creating a story from a single sheet of paper. An idea for a new piece will often start with a continuous line drawing with the intention to mirror nature's indomitable spirit of constant change and movement. Flow, energy and pattern figure as key principles within the work she creates.

When making the sculptural pieces Suzanne finds the delicate yet strong characteristics of paper make it an interesting and versatile material to work with. It is this contradictory nature that fascinates her, and its ability to continually reinvent itself never ceases to amaze.

Suzanne currently exhibits and sells her work through selected galleries within the UK and her website. She is also happy to work on commissioned pieces. Please contact her for further details (see index page 151).

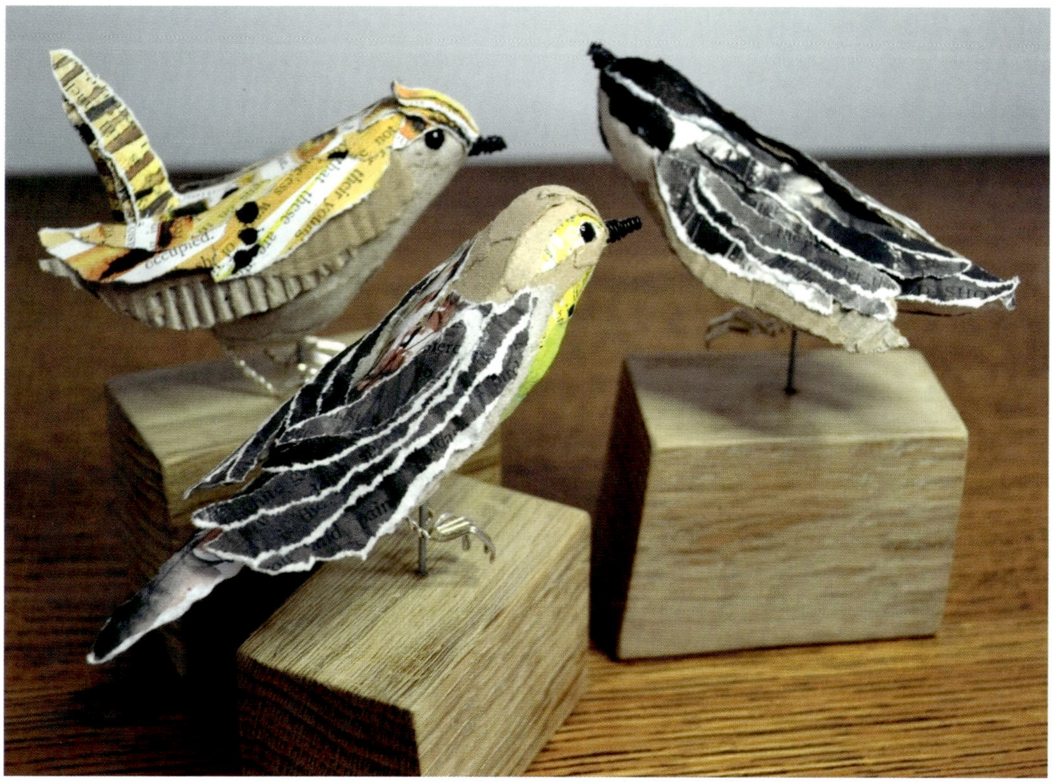

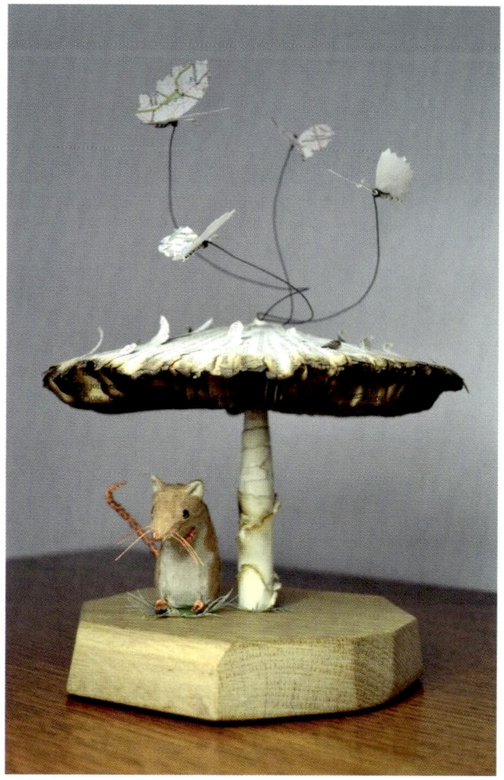

Mark Glassman

Artist

Mark Glassman's recent paintings express the on-going dialogue between the artist's vision and the Sussex landscape that surrounds him, where he continues to experiment with the fluid and textural qualities of paint, abstracted forms and graphic simplicity based on feeling and observation.

A local sculptor in Lewes, Serena Thirkell, recently said of Mark's work:

"I love Mark Glassman's work. I have his painting of a Norman country church, its pointed hat tower stark against the fields and sky as I see it whenever I go past. He has a strong, evocative and highly original style when painting Sussex: its cliffs, seaside, fields and lanes. His record of a time and place on the Sussex coast has to me an unparalleled truthfulness and graphic beauty."

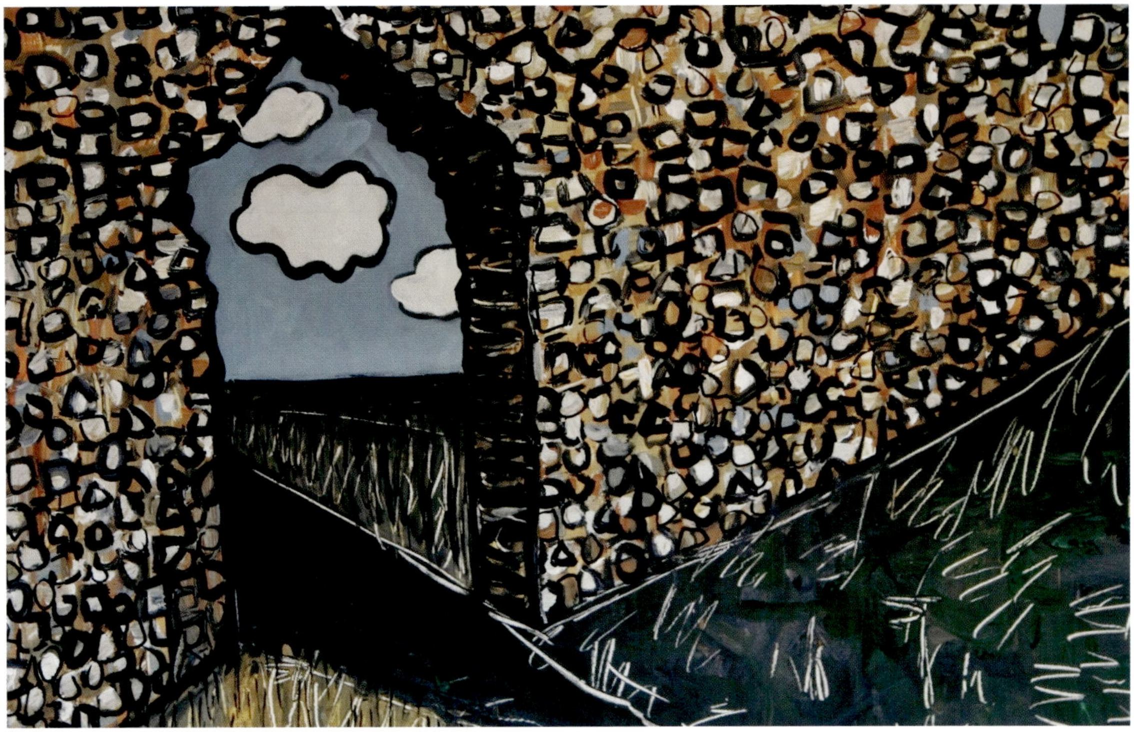

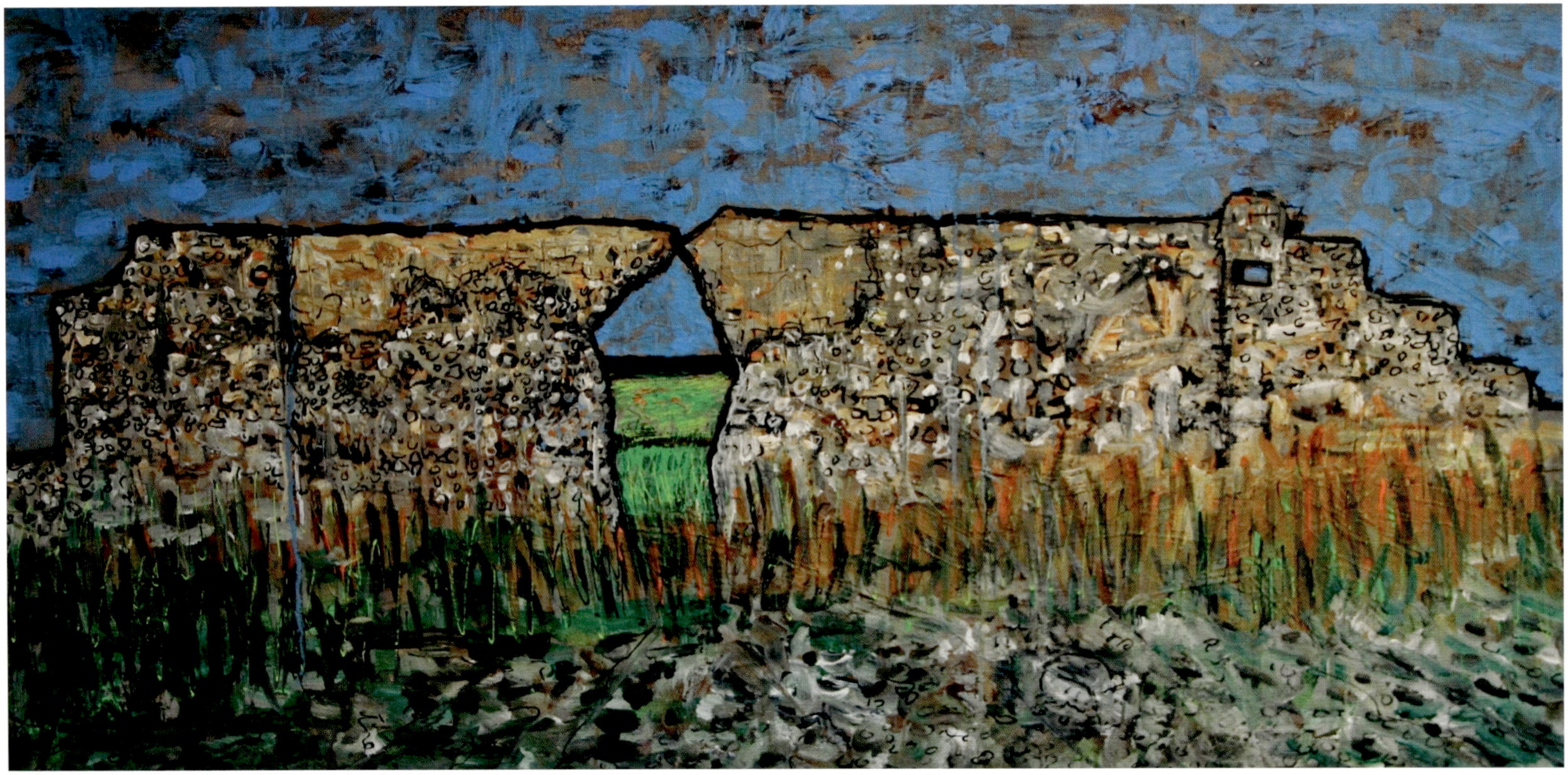

This page: Rocks 99
Opposite page: (top) Tide Mills 102,
(bottom) Tide Mills 101

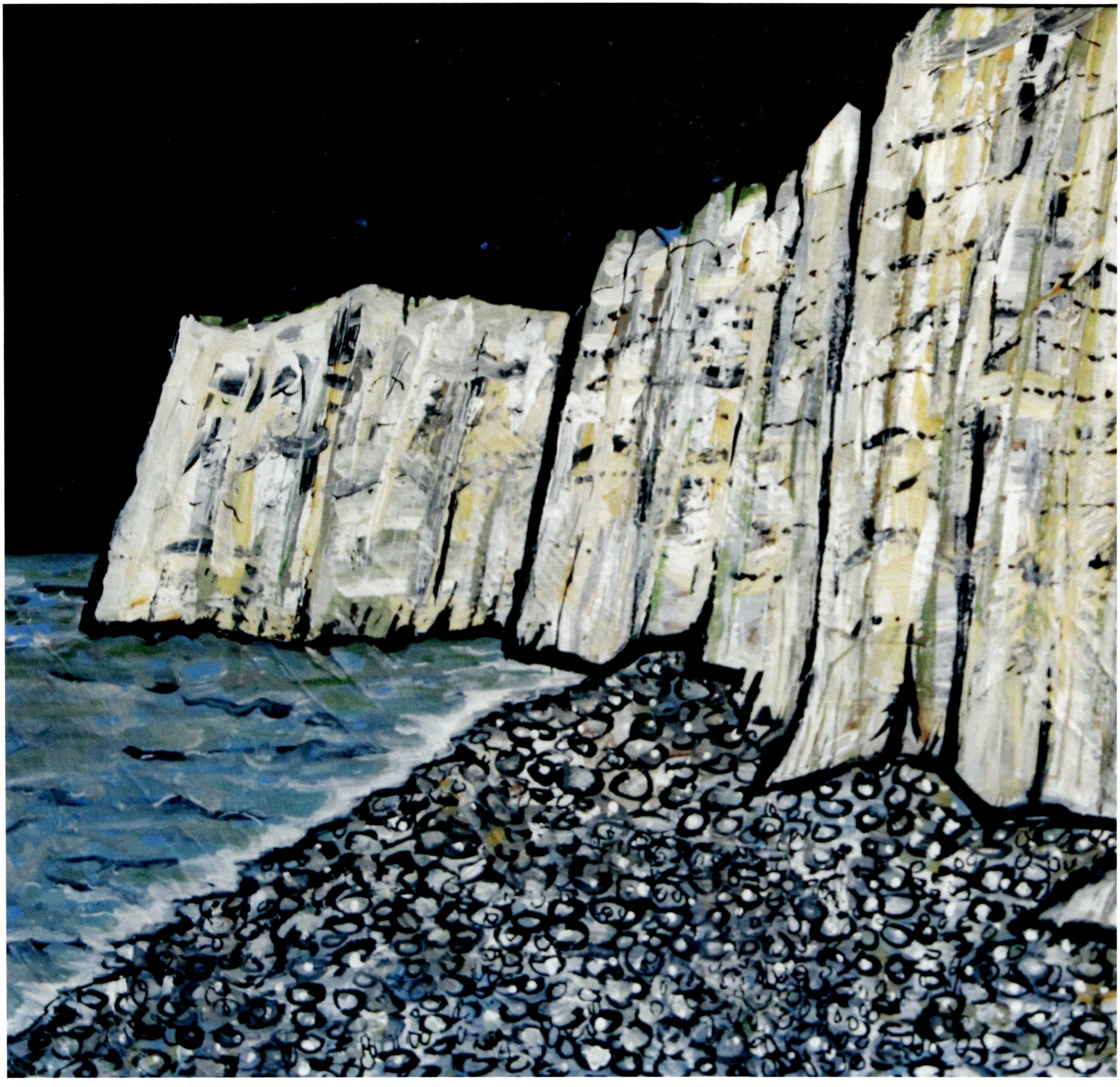

The Private Press

Screen Printing Studio

Clockwise from top: A Field in England film poster (printing 3 colours), artwork by Luke Insect and Kenn Goodall; Lucky Strike A2 print (printing 4 colours including a metallic gold) artwork by Tom Love; 'A' limited-edition poster (printing white ink onto 2 different substrates) artwork by Anthony Burrill

The Private Press is a contemporary screen printing studio based in Brighton, specialising in making hand-pulled prints for established and emerging artists and illustrators, alongside short-run bespoke commissions.

Working closely with clients, they make sure every print is of the highest standard and take time in choosing the right paper, selecting the best inks and assisting in the preparation of artwork. Printing up to A1 in size, all prints are made with exceptional attention to detail, and making sure work is ready in time for major events (such as the Brighton Artists Open Houses) is a top priority.

The Private Press are passionate about the possibilities of creative screen printing and making beautiful prints. Sustainability is also important: all papers used are environmentally sound and all inks are water-based.

The definition of a private press is 'a printing establishment operated on a small scale by a private person or group, in which the emphasis is on quality and individuality' – which perfectly sums up what this studio does.

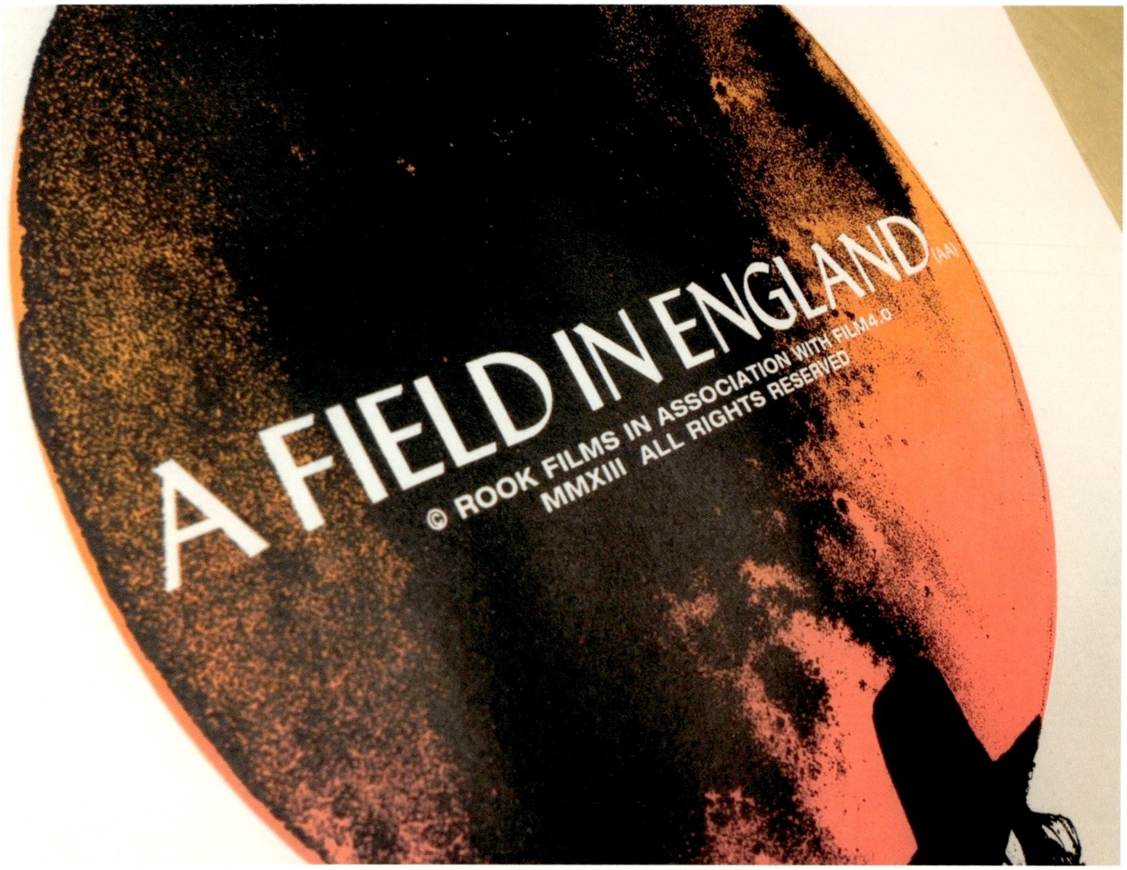

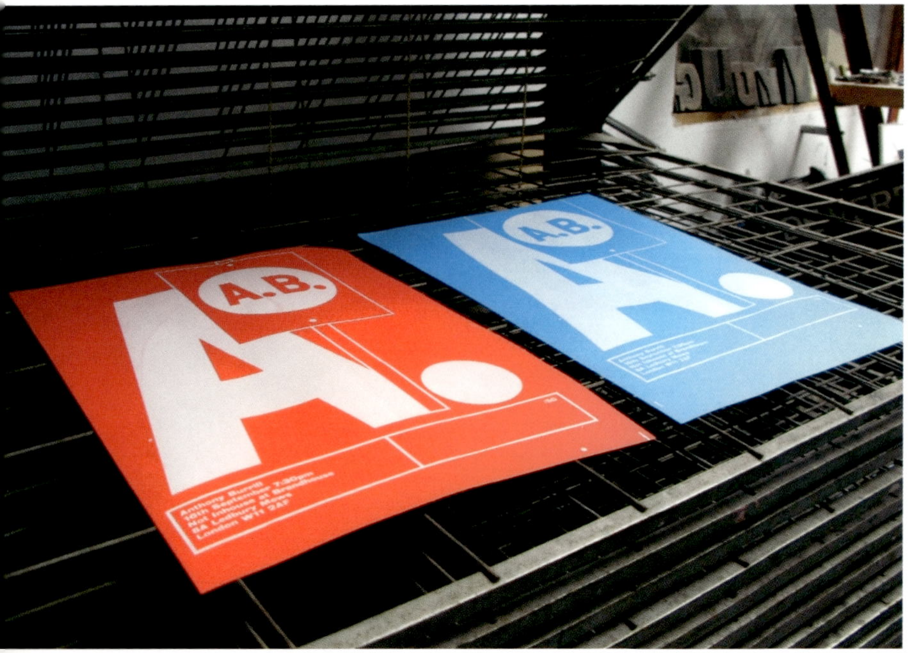

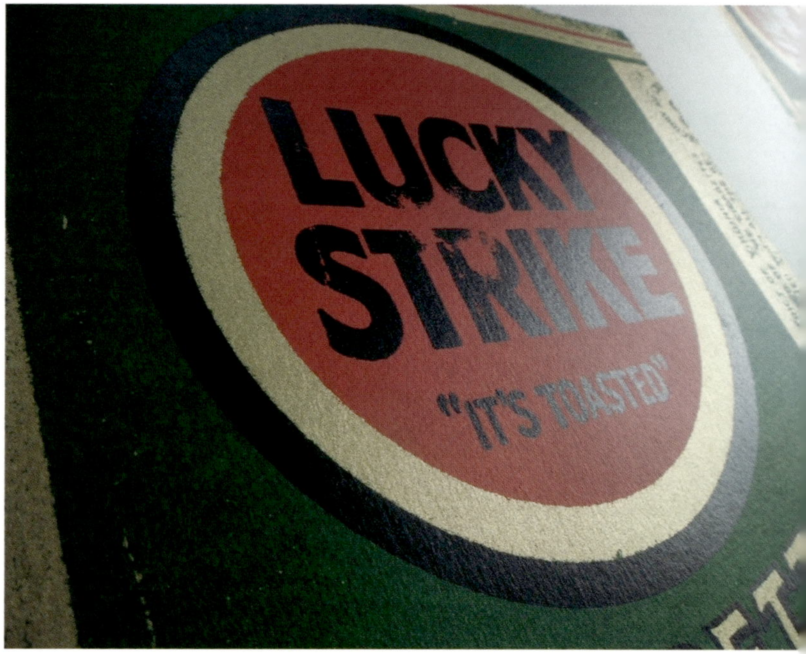

Jan Irvine

Artist

Clockwise from top left:
Olympic Drawing; 20-min Drawing; Collage;
Movement Drawing; Oil Portrait Detail

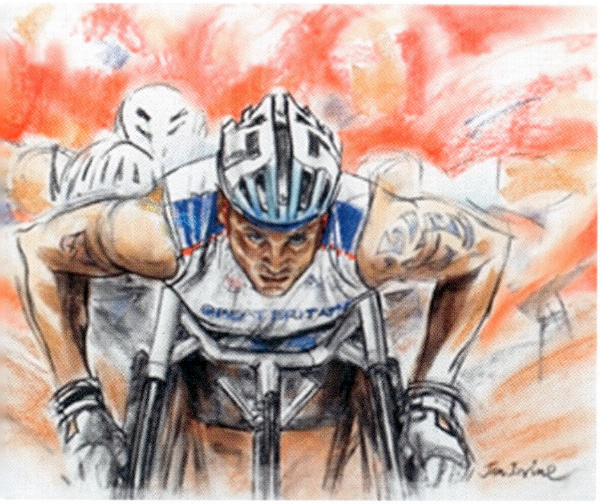

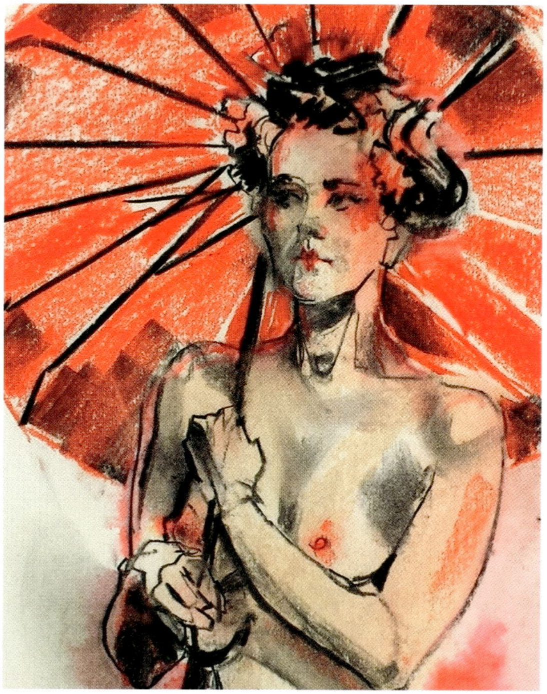

Jan Irvine is perhaps best known for her 'live' drawings; capturing the energy and beauty of the body in motion. Her lines are fluid, strong and confident, and yet on occasion, when a likeness is required, can take on great sensitivity.

She has always felt she is best working at speed; too much time and she just might lose something of the magic... However, two of Jan's other practices prove this to be wrong.

Her vibrant collages, which are much coveted, and her new, equal passion, oil portraiture both evolve over time, and focus much more on colour, shape and texture, but give her equal amounts of pleasure.

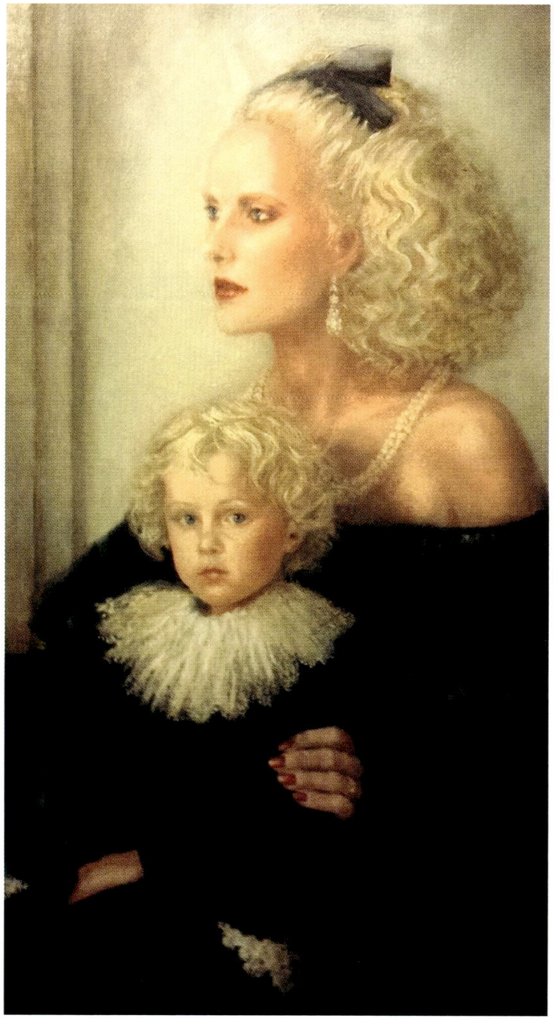

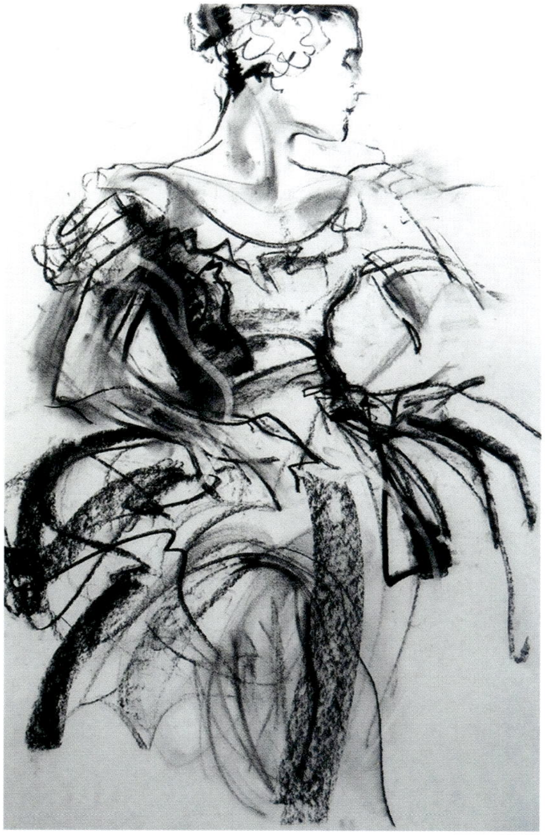

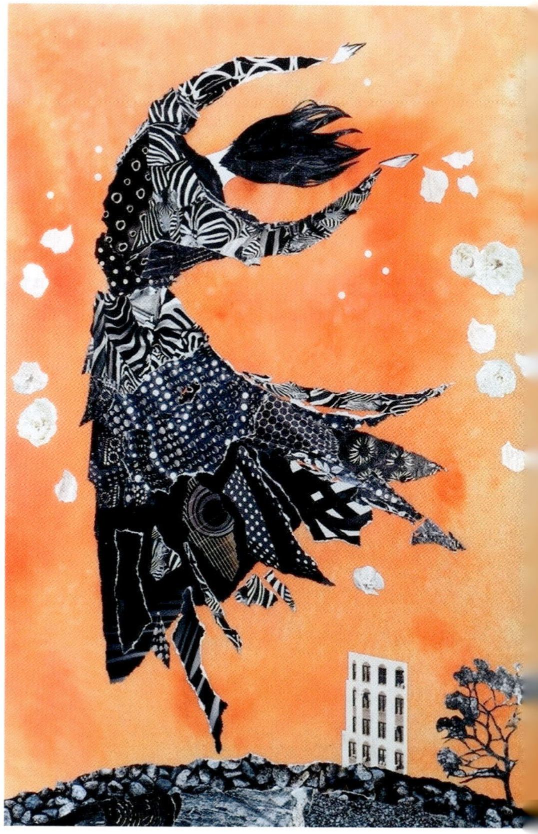

Geoff Hands

Artist

The current work of Geoff Hands ostensibly suggests abstract pictorial constructs made in response to recalling walks along coastlines. However, the artist understands the paintings more as performative acts, intending to be bold, demanding, ambitious and commanding of attention. These are studio paintings, but they could not have been made without referencing experiences that are contingent: the sea and skies, the time of day, weather conditions, sounds and memory.

When out walking, Geoff will draw spontaneously in a sketchbook: inviting reverie with a contradictory sense of stillness and movement. He finds that something similar can happen in the studio – gestural actions and decision-making, punctuating contemplation.

Geoff strongly believes that paintings should be made to be experienced, and hopes that some connection with his work will resonate with the viewer – so that this shared enquiry is conditioned by a visceral, visual and tactile empathy.

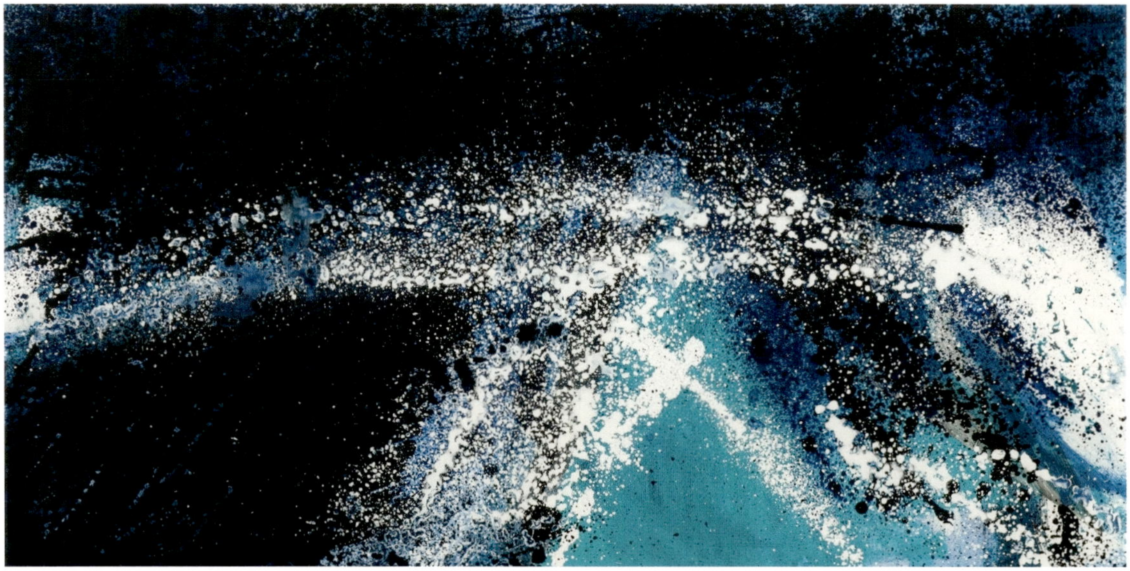

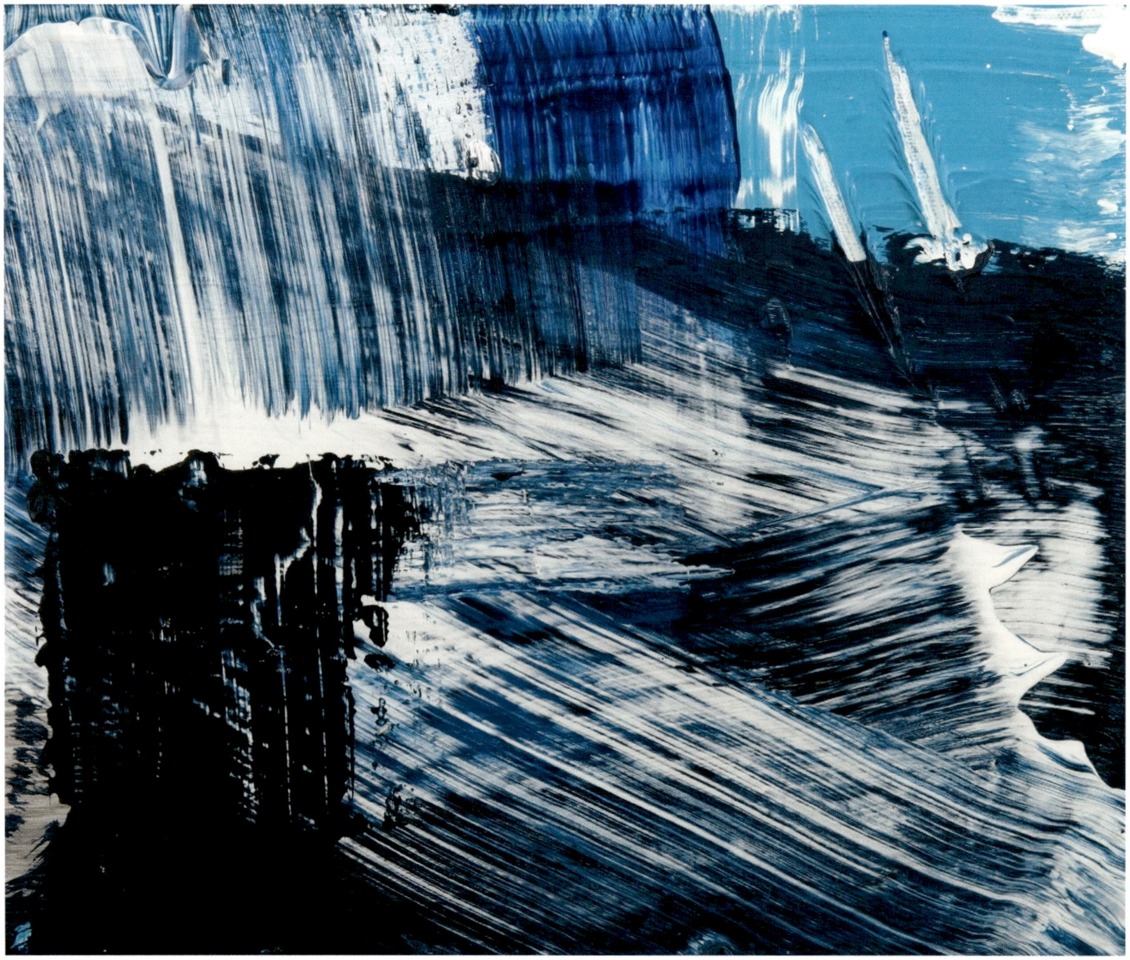

This page: (top) Nanjizal IX, 2013,
(below) Sennen Wave Walk III, 2013
Opposite: Sennen Wave Walk VI, 2013, Nanjizal Study II, 2013

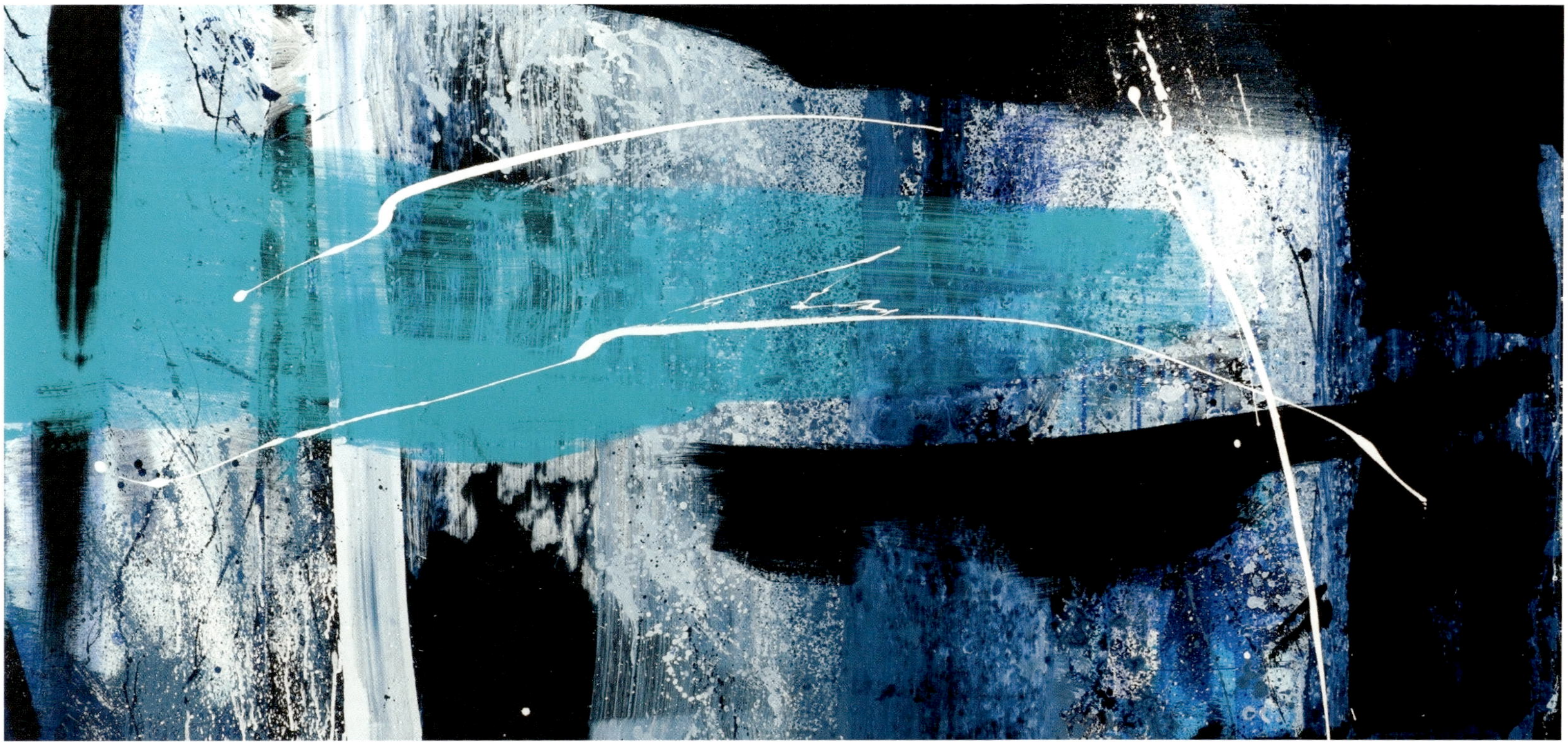

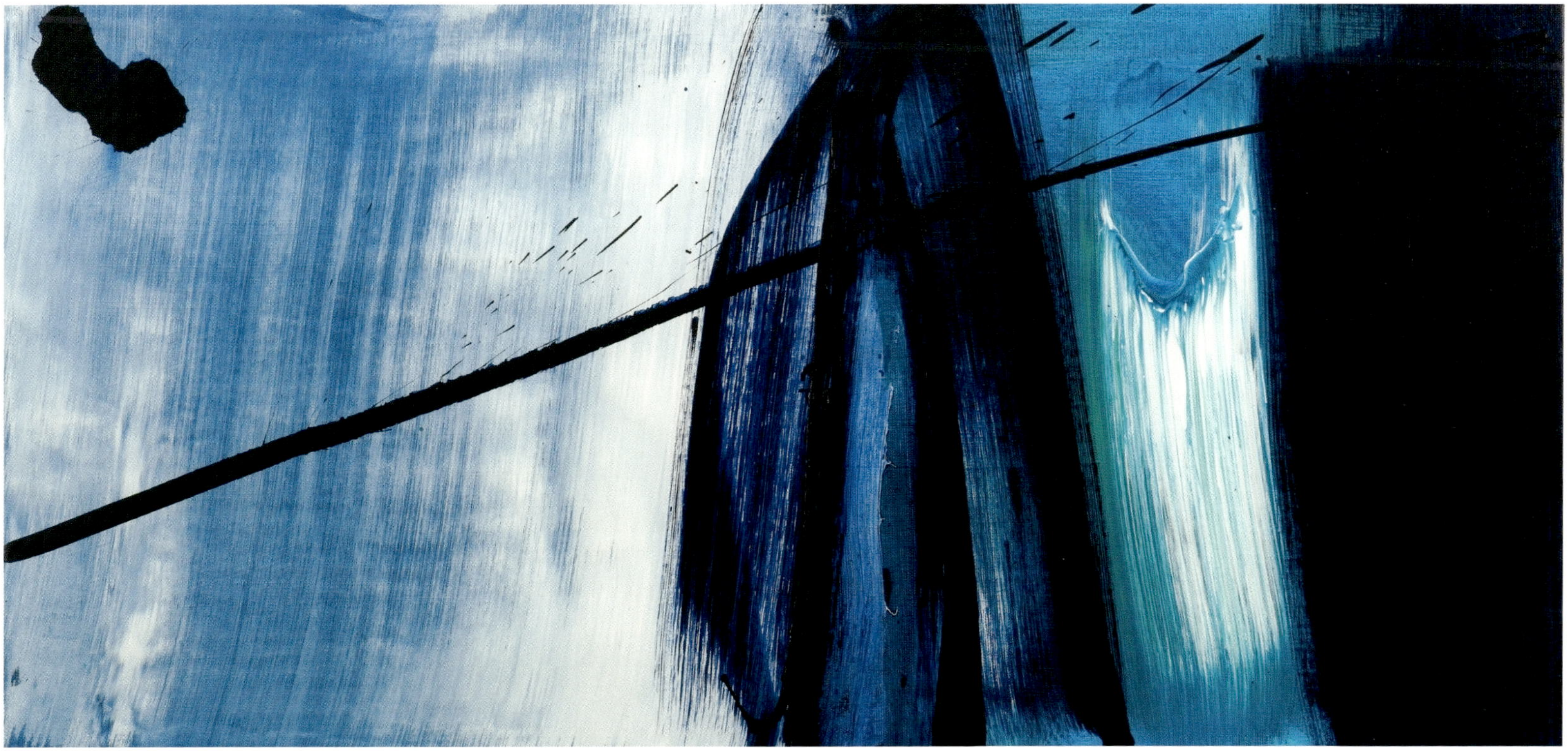

Betty Shek

Felt Arts, Button and Up-cycled Jewellery Artist

Clockwise from top left: Starfish & Coral Freeform Embroidered Felt Brooch; Turquoise Beaded Seahorse Felt Brooch; Coral & Turquoise Beaded Shell Design Felt Brooch; Vintage Buttons & Turquoise Jewellery; Coral & Turquoise Beaded Shell Design Felt Brooch

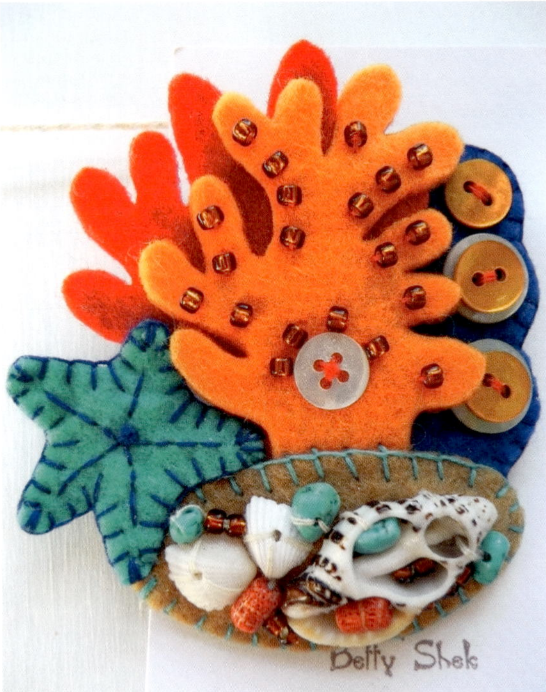

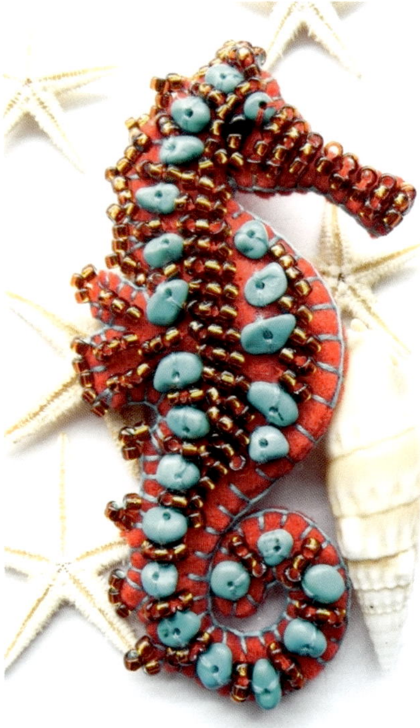

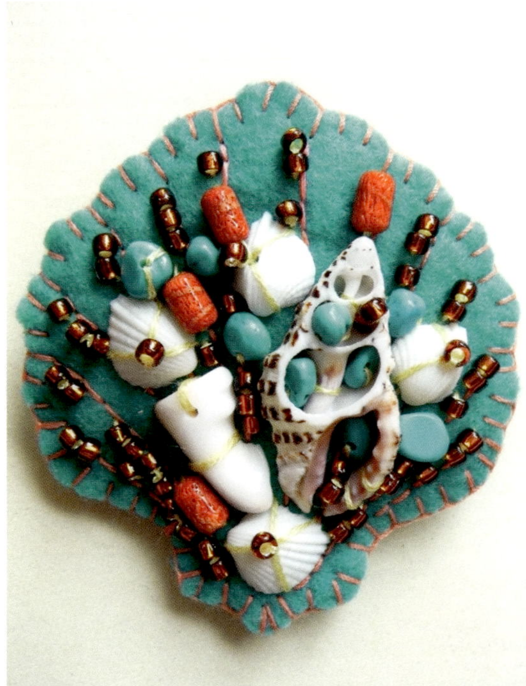

Betty Shek has a background in fashion and textile design, and she enjoys creating unique pieces of felt art, using vintage buttons and up-cycled elements to create her work.

Betty creates all her pieces with her original designs and freeform embroidery technique for each individual piece. She uses vintage buttons and up-cycled elements for her one-of-a-kind jewellery.

She used to travel to Japan very frequently for her job and worked with a local textile designer – and you can tell her works have been influenced by Japanese culture.

Betty's works can be found on etsy.com, folksy.com and at iO Gallery (page 124) and Cactus Gallery in Brighton.

Her studio will open in May with a selection of talented artists showing their works. More information can be found on Betty's facebook page facebook.com/BettyAndFriendsArtistsOpenHouse.

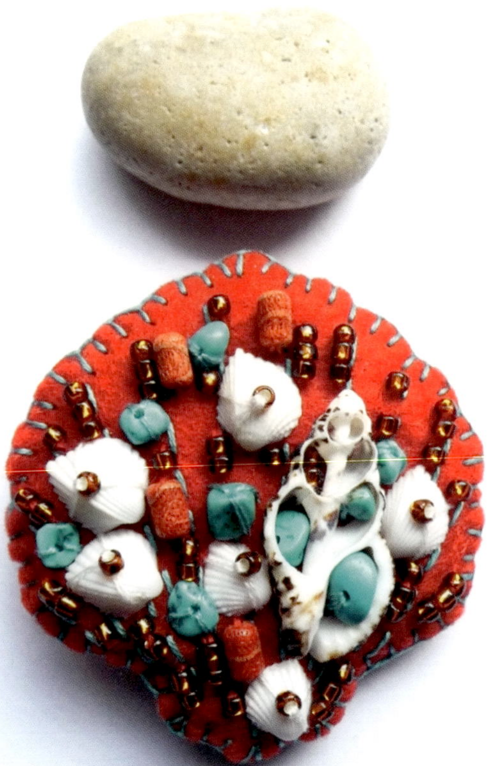

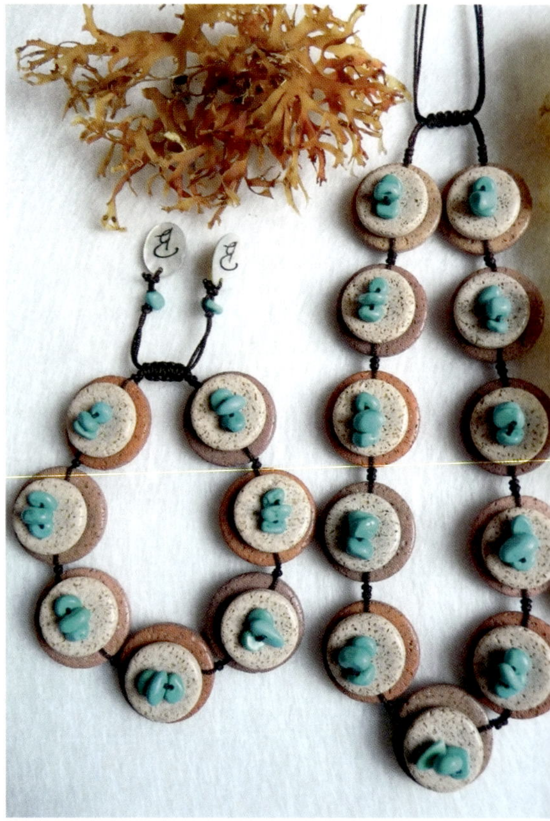

Clockwise from top left:
Dr Who and the Daleks; A little trip to Brighton 2;
Mary Poppins; A little trip to Brighton

Heidi Jane Rhodes

Artist

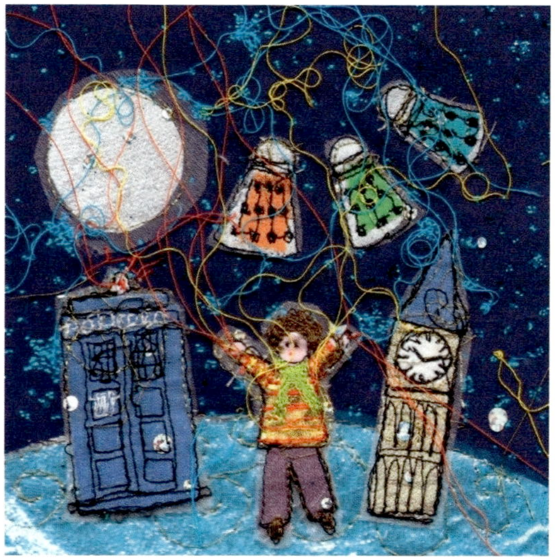

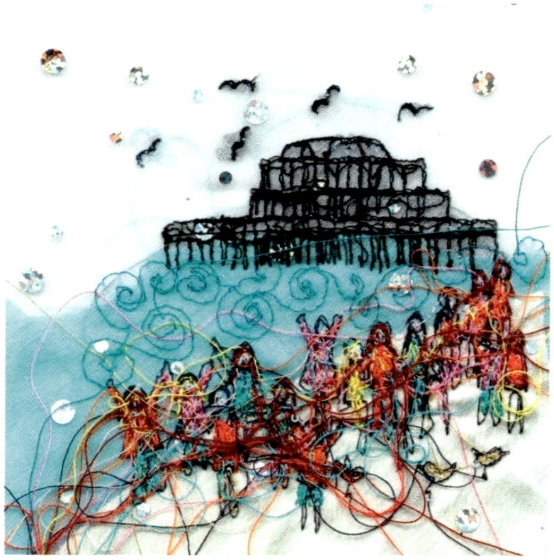

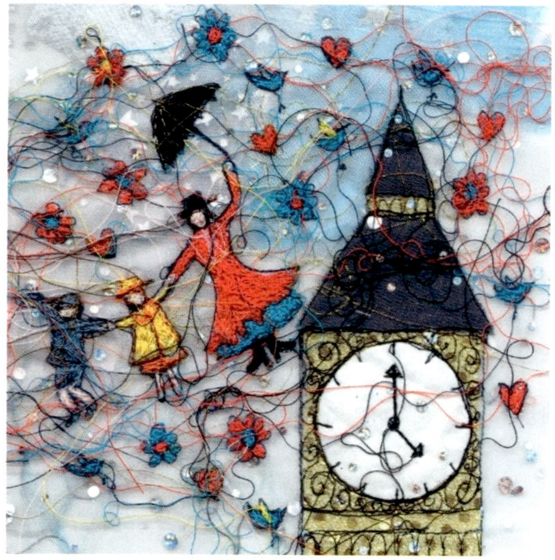

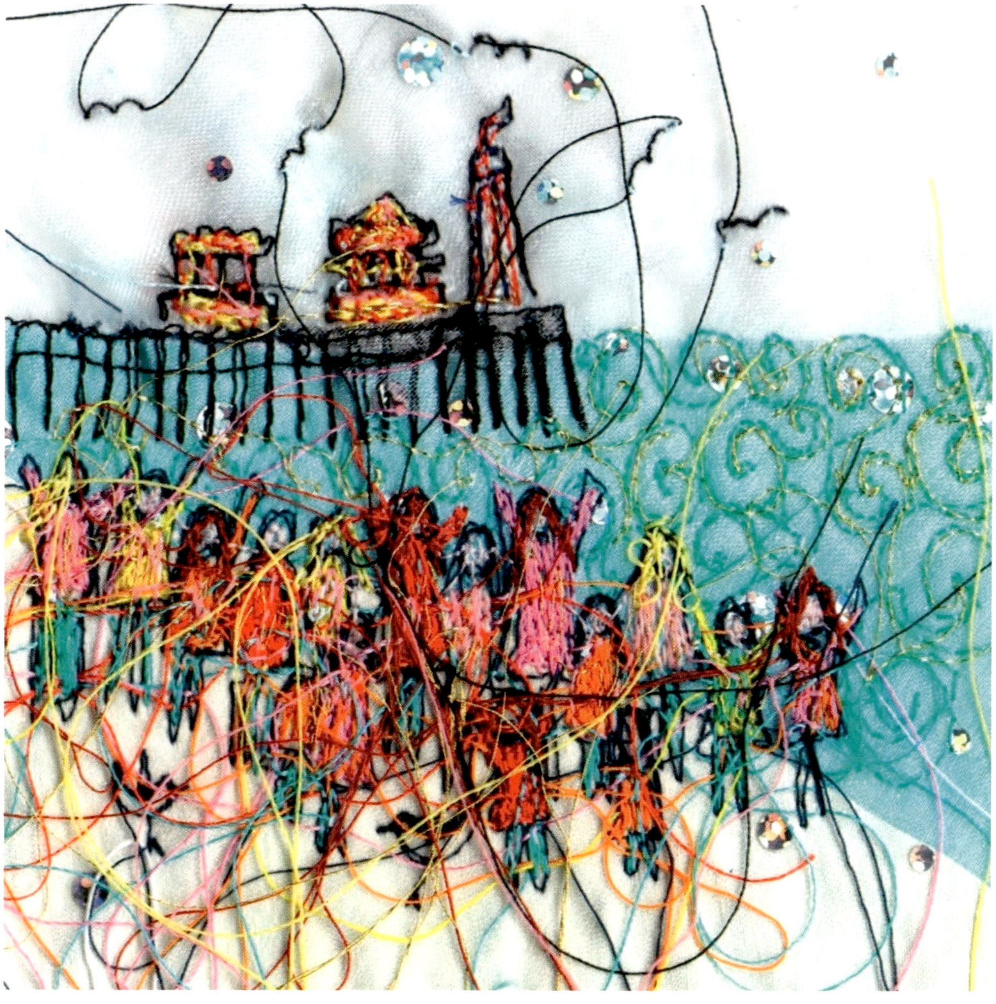

'Pictures to make you smile'

Heidi loves to capture anything in stitch! Using techniques she has developed, she makes unique and vibrant images with her trademark loose threads that lend an energy and movement to her work. Heidi draws her inspiraton from her surroundings and is particularly inspired by iconic buidings and how people and events interact with them. Her work has a nostalgic, magical feel, often with a touch of humour, made, she says, for the 'child in you'.

As a Brighton-based artist, Heidi is continually inspired by the beautiful architecture on her doorstep and has captured many of its iconic scenes in stitch, including the Palace Pier, the West Pier, the Royal Pavilion and the bandstand. In 2012 she produced a collection of textile pieces to celebrate the Diamond Jubilee and the Olympics, which perfectly suited her sparkly, celebratory approach to her work.

Alongside this, Heidi contiues to create a series of magical pictures inspired by childhood, including Mary Poppins, the Clangers, Peter Pan and Doctor Who and the Daleks! Often taking the characters out of context, such as: Dorothy goes to Brighton; the little Daleks go on a city break; and a fairytale in London.

Heidi and her work can be found at the Naughty Pirates Gallery in the Artist Quarter – her latest adventure with her partner Stephen Connett – or at one of the art or craft fairs she shows at throughout the year.

Pathway

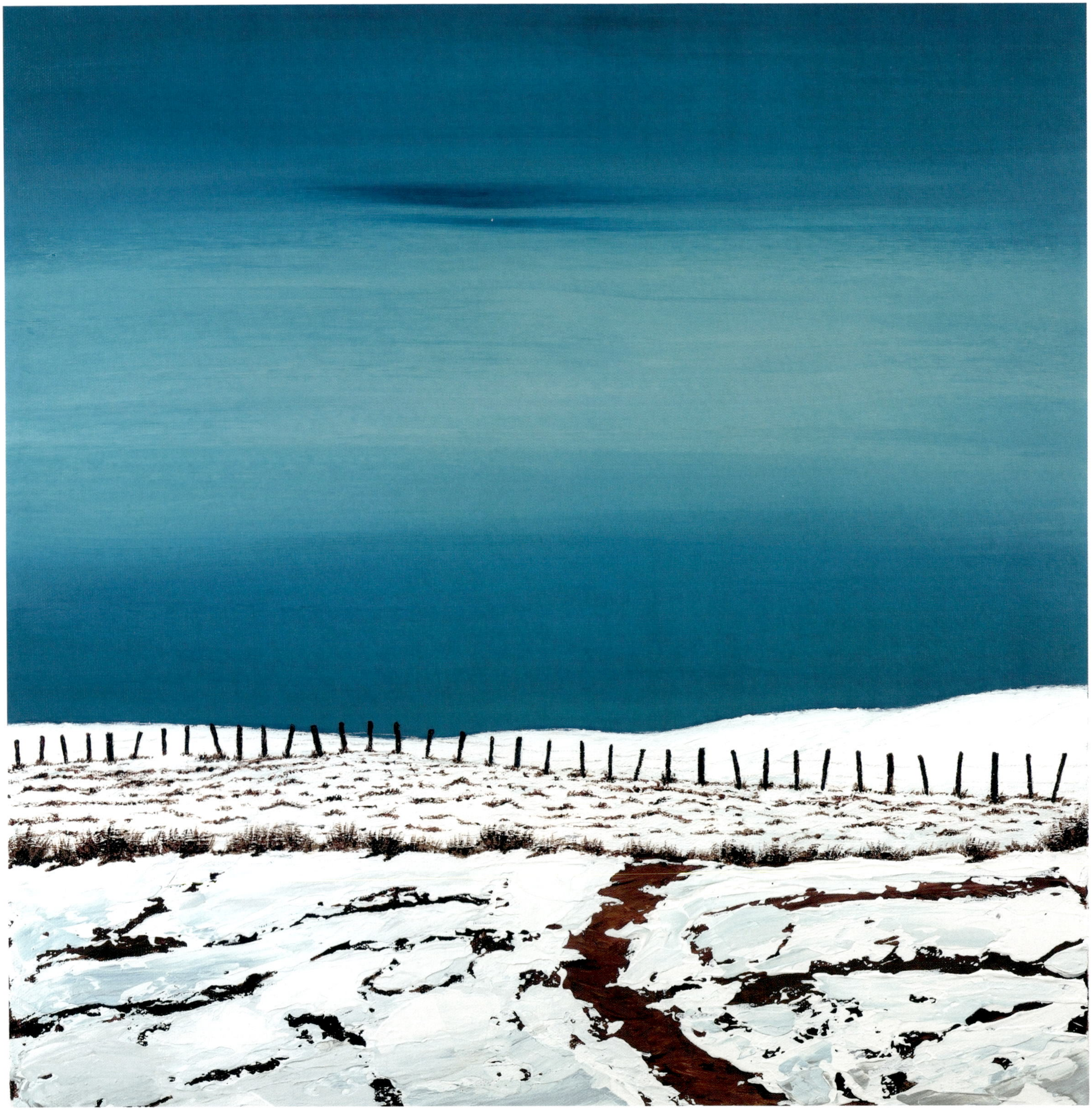

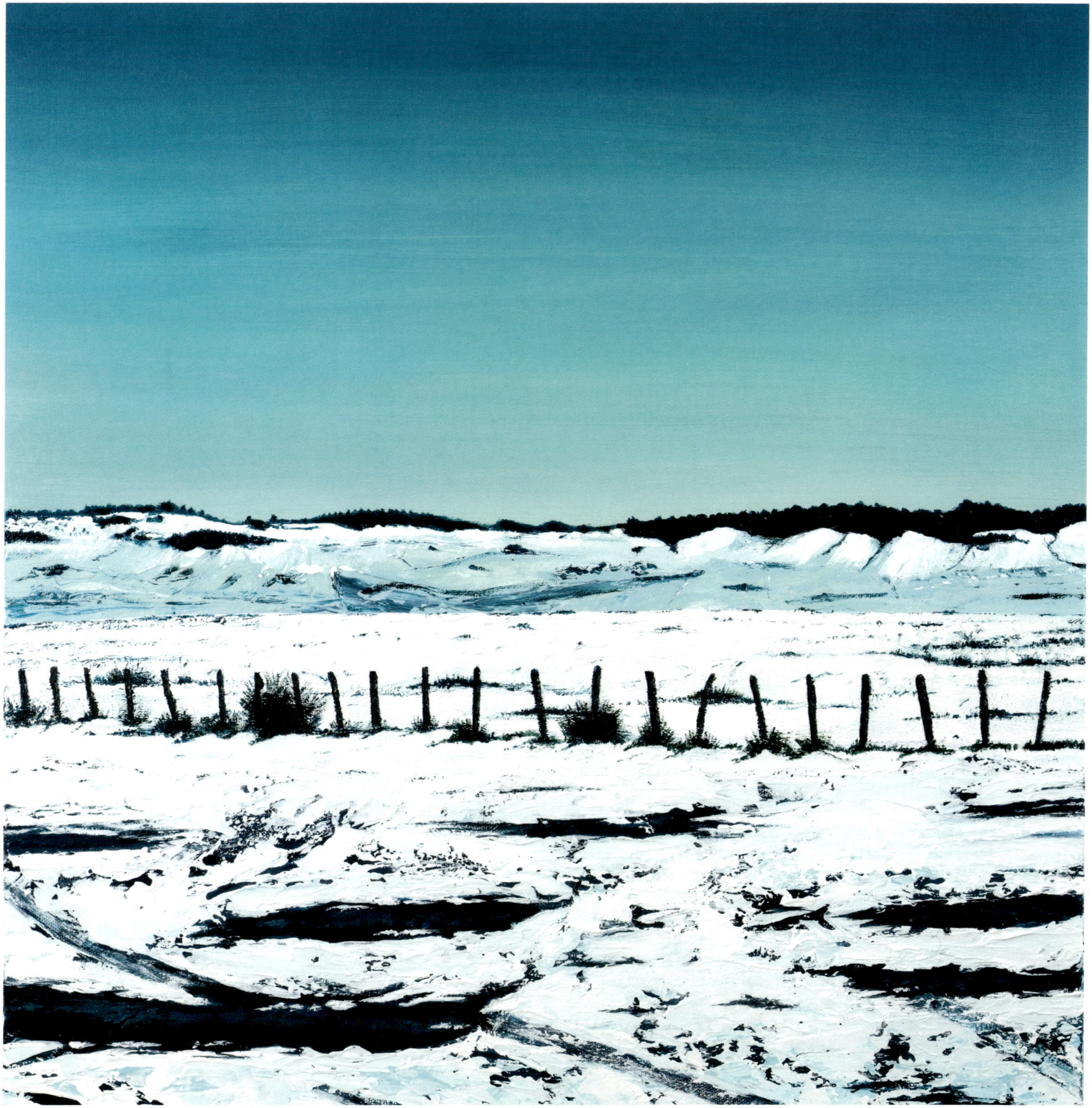

Graeme Richardson-Locke / Eye 4 Colour

Print Studio

Clockwise from far left:
Cozmo, by John Marshall; Joe Strummer, by Simon Dixon;
Metagraf, by Ben Allen; Terrarium II, by Chris Kettle

With more than 25 years' experience, Graeme Richardson-Locke really understands the finer points of the printing process. And through his company – Eye 4 Colour – he is committed to delivering only the best quality giclée reproductions on the finest papers. If you wish to add something very special, Eye 4 Colour will also manage flocking, foiling, glow in the dark and overprint varnishing. Graeme has experience of working with artists, photographers, art-publishers, galleries, graphic designers, interior designers, private commissions and charitable organisations. He currently produces prints for local artistic luminaries that include Ben Allen, Chris Kettle, Simon Dixon, Steven Wilson, Patrick Bremer and fine art photographer Gill Orsman.

You can buy limited editions of their prints, and others, at the Eye 4 Colour website. Eye 4 Colour is an accredited member of the Fine Art Trade Guild, giving the reassurance that prints are independently validated and tested to meet the highest expectations set by the Guild.

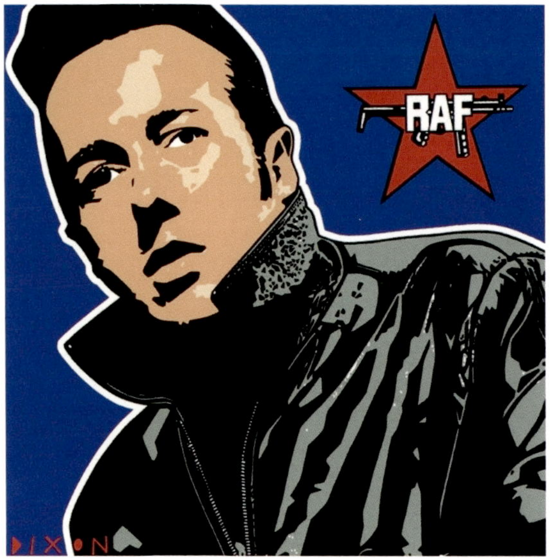

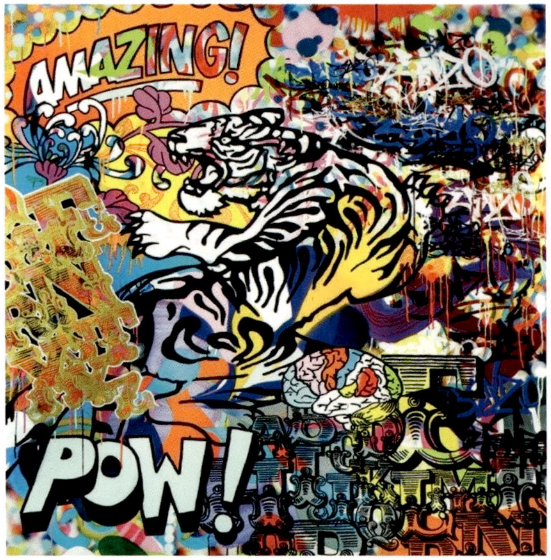

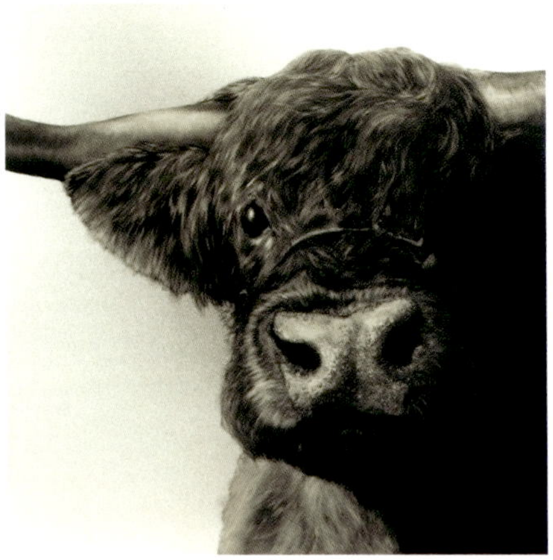

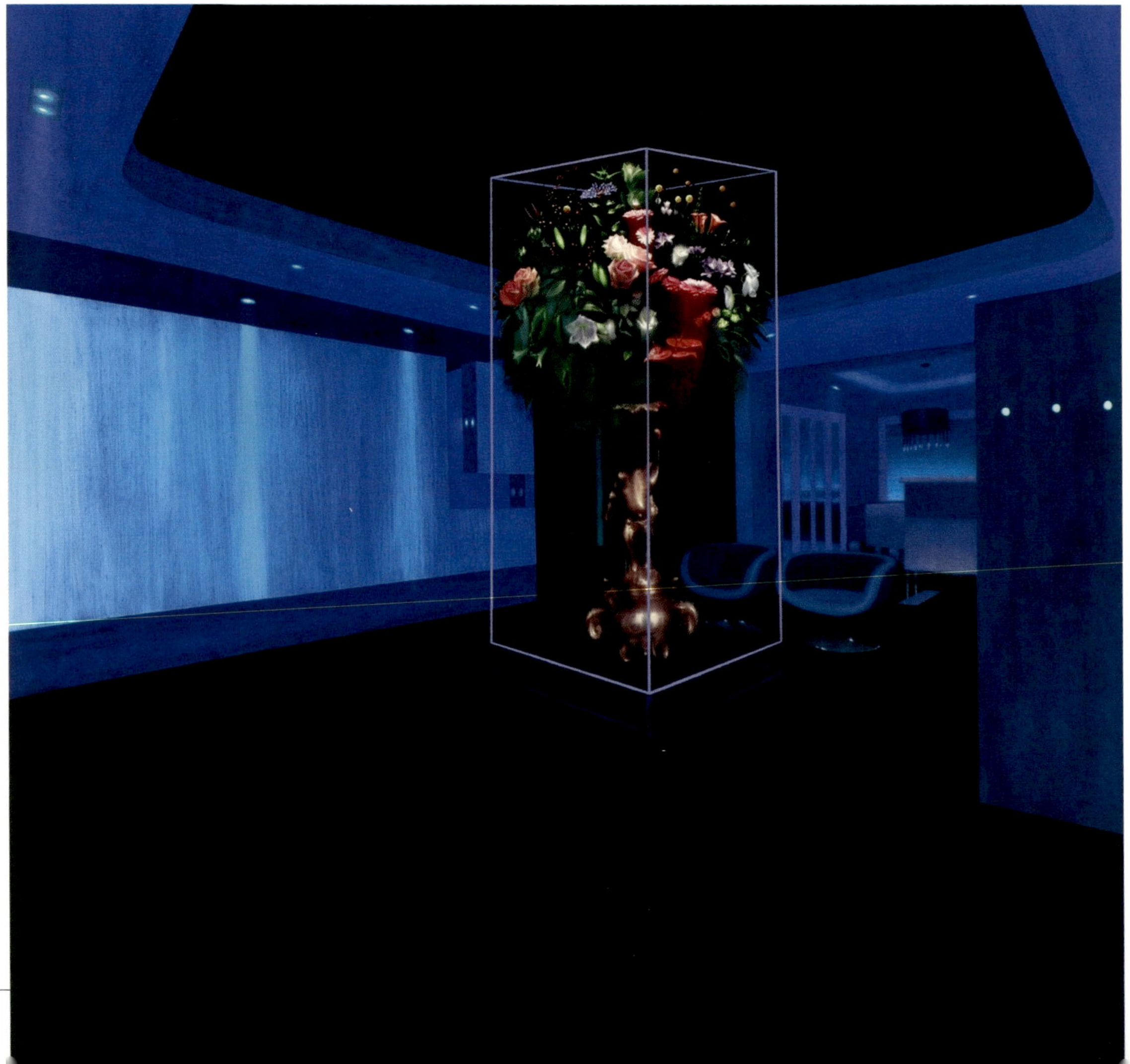

Clockwise from top left:
Well Hello; King Bear; Octopussy;
Is This It? and Fetch

Eve Poland

Artist

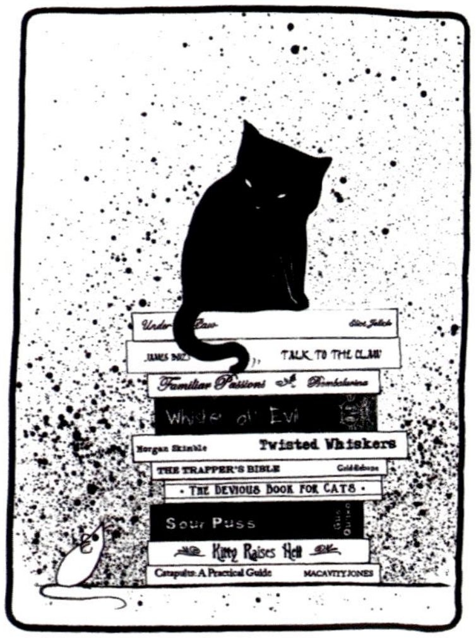

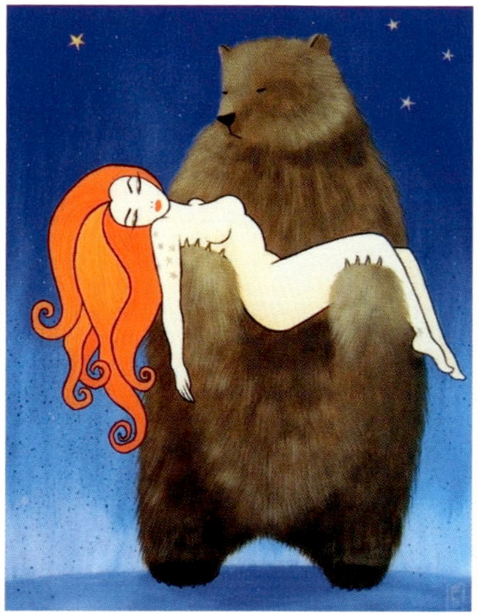

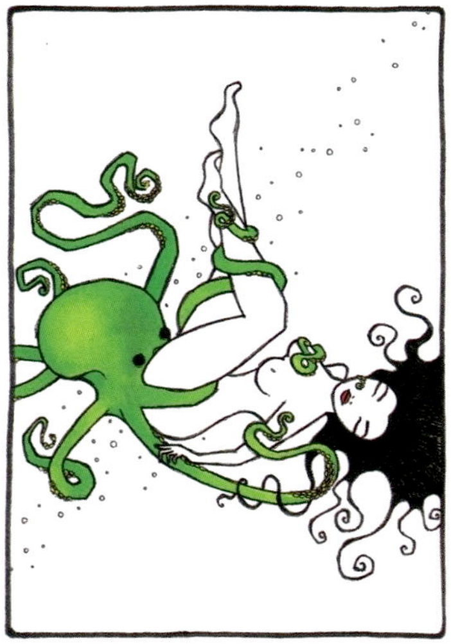

Eve Poland produces paintings and hand-printed silk screen prints in a bold, illustrative style. Her striking original artworks feature twisted kitties and peevish tigers, not to mention lascivious foxy ladies, populating a world where naked nymphettes cavort with obliging octopuses and clever, mischievous kitties will always win out over their cosseted canine counterparts.

Each piece captures the essence of its subject's identity in a deceptively simple execution; Eve employs traditional manual techniques rather than working digitally as she enjoys the characterful imperfections which arise from such handmade processes.

Eve has secured a reputation for intelligent work which reflects her own quirky sense of humour – with an undercurrent of darkness.

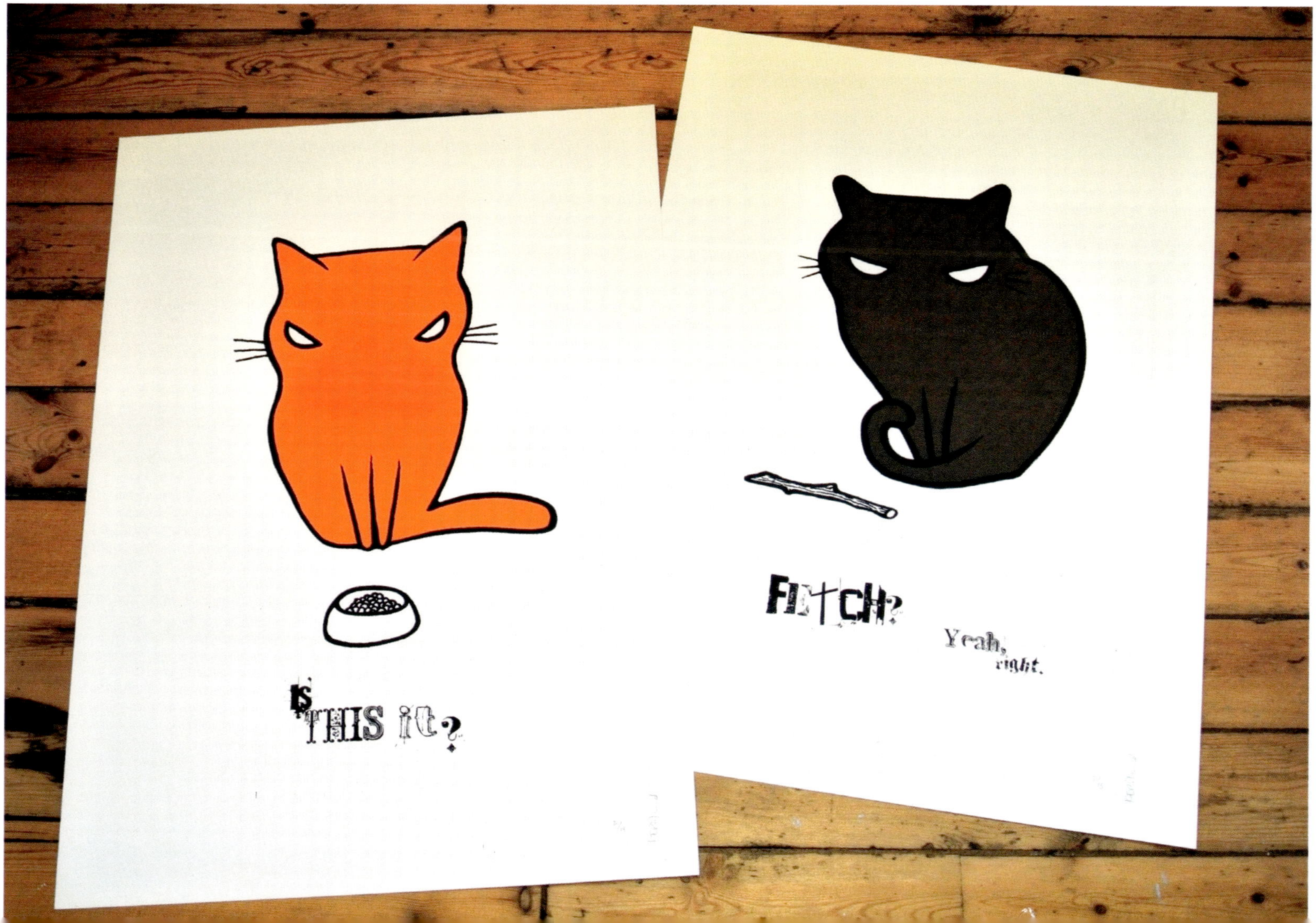

Kellie Miller

Artist

This page: (clockwise from top left)
A Stroll in the Park; Bella Bellis; Maybe Rain
Opposite page: Follow your Path

Kellie Miller has always been interested in 3D, perspectives, materials, texture and colour. She approaches her work by addressing and balancing these aspects, with the aim of making her work approachable to the viewer. The techniques she uses are complex – with some of her pieces requiring 27 separate stages before they are complete, resulting in tactile, carved paintings.

Kellie produces her work from the deep within herself, from a place she does not recognise in the outer world. The work is often described as peaceful, beautiful, reflective and calming. Although she sometimes struggles to achieve these qualities in her everyday life, they easily flow in her work. She knows that she will forever ponder the question – how is this possible?

Kellie does not feel the need to be controversial or sensational with her art. The style and techniques are challenging enough without having to go to extremes of shocking audiences. Besides, she thinks we have become desensitised to controversy and it has become everyday. However, more awareness is required to read works that are subtle, simple, gentle and perhaps wise.

Her subject matter is often drawn from nature and travel. She enjoys using these, together with words and feelings, as her starting points.

Because of the 3D elements, texture and colours of her work, it does not always translate well into a 2D format. A photographic image can only convey an impression. The work has to be seen first hand to truly experience it.

Kellie graduated from Camberwell School of Art in 1991, then Brighton University in 1994, and gained her MA in Arts Criticism from City University, London in 2001.

In 1996 she set up Biscuit Studio, where many artists and designers have worked, including makers from Japan and Turkey. She is a founder member of Hove Arts, an organisation linking artists' houses, studios and workshops as part of England's major arts festival.

Kellie's relationship with Japan started in 2002 when she spent several months in an artist residency. She was selected to exhibit her installation of 101 Couture Cups at Mino Museum's 8th International Ceramics Festival 2008. More recently, she had a solo exhibition in Orie Gallery in Tokyo and has been commissioned to produce a ceramic installation for the foyer of Nakatsu Hospital in Kyushu, Japan.

In addition to exhibitions in the UK, Denmark and Germany, Yingge Ceramics Museum, Taiwan, Shigaraki Ceramic Cultural Park, Japan, and Brighton and Hove Museum, England, have all added her work to their collections. Her work has been featured widely in the UK press, including *The Times*, *The Guardian*, *Elle Decoration* and *Homes & Gardens*.

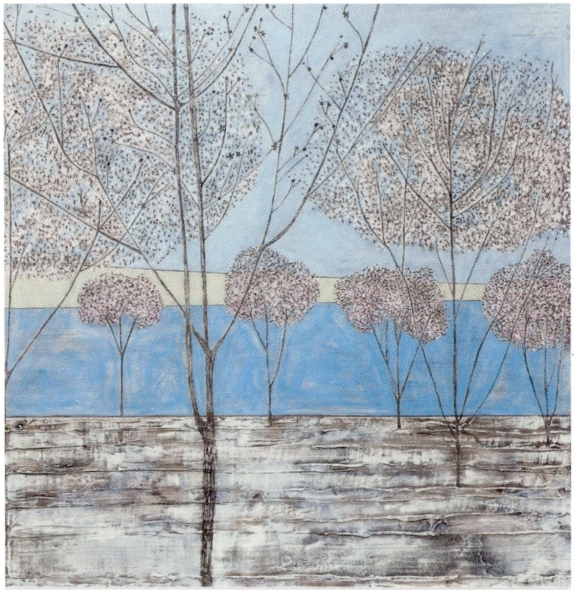

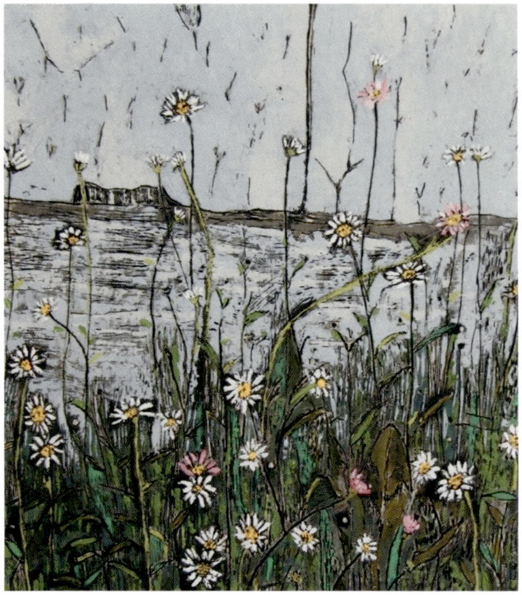

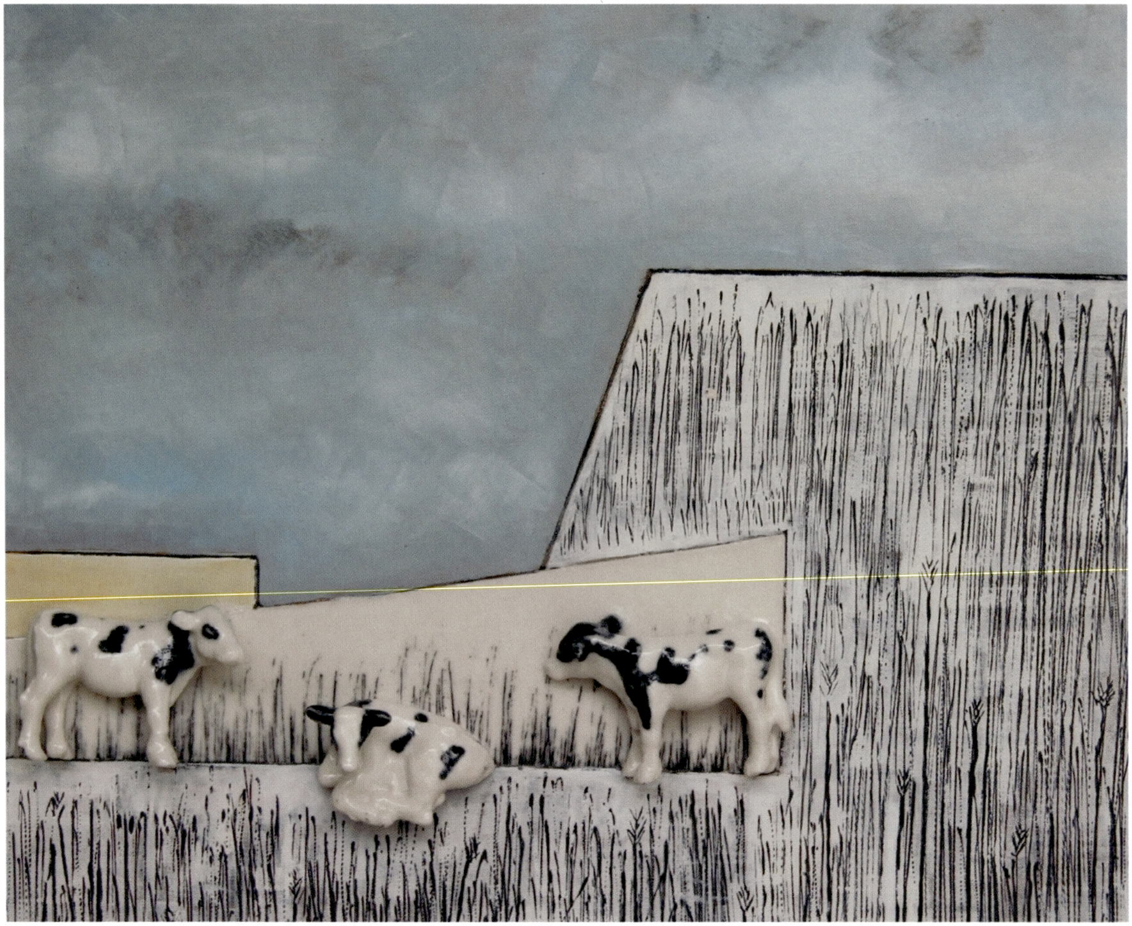

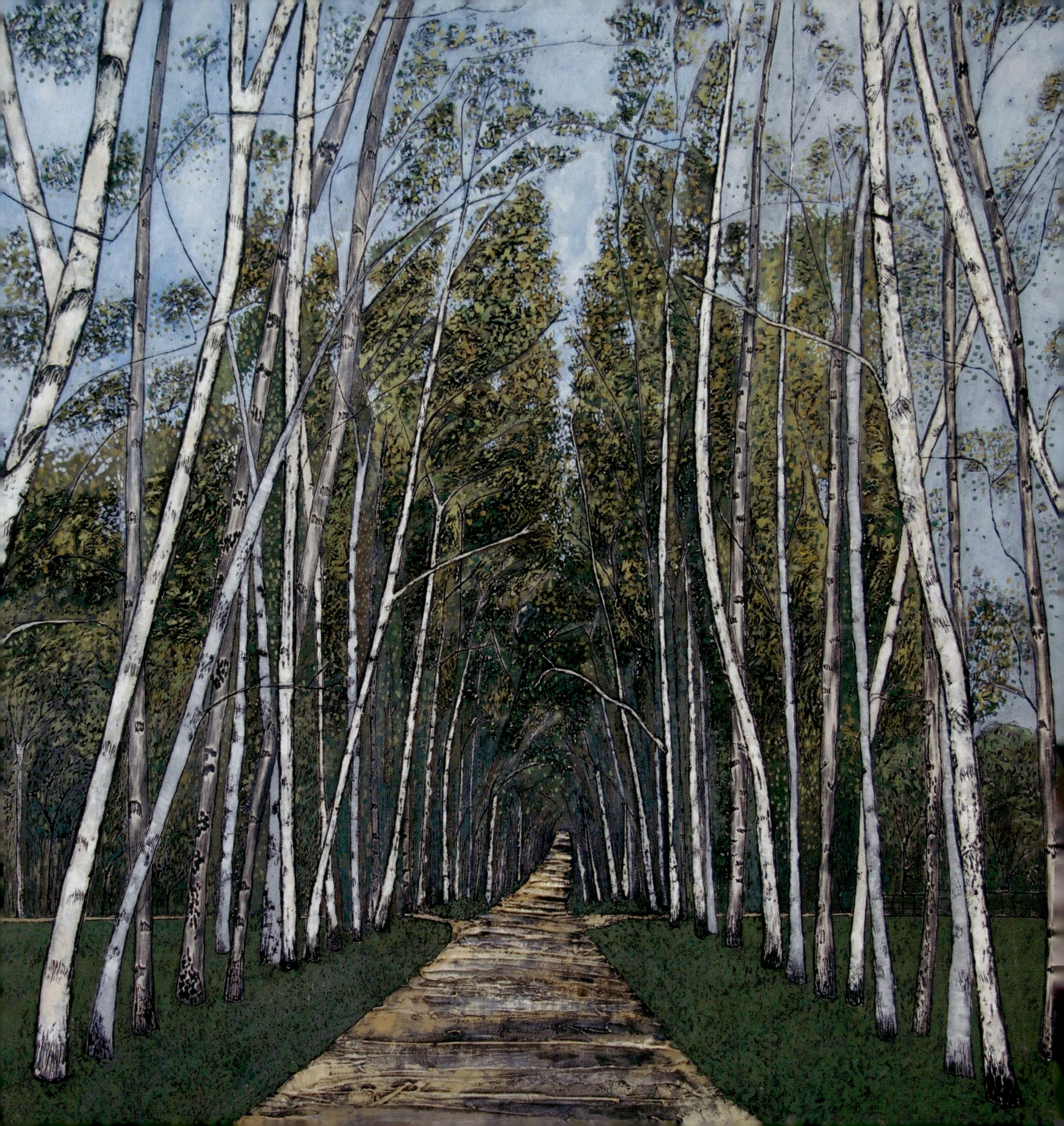

Alexander Johnson

Artist

This page: (clockwise from top left): Portal 2; Roundel 6; Portal 1
Opposite page: Viaje 5

Arriving at art college in 1980, Alexander was very much a child of his time. His formative visual inspiration came from the ground-breaking graphic styles of the original punk movement, which he continues to pay homage to today with flashes of fluorescent colour combined with his signature greys and blacks. Recent paintings use reconnaissance photographs taken by his father from a Spitfire in WW2 as a starting point. The paintings have an initial impact and enormous vitality that reveals depth as you spend more time with the work.

Most recently working with the Modern ArtBuyer agency, Alexander had a successful solo show at The Four Seasons Hotel in Canary Wharf in 2012. Since then his work has been increasingly in demand after a sell-out show in the Brighton Festival Artists Open Houses in 2013 and the Affordable Art Fair in Battersea, London 2013.

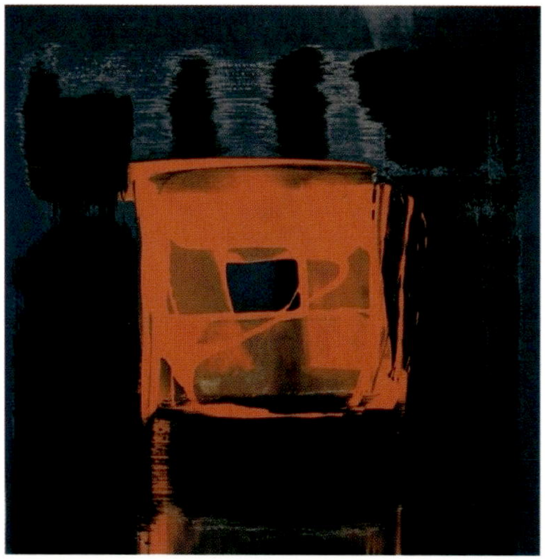

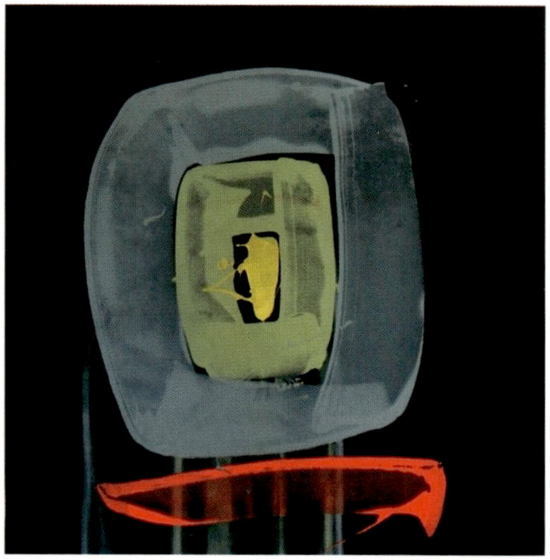

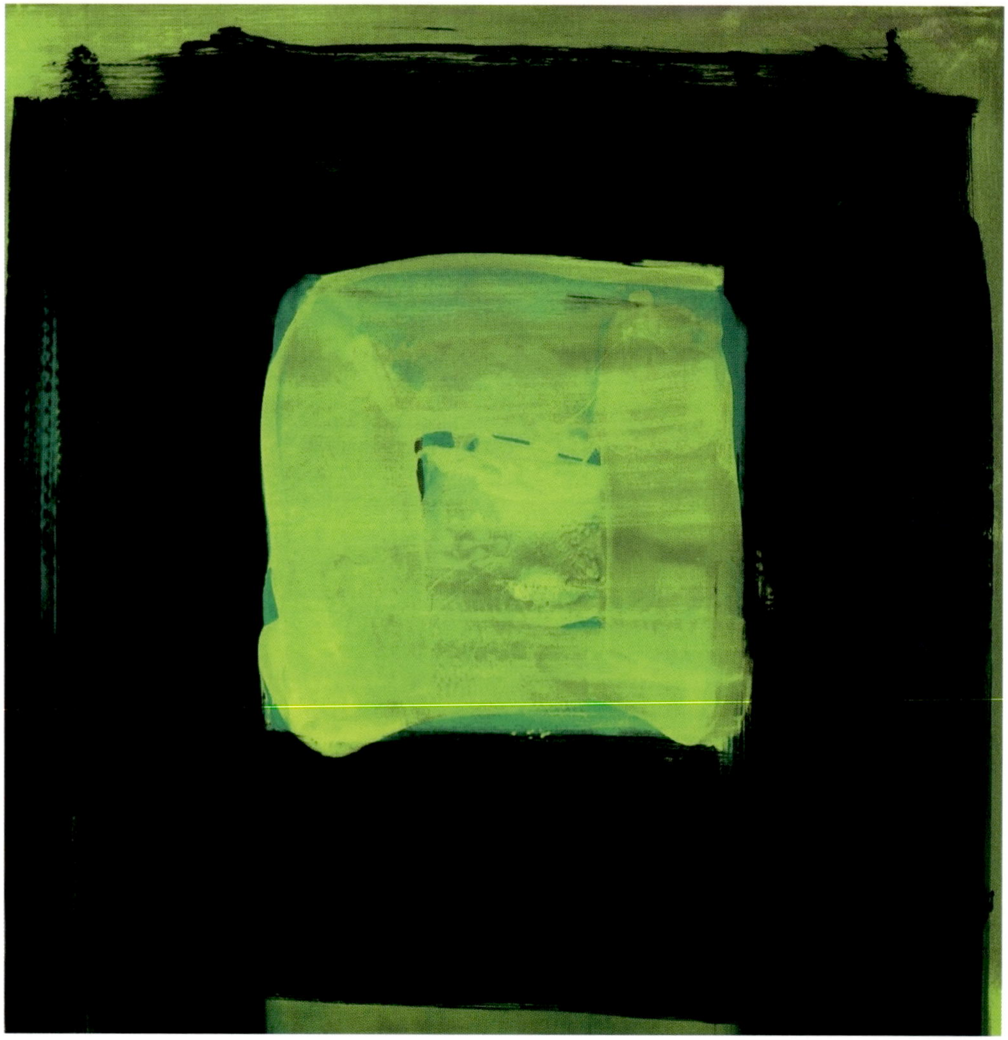

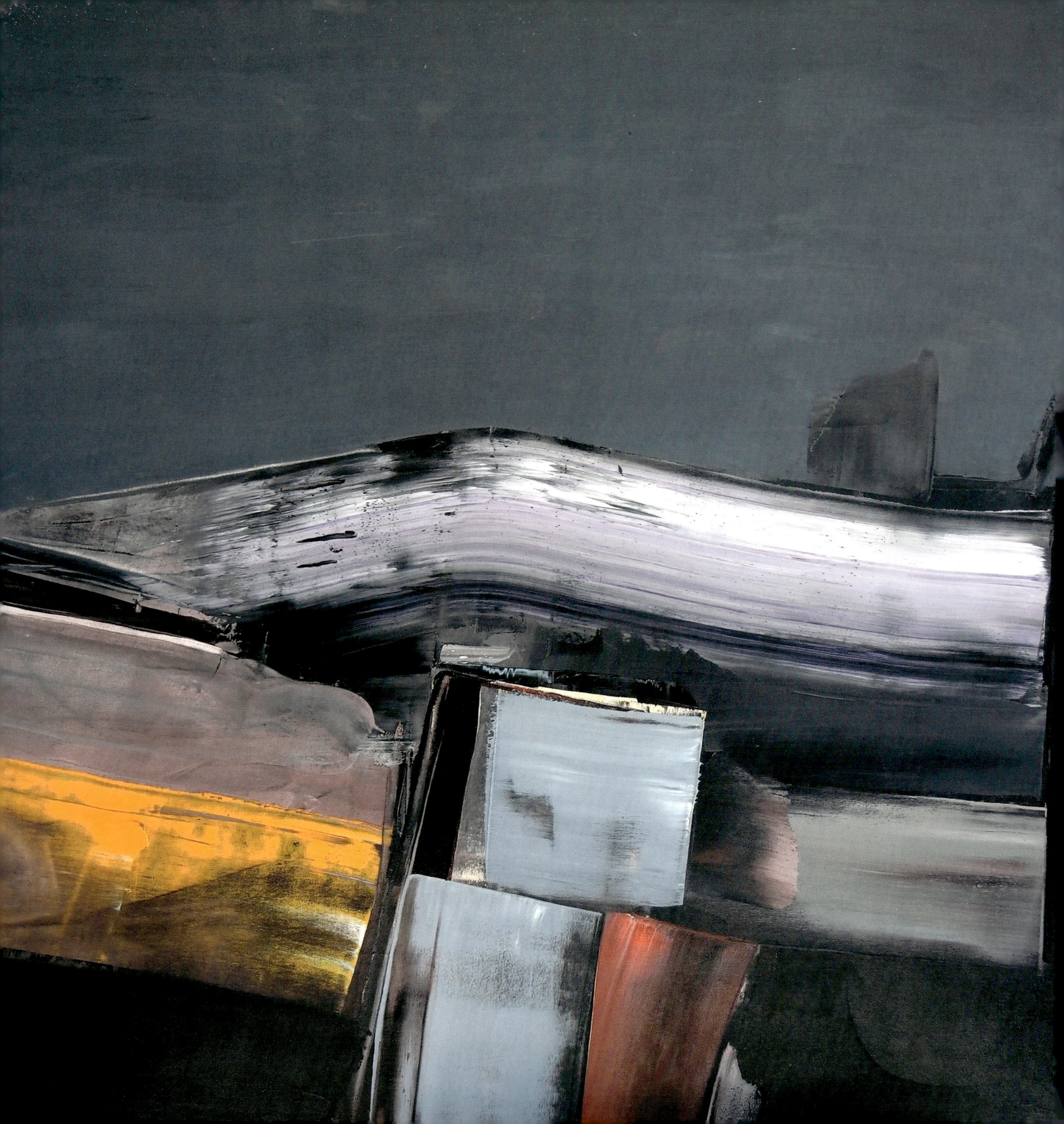

Chanchala Ariyaratne

Jeweller

Clockwise from top: Victorian Salvage Necklace; Steampunk Mantel Clock; Steampunk Desk Clock; Eric the Half-a-Bee Brooch

Chanchala Ariyaratne first started making her Steampunk-inspired jewellery with the remains of old timepieces recovered from her father's shop after it was caught in the 2004 tsunami. She finds great joy in turning these pieces of history into wearable art.

Chanchala grew up in Sri Lanka and has a PhD in Engineering from the University of Nottingham – she has a flair for weaving these influences in novel ways, and loves when things are both beautiful and functional. Her recent range of Steampunk-inspired clocks is proving extremely popular, with each one a unique design.

She can generally be found scouring antiques markets and boot sales in and around Brighton for ideas and inspiration.

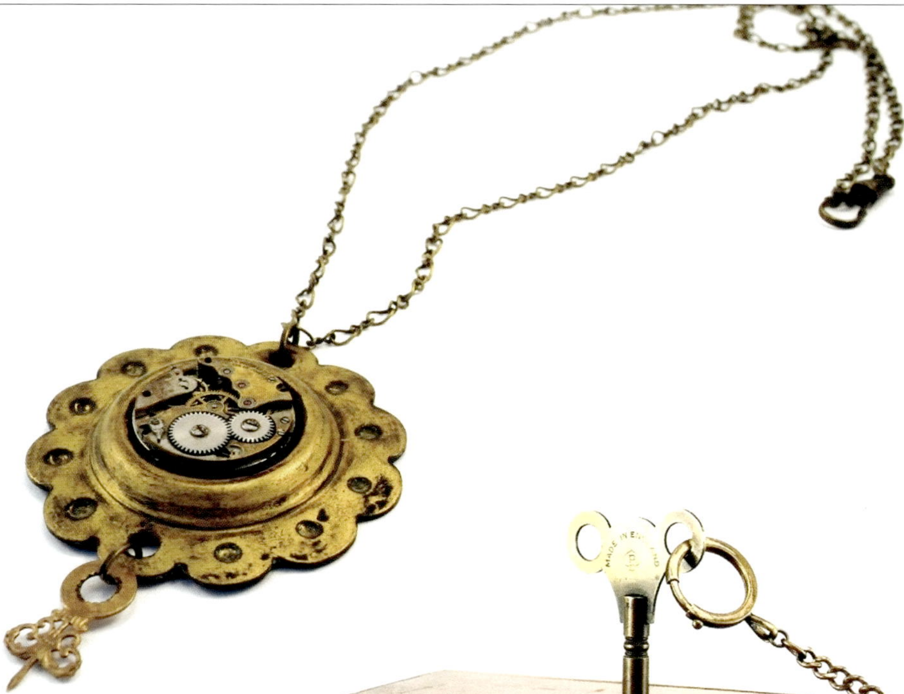

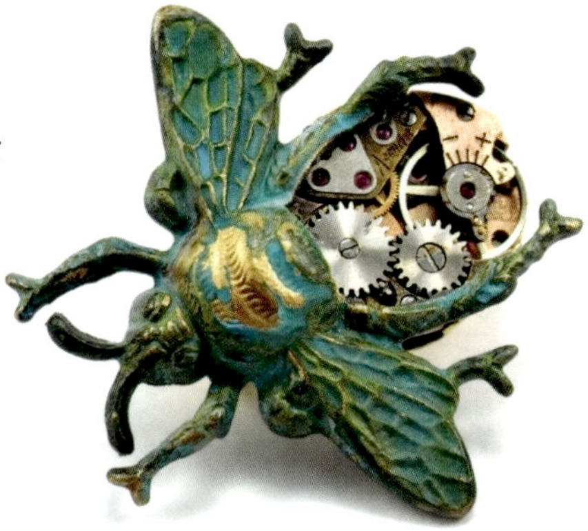

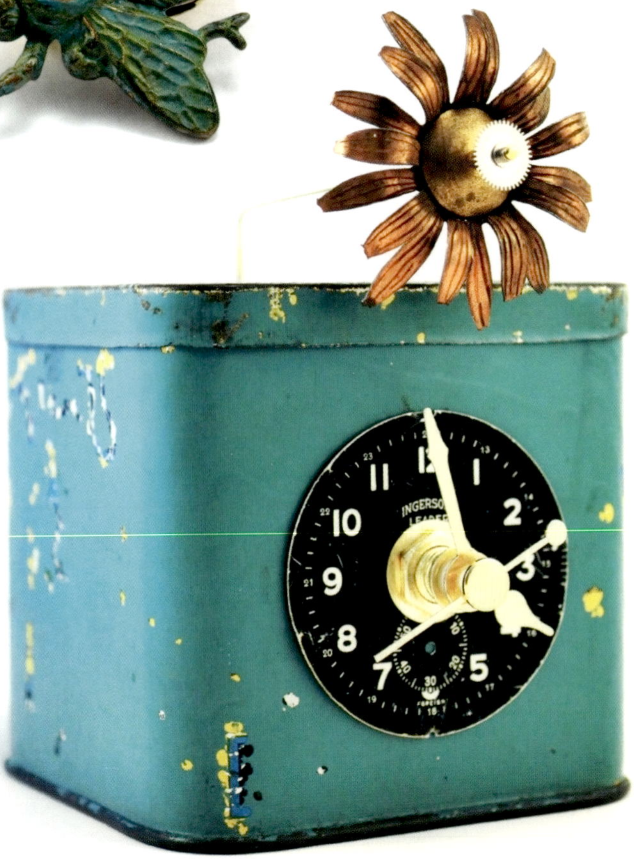

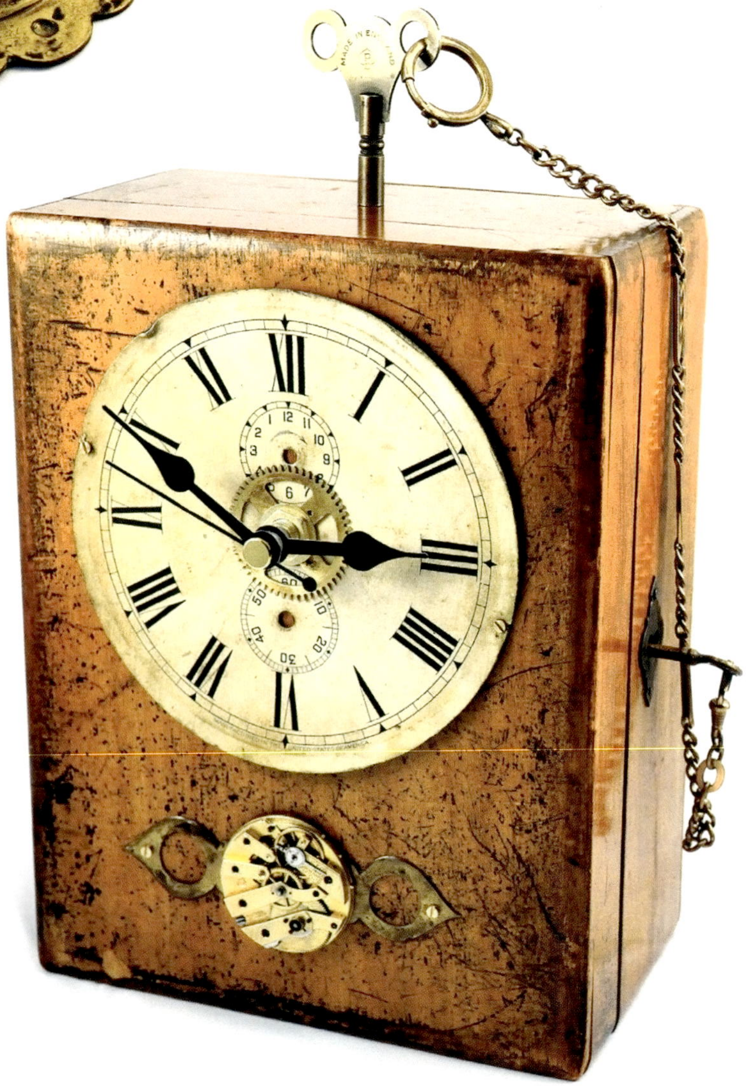

Caia Matheson

Artist

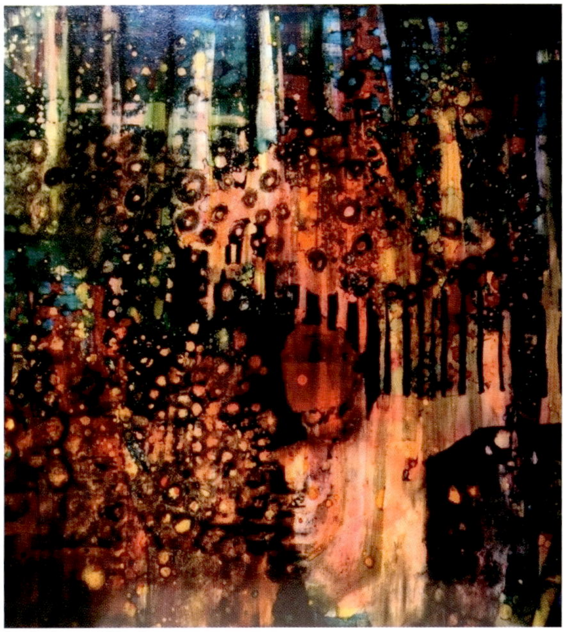

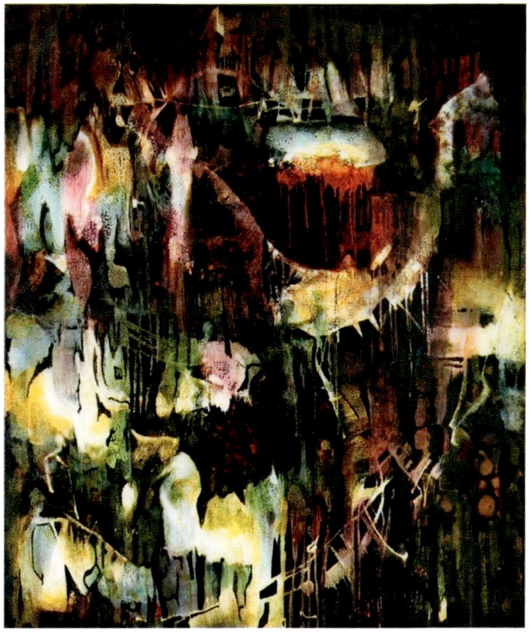

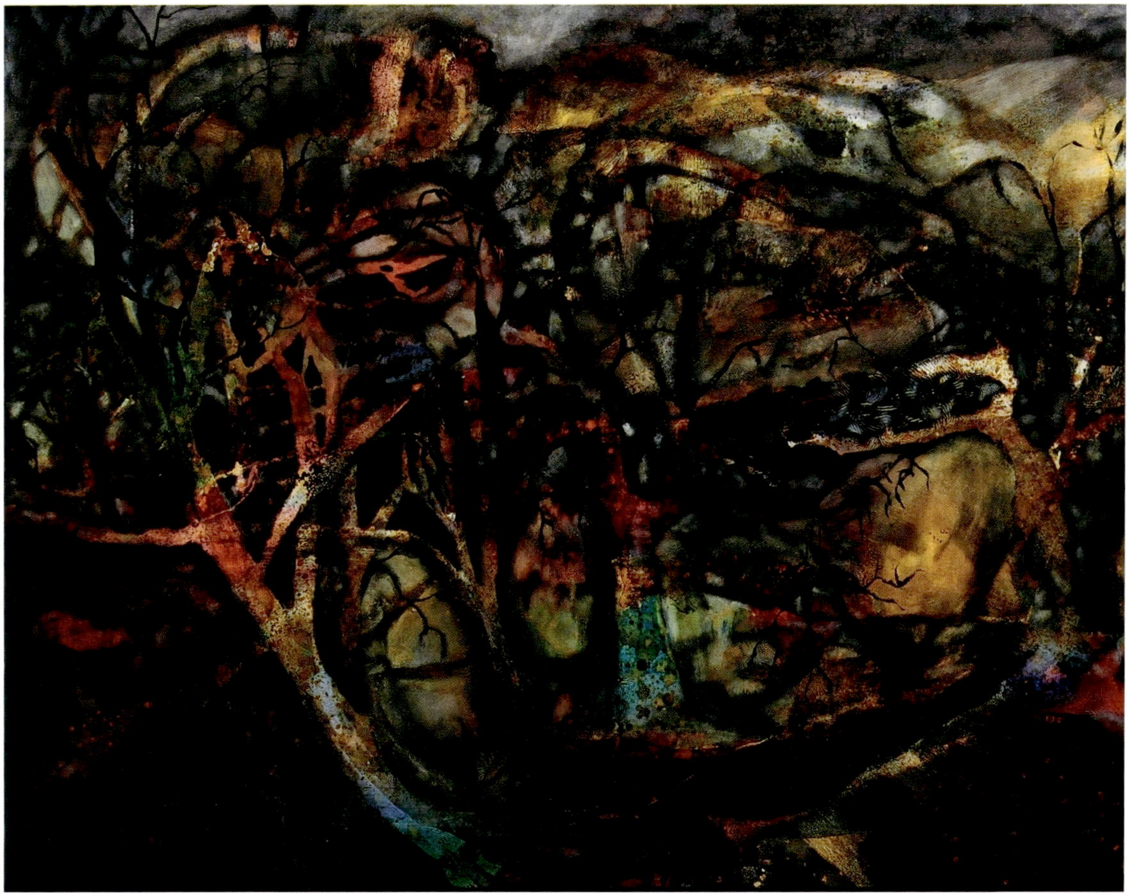

Clockwise from top left: Remembering, Enter the Dragon, When Darkness Falls

Caia Matheson is an award-winning contemporary British painter based in Brighton. She was born in Johannesburg and educated in Tokyo and London. Caia has exhibited alongside Billy Childish, Jamie Reid, Yohji Yamamoto, Sir Paul McCartney and David Freud.

As a child Caia was fascinated by Lowly Worm in the Richard Scarry books. She loved scouring each page to seek out that worm, and when she found it would feel most content – as if she had discovered a piece of secret truth that would uncover all the answers to her questions about the universe. There are some Lowly Worms in Caia's abstracts – albeit in symbolic form.

Caia is inspired by wabi sabi, or the beauty of imperfection. She loves to mix paint mediums and experiment with the effects. This can be the most exciting part of the creative process. Her mediums are oils – tubes of oil paint, oil bars, oil pastels and mixtures of oil paints and dyes. She enjoys the texture, consistency and smell of them. Caia paints with her hands and washing-up sponges onto canvases laid flat on the floor. It is a physical process.

"I begin painting with a specific colour that I have in my mind's eye. I then introduce other colours and begin to build layers on the canvas. These layers are then scratched off and layered over again like a palimpsest literally meaning 'scraped clean and used again'. I love the idea of previous markings that are not visible but are still an inherent part of the composition."

The layers are designed in a way to expose different subjects of the composition. These subjects are buried in the dark and light spaces and come out and disappear as the light changes, presenting different aspects depending on shifting light conditions and mood.

"I consider each successive layer a generation to populate or depopulate the canvas as needed and create my own world as I go.

I like to create a world within worlds."

Nominations & Awards

Painting selected by author Neil Gaiman for book A Calendar of Tales 2013. Winner Brighton Artist of the Year UK 2004. Nominated for the Ambassador's Art Prize Belgium 2005. Nominated for the Women's Art Show Basingstoke UK 2005. Short listed for the Brighton Festival Art Prize UK 2004

Emma Troy

Multimedia Artist

Clockwise from top left:
Pandemonium (RHS); What Will I Be Believing;
Desidero (Stardust)

Emma Troy is a multimedia artist based in Hove, East Sussex. In her current work, Emma uses drawing, collage, photography and printmaking to reinterpret familiar and iconographic images and text. The hazy areas of memory and longing are explored through re-imagined creatures, ancient trees and landscapes created from old magazines and newspapers rescued from the recycling box. Nostalgic and evocative verses, often borrowed from old song lyrics, are embellished with gold or silver leaf.

Emma completed her MA at the Royal College of Art, London in 1998. Also working in live art, installation and video, her work has been seen widely around the UK and Europe. Several of her works have been shown on Channel 4 and in the British Short Film Festival. Emma's prints are now exhibited in galleries around the UK and are available directly through her website (see index page 150).

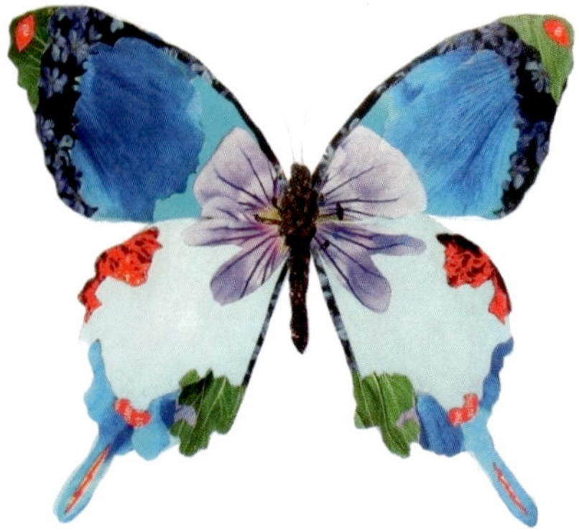

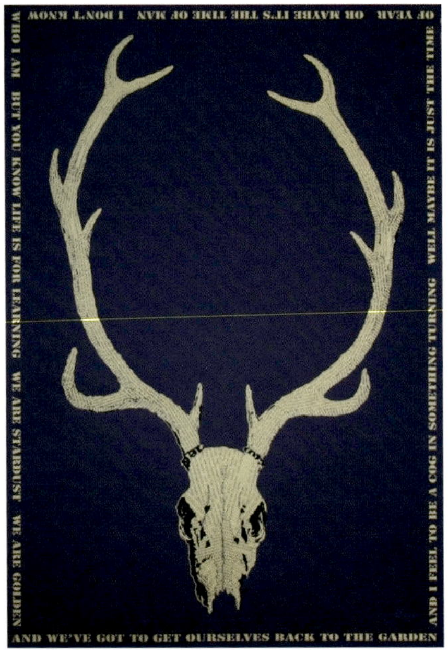

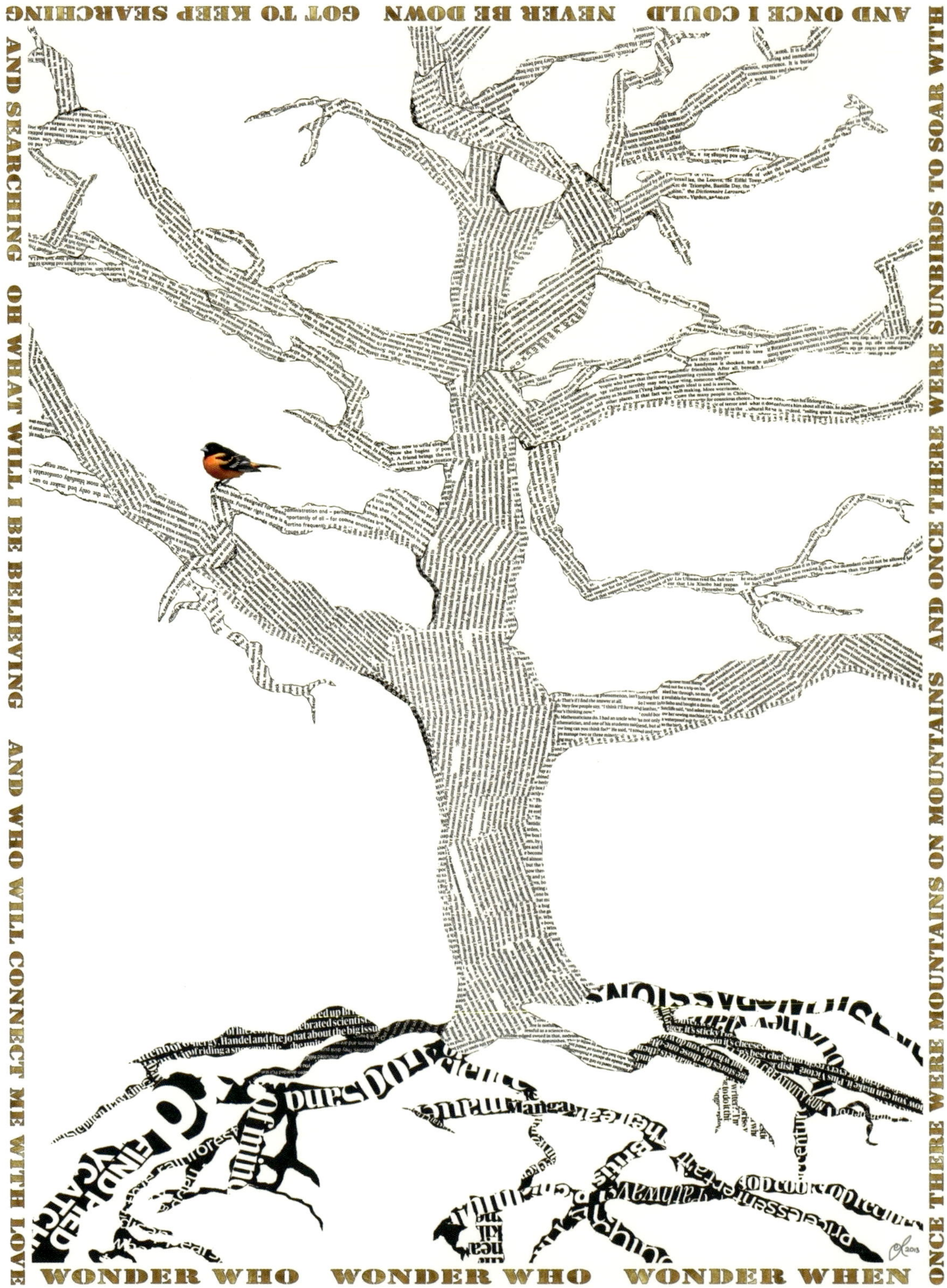

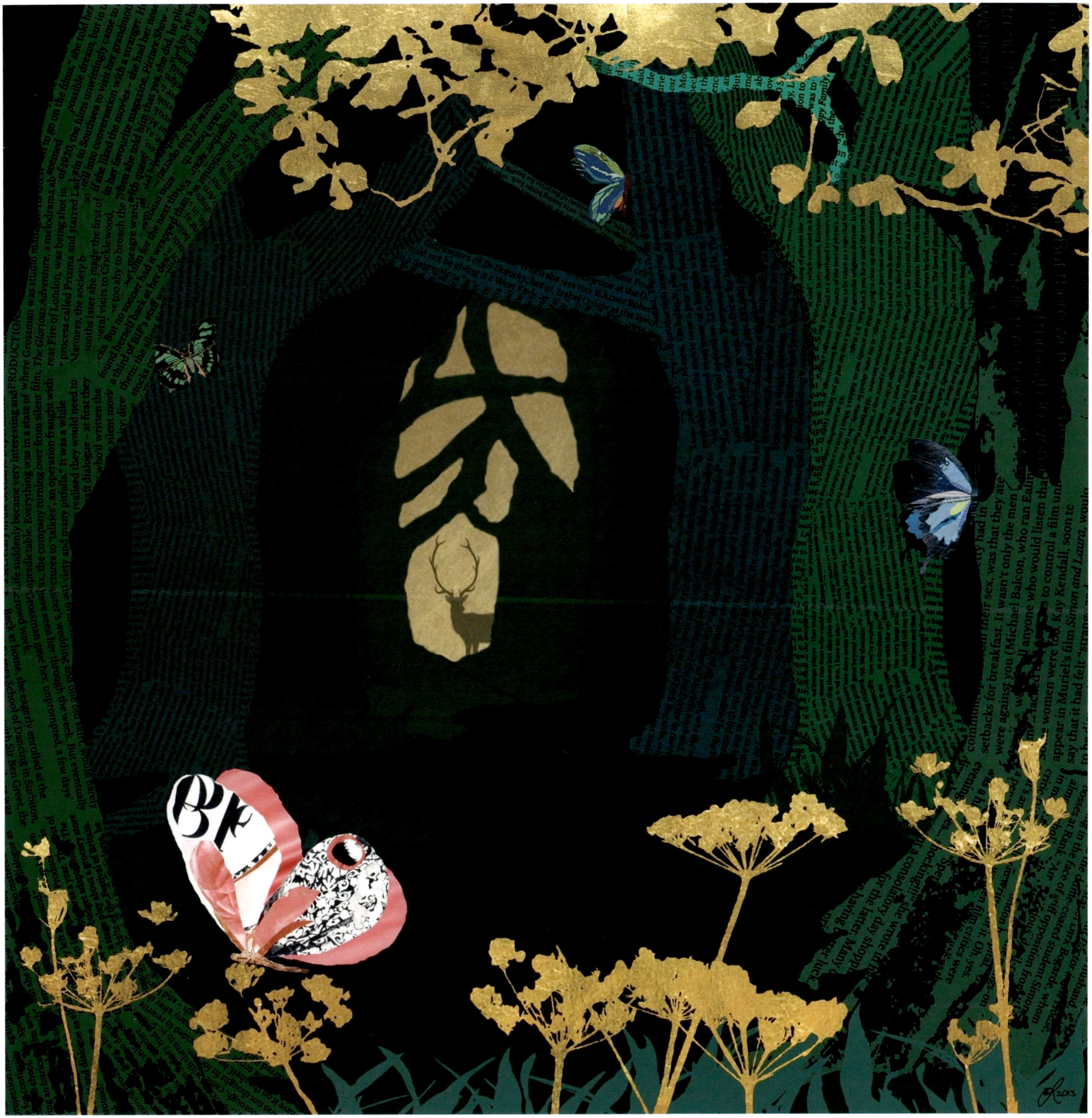

Lizzie Thomas

Artist, Author & Illustrator

Clockwise from top: Hidden Forest; They said a King Once Ruled the Forest; Hidden Winter; Hidden Spring (detail)

Lizzie Thomas is an artist and children's author/illustrator. Narrative is central to her crafted work. She writes with materials and images rather than words, and her aim is to draw out the lyrical qualities that exist in wood and paper.

Lizzie enjoys using sheet materials to create moving mechanisms and is passionate about 'pop-ups'. She loves the theatricality of their mechanism: something secret waiting to burst out and surprise the viewer. Her aim is to push the boundaries of pop-up towards beautiful hand-crafted sculpture by combining her skills in paper engineering, detailed papercutting, bookbinding and woodworking.

Lizzie has just finished her first children's picture book starring folk doll 'Coco Kokeshi' and her magical Spirit Cat companion 'KamiCat', and is hoping to secure a publisher soon. She exhibits her work in the UK and internationally, including South Korea, Berlin, USA and Japan.

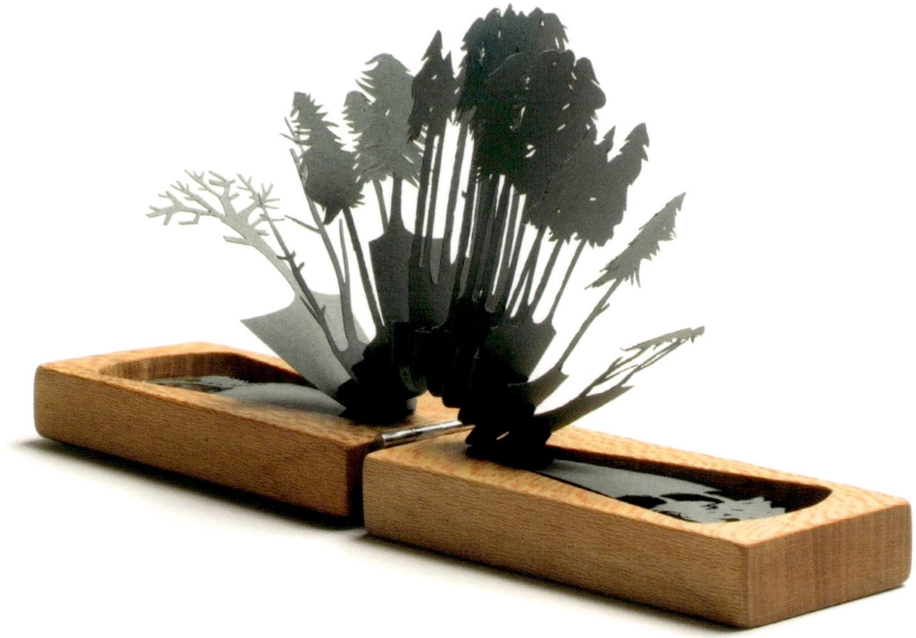

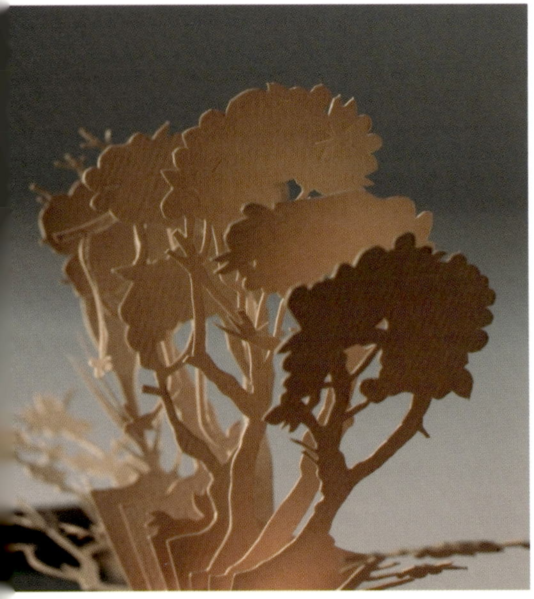

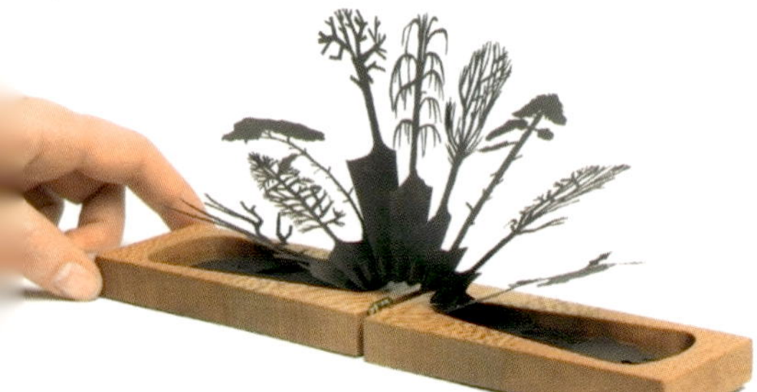

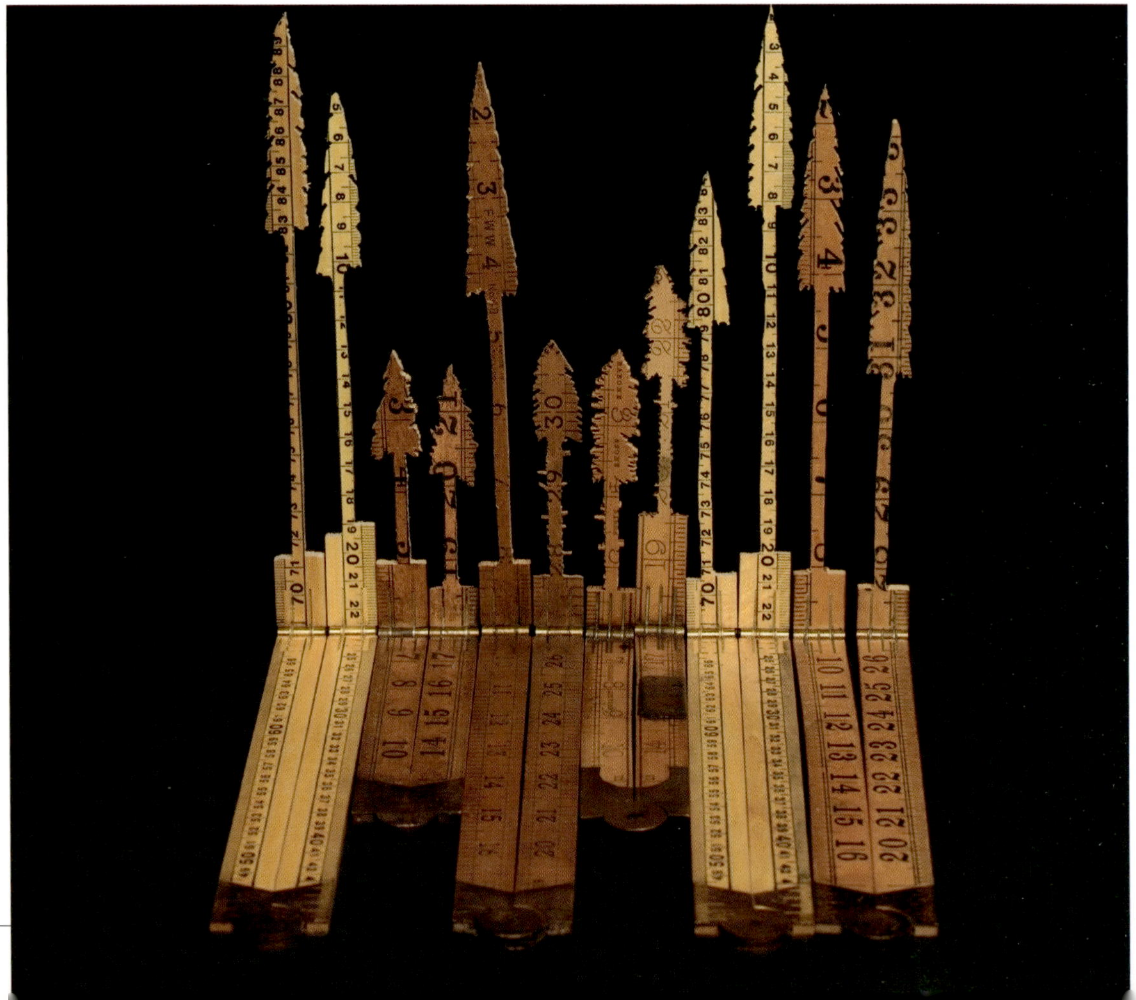

Clockwise from top left:
Brighton Sunset X; Lewes Sunset I;
Brighton Sunset XI

David Moore

Artist

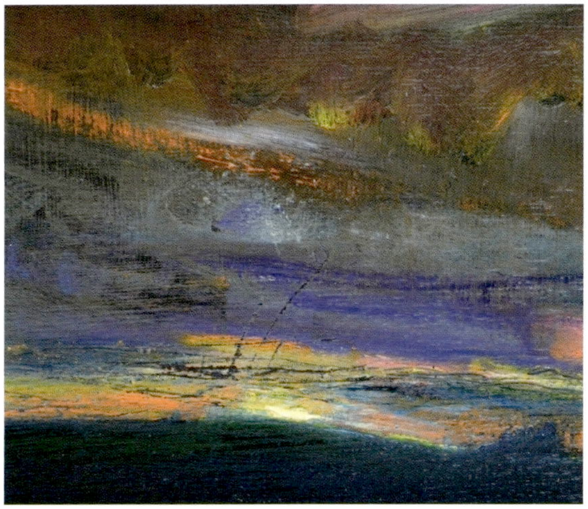

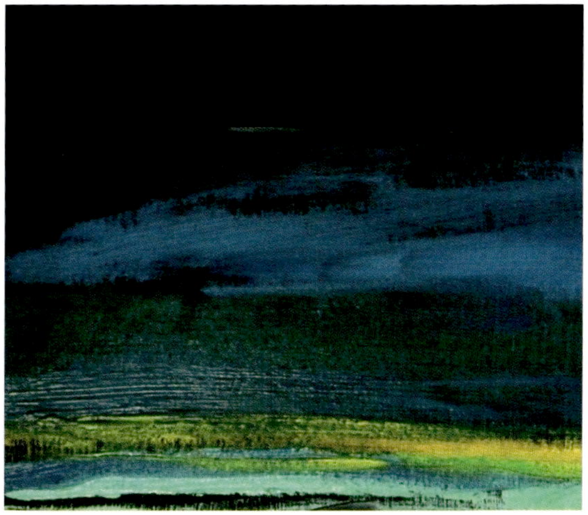

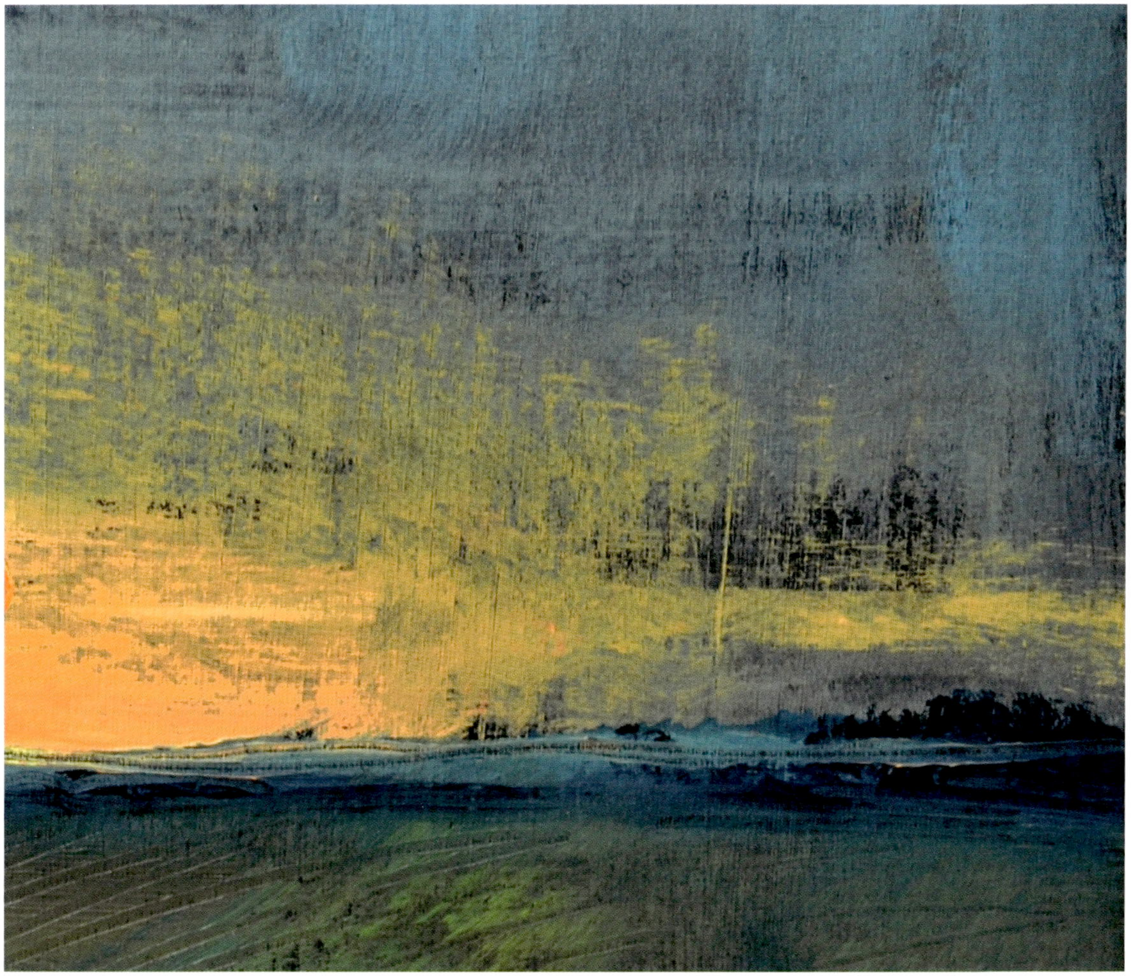

David Moore, a Phoenix Brighton studio artist, is currently showcasing his latest work 'Sunset Series I'. His work can be found as far afield as China and Australia, although he mostly exhibits his oil and acrylic compositions in London, Brighton and the South East. His bold experiments in light and colour moods; his contrasts in high key and low key tones, convey the drama and atmosphere of British landscapes.

David believes that painting outside, directly from the subject, is excellent for appreciating how to capture the movement in light from a sunset. He uses this method to drive the site studies of his present work, which are linked by the central theme of lines of light on landscapes.

The deep and distant Downs surrounding Brighton, Hove, Lewes and Ditchling provide the artist with fascinating horizons that are perfect for anchoring fleeting skies and staging an ephemeral sunset. Every one leads to a unique composition, even when painted from the same site and at the same time of day. David responds quickly and intuitively to the setting sun, applying glazes and rhythms of patterned marks over bands of exposed layers and textures.

The Gilded Cage

106 St James Street, Brighton BN2 1TP

Clockwise from top left:
Inside the studio;
Bird Skull Goddess; Bird Heart

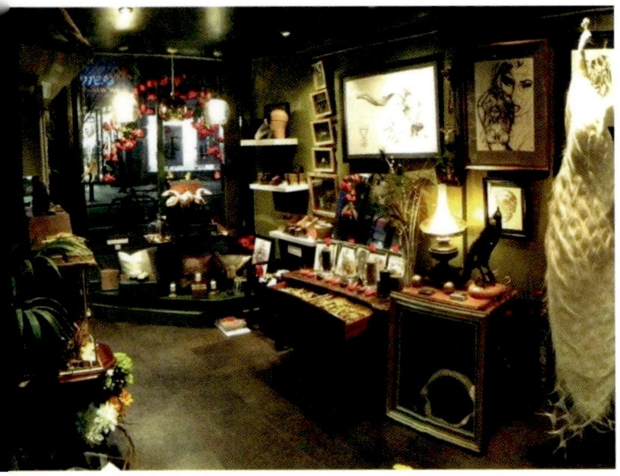

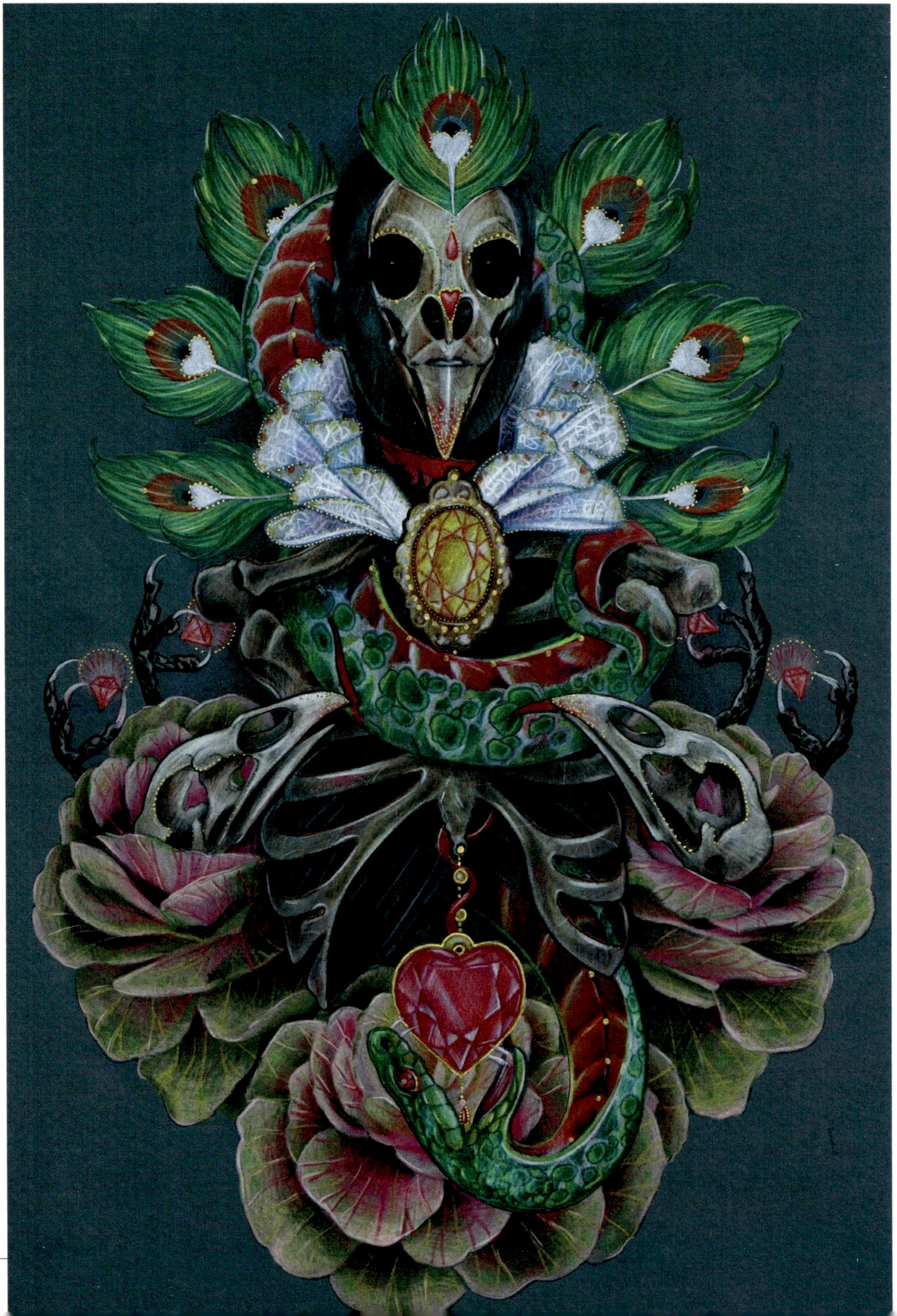

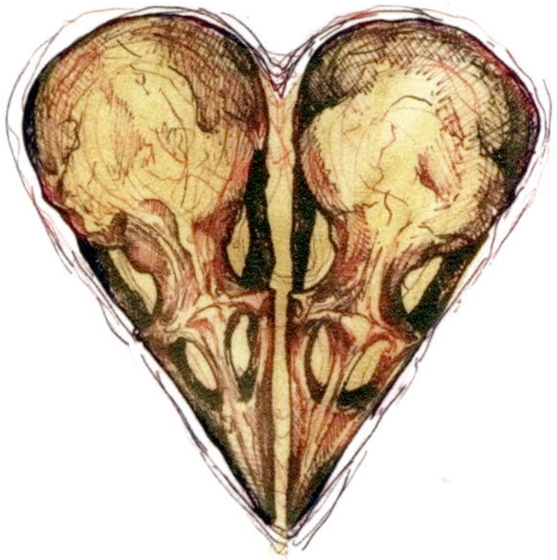

The Gilded Cage is a tattoo studio and boutique in Brighton, and is the home of tattooist James Robinson. The studio has made a strong impression on St James Street. It has built up a solid reputation for creating distinct, beautiful tattoos with a strong influence from nature, religion, mythology and the macabre.

All James's designs are custom made; and not only for the wall, but transgress to the human flesh, really bringing his designs to life.

Designs are researched for the individual customer, roughly drawn as thumb nails, sketched out large, then worked back into with mixed media, paint, graphic pens, pencil and usually embellished with Swarovski crystals and glitter for a hint of vibrancy.

James works alongside other influential artists in Brighton. The studio has a gallery space upstairs, which displays Brighton's finest and a collection of outstanding original styles.

If you haven't entered the Gilded Cage yet, make sure you stop by. Be prepared to enjoy a lavish, eye-catching environment decorated with vintage splendour. If not for a tattoo, you will want to return time and time again to soak up its luxurious atmosphere and maybe even take a way a piece of artwork on a cushion or wall hanging, which you would be proud to hang in your own home.

Clockwise from top left:
Great Great Great; Carpe Noctem; By Beast or By Bicycle; Ayahuasca-Vine of the Soul;
Year of the Horsicorn

FOX

Artist & Printmaker

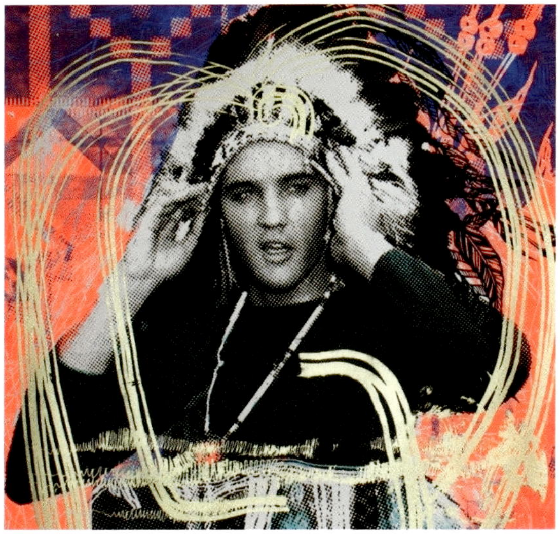

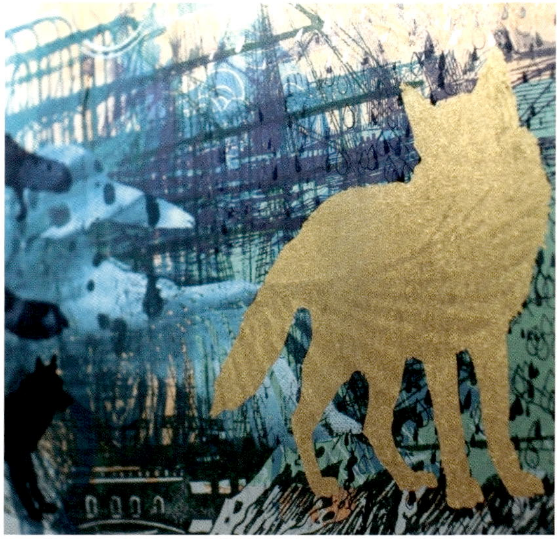

Raphael Fox, known as FOX, founded Studio Salute, for screen printing and other creative adventures, including design, illustration, animation and film. He creates fascinating mixed media prints inspired by the aesthetics of the hand-drawn vs. the clarity of the digital.

After completing an MA in Sequential Design & Illustration, FOX began teaching screen-printing and digital prep at Ink Spot Press and selling his work at artrepublic gallery. He is also acknowledged on *The Independent's* Pink List for raising awareness of trans issues, after taking part in *My Transsexual Summer* (Ch4), co-founding *My Generation* (a film series about gender variance), engaging with the mainstream media and setting up Trans Pride.

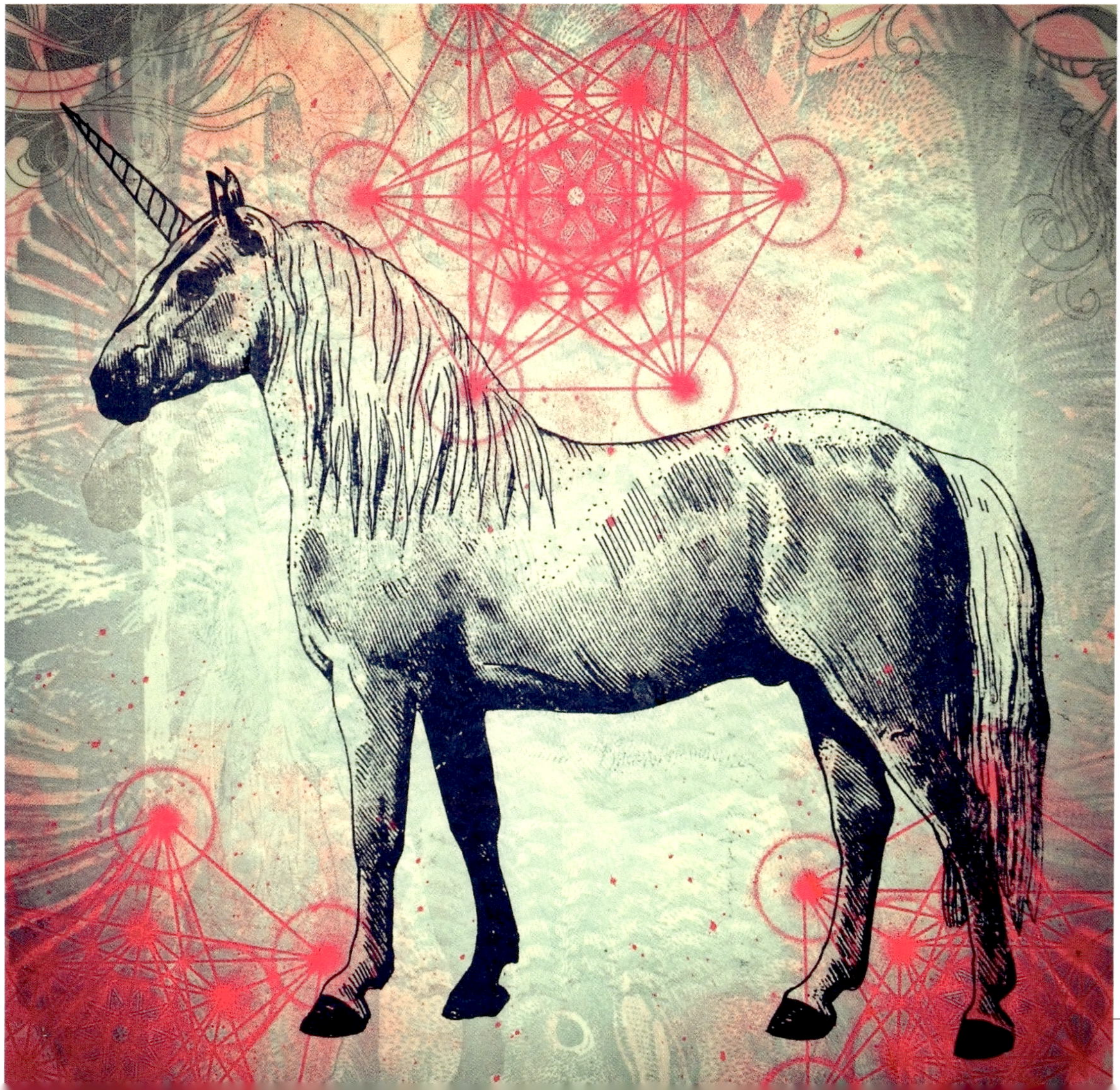

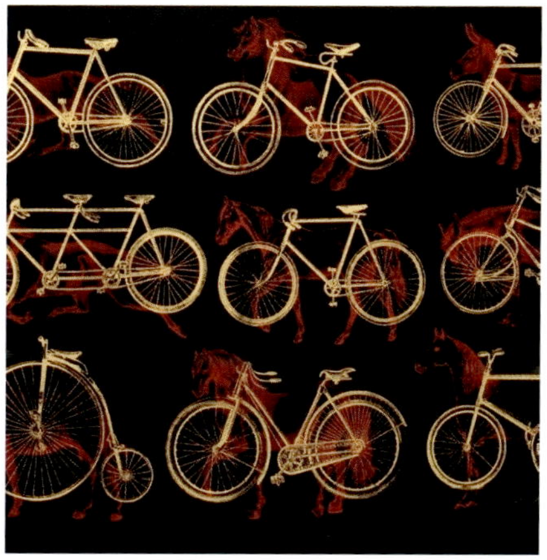

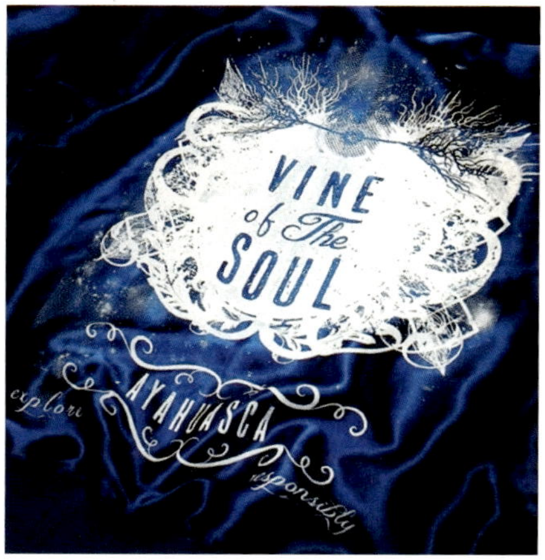

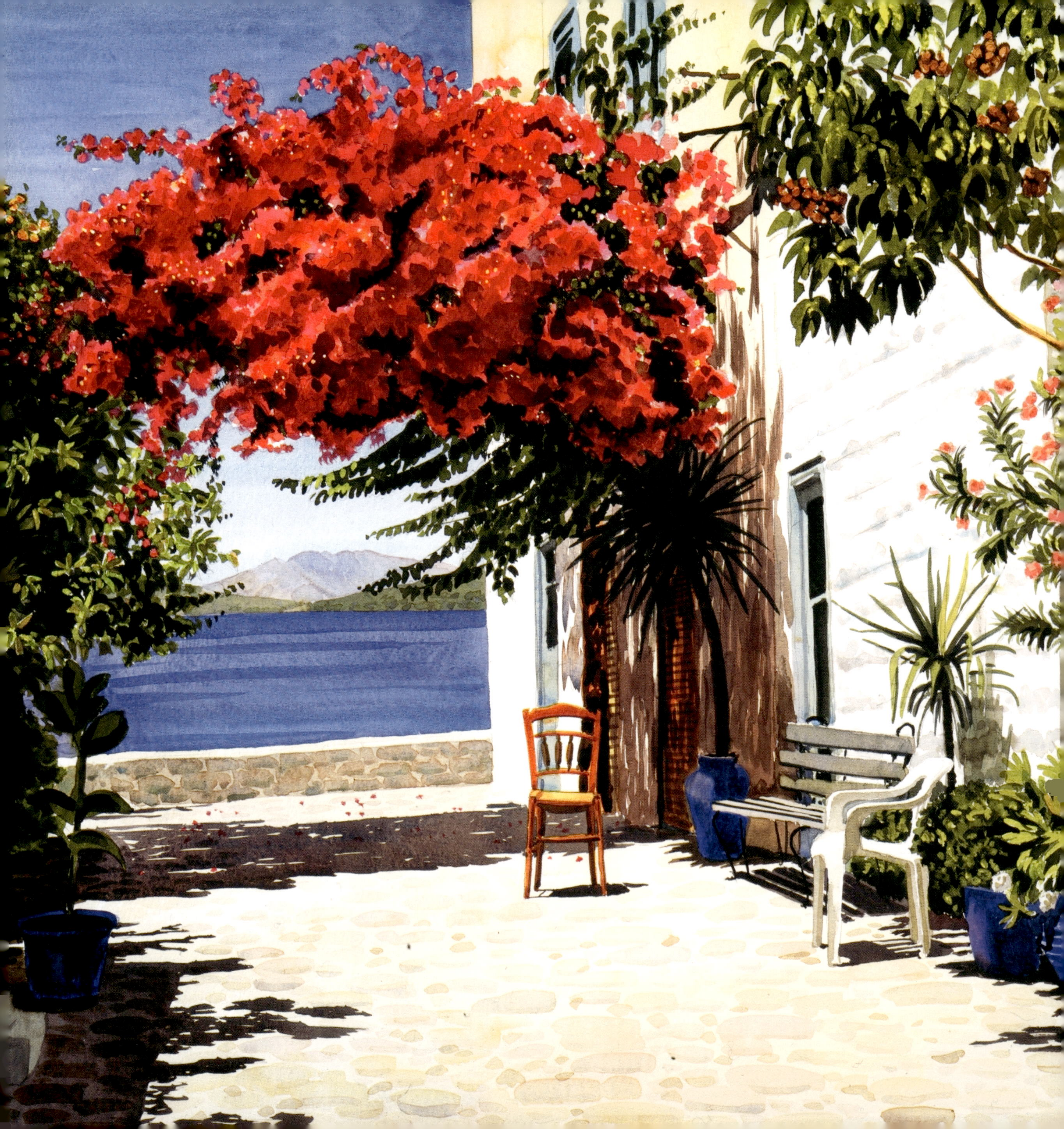

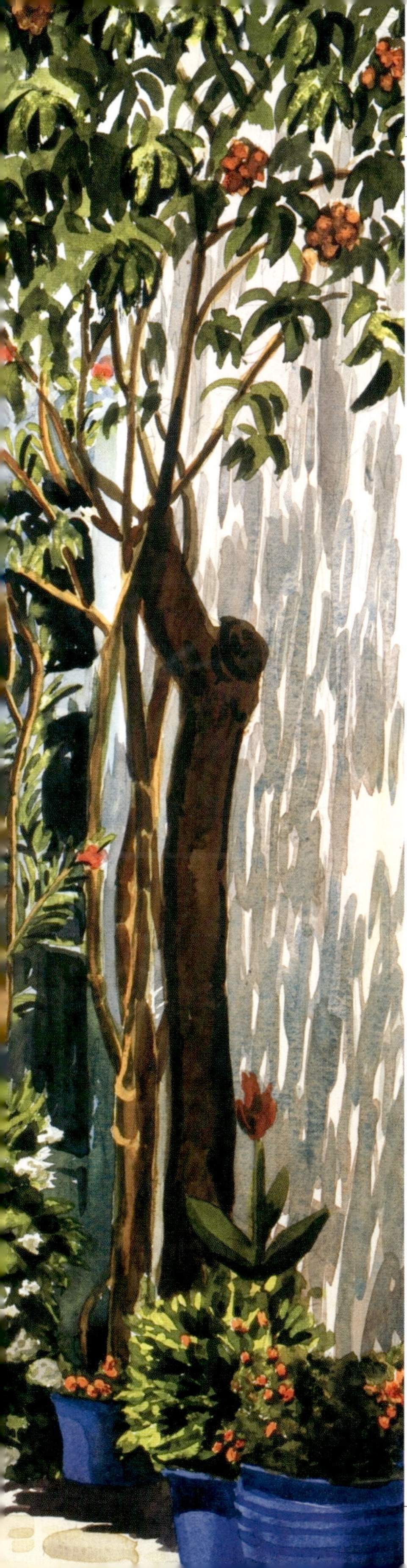

This page: (clockwise from top): Cassiss on a hot day; Poles St Georgio; Scotch House; Courtyard, Marrakech; Vine Terrace, Domme.
Opposite page: Bougainvillea Arch

Ilana Richardson

Artist

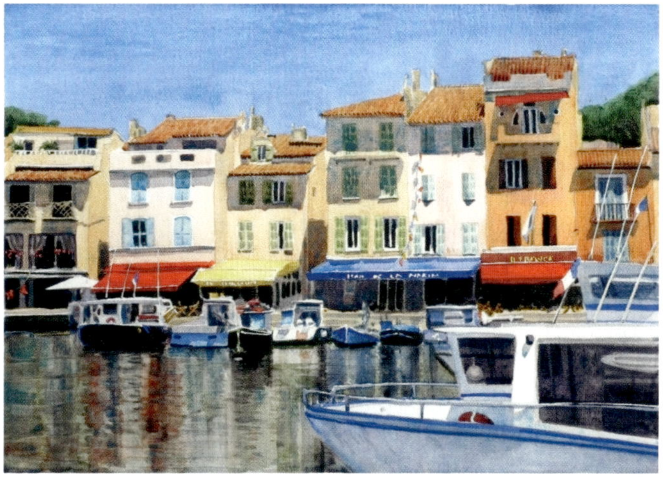

Ilana is based in Brighton and enjoys an international reputation, with many exhibitions in England and abroad. Her evocative, sun-drenched Mediterranean paintings and prints radiate heat and light.

Ilana's inspiration comes from her love of travel. She is at her best depicting the interplay of light and shadows, and favours subjects that contrast lush vegetation with the whitewashed walls of Mediterranean architecture or the vibrant colours of Mexican houses. Onlookers can feel the heat and are drawn into the light and warmth.

Her work is included in many collections and she regularly undertakes painting commissions.

Ilana welcomes visitors to her Open House during the Brighton Festival in May and any time throughout the year by appointment.

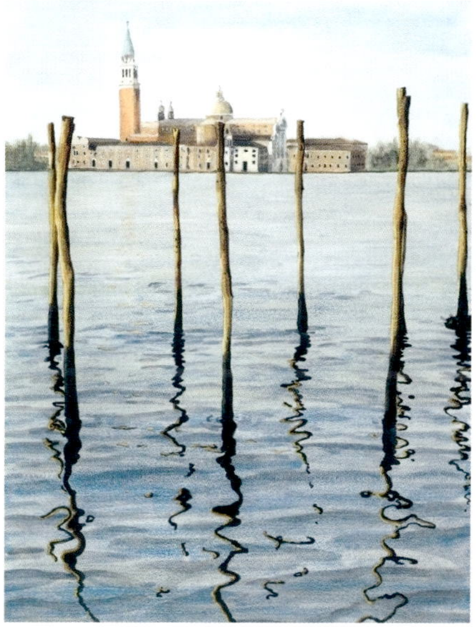

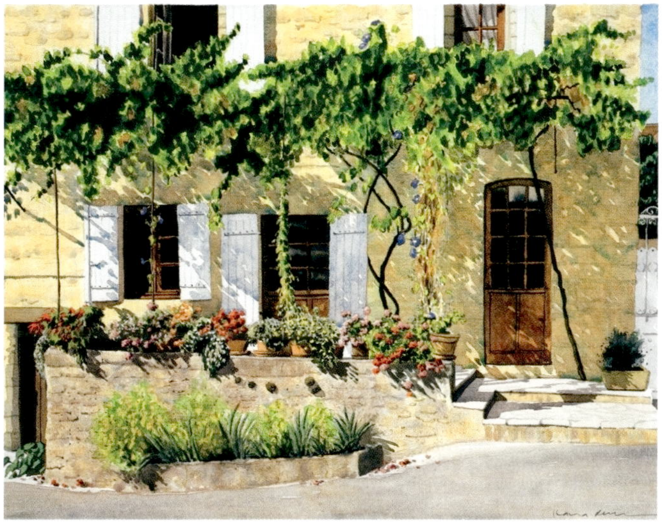

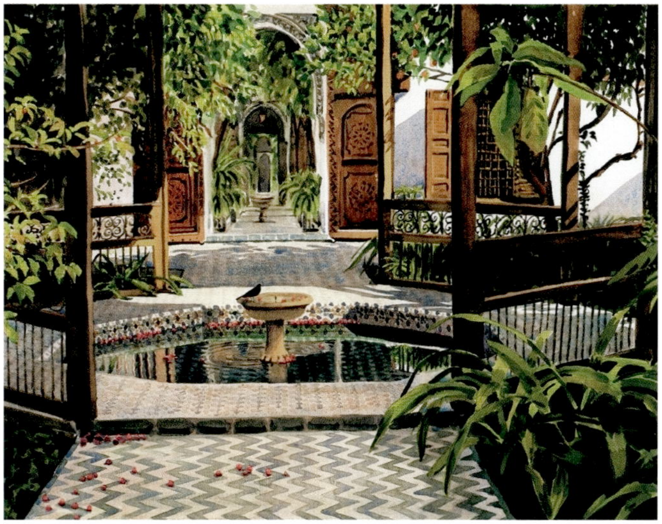

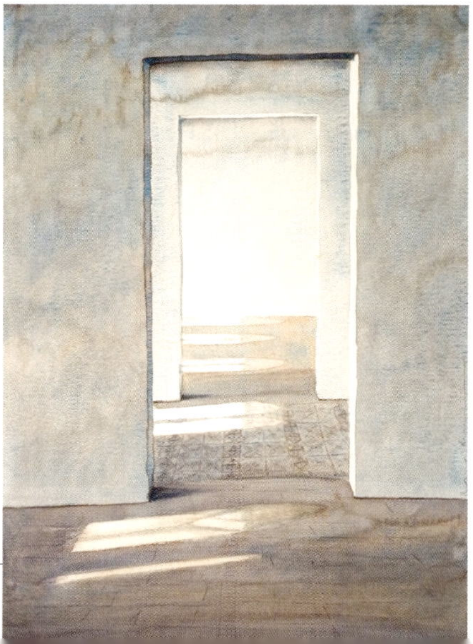

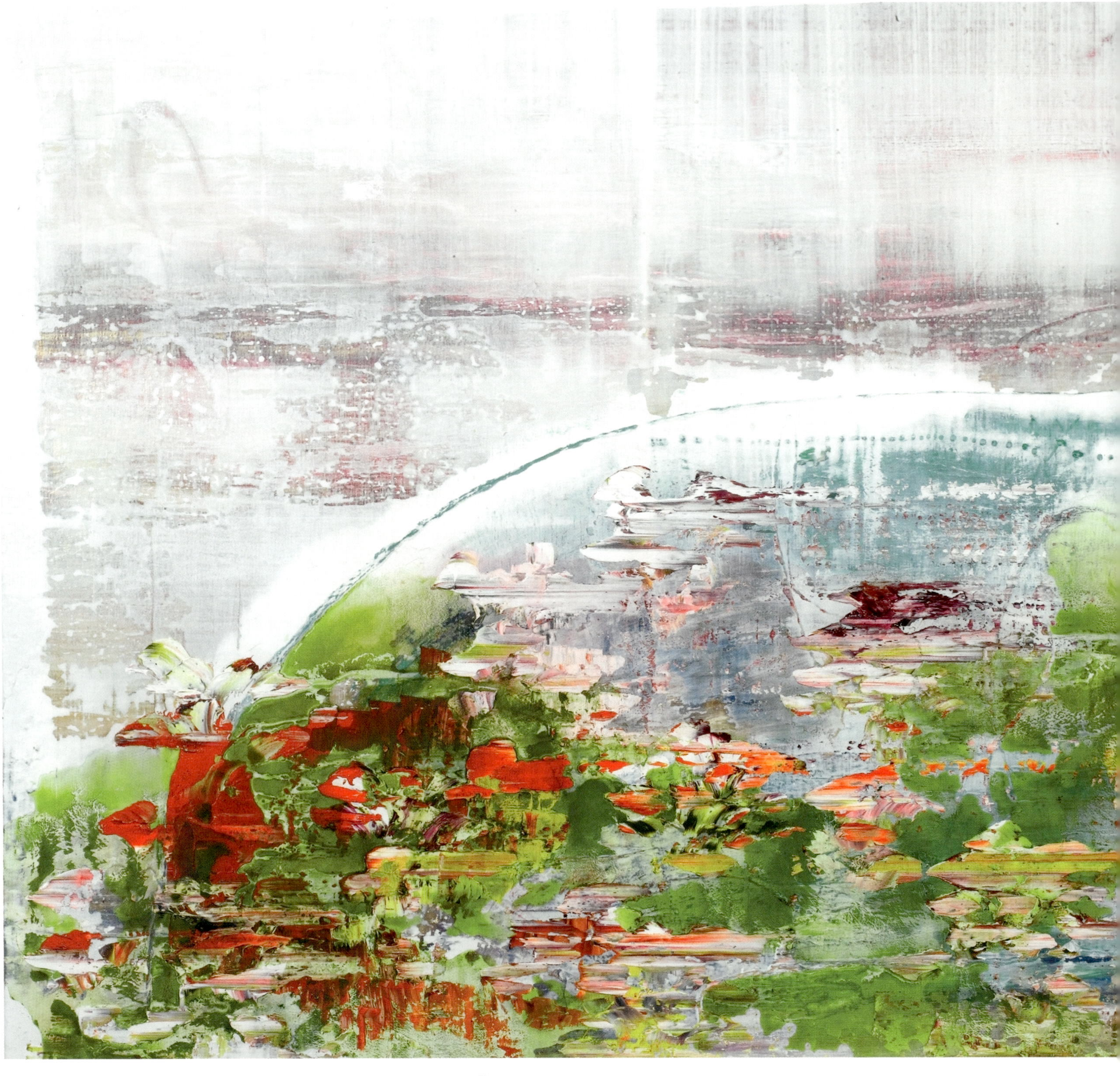

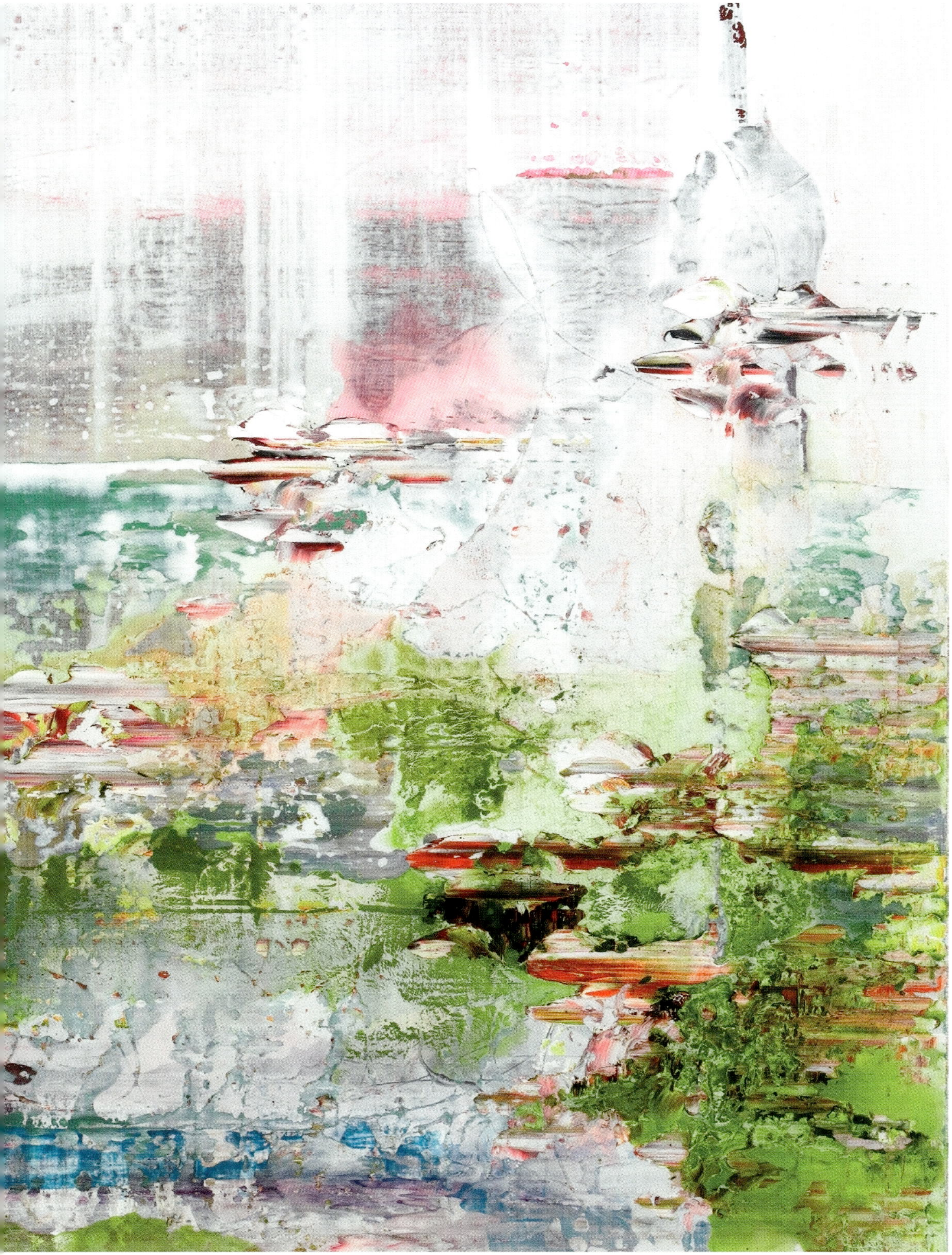

Jessica Zoob now has a range of limited-edition prints available on paper, canvas and diasec. Also available is a range of textiles, cushions and wallpapers in collaboration with Romo Black Edition. Check out the shop section of her website for further information (see index page 150).

"Zoob's use of line, texture and colour recall the work of Gerhard Richter's abstract paintings and the poetic quality of Claude Monet's later works. However, they are rich in imagination with an innate energy and beauty all of their own."

Leonie Irvine, Medici Gallery

"Electrifying, elemental and powerful."

Art of England

"Truly beautiful."

Bernard Jacobson

"Stunningly beautiful and unique. A photograph cannot do justice to her paintings. Abstracted and atmospheric, the textures and vitality of her paintings need to be seen to be appreciated."

Mary Fox Linton

Karl Smith

Sculptor & Jeweller

Clockwise from top:
Oak Dining Table with Pewter Inlay; The Bench;
'Caress' Alabaster; Tryptic of Platinum, Gold and Diamond Rings;

Karl Smith's work is often inspired by his beloved Sussex landscape, the human form and elements from nature. His pieces have a sensual fluid energy and simplicity.

He enjoys working with different mediums and in different scales, for example the juxtaposition of steel and timber in his epic sculptural furniture, as recently featured in *How to Spend It* magazine. However, he is equally at home carving alabaster into organic forms or creating exquisite heirloom pieces of jewellery.

The slow process involving hand tools allows Karl to discover the hidden beauty within the timber, or stone that could so easily be lost with the use of power tools. History naturally occurring during the creative process is treasured and explored. These tooled marks are an integral part of his aesthetic.

Karl enjoys working in collaboration with his clients, who have included interior designers such as Intarya, on commissioned pieces. Thus enabling him to create the perfect end product for their environment.

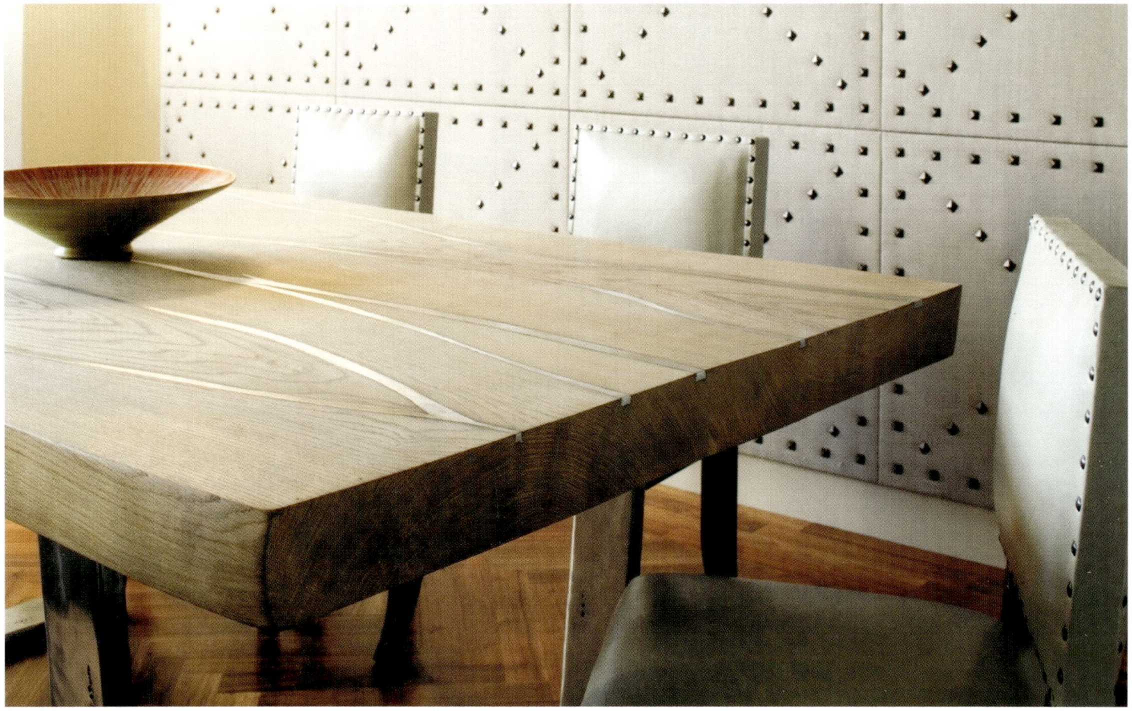

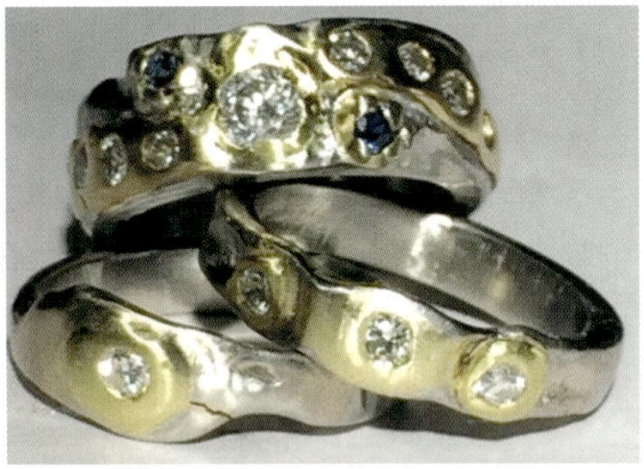

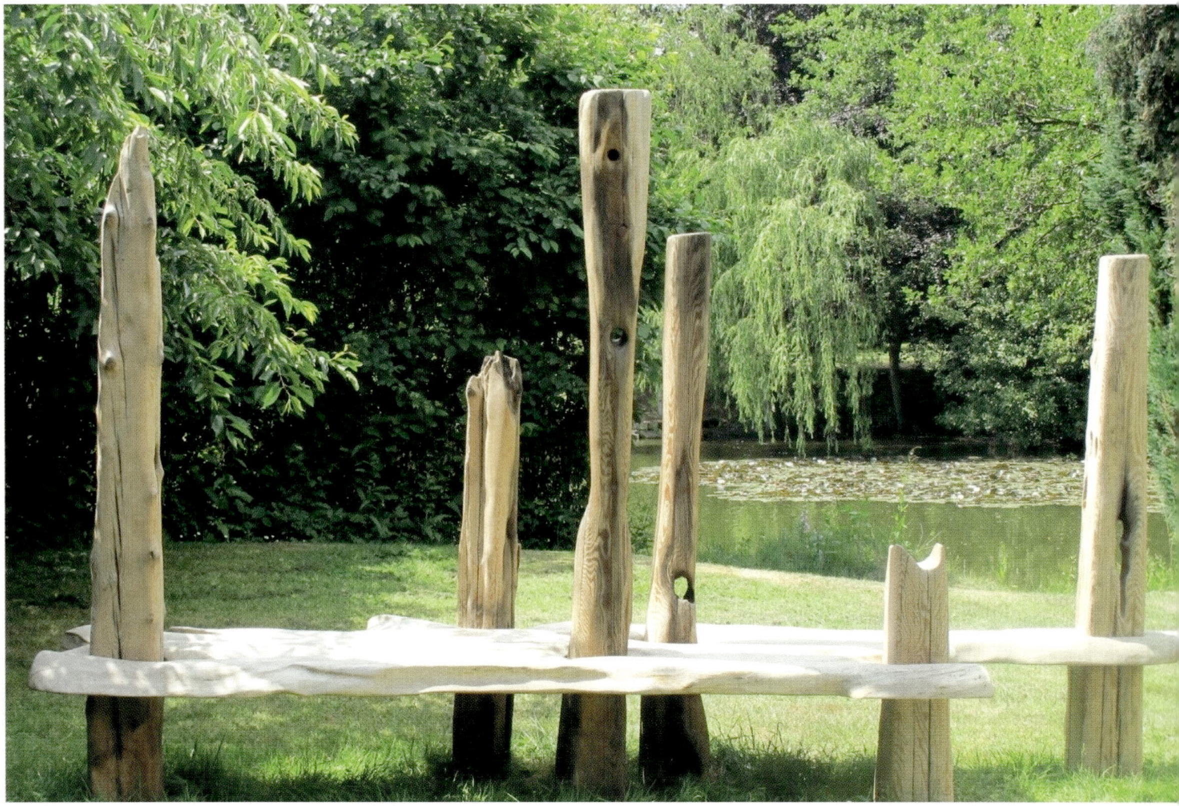

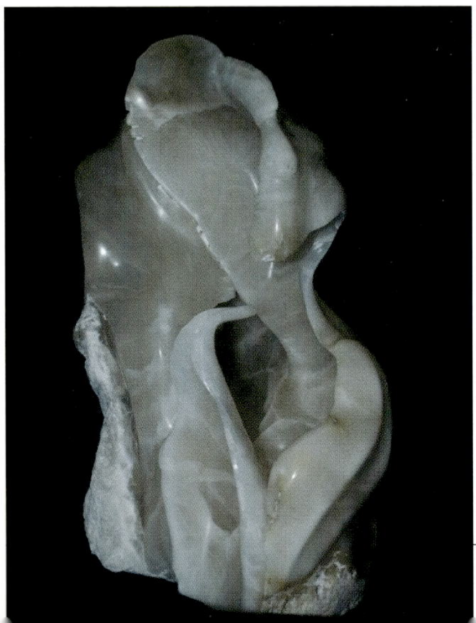

Angela Newman

Artist & Photographer

Clockwise from top:
West Pier & Gull on Spruce;
Bandstand on Pine; West Pier & Gull on Oak Slice

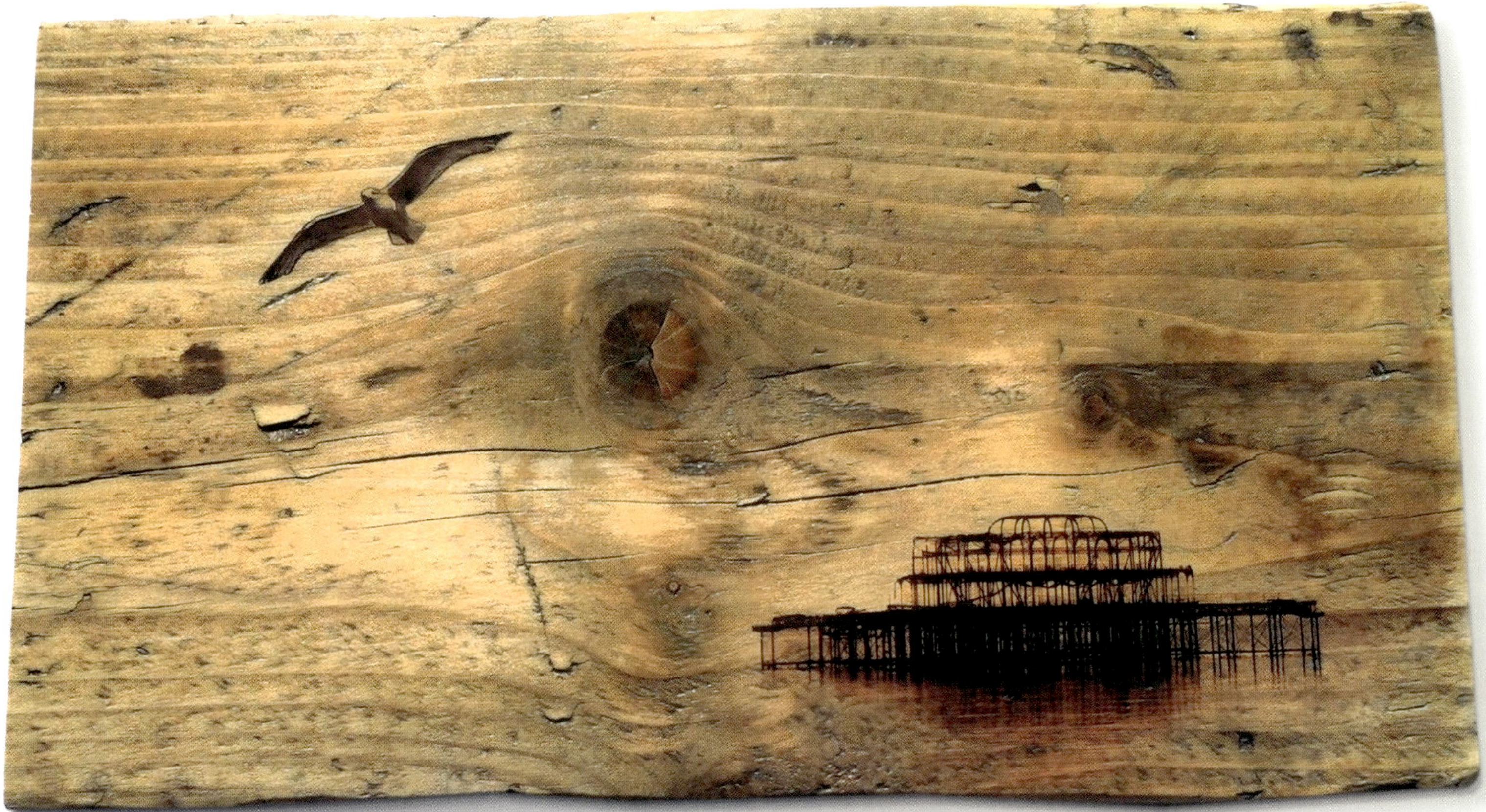

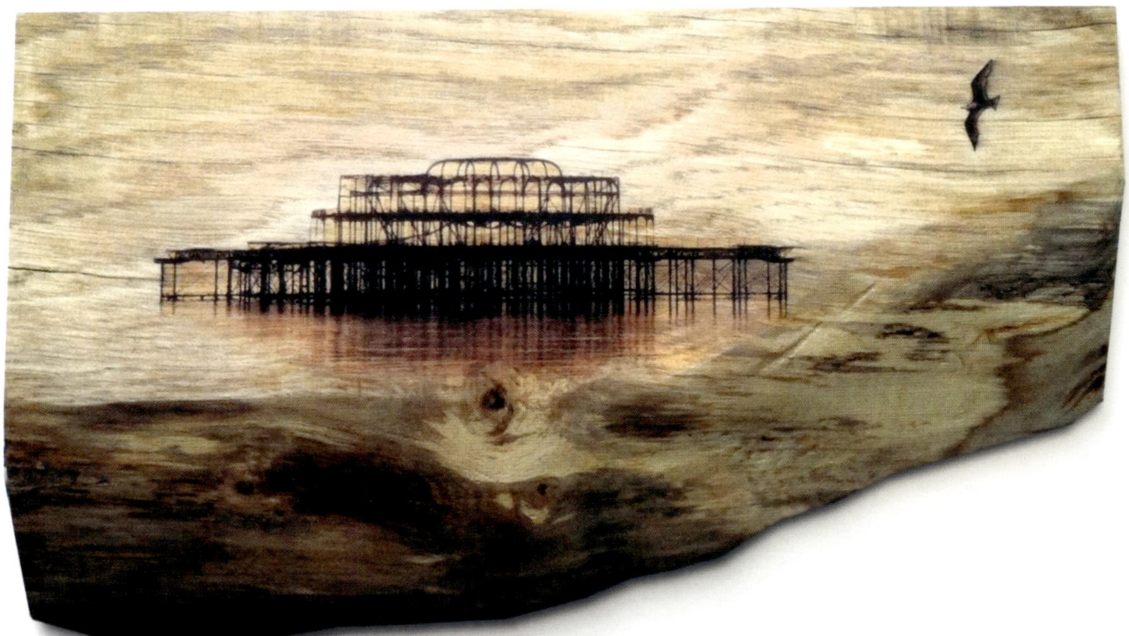

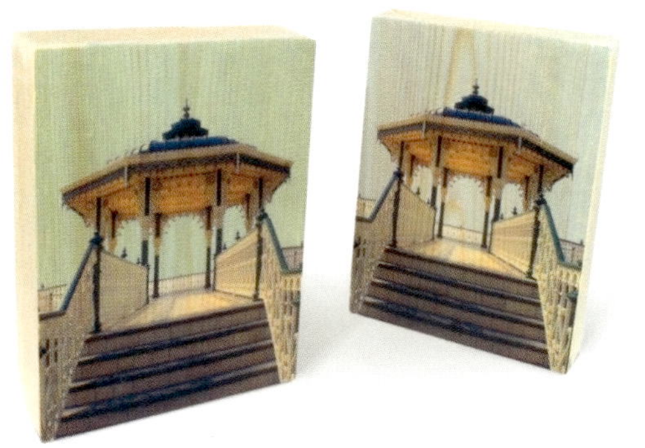

This Brighton artist/photographer creates striking wood blocks by transferring her own images – by hand – onto a variety of locally sourced, reclaimed wood of all types, shapes and sizes. The Royal Academy of Arts Summer Exhibition 2013.

rubandagar

Digital Artist

Clockwise from top left:
Forgiveness Psychedelic; Map Red Actually!;
Sunset Dawn; Pavilion Pink; Vurt Cat

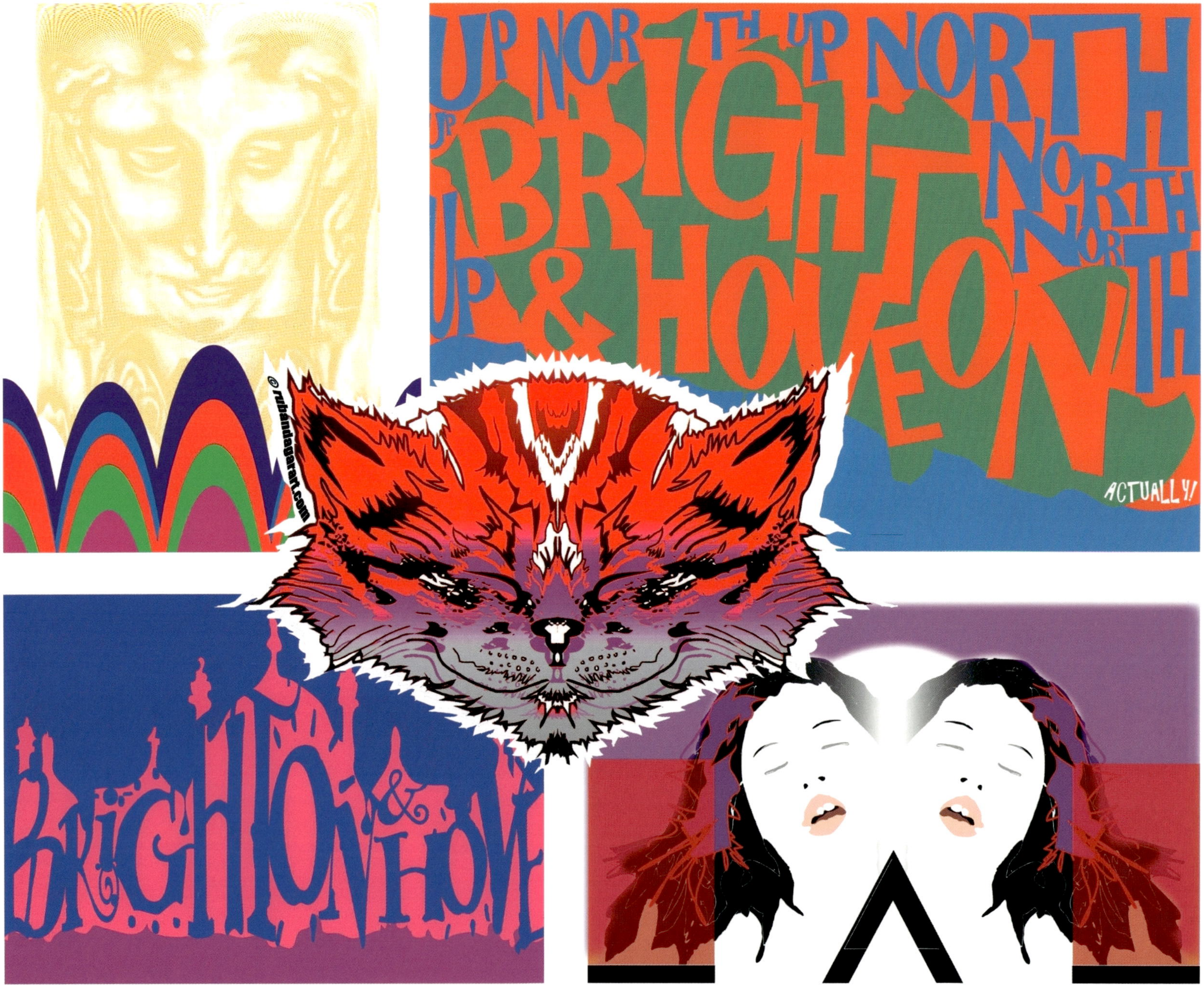

Psychedelic, typographic and fantastical. rubandagar produces striking, thought-provoking images, encouraging the viewer beyond a first impression. A love of surrealism, comic book art and things of beauty are all influences. Inspirations are everywhere. Primarily a digital artist, he experiments with styles and techniques, from graphic to fine art, trying new ideas, working in pencil, paint, Photoshop and Illustrator, his favoured medium by far. Vectors.

Clockwise from top left:
Chance; Mind Games;
Clowns; Men in Ties

Robin Cooper Hannan

Artist

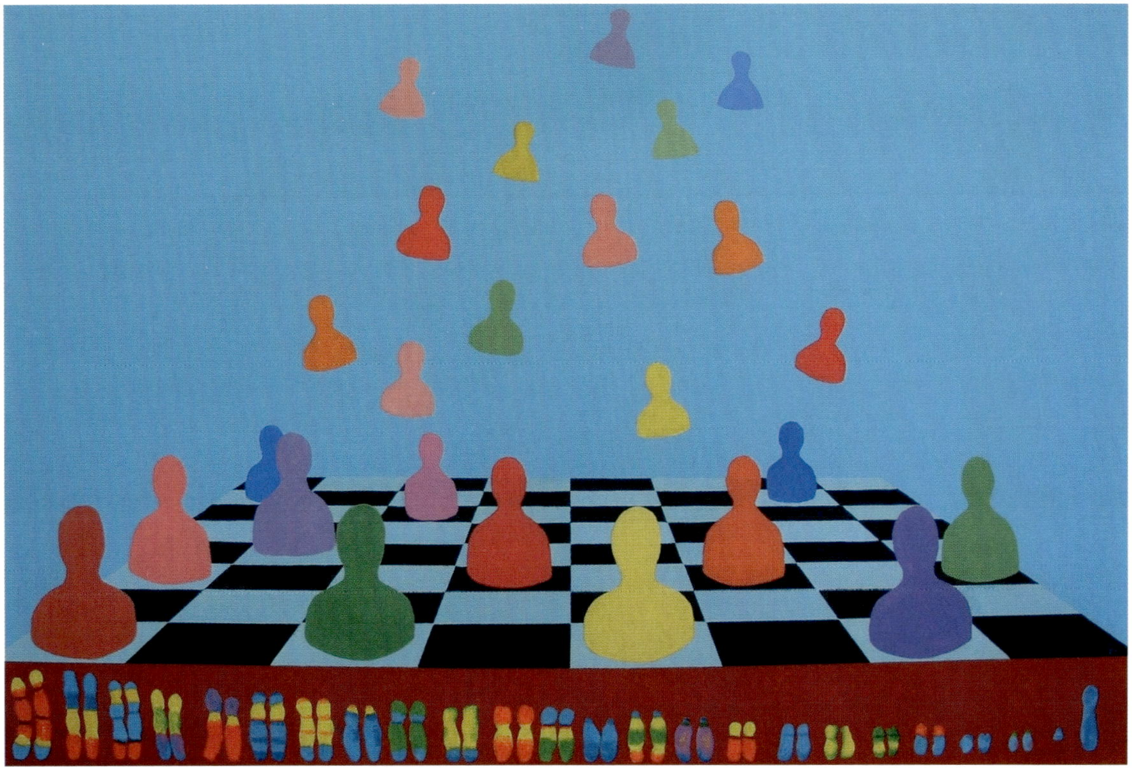

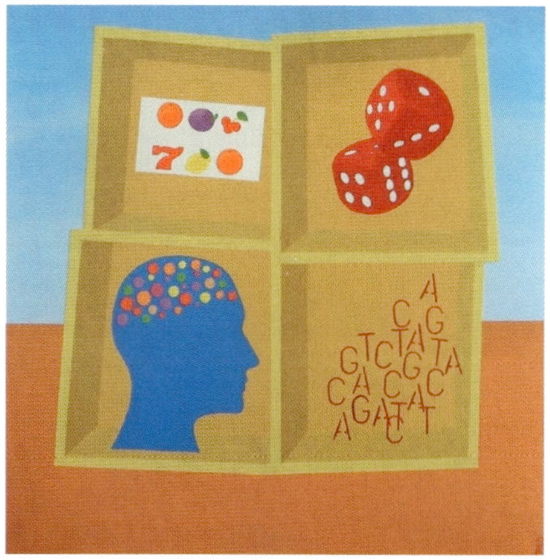

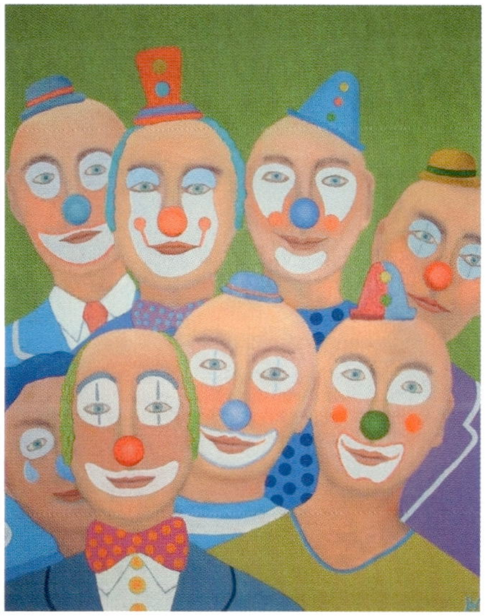

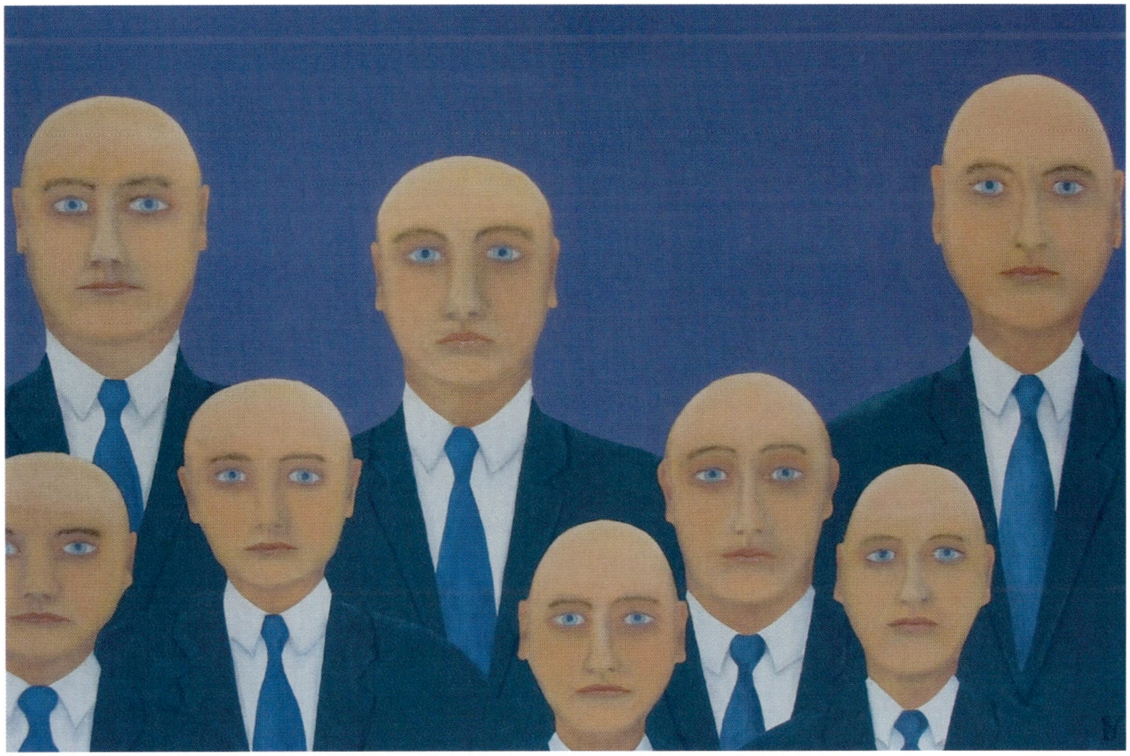

Colourful and thought-provoking, Robin's recent paintings have become representative and bring together personal and scientific narratives on the human condition.

Working in oil on canvas, subjects range from chromosomes to identity in the corporate world, with imagery including the comic and tragic. Abstract work continues with exploration of the natural sciences at cellular and sub-cellular levels. Art and science have more in common than opposition, there is no art without investigation and no science without imagination.

Robin views creativity as a journey with each composition attaining a life and vitality reflecting our strengths, uncertainties and ability to relate with ourselves and others.

Penelope Oakley

Artist

Right to left:
Elenin;
Sempertina

International artist Penelope Oakley's unique and distinctive style is inspired by the beauty of nature and of the human spirit. The desire to express not purely the external beauty but that which lies beyond and within. Seeking to dig deep and peel back the layers reveals the real vision, the essence of who we really are. Crossing over any boundaries of specific cultures and origin, distance and time.

"To any artist, worthy of the name, all in nature is beautiful, because his eyes, fearlessly accepting all exterior truth, read there, as in an open book, all the inner truth."

Auguste Rodin

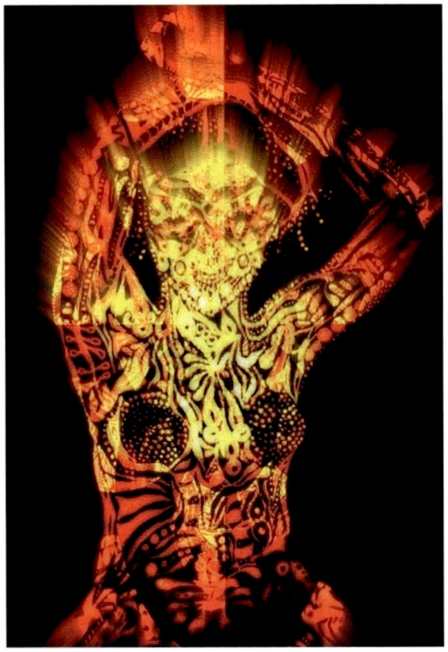

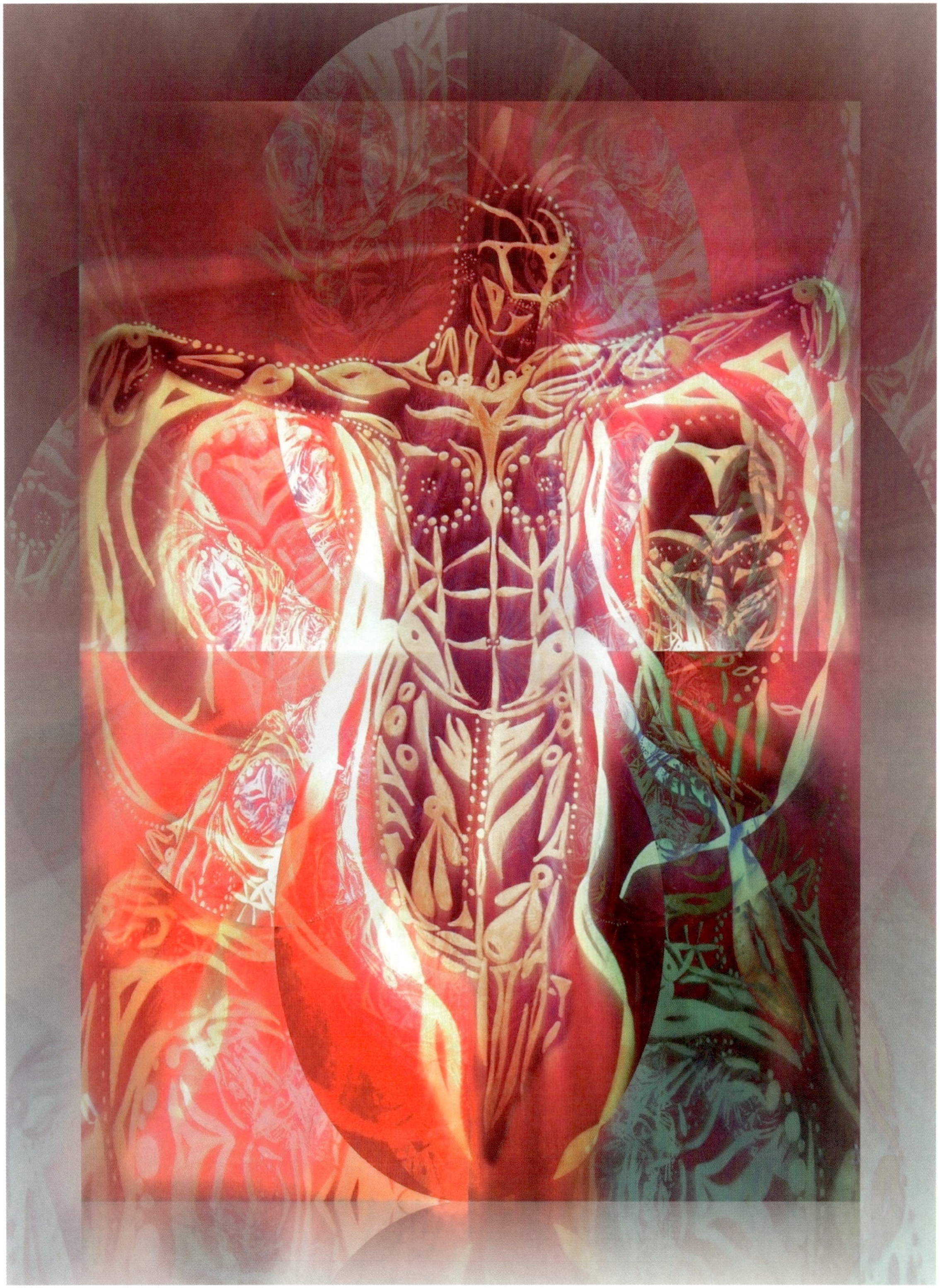

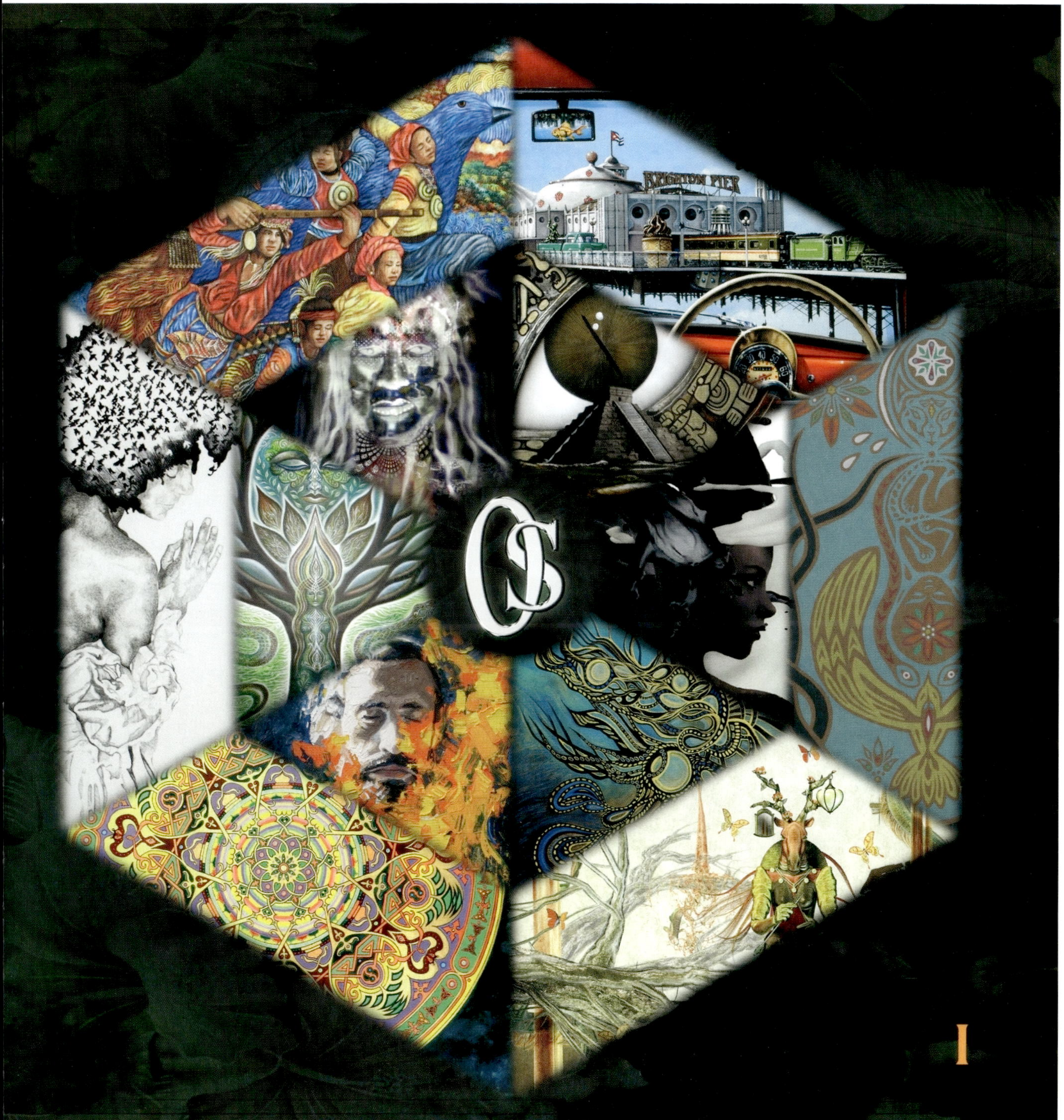

Omnia vivunt, omnia inter se conexa

"Everything is alive. Everything is interconnected"

Cicero

Be a part of our exciting collaboration and exhibitions – show your art in the UK and abroad in one of our upcoming collective shows in 2014. Long-term promotion and visibility for all artists who exhibit their original works in the exhibitions – alongside your art being part of the ever expanding Omnia Scroll, which highlights and joins each artist's work to the next.

The theme of the exhibitions is the interconnectedness of all things.

Now accepting submissions for new artists to join us and details of our fourth collective show.

Email submissions and queries to curator Penelope Oakley at omniascroll@gmail.com.

Together we create
~ The Omnia Scroll ~

Dinah Dufton

Artist in Practice

Clockwise from top: Audio; QR code; Pintograph

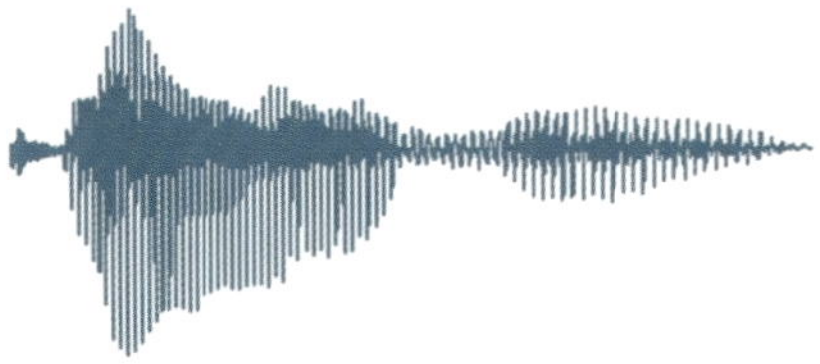

Often described as playful, witty and smart, Dinah Dufton's work is project-based and so differs from collection to collection. But it builds on earlier skills and ideas while always looking fresh and deceptively simple.

From original paintings and prints using typography to map hyperreal figures through to a series of works with toys inspired by her son, and now a return to earlier personal interests in codes, mechanical intervention, puzzles and mazes.

Exhibiting internationally since 2000, her work has been commissioned by the BBC and other public organisations and is in many private collections.

Dinah & Co jewellery and design are new additions that are becoming estabished in their own right.

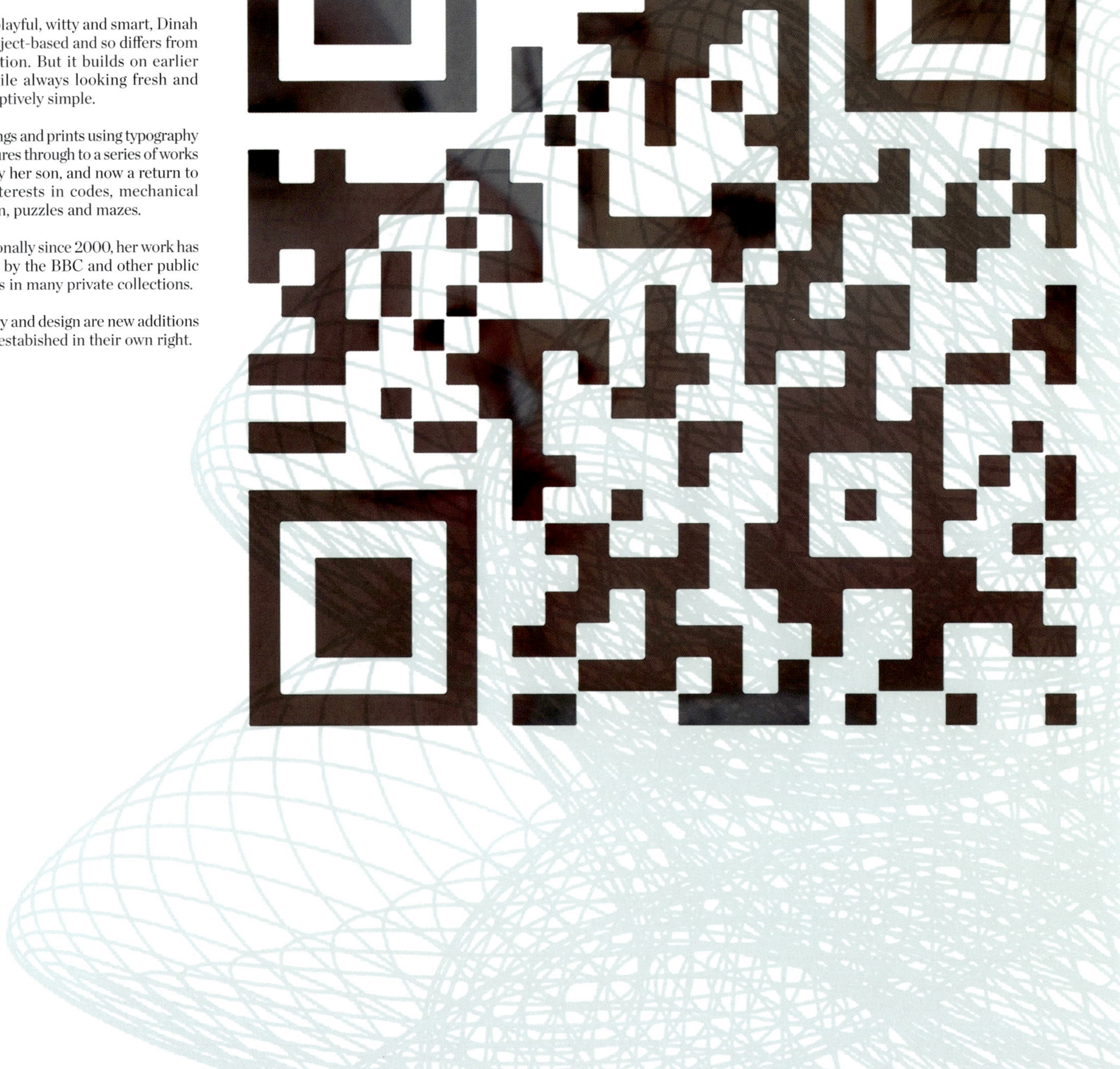

Clockwise from top left:
Brighton Seagulls; Hove Bandstand;
Hove Beach Huts; Life is Sweet in Brighton

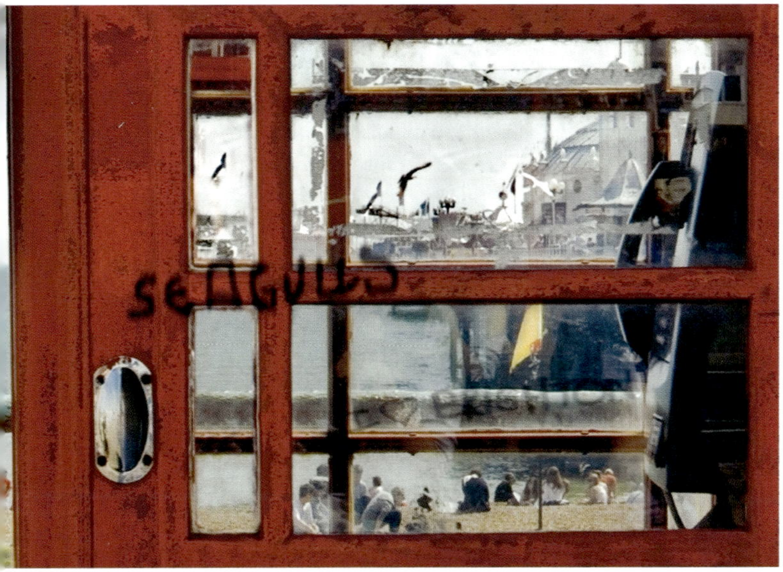

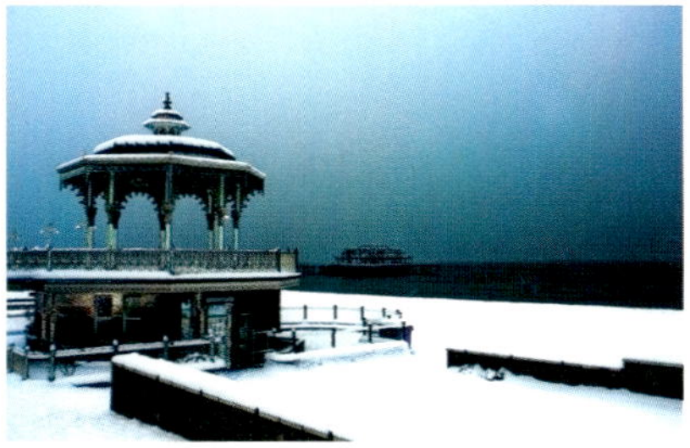

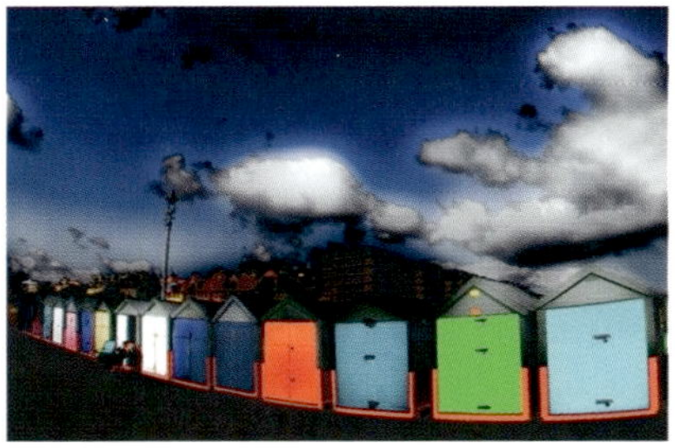

Nicole Carman is an award-winning, professional fine art photographer living and working in Hove. Through the combination of traditional photographic techniques and digital processes she seeks to capture the colourful spirit of Brighton.

Nicole's limited-edition prints and canvases are available to buy in the Frameworks Gallery in Brighton's North Laine and online via her website www.brightonandhovephotos.com.

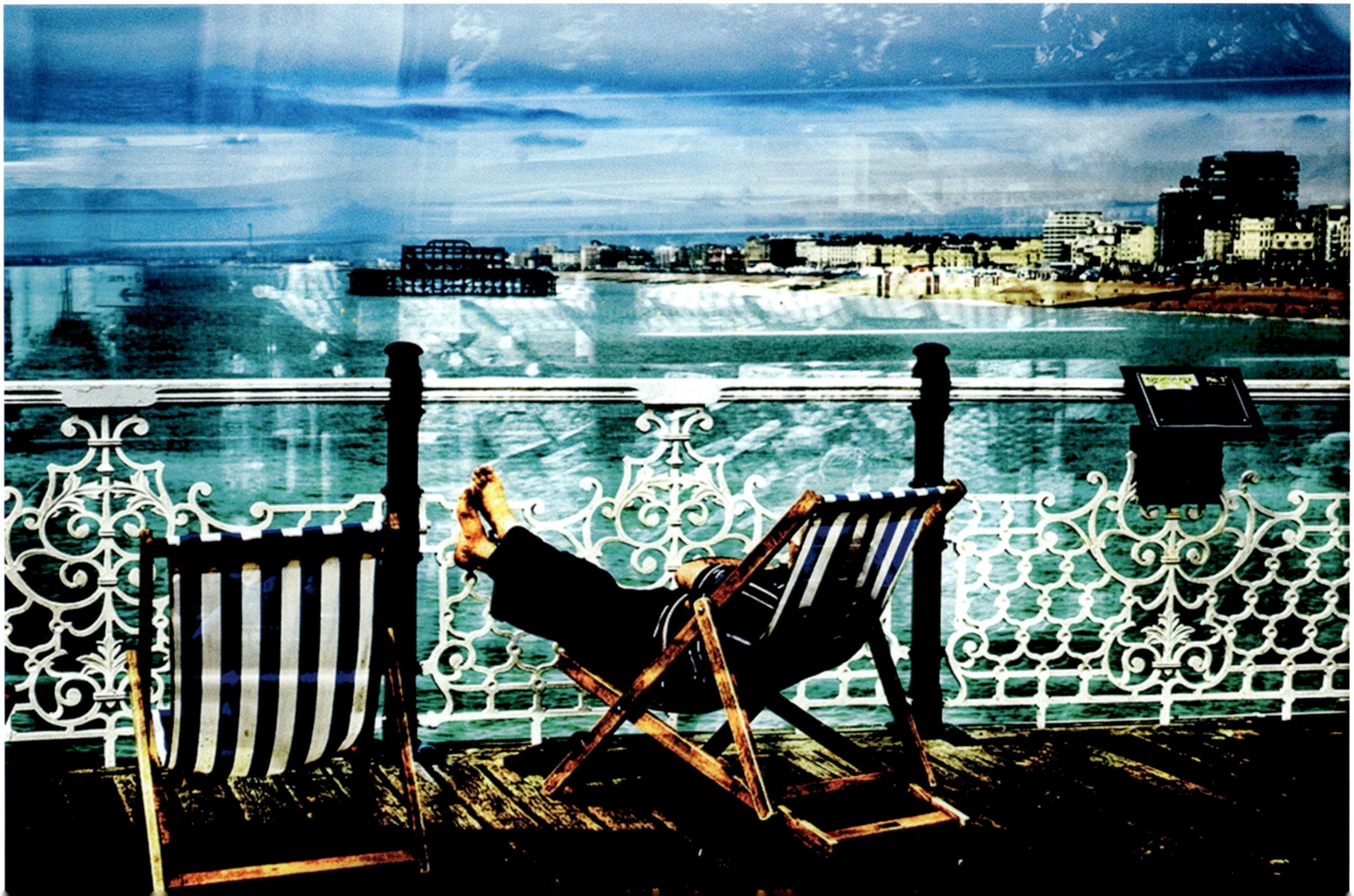

Lisa Ridgers

Artist

Top: Country Scene
Below: Serene Moments IV

Lisa Ridgers was born in Shoreham in 1968 and is an internationally established artist who has been living in the USA for the past 20 years. She has recently returned to the South Coast to bring her unique brand of artwork to Europe and looks to Brighton as the place to allow her creativity to run free.

Lisa began painting professionally in 2000 in Phoenix, Arizona, under the tutelage of two prominent contemporary artists, and has continued on as a primarily self-taught artist, developing her own unique methods and processes for her paintings. She finds that the rich colours and drastic scenery of the Sonoran desert influence her work still; yet now, finds a harmonious balance brought about by her new surroundings near the sea.

Says Lisa: "My passion for the diversity found in nature, combined with a personal quest for balance and serenity, inspires my work. My goal is to fuse these elements together with a contemporary twist so that the viewer is invited to take a journey that is not only a visual experience, but also an intimate, emotional contemplation."

Her work, predominantly acrylic accented with a range of mediums and techniques, has been described as 'a fusion of organic palette, natural elements and inner meditations'. The contradictory nature of her process creates a complementary and uniquely fresh look at subject matter ranging from bold, minimalist representations to vivid and earthy abstracted landscapes.

"I prefer to work spontaneously, drawing inspiration from many sources, including my love of the outdoors and travelling. Also, the process of the work itself; which, by its very nature, can often produce unexpected and delightful results."

Lisa's original works are collected internationally by private and corporate collectors and have also been seen on various US television programmes and advertisements including *The Big Bang Theory* and *Two and a Half Men*. Her work is published internationally by Third and Wall Art Group, based in Seattle, and she is excited to now be able to offer her work more extensively in Europe to the public and the trade. More information regarding representation can be found on her websites (see index page 151).

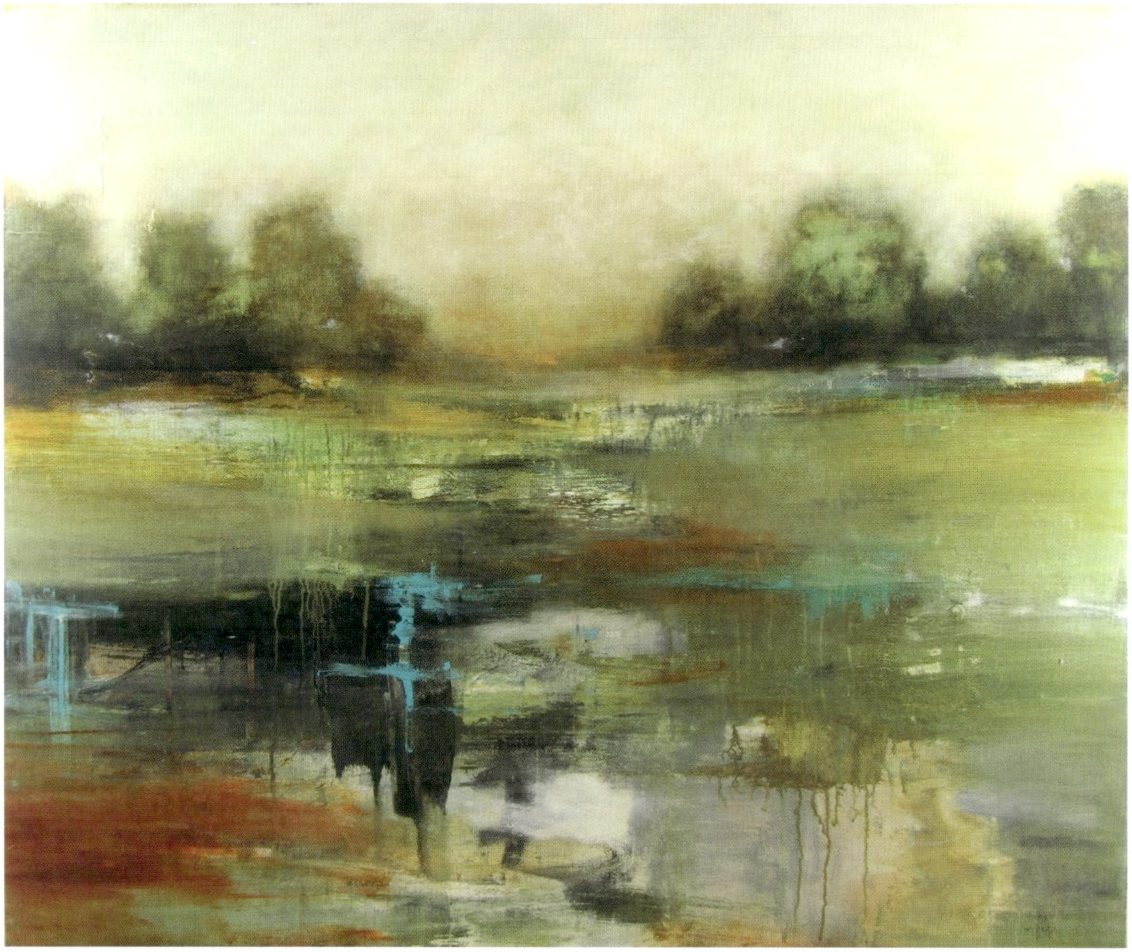

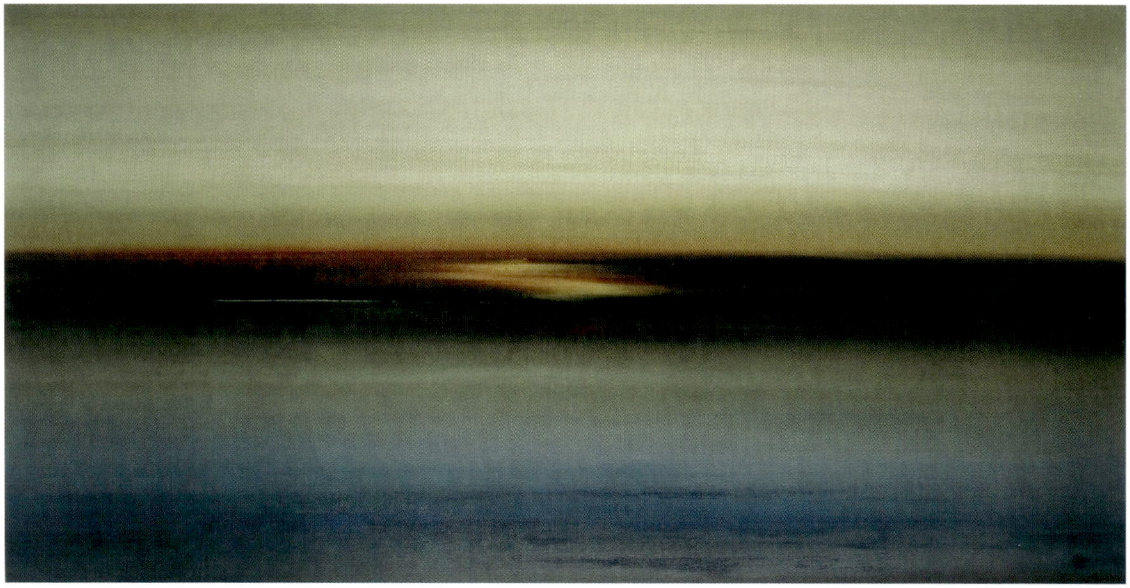

Clockwise from top left:
Drifting Away; Romantic Memoirs;
Elegant Moment

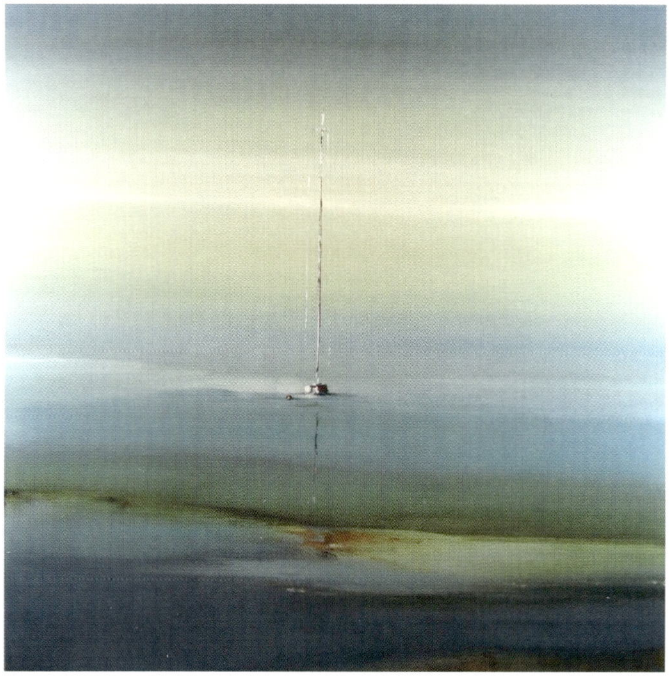

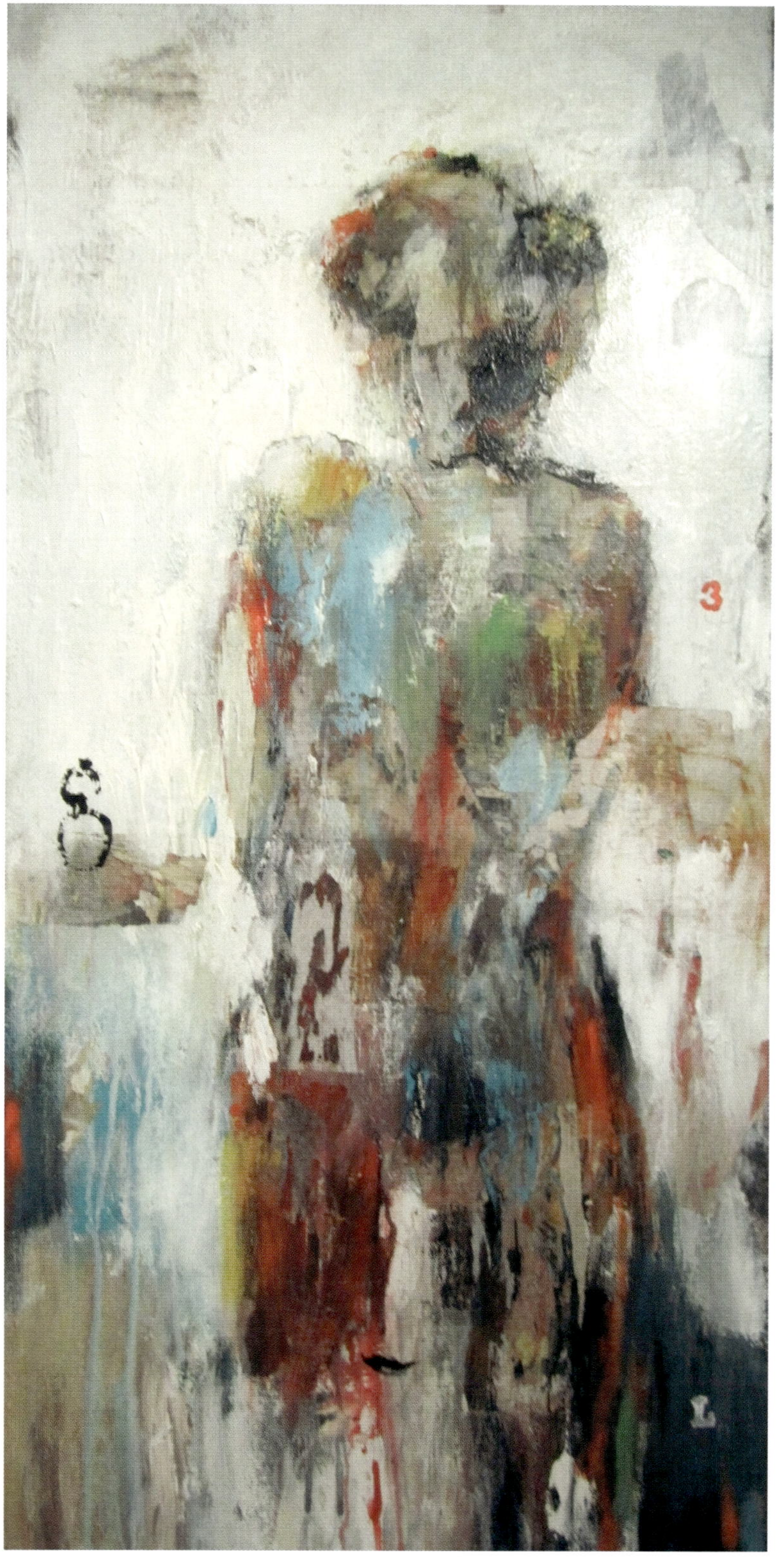

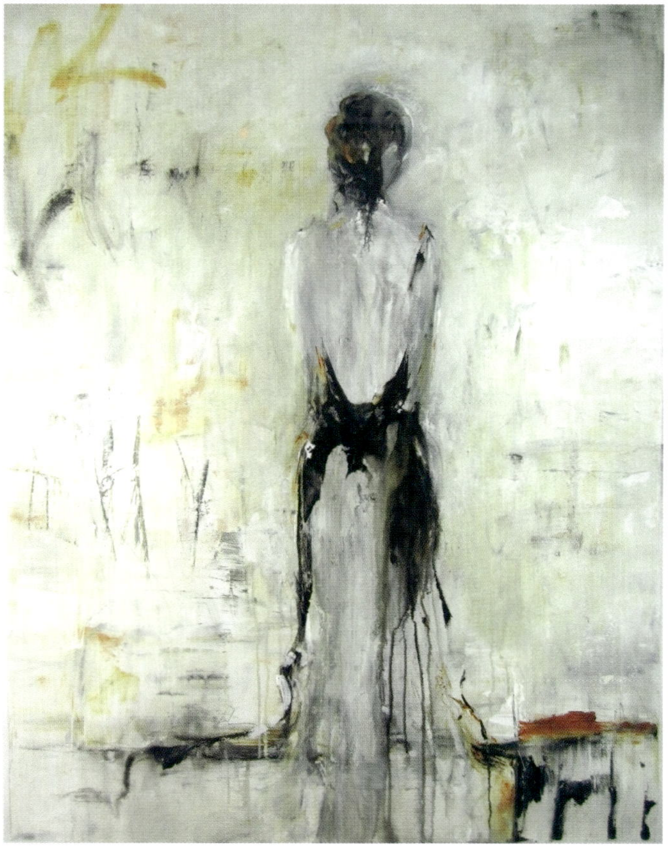

*"Swarms of maple leaves hung,
one hundred paper moths waiting a swell of autumn wind."*

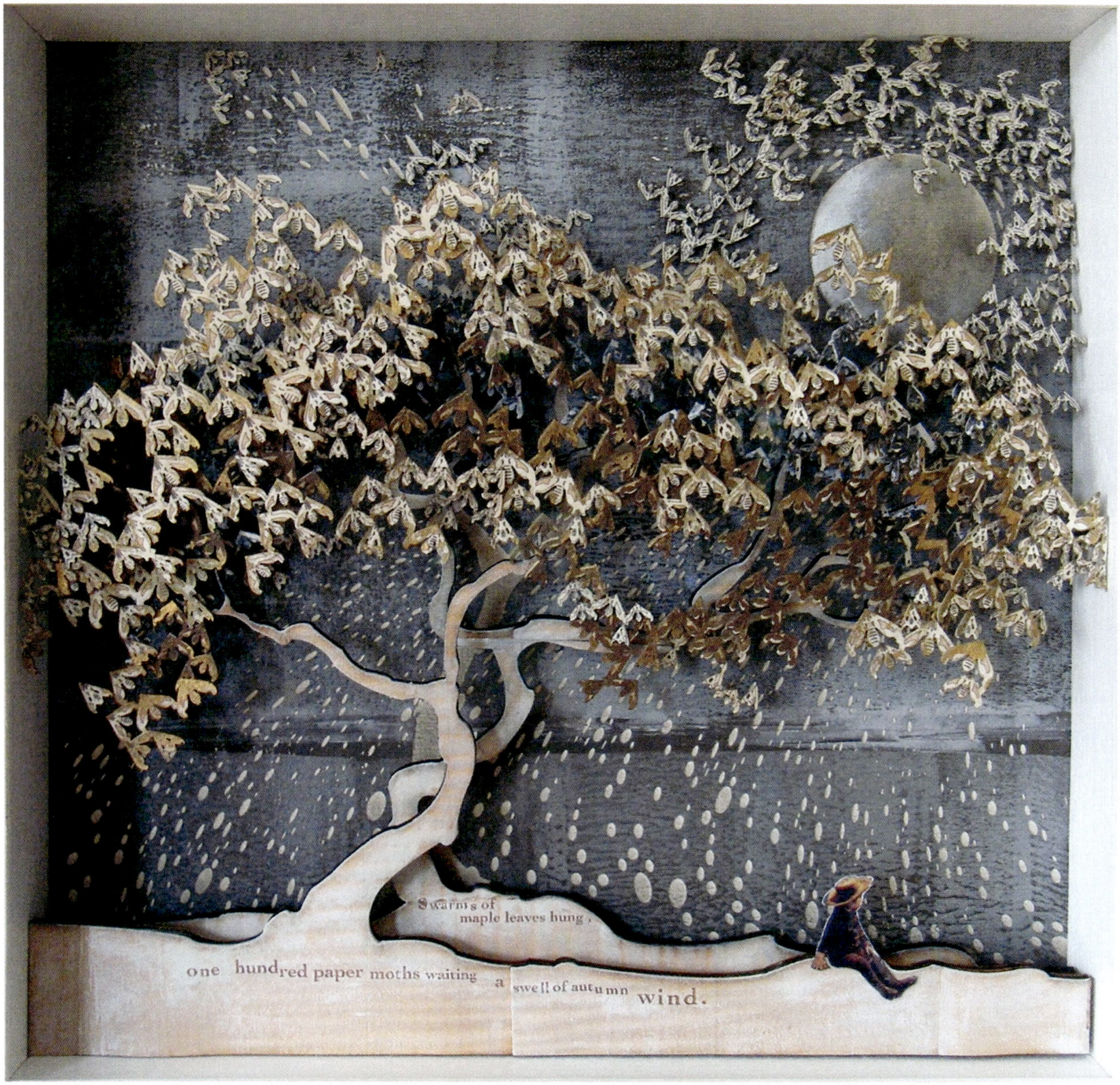

Mark Oliver

Artist

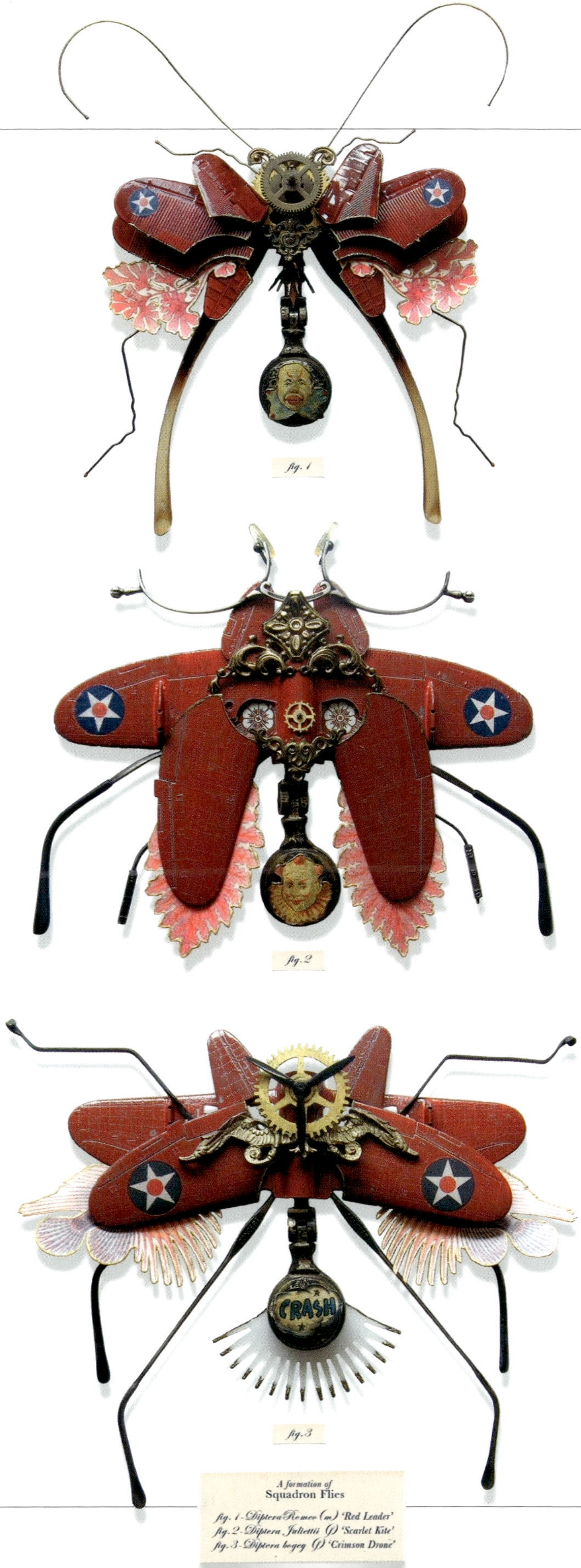

Artist and illustrator Mark Oliver has long been fascinated by the Victorian obsession with collecting and cataloguing insects. He finds himself drawn to the really large, exotic or scary specimens among the displays in museums of natural history, each one a tiny time capsule with a story.

The artist observes how the objects we throw away are left to rot and rust, getting stained, burnt and changing their appearance as they try to return to nature. He collects these and re-assembles them into an insect time capsule to recreate their story.

Opposite page

Linsay Oliver is inspired by narrative and theatre, and also the formal structure of set design. Her resulting three-dimensional artwork is a composition of creative writing, cutting, engraving, painting, staining and collage.

Louisa Crispin

Artist

Clockwise from top: Little Owl; Lichen on Gleditsia III; Shetland Wren

In Detail – Drawing From Nature

Living in the countryside has given Louisa a rich education in the local flora and fauna. Studying with the Open College of the Arts has opened her eyes further, and she is constantly exploring and finding a new understanding of art while enjoying the challenges ahead.

Louisa is a member of Chalk Gallery, Lewes (page 136), and Selected Artist for Pure Arts Group, winning Best Drawing Prize 2013 at the Autumn Show, then exhibited at the Saatchi Gallery, Strarta 2013.

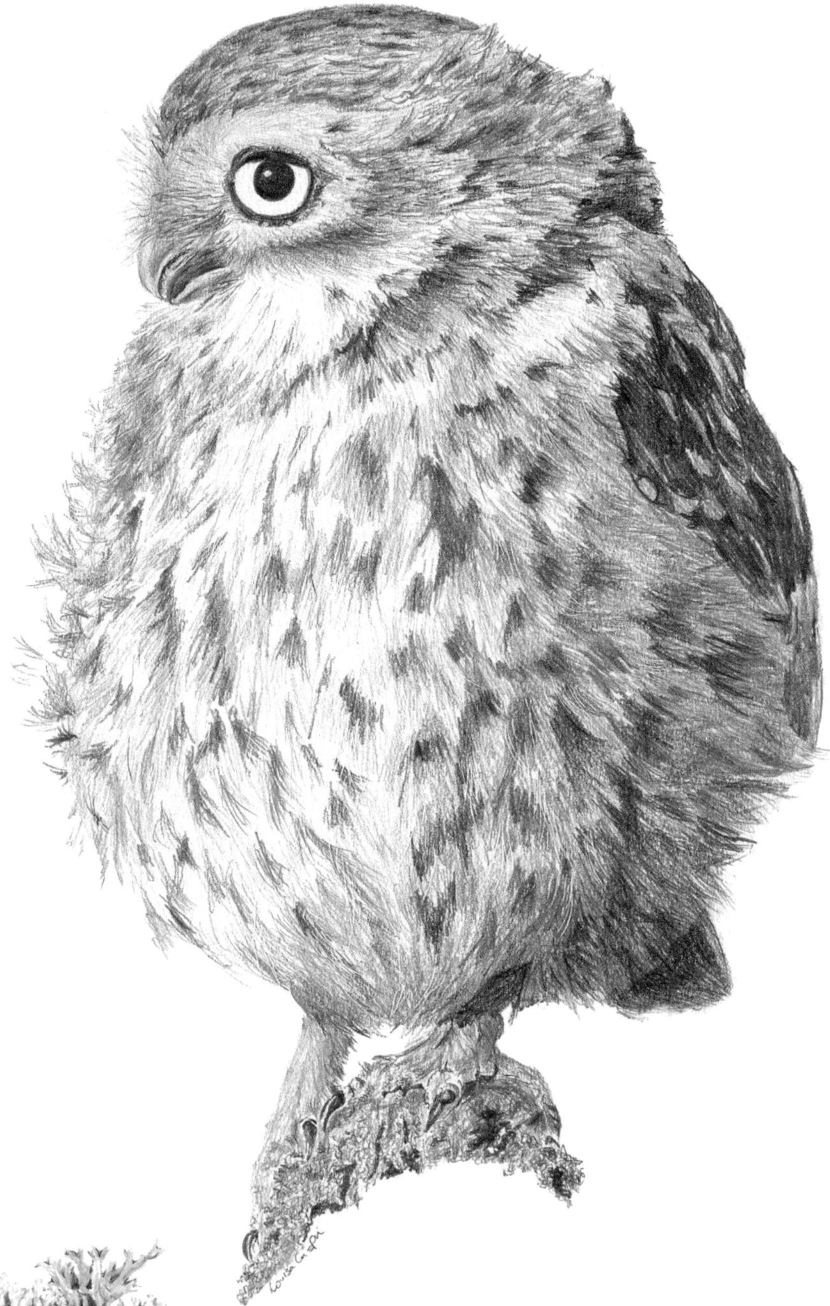

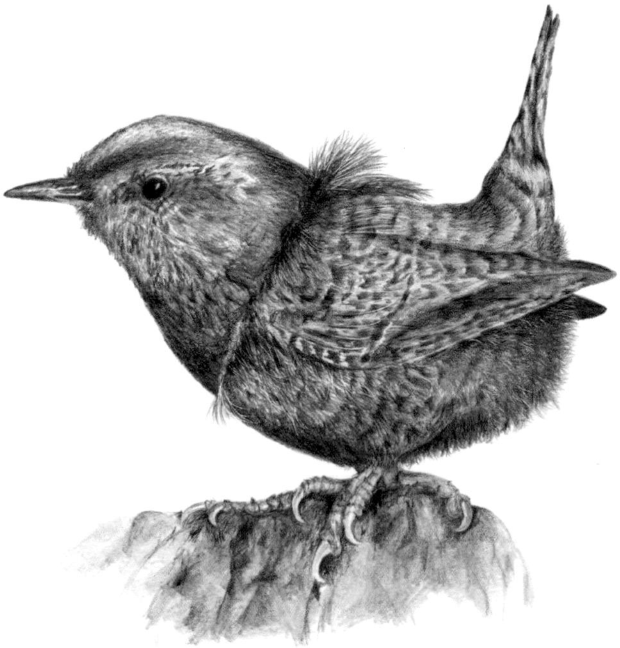

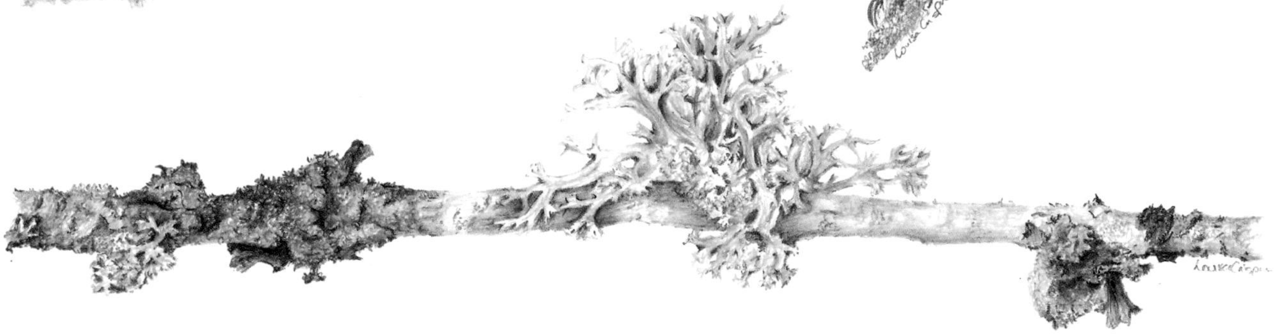

Clockwise from top left:
White; Ferns;
Tree; Gold

Angie Meaden-Bonnel

Artist

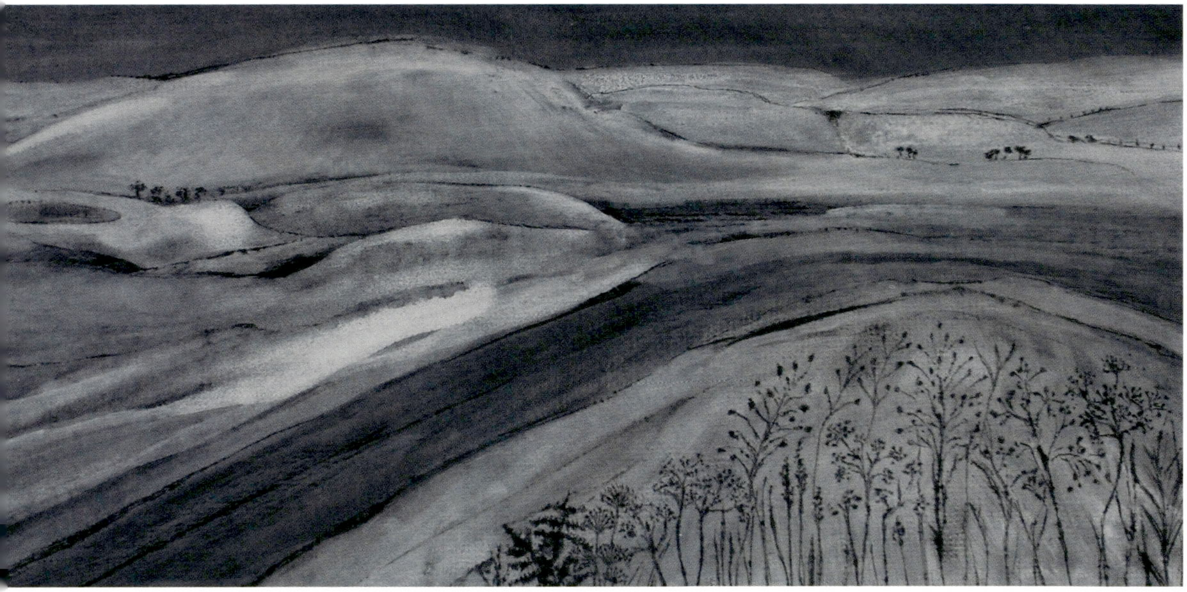

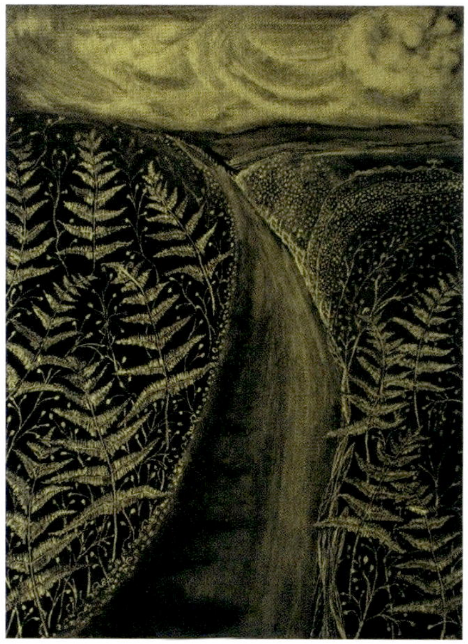

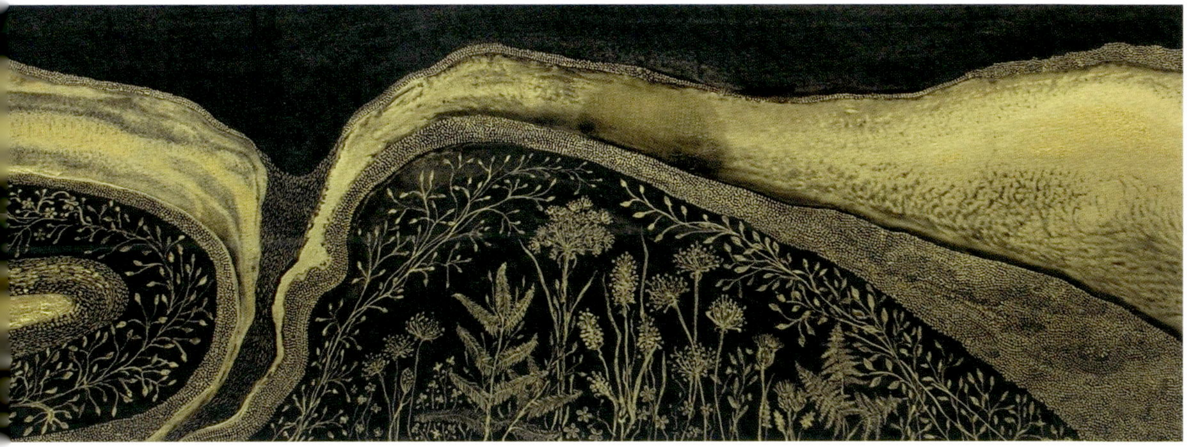

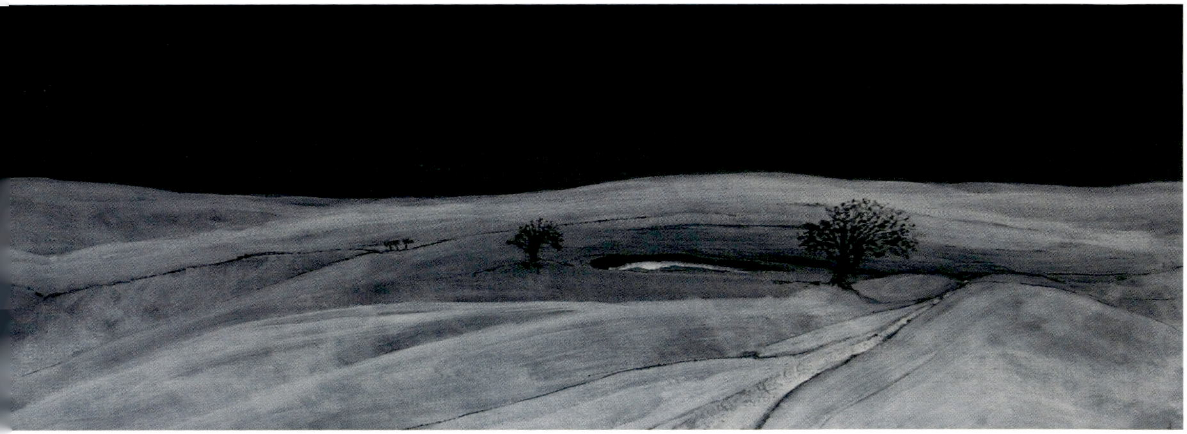

Angie Meaden-Bonnel draws with mesmerising intricacy, resulting in artworks that exert their own quiet power over the viewer, captivating and always offering new details to discover.

She studied fine art textiles at Goldsmiths, London, and describes her technique as repetitive mark making, very much like the stitching she used to do. Her tools are traditional pens with ink, which she waters down to create varying effects, and her chosen palette is a very deliberate black, white and gold. This enables Angie to focus on textures, meticulously working the layers away to uncover the intriguing visual narratives.

Angie has become known for her moody, evocative landscapes, which reference her penchant for long walks on the Downs. These are informed by memories rather than specific Brighton landscapes, with all manmade facts – such as pylons – removed – to enable the artist to focus on elements such as the weather and the emotions of the people she was with.

Dawn Stacey

Artist

This page (clockwise from top left): Silent River Reflections 8285, Path to White Lodge, Winter Woodland, Blue Island 7548A4; Opposite page: Morning Flight

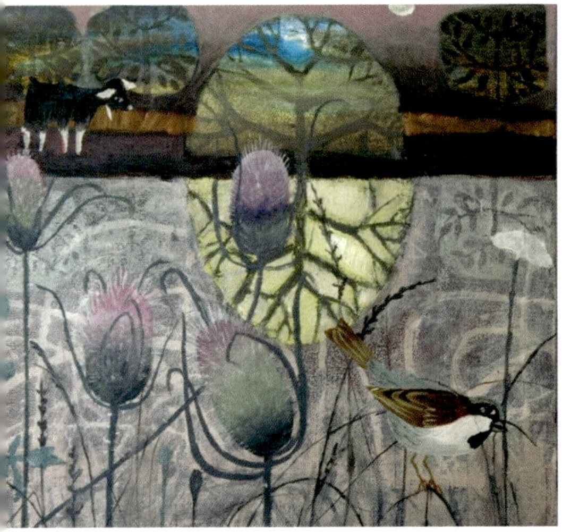

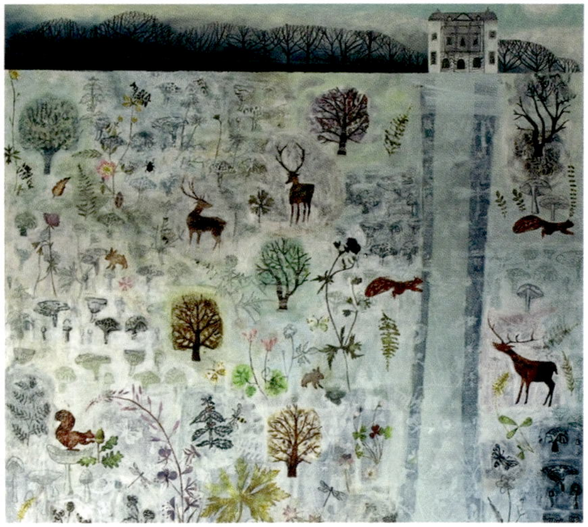

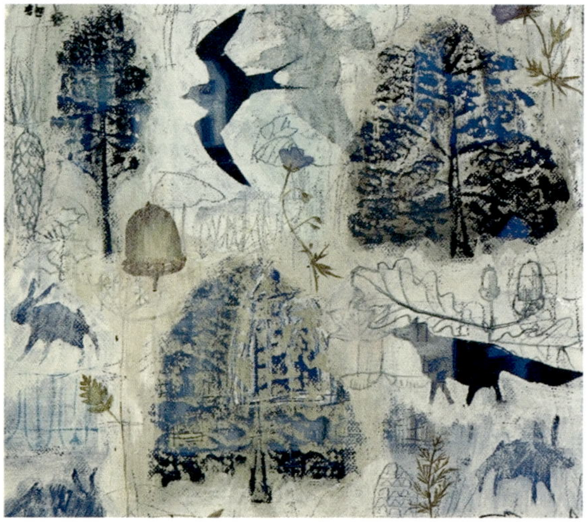

Dawn Stacey studied textiles at Derbyshire Art College and later gained an MA from Brighton University in Sequential Illustration.

Her paintings are usually based on nature in the landscape and evolve from walks with her dogs on a local nature reserve or surrounding landscape where she absorbs ideas, memories and nature in the landscape. Dawn's paintings are built from layers to reveal imagery – perhaps incorporating a frosted leaf, teasels or embedded wild flowers intended to capture the essence or mood of a place.

Dawn exhibits throughout the UK, and a collection of her paintings has been bought for a Brighton Hospital Trust and St. Wilfrid's Hospice. She has also been featured on the front cover of *Latest Art* and the *Artwave* brochure. Her paintings were recently reproduced for a collection with John Lewis.

You can view and purchase Dawn's work at South Heighton Pottery, Newhaven (weekends during May 2014), and the Artwave Festival in Lewes at 14 Toronto Terrace, BN7 2DU.

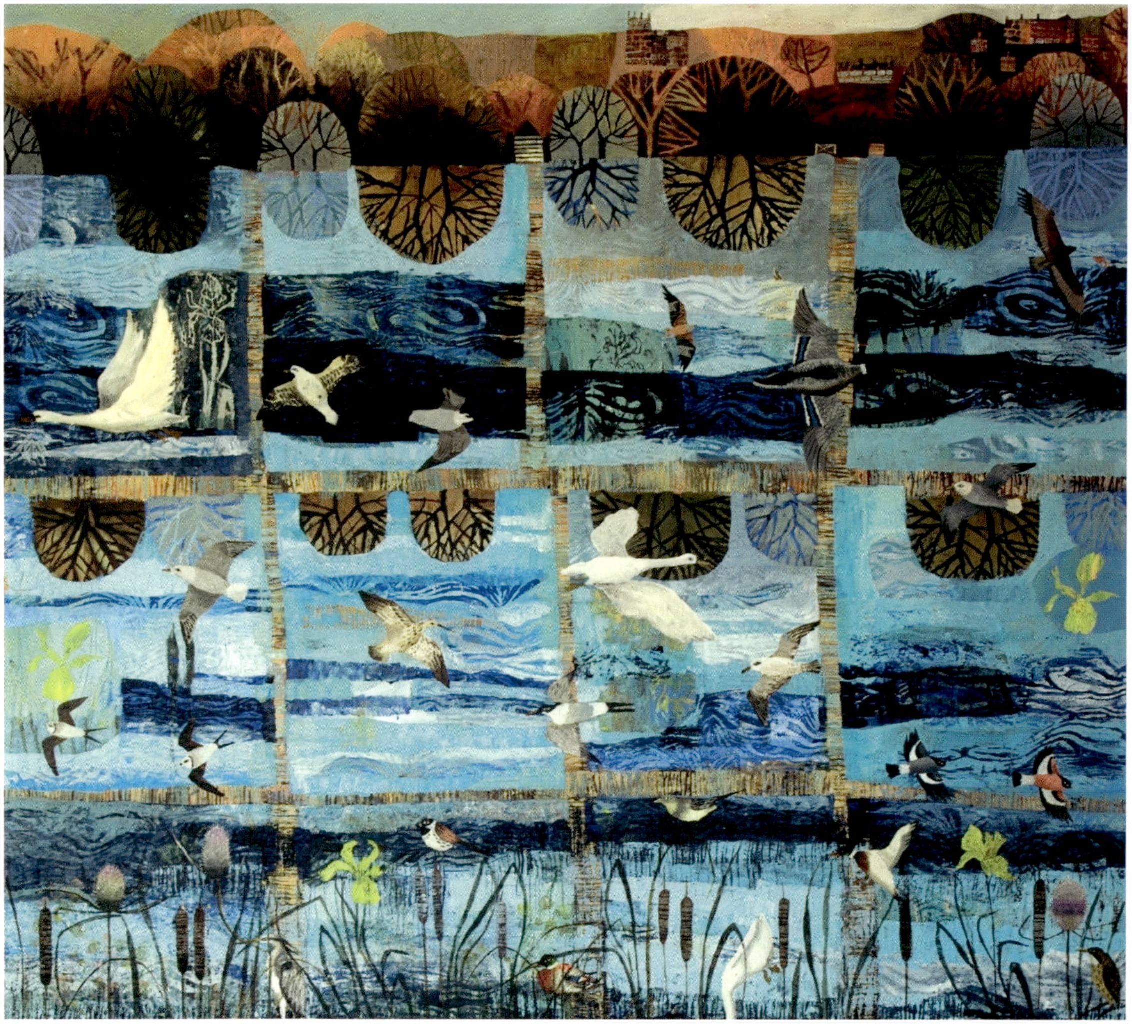

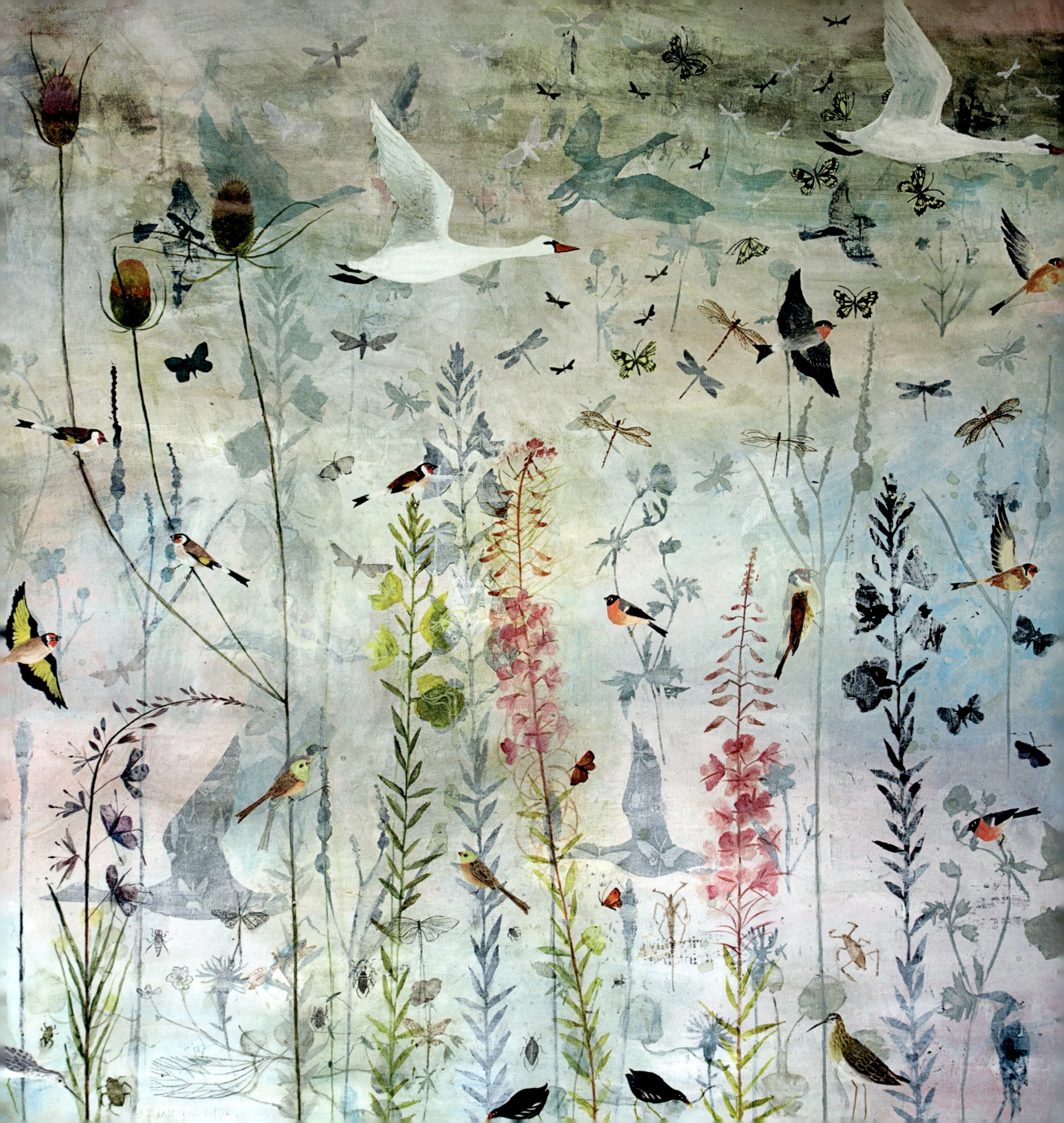

Steve Carroll

Artist

Clockwise from top left:
Shoreham Airport; Angel Pier; Pavilion Gardens;
Kolkata Princess; Autumn Houseboat

Steve Carroll is a freelance graphic designer and a teacher of Art and Art History to adults at local colleges. His favourite saying when talking about his artistic career is the word of advice John Lennon gave to his son, Sean: "Life is what happens to you when you're busy making other plans."

"When I look at the work of artists like Titian and Rembrandt, how can I compete with that? I have to create something completely different that will not be compared with the great art of the past."

Steve trained in graphic design and illustration at Berkshire College of Art and Design, graduating in 1982 in a pre-digital age when designers had to be able to draw. And one thing Steve is always doing is drawing. He is the co-ordinator of 'Sussex Sketchcrawlers', which organises drawing days around Sussex towns. (Find them on Facebook). His digital prints are a fusion of on-the-spot drawing and design. They have a fresh 'as it comes' look, together with a strong sense of colour and design.

Most of Steve's images are drawn with Indian ink on old-fashioned Bristol Board, then scanned into the Mac and coloured in Photoshop. They have the appearance of screen prints, an application he has explored and would like to develop. However, he likes the fact that running out his work as digital prints makes it affordable to everyone.

Steve moved with his family to Sussex in 1998 to work at a design and print company. He was made redundant in 2001, but was adamant about staying in the area because of its beauty. He did absolutely anything to support his family, including writing a series of graphic novels called 'Riddler's Fayre', set at the time of the Crusades as a comment on George W. Bush's 'War on Terror'.

His exposure to the graphic novel industry was one of the greatest revelations of Steve's life. He realised that it was limitless in subject matter and so varied in style. He thinks of his images as 'Frames from comics that haven't been written'.

On his website you will find Steve's collection of Sussex images, alongside images of Calcutta! Steve was in India in February 2013 teaching art to children in slum schools, where he saw beautiful little girls being groomed for prostitution because it was the only thing they could do to earn money. Steve wants to go back and teach these children – giving them a trade will rescue them from such a terrible life. All profits from sales of his India pictures will go to the work of educating such children.

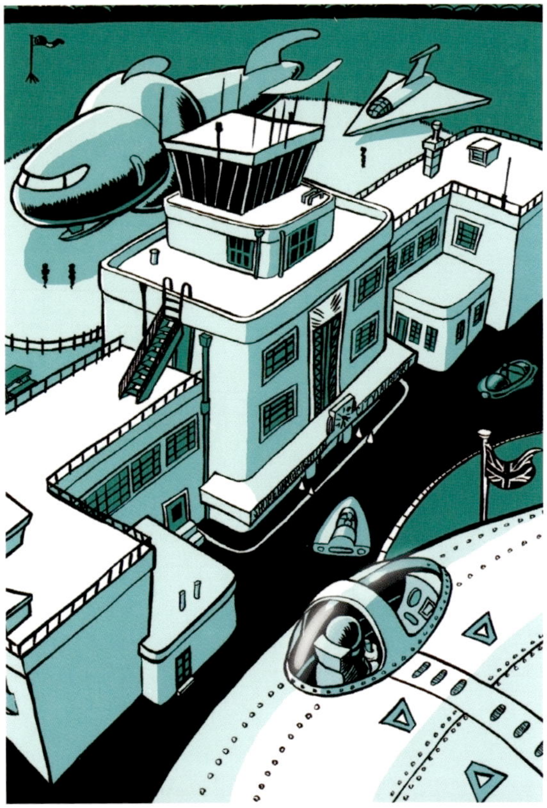

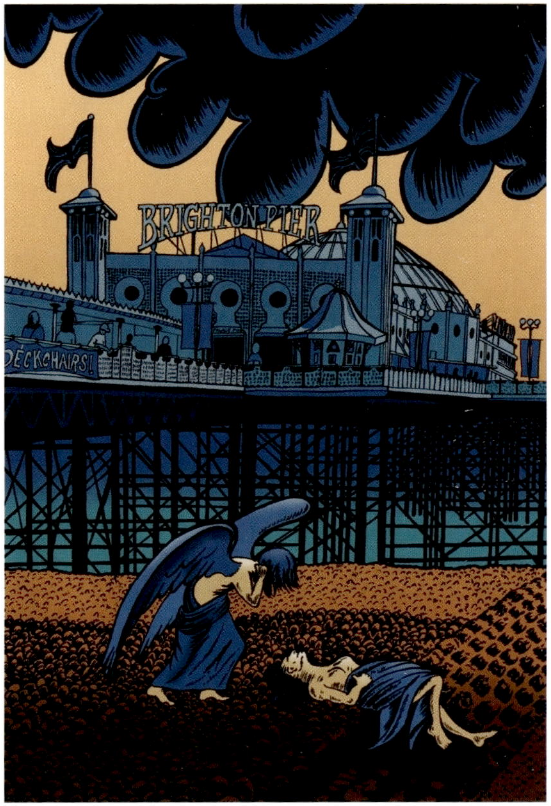

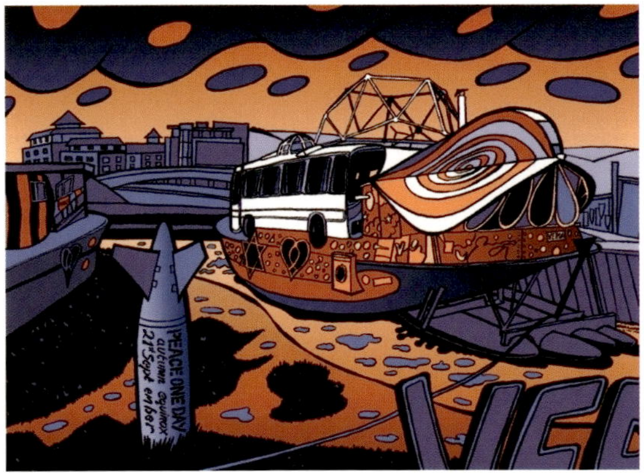

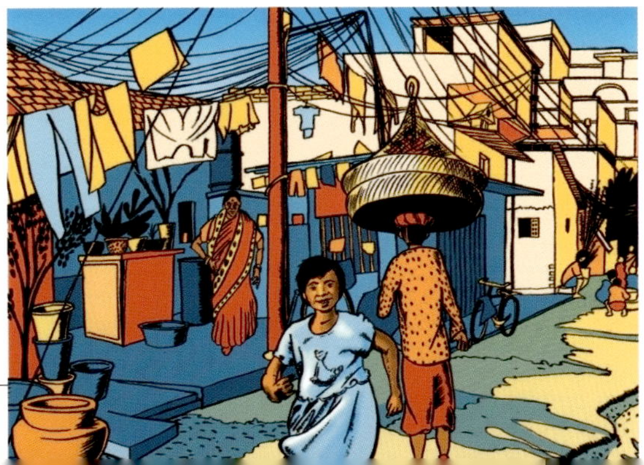

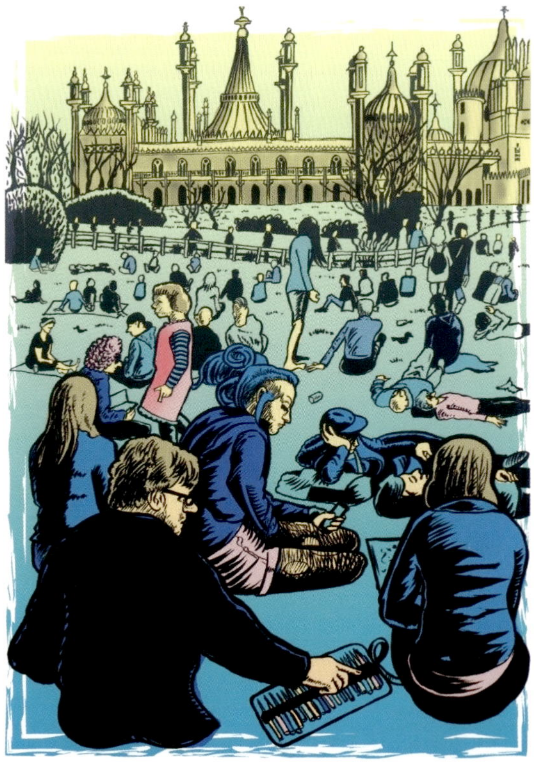

Clockwise from top left:
Lampshade Red; Pink Jug;
Dive 35; Landscape without Trees

Min Cooper

Artist & Printmaker

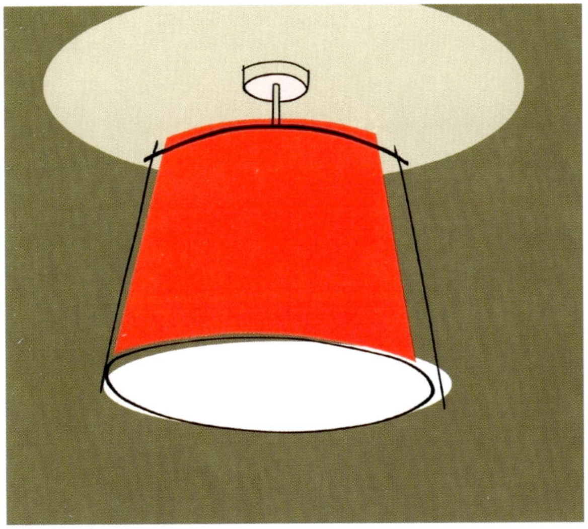

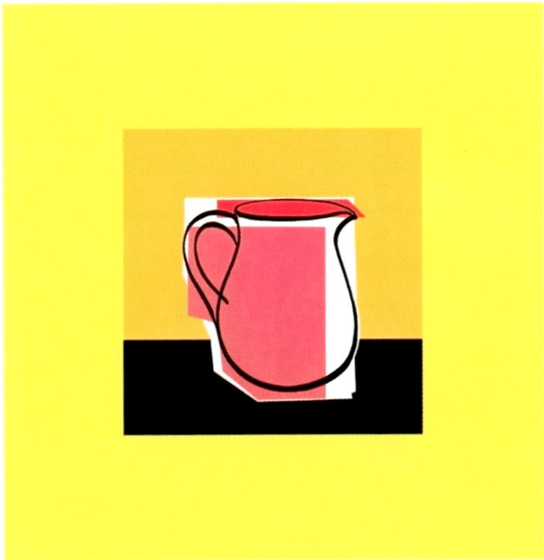

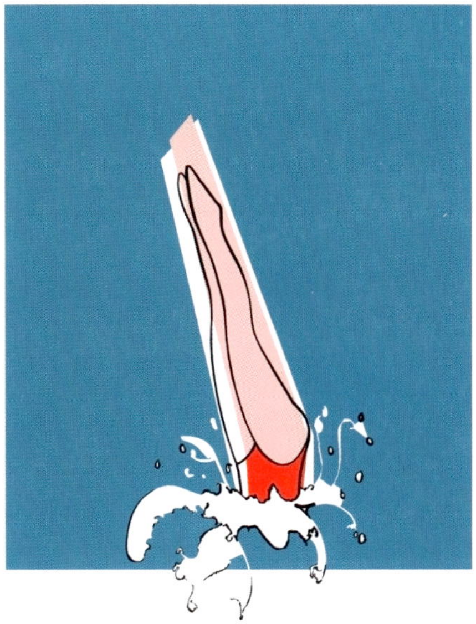

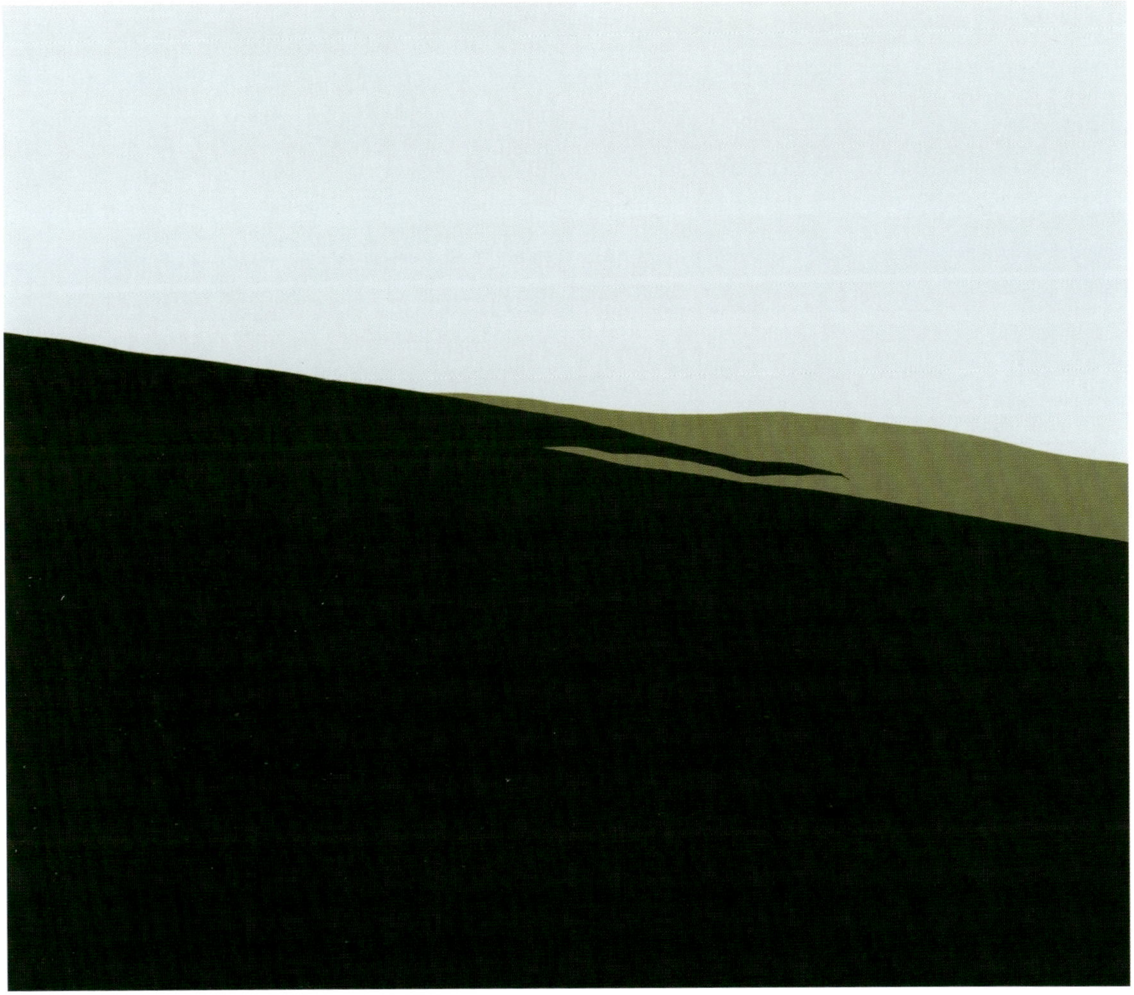

Min Cooper was best known in the 90s for her award-winning illustration and cartoon work for newpapers and magazines. A move from London to Sussex prompted a change in direction and Min now produces these beautiful, vibrant prints, utilising and celebrating the beauty in the everyday.

The online gallery is the best place to view and buy Min's work (see index page 151).

"These are the things that surround me. We are surrounded by stuff we tend to overlook, beautiful things in beautiful colours. I want to celebrate them."

Alison McGechie

Sculptor

Alison takes her inspiration from the human form and the human condition. Life drawing is at the root of her artistic practice and her sculptural work stems from it.

Over years of intense observation her interest has moved from a concern with form to focus on layers; what lies beneath the surface, and issues surrounding the changes that are wrought on human flesh over time.

"My aim is not to produce life-like representations of the body but to use the materials to hint at elements of the human condition that resonate with the viewer in a more poetic/metaphorical way."

She works in a variety of media; ceramics, wood, metal and stone, as well as continuing to explore techniques and the possibilities of different materials in her 'Life' studies.

Alison's 'Brain Piece' (right) is from a recent body of work about mutability and the cyclical nature of life – decay and regeneration. It was informed by her life-long fascination with the human body and developed through a dialogue with the materials.

For these pieces Alison used rotted tree stumps as the basis of her sculpture, melding the carved wood with forged, cast and etched metal.

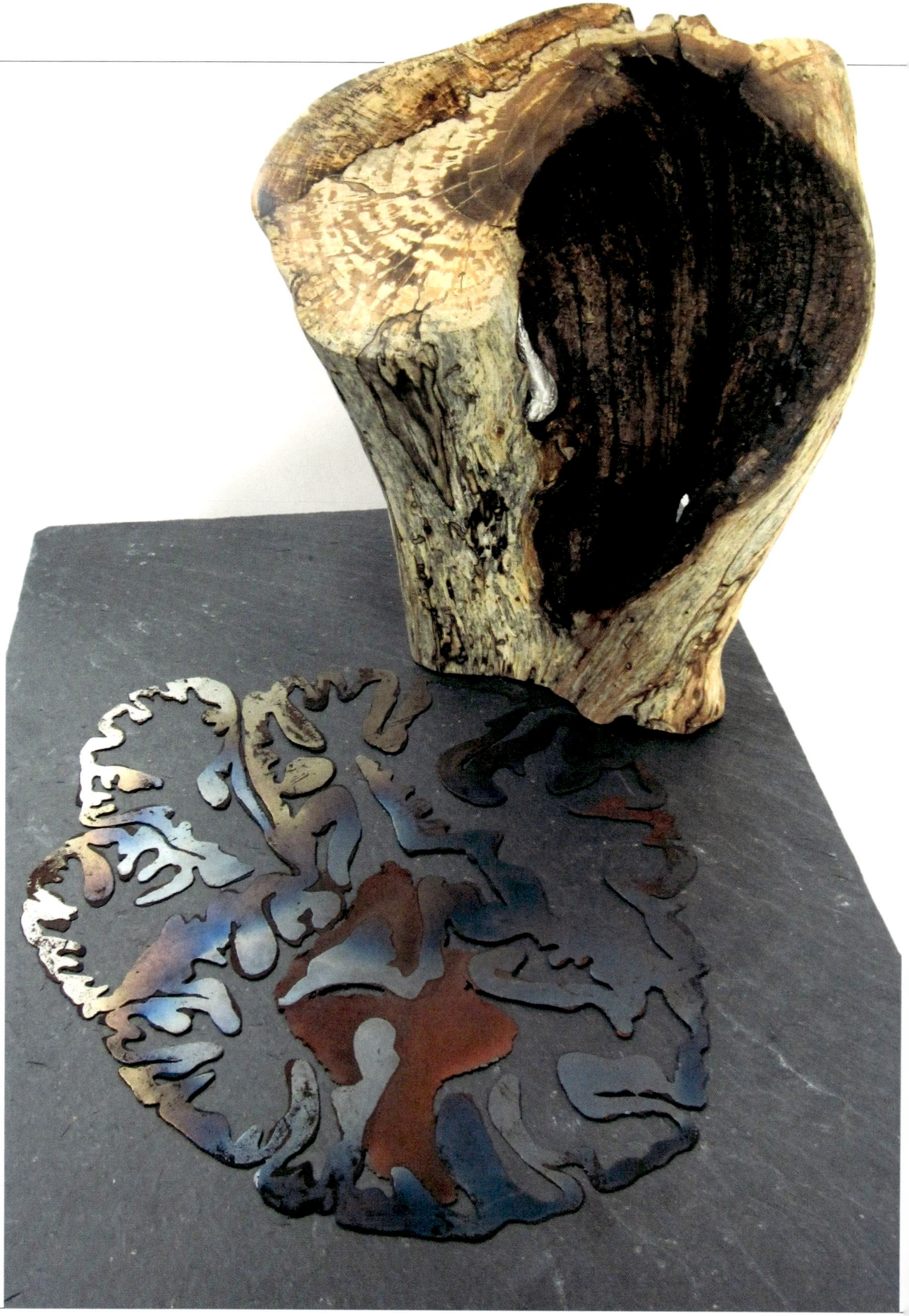

This page: (clockwise from top) Convoluted Form; Only Dreaming; Mother & Child
Opposite page: Brain Piece

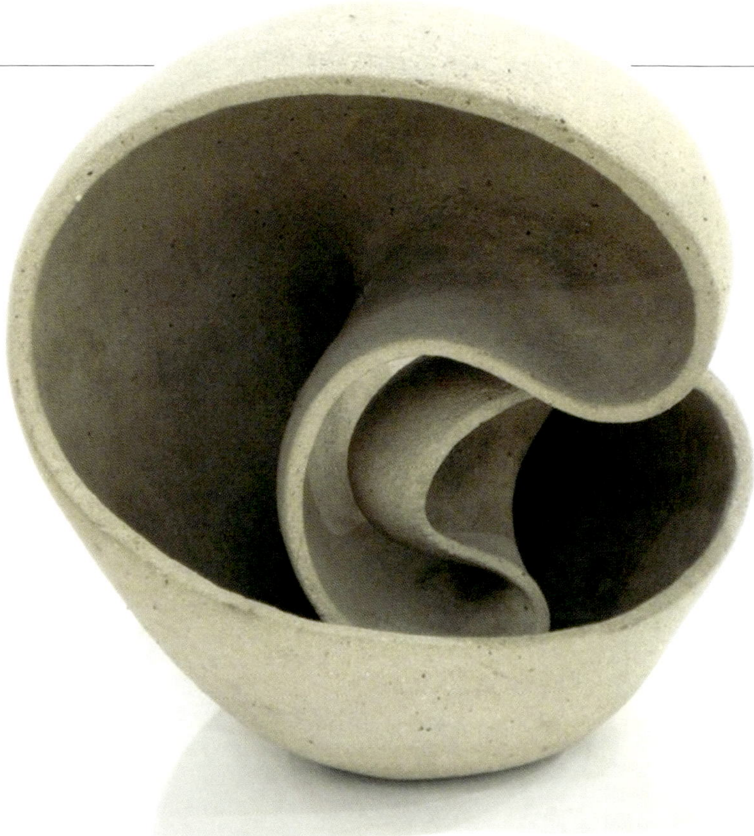

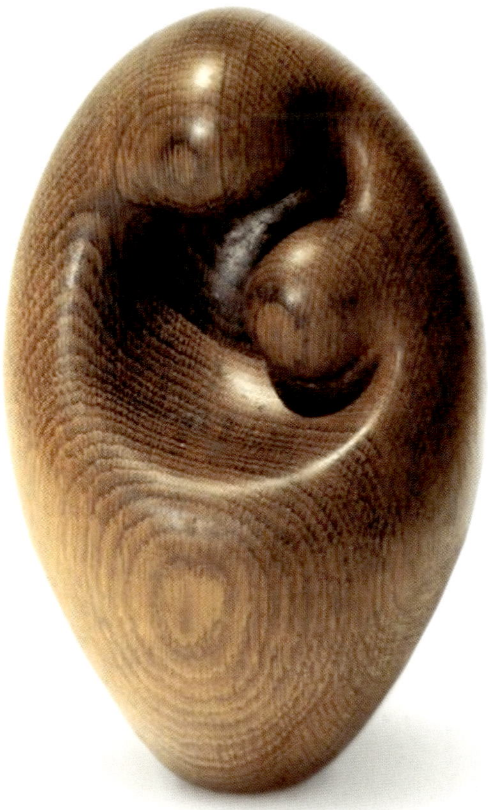

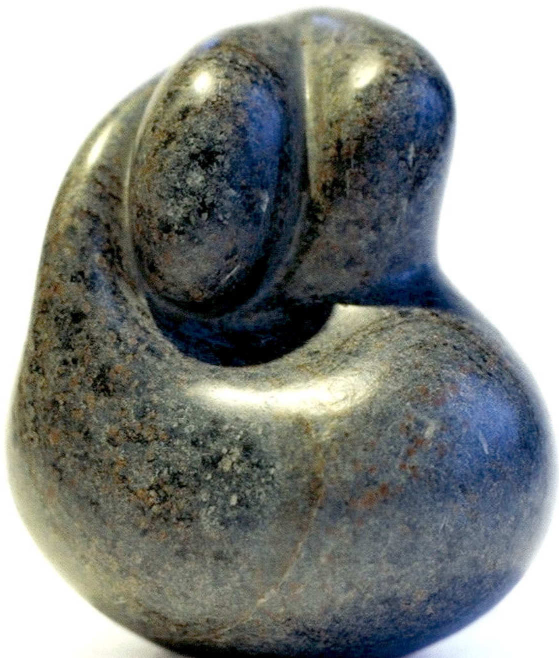

Sue Collins

Printmaker & Painter

Clockwise from top left:
A Dog's Life, The Red Arrows,
The South Downs and Three Hens

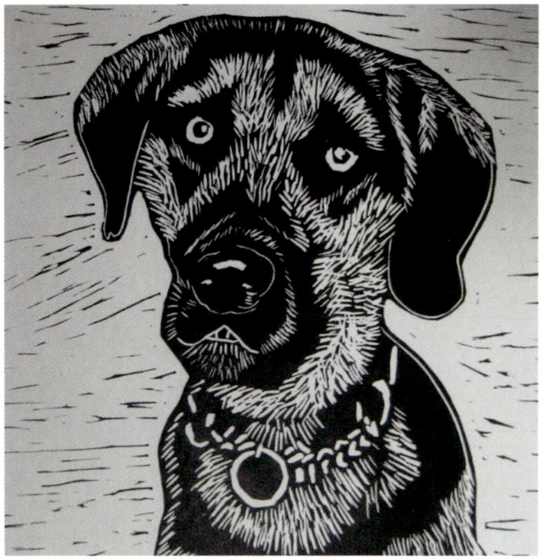

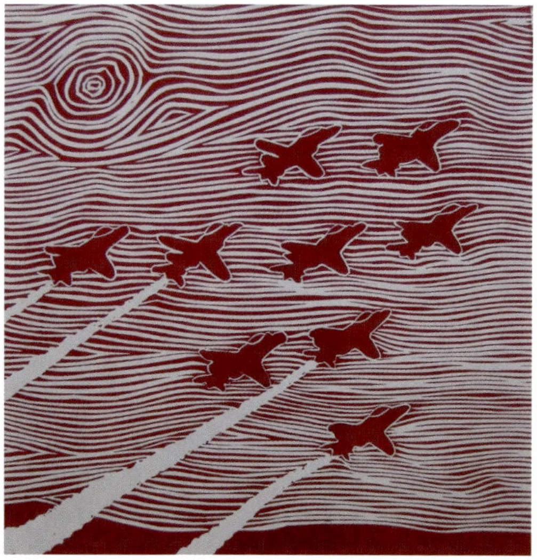

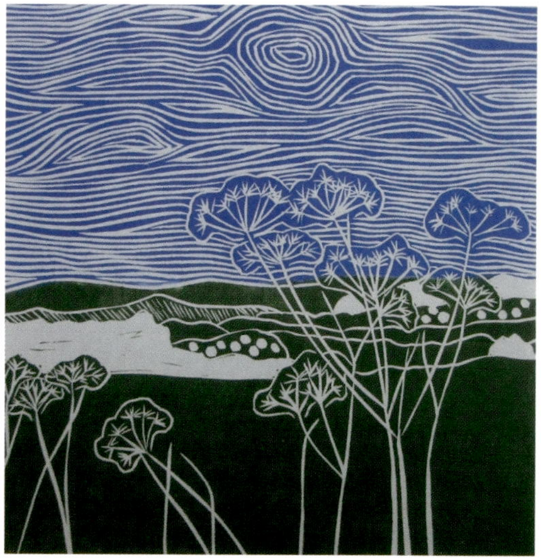

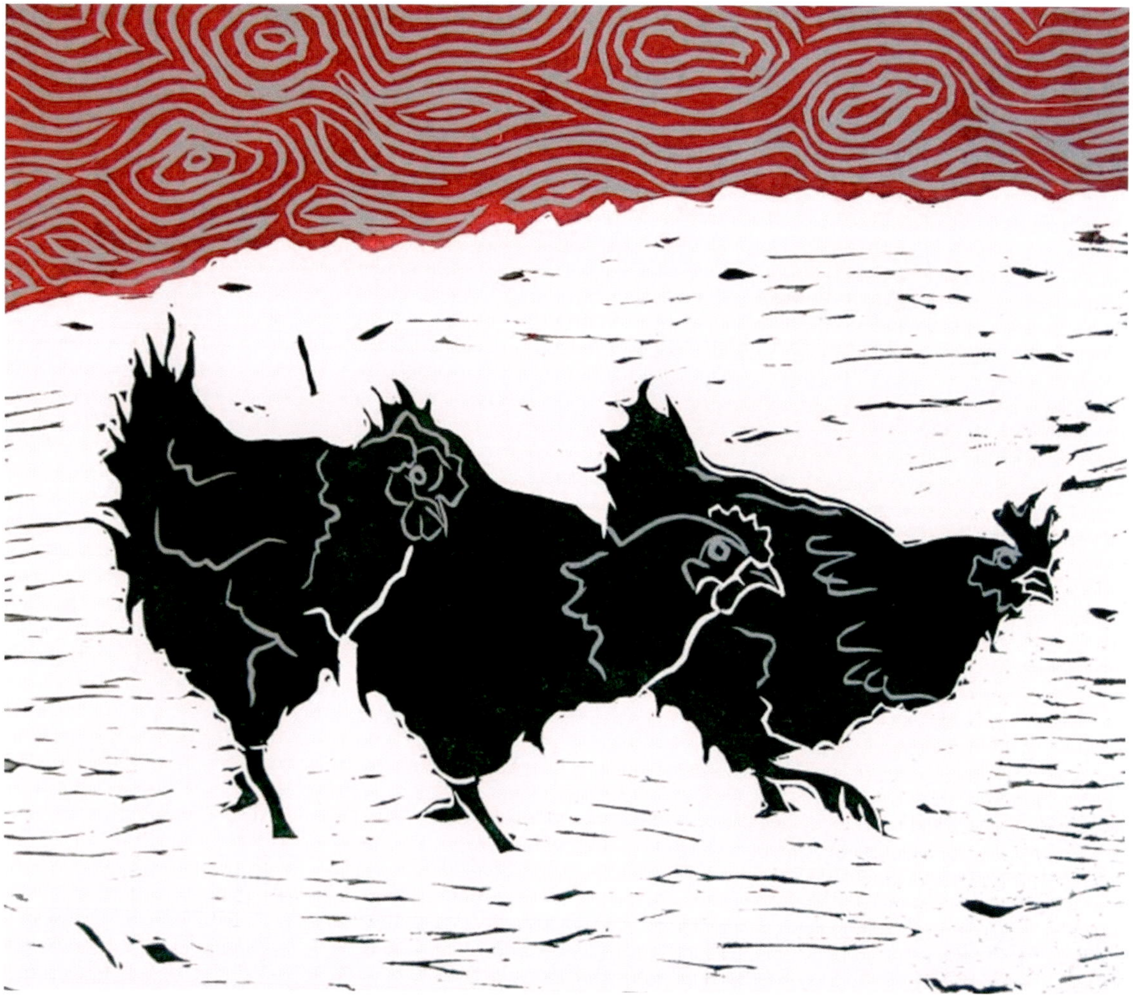

Sue is a printmaker and painter working from her studio in Hassocks. Currently her work is predominately printmaking with lino. Using a combination of photography and sketching, as well as drawing on her own personal experiences and memories, Sue creates images that are primarily of Sussex and the surrounding area.

Sue loves using colour and producing work that creates, or evokes, happy memories. She has a Fine Art Degree and has been selling her work through galleries since 2011.

In the past two years Sue has enjoyed exhibiting at the Artists Open Houses in Brighton and Horsham. She also plans to be part of the South East Open Studios in 2014.

Firb

Artist & Fixer

Clockwise from top left: I Stalk Women on the Internet (2.1); W.A.S.; I Stalk Women on the Internet; All I Ask is a Tall Ship; My Life's a Fucking Car Crash

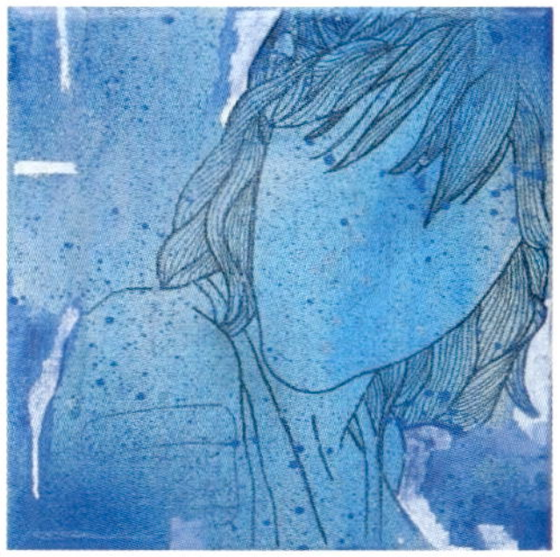

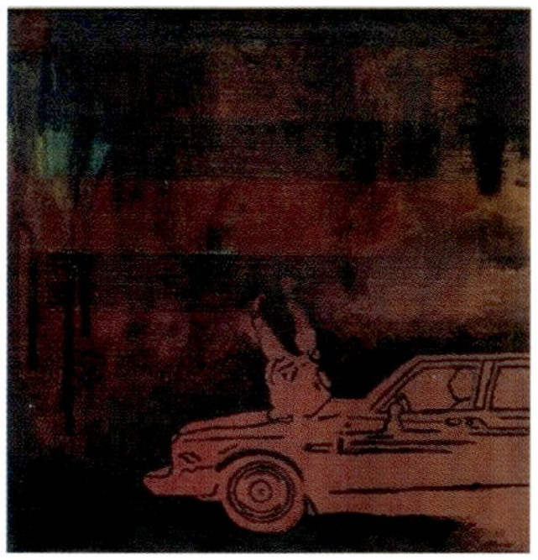

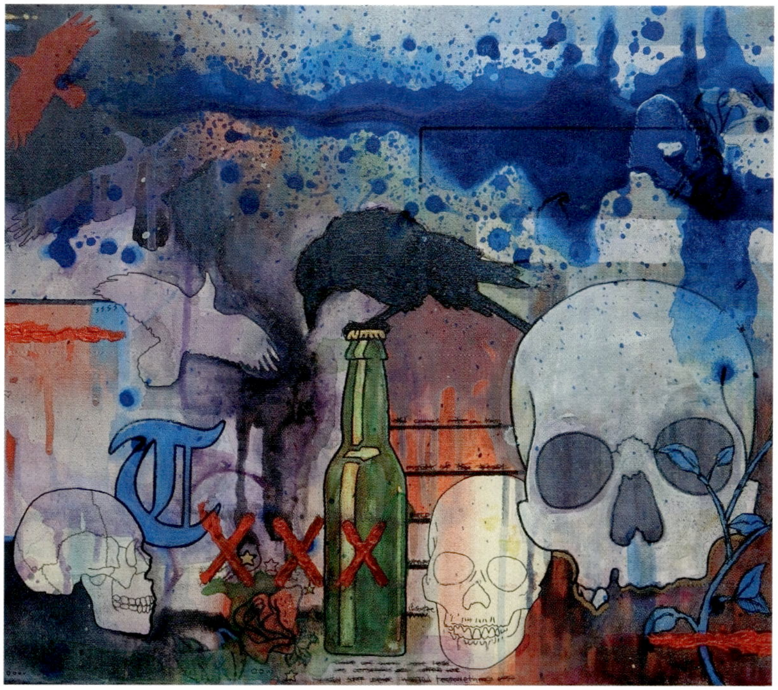

Firb describes his work as contemporary paintings based on old-fashioned subject matter. Some are illustrative. Some are more painterly. He can work in a heavy-handed, textured way, or much lighter using multiple washes. Whatever his technique, the result is always to build up atmosphere and portray a mood.

Although Firb describes his approach as "a fairly standard formula" it's perhaps not quite as simplistic as he'd like you to believe. This is an artist who puts a lot of work into researching the imagery and subject matter that inspire him. And the results can be as varied as a sensitive portrait to a bold montage.

Firb is also the force behind contemporary creative arts company Wolf & Pigeon. Follow him on facebook.com/wolfandpigeon and discover all the exciting stuff that's brewing.

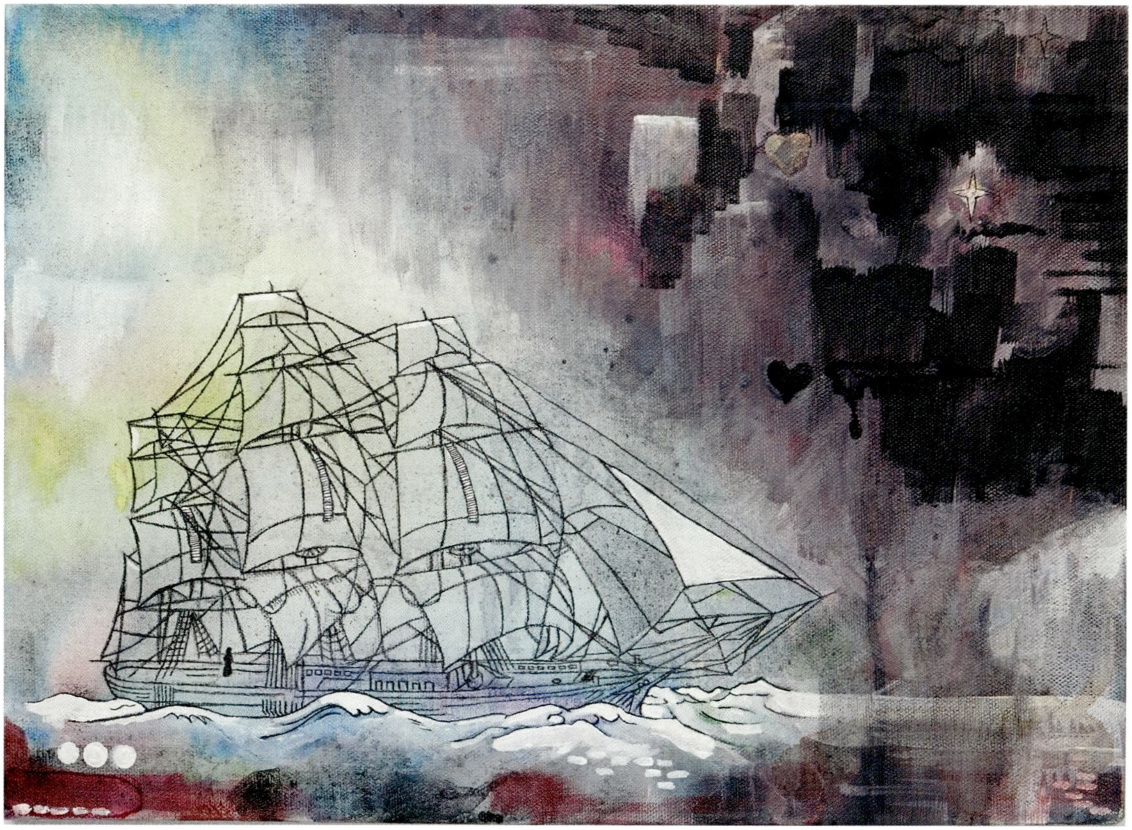

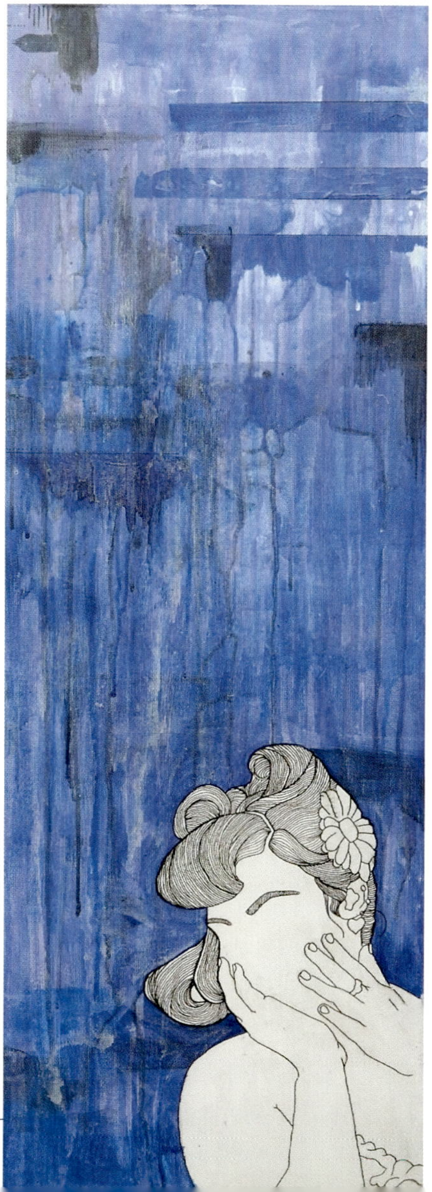

Viv Martin

Artist

Clockwise from top left:
Becoming; Fragmentation;
Like a Bat out of Hell; Beyond Time

Viv Martin's art reflects meanings she constructs from her experience. She is interested in traces left through time, in natural cycles of the seasons and in evidence of earlier lives. The image 'Fragmentation' is part of a series of work about the transient beauty of blossom and its fragility. The transition, from bud to full bloom and fall, reminds us of our own mortality but also of our place in a very long series of similar cycles. 'Fragmentation' is a collage on paper, using woodcut, linocut, stencilled and screenprinted images. Many of these images are fragments from associated work and carry additional meaning in their connections, as in 'Making Connections' and 'Fall', which are also from this series but use canvas and paper prints collaged onto printed board.

Viv is also drawn to marks and objects left by people who lived in much earlier times. When she was at college in the 1960s (at Corsham, Bath Academy of Art), Viv travelled to Italy to explore Renaissance art and won a scholarship to Paris. She then discovered the ancient art in Turkey and became interested in Greek and Roman art. Later, at Goldsmiths, Viv won a scholarship to Egypt, where she was amazed by how clearly the marks and ideas of ancient artists continue to communicate, particularly in places that were less formal.

More recently the artist has found surprisingly similar connections with art in prehistoric caves, where the marks and fingerprints remain after 30,000 years. 'Becoming' (acrylic on canvas) is drawn from a series of monotypes that reflected on prehistoric Venus figures. Viv works with a mixture of drawing, printmaking and painting, often incorporating these in multi-media and collaged work that frequently includes drawings made to record responses and impressions.

Viv layers her work with the visual evidence she collects, but also often incorporates references to the myths and legends that are associated with particular places and the attraction that has drawn visitors over the ages. Many of the drawings she made in the dark in the prehistoric caves of the Dordogne were embedded in collage in another series of monotypes including 'Beyond Time', 'Like a Bat Out of Hell' and 'Walking the Mysteries'. 'Hidden Cave' is a woodcut that links themes of people with blossom and caves.

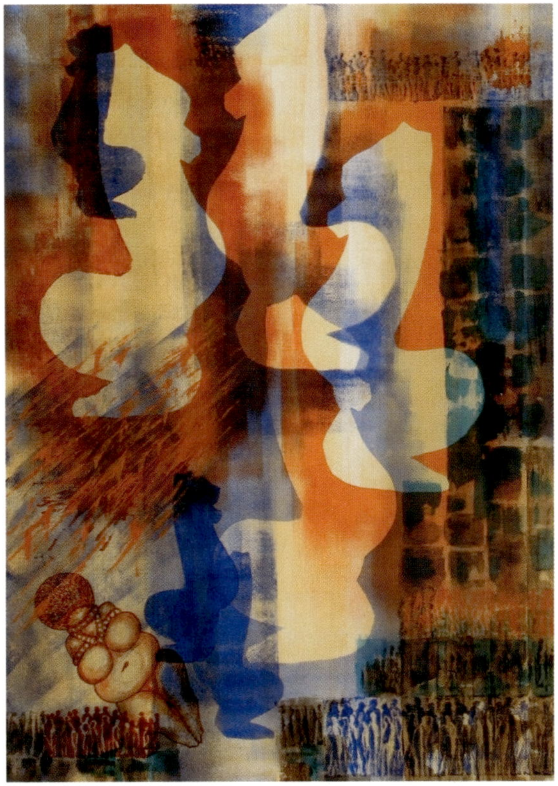

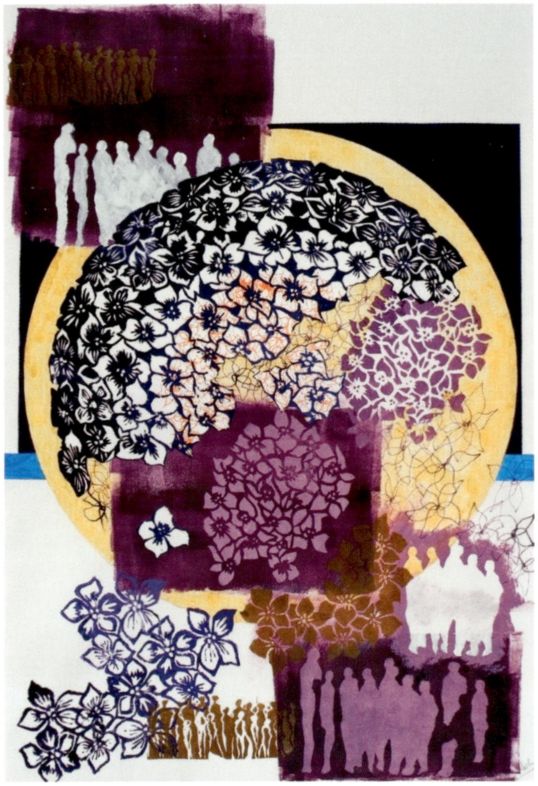

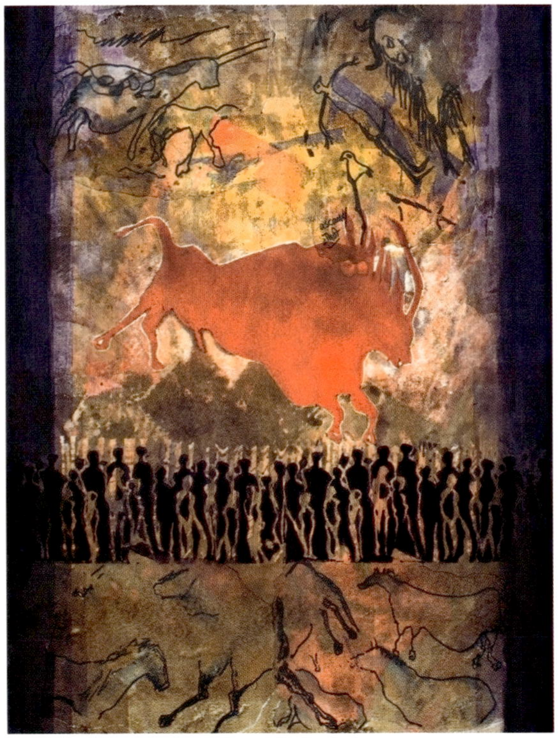

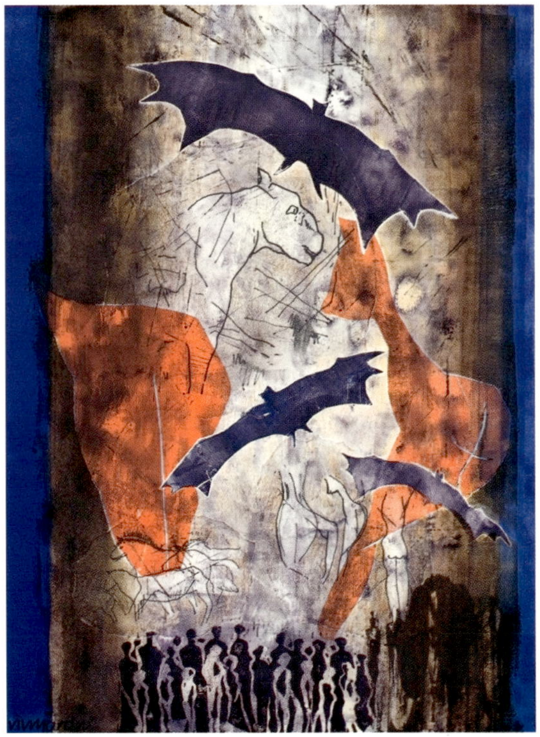

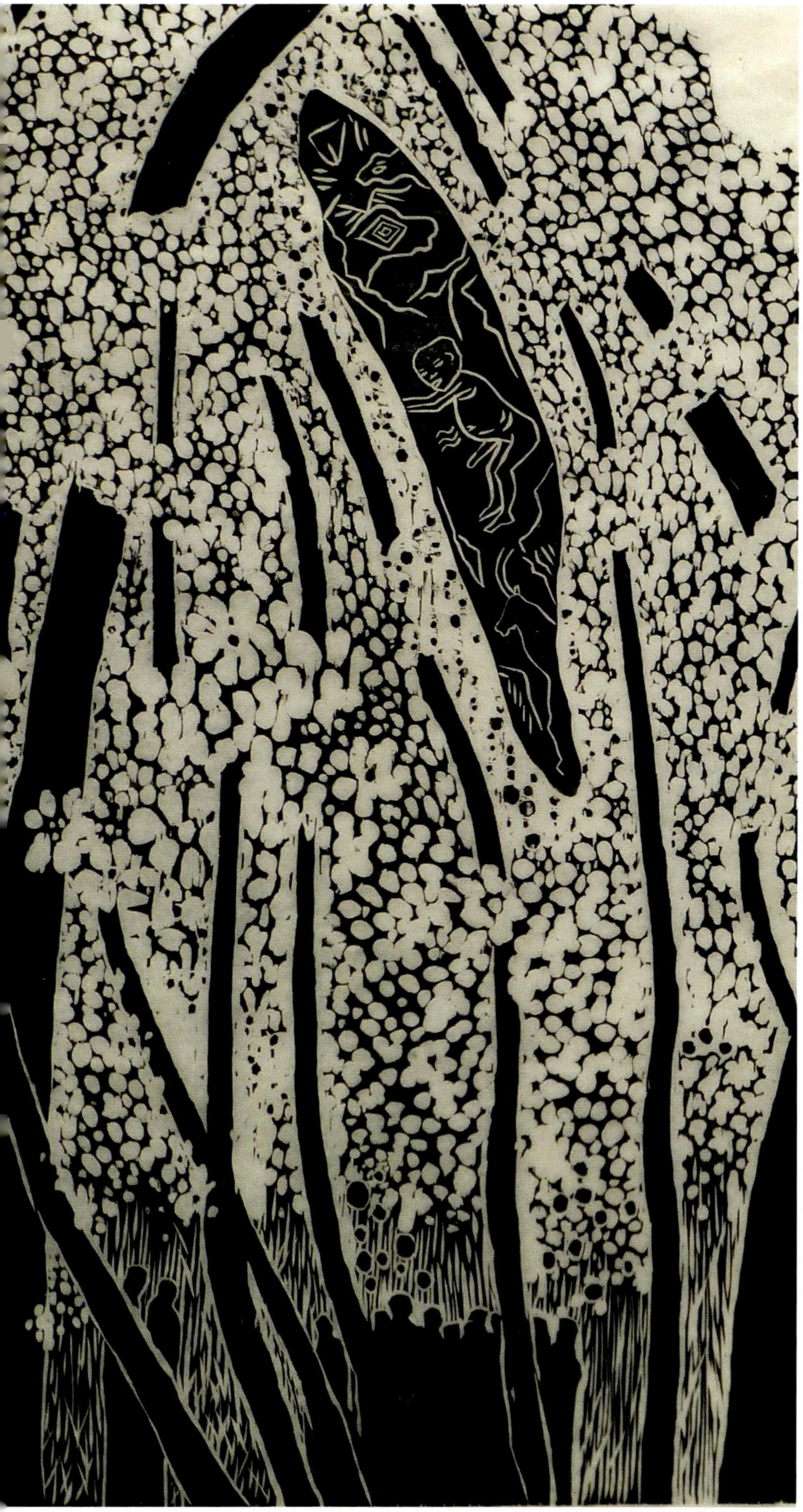

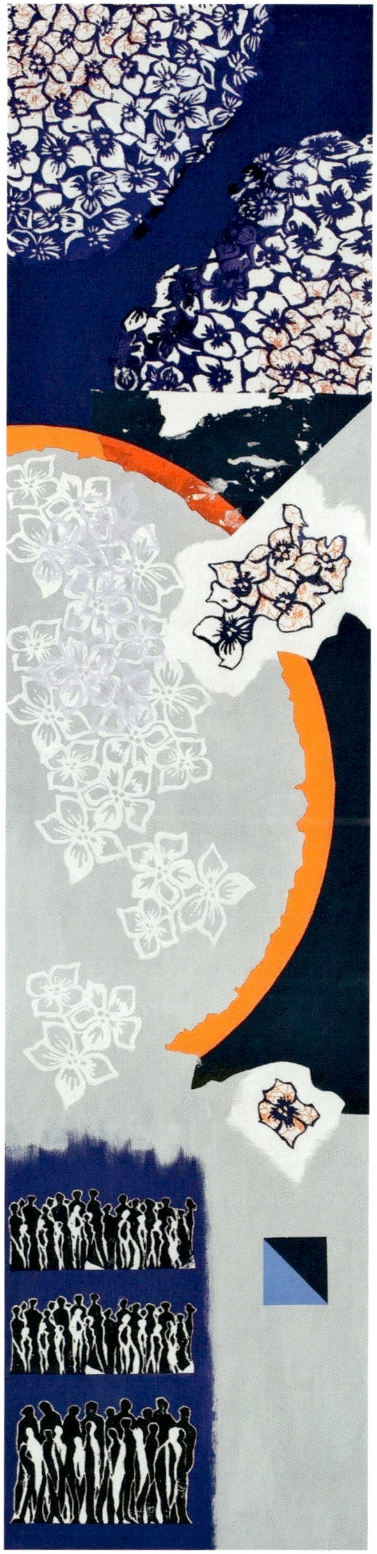

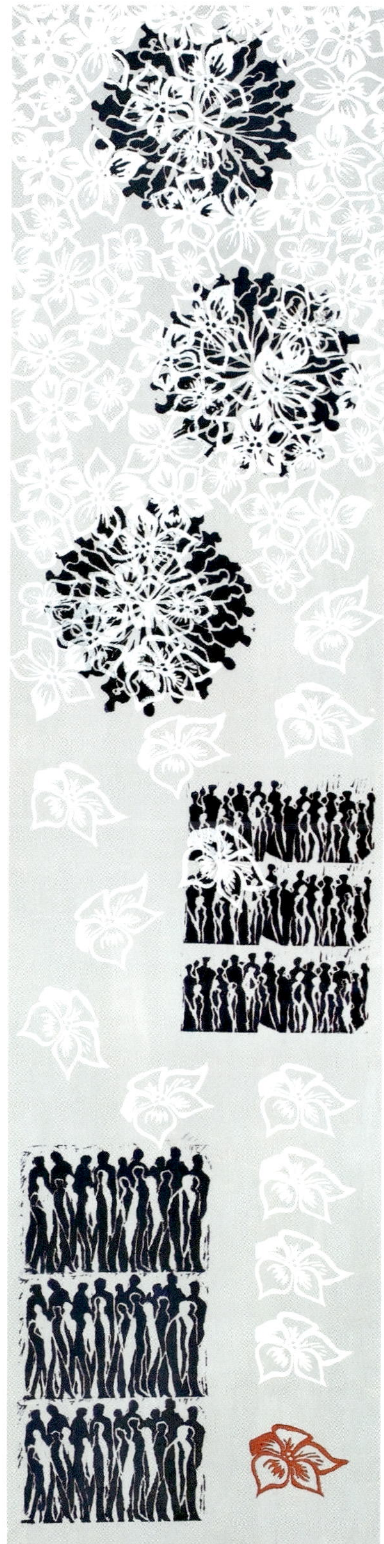

Left to right:
Hidden Cave,
Making Connections, Fall

Katja Dell

Artist

Clockwise from top:
Hello Beautiful,
Esther; Kitty; Marilyn

Katja's artistic journey began in 2004 when she gained City & Guilds and BTEC certificates in Photography at Richmond and Lambeth College in London. She later re-trained in illustration and was awarded a Master of Arts in Sequential Design/ Illustration from the University of Brighton in 2011.

Her passion for boisterous lacy fashion, fancy hats, burlesque theatre, antique dolls, tattoo art, haunted mansions, vampires and cupcakes has always provided an abundance of inspiration for her work. She is fascinated by Pop Surrealism, the Steam Punk revival and anything remotely Victorian.

Over the years her artwork has been highly influenced by the dark humour of Tim Burton, Edward Gorey, David Roberts and the visually stunning world of Mark Ryden, Nicoletta Ceccoli and Benjamin Lacombe.

Katja is a part-time freelance illustrator and has exhibited at the highly acclaimed Egg House, nominated for the Best Open House Award in 2009. Other venues include the Cactus Gallery, Starbucks and the UB Visual Arts Graduate Show 2011.

She loves to scour vintage markets and rescue second-hand books and treasures that can be given a new breath of life, and has a soft spot for decadent patisseries and Saint-Honoré rose.

Katja is one of the resident artists at the Naughty Pirates Gallery on Brighton seafront, and a regular at Waterstones, where she spends most of her weekends sipping tea with a Baron and creating unique and quirky characters that are becoming increasingly popular.

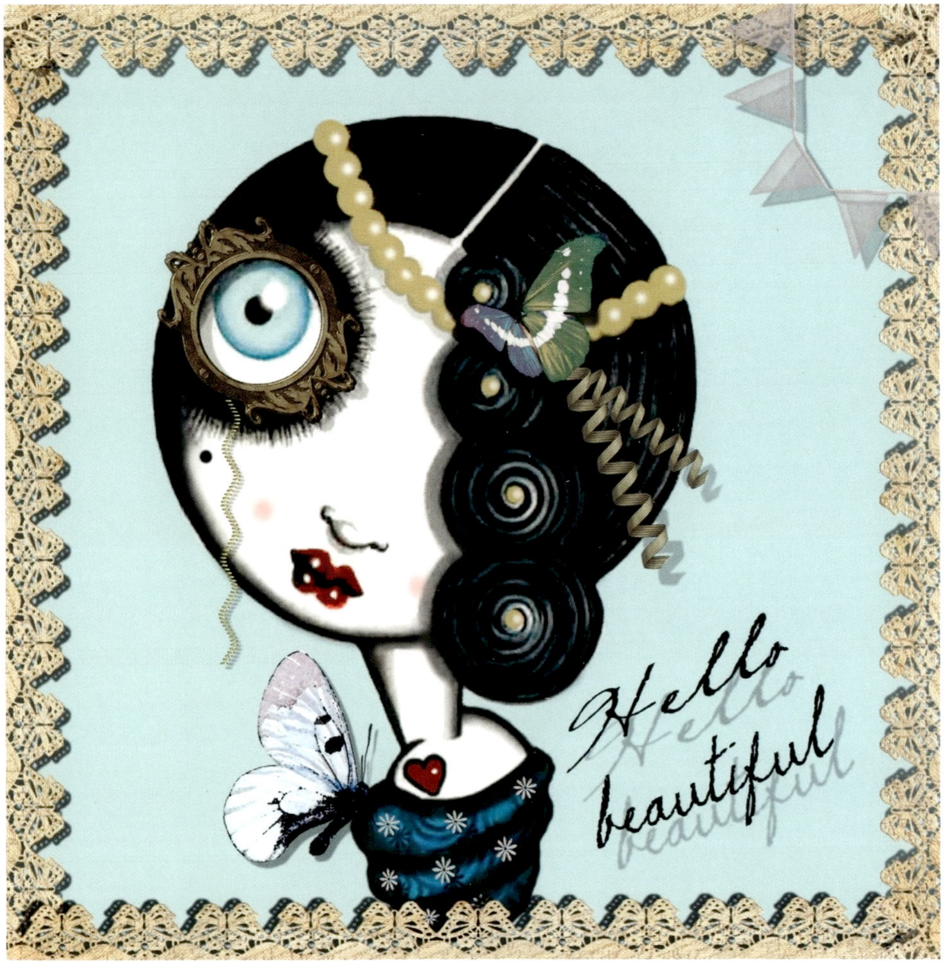

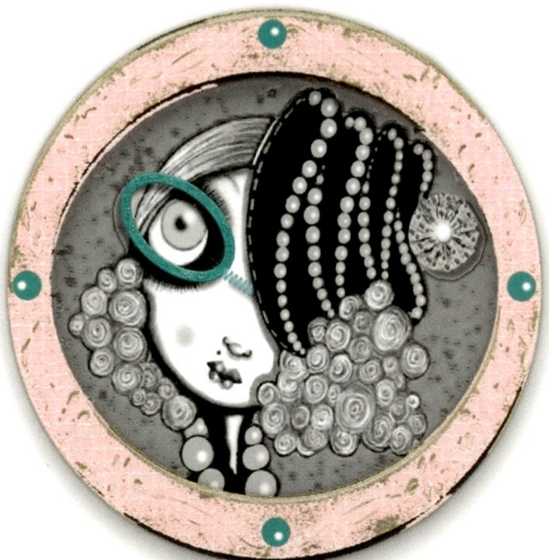

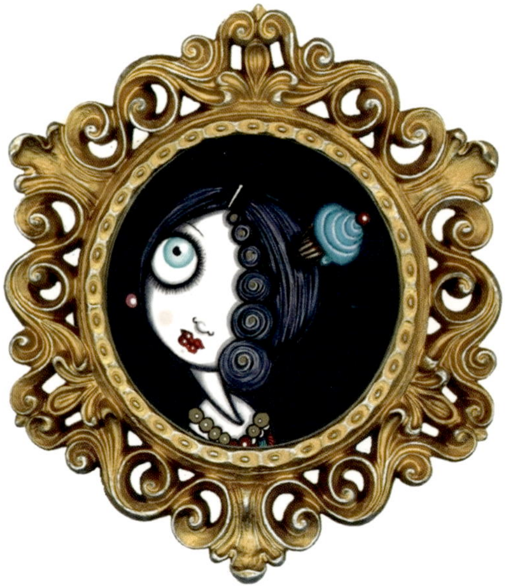

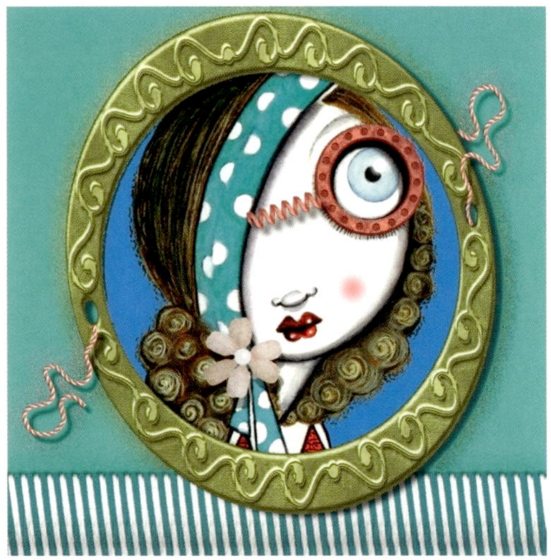

Clockwise from top left:
Dew Pond; Dark Side of the Downs;
Undertone

Jo Watters-Pawlowski

Artist

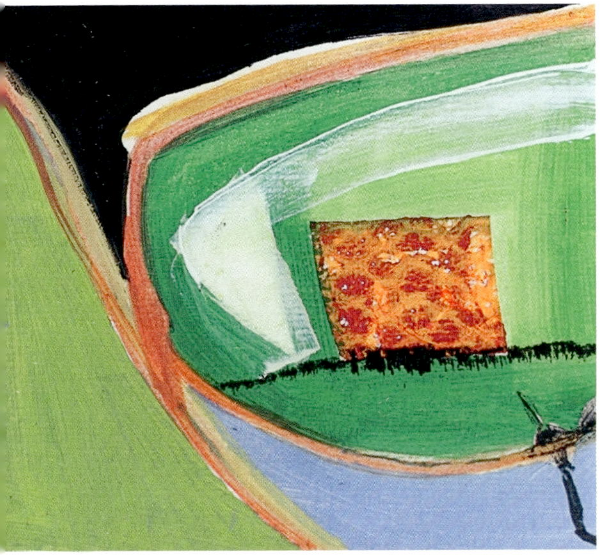

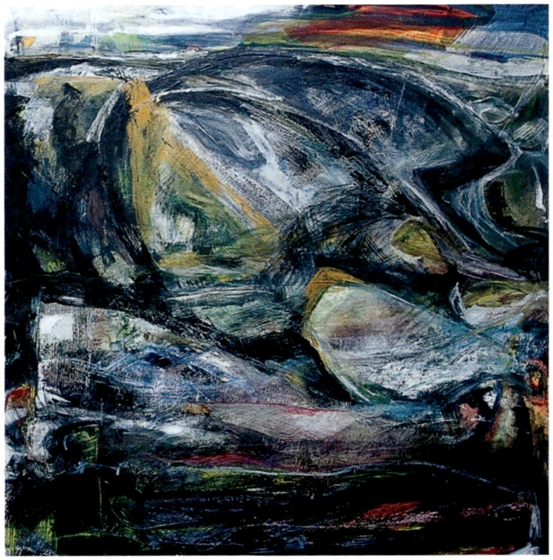

Jo's current paintings are based on influences and emotions drawn from landscape. Her observations explore the intensity of colour and form to create subtle abstract statements. Layering techniques, using oil and acrylics, lend a spectacular intensity to the finished painting.

Jo's work ranges from small coloured and black and white drawings to larger canvases. She successfully sells work through the Artists Open Houses Festival, working to commission and selling to private collectors.

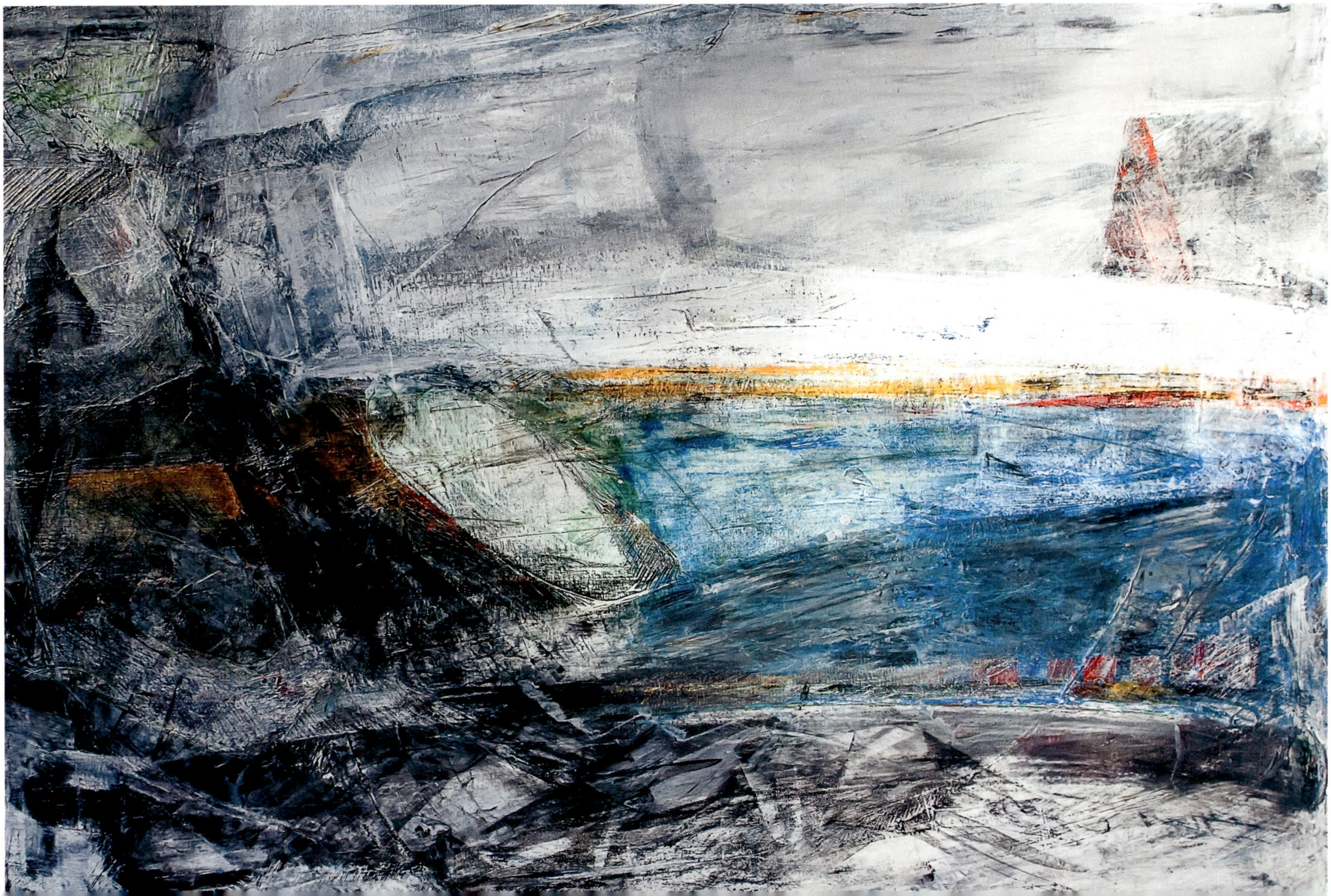

Auricula

12 Turner Dumbrell Workshops, North End, Ditchling BN6 8GT

Clockwise from top: Beihai; Isis; Seascape; Rococco

Auricula is a treasure trove of tempting beaded gemstone jewellery tucked away in the Turner Dumbrell Workshops in Ditchling. From here, Natasha Caughey designs and makes her fabulous jewellery collections. Natasha started trading in Ditchling in 2006 after five years working as a jewellery buyer and designer in central London.

Natasha loves to experiment with colour and texture in her designs. She hand-selects the gemstones and freshwater pearls on her trips to China and India and is always on the look-out for unusual cuts and colours. The selection of jewellery on offer is constantly evolving and commissions are welcome.

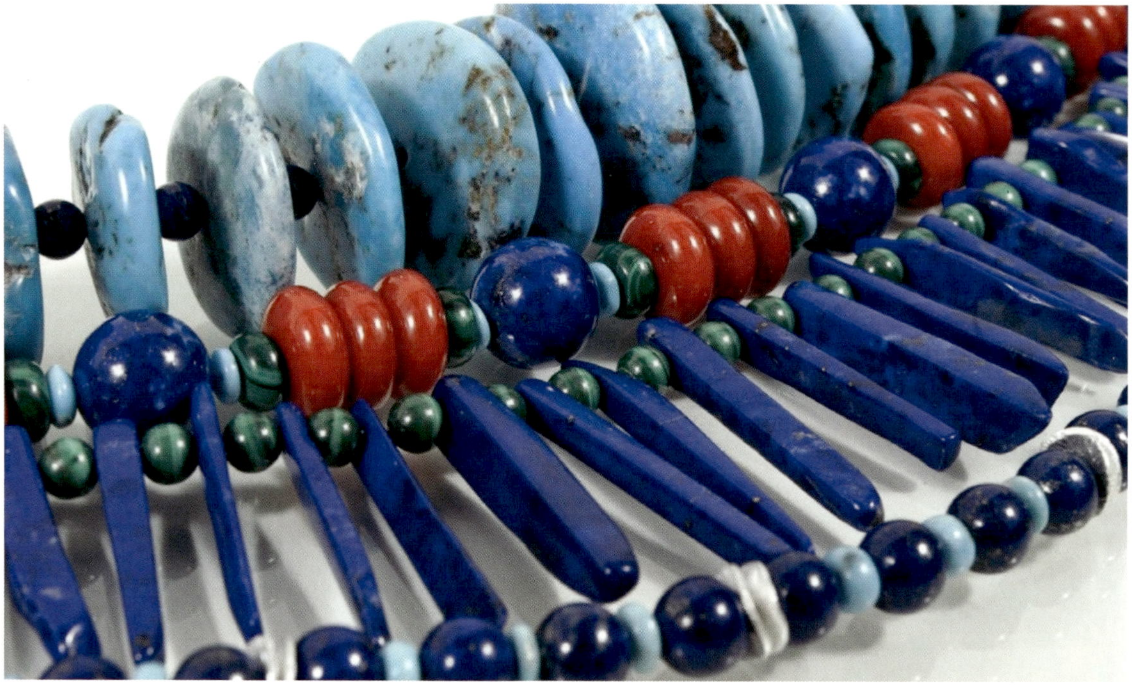

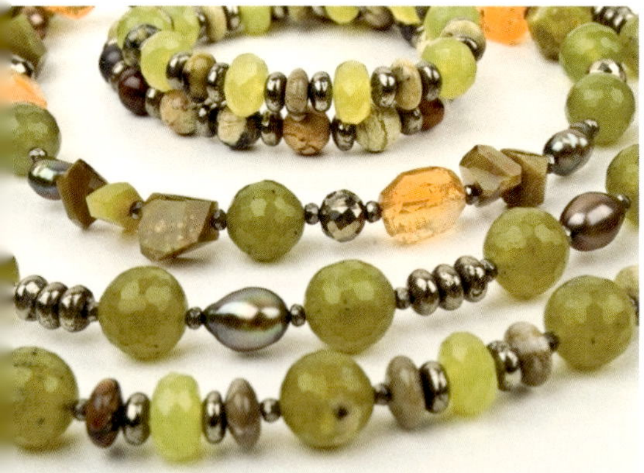

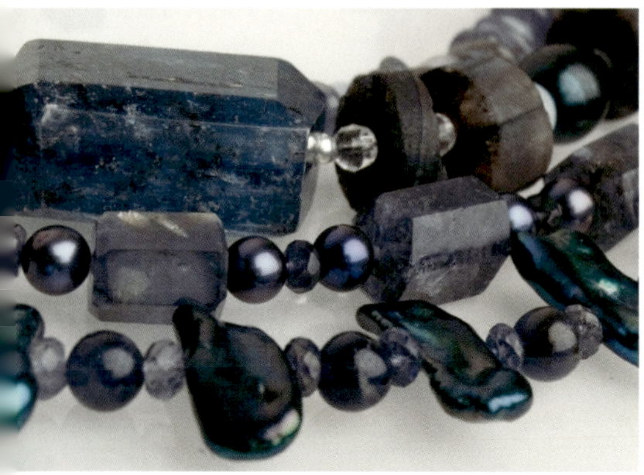

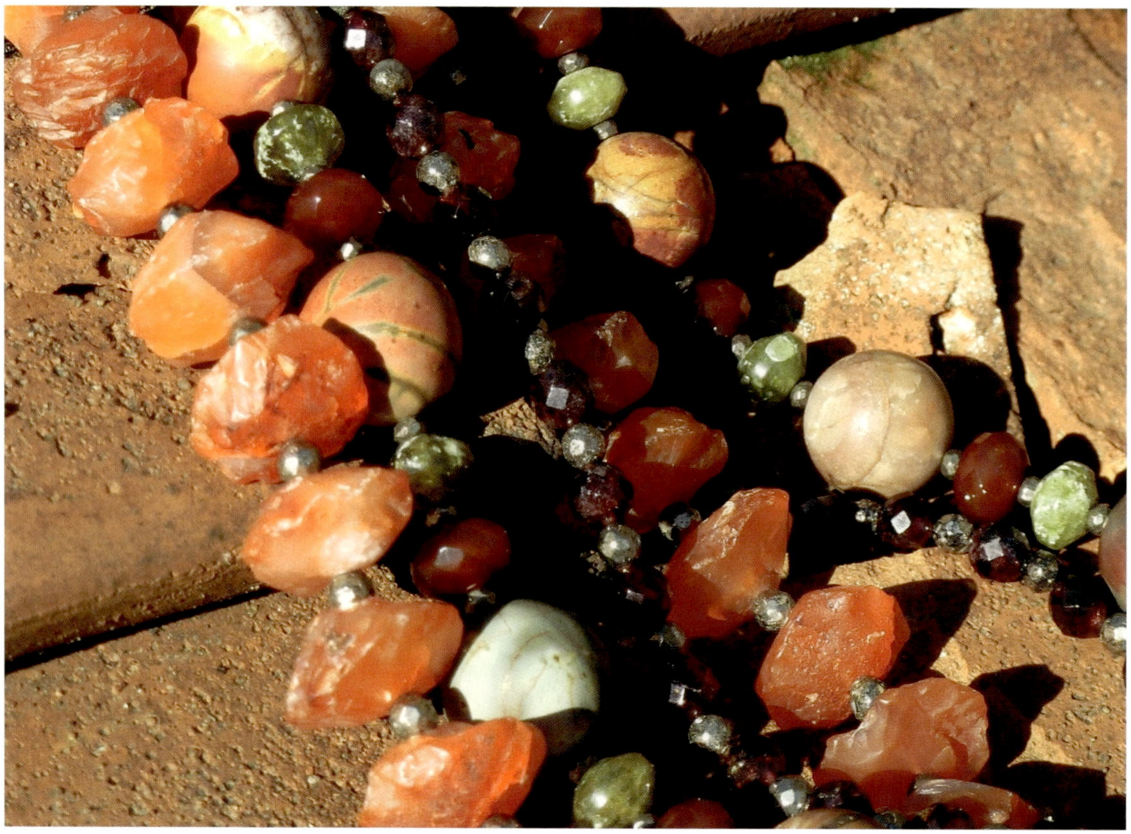

Clockwise from top left:
Woman standing behind a Sculpture;
Vulva Landscape; Sepalia in red; Feminine Energy

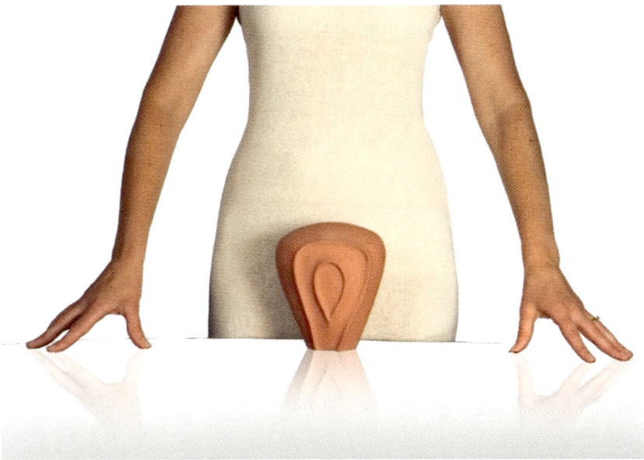

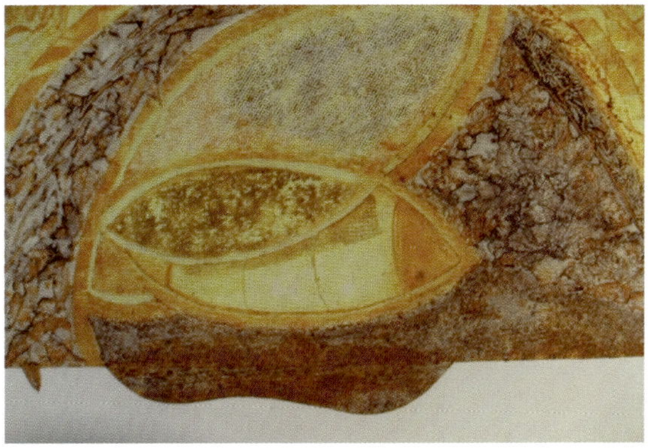

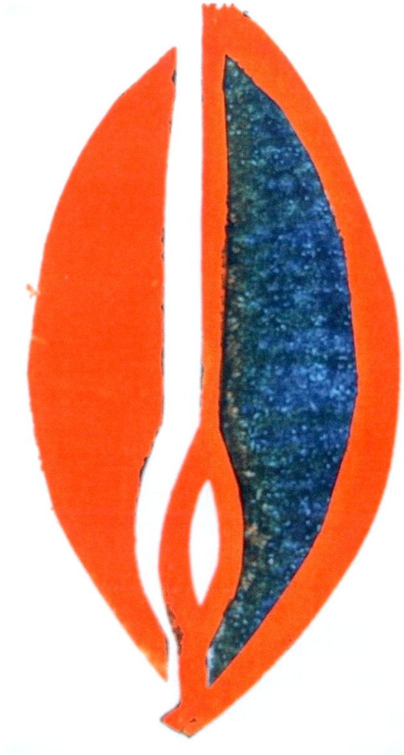

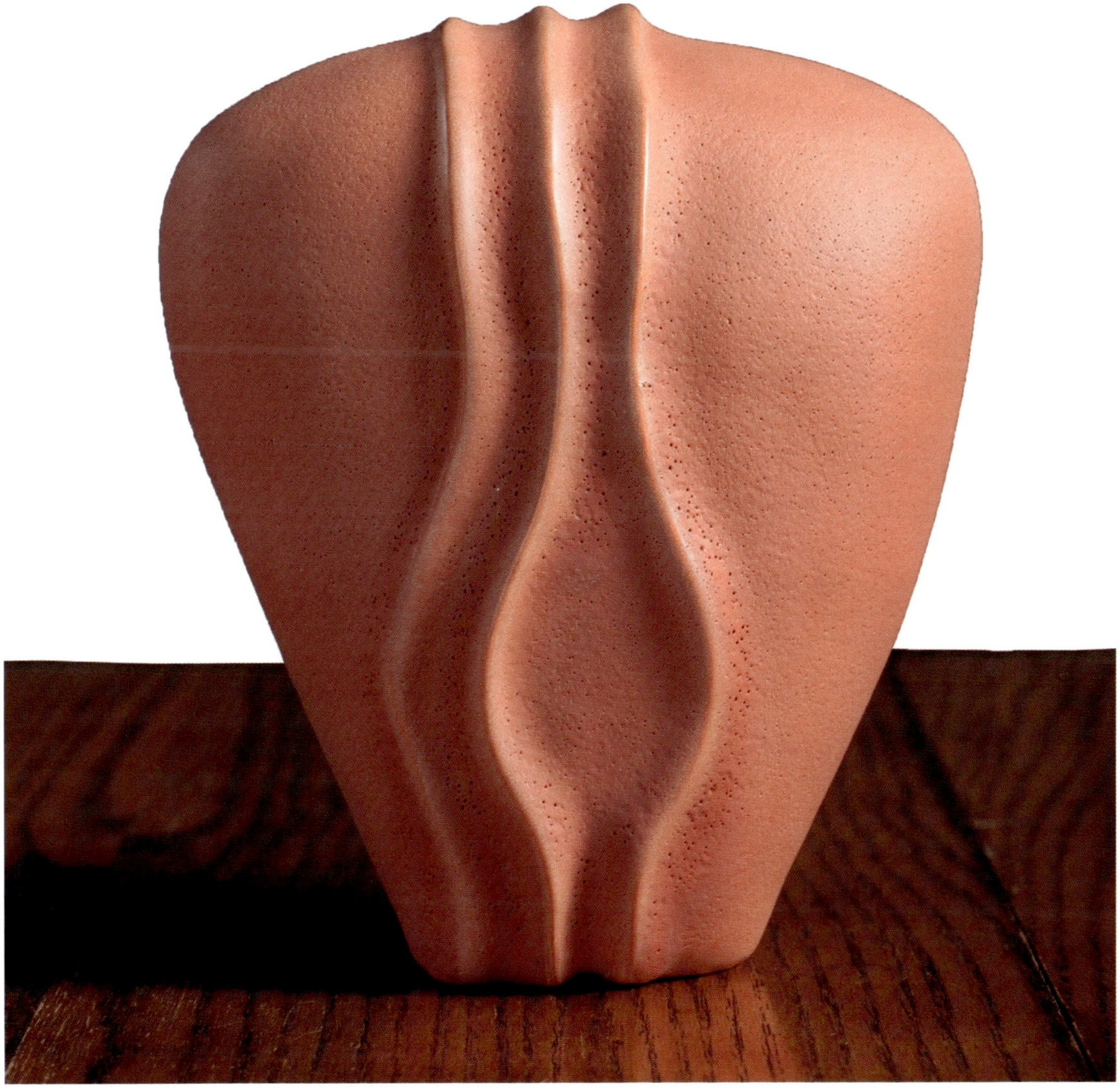

Expressing feminine energy

Marga Beuth is a sculptor, printmaker and artistic anthropologist. Alongside her art, she offers observations about the human condition and specifically about feminine energy and its place in the world.

Currently, Marga's art revolves around a triangle of issues: representing the most feminine body part (the vulva), creating new female symbols and thirdly exploring the essence of 'The Feminine'. She uses the vulva to represent 'The Feminine' and feminine energy – offering in effect new symbols of feminine power.

Marga believes that if women feel uncomfortable with a defining characteristic of their gender, they can never act in a relaxed and powerful way in the world. In her view the vulva represents womanhood, just like a penis represents manhood. It's as simple as that!

Marga has worked as an artist for about eight years, while working as a consultant for publishing companies. Her recent work has focused on printmaking, embedding the simple almond shape of the vulva into a well known context such as semi-abstract landscapes.

Sarah Shaw

Artist

Clockwise from top left: Unearth; Rorschach Head II; Roads; Monolith V

Sarah Shaw's paintings hover in a place between figuration and abstraction which allows the viewer the space to impose their own interpretation. Time collapses as past, present and future are represented in oil paintings that obey a non-linear chronology: they stand simultaneously as a visualising of the past and as a perception of the present. Some of the work's imagery springs from the artist's imagination, while other work explores metaphorical or symbolic images/barriers/passages and evokes ideas about living through time.

Characteristic of Sarah's work, the process revolves around the building up and stripping down of imagery, and the exploration of different painterly languages, eventually being reduced down to the lowest denominator where an edgy quietness falls. They are not whole images, but snatches of images, sounds and thoughts, forming into coherence briefly... like a painterly slideshow of memory. Ultimately the paintings speak of a belief in the enduring vitality of painting as a primary form of visceral and visual communication.

"These recent paintings were inspired by Rorschach inkblot tests and the theory behind them - that the subconscious/unconscious mind can be revealed by the study of ambiguous replicated imagery. The act of painting in itself seems to echo this process, revealing one's own subconscious thoughts, though this does imply a lack of control over the imagery. I see the painting process as being not so much unconscious but rather a kind of accelerated consciousness in which decisions are being speedily made during the painterly dialogue. I wanted to make a body of work which was ambiguous enough to allow the viewer to be transported by their own thoughts rather than dictated to by my own, and for the paintings to continue to reveal themselves the more they are viewed."

Sarah studied at Falmouth College of Art. Her work has been purchased by private collectors in the UK and abroad, and most notably by Ronnie Wood. She has featured in many notable competitions, including the National Open and the Aesthetica Art Prize and was recently shortlisted for the prestigious Threadneedle Art Prize.

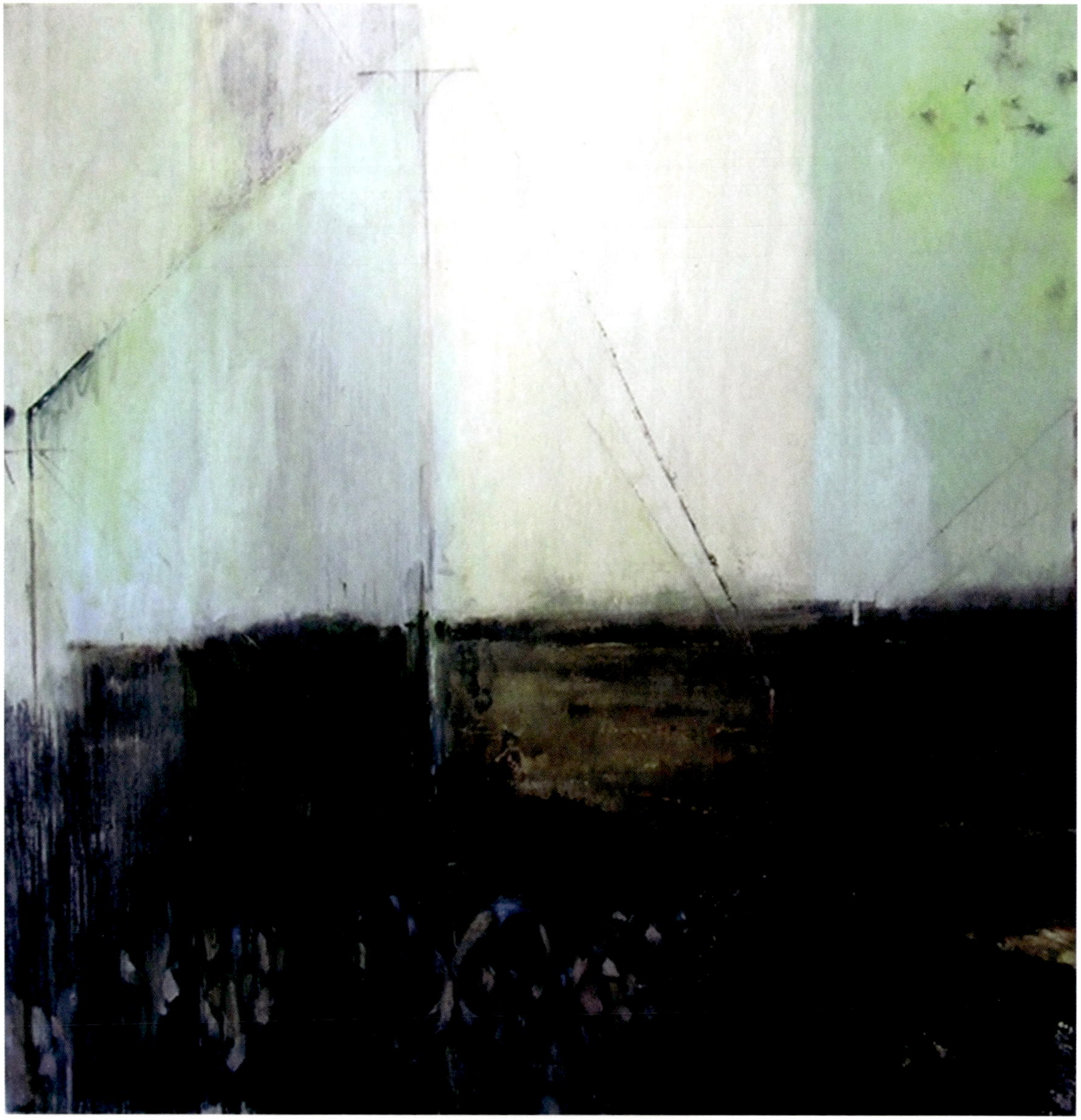

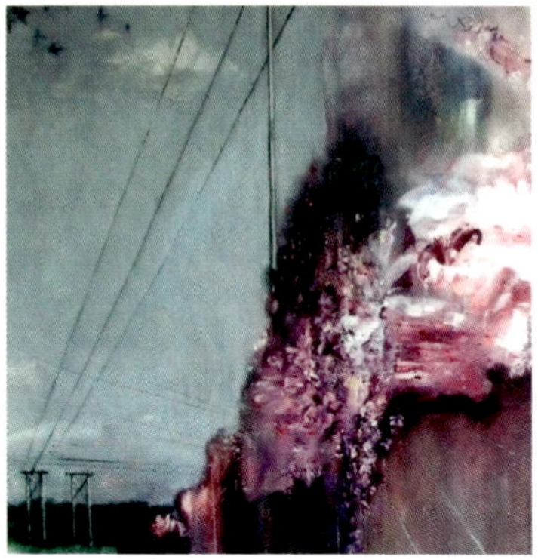

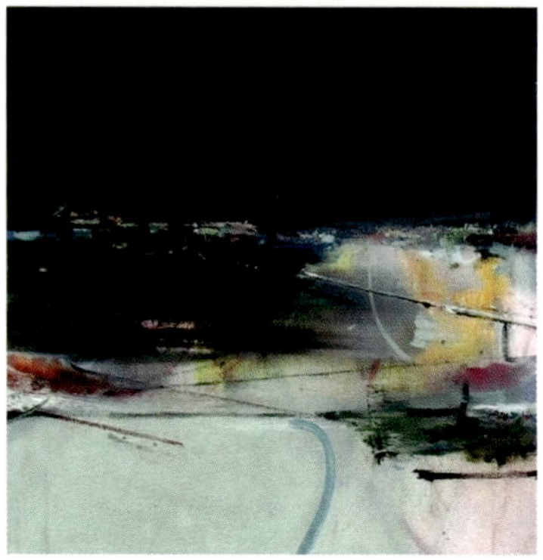

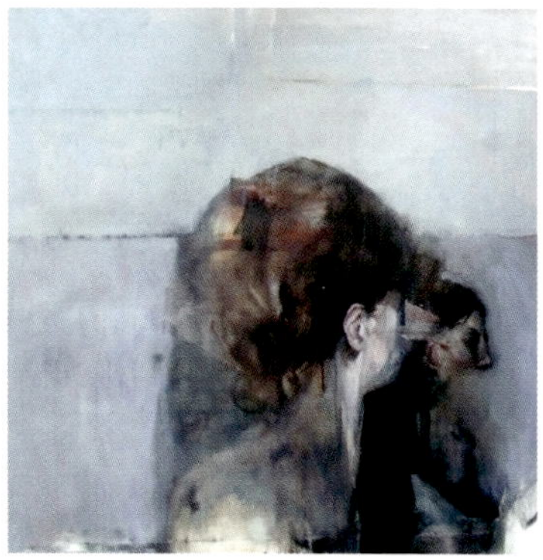

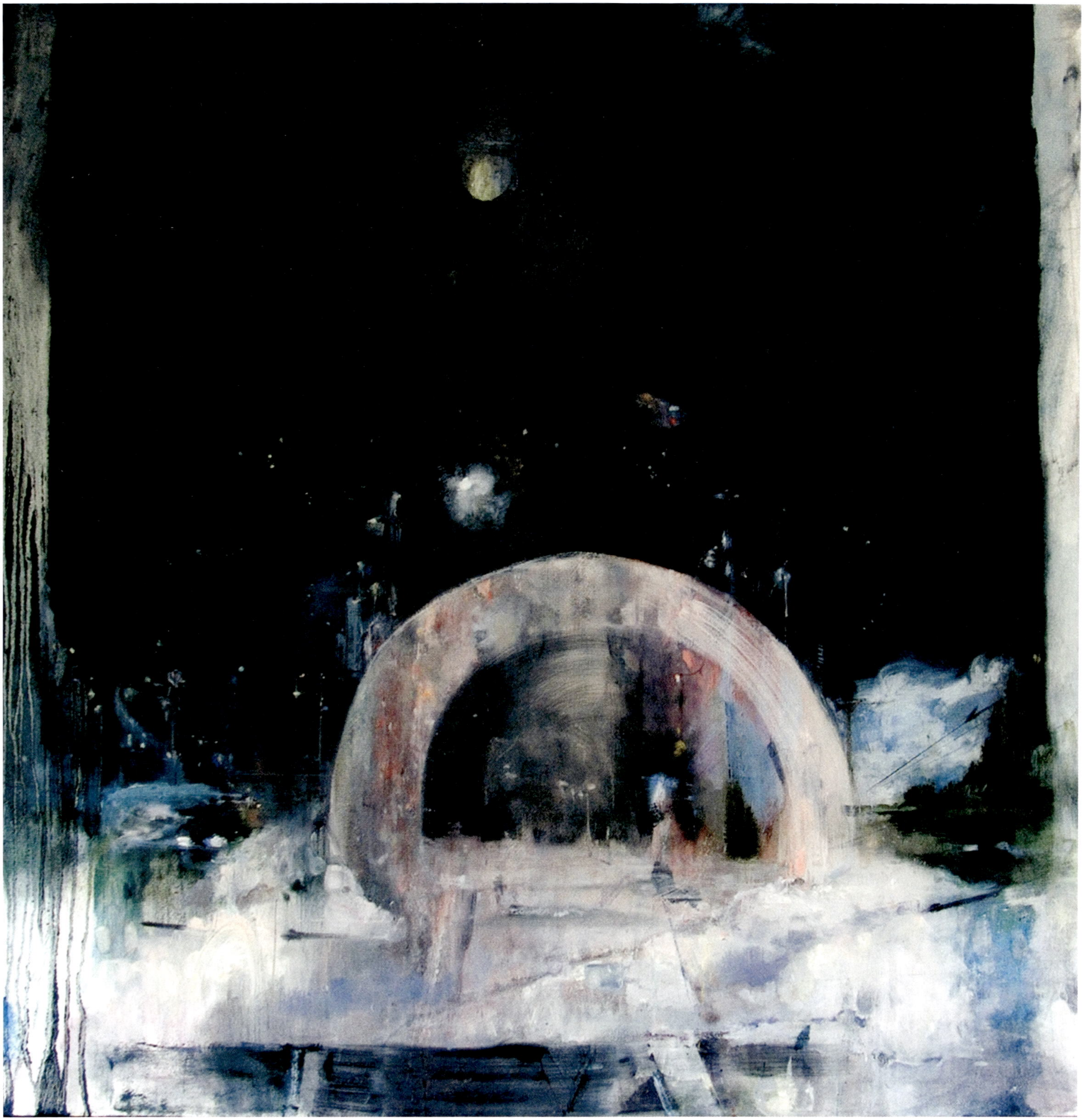

Harriet Butler

Artist

Left: Big Ben
Right: Blue Note

Harriet Butler will take you on a magical journey through history and time with her unique perception of the art of storytelling. Guided by her love of architecture and all its beauty, Harriet's drawings encompass all the quirky facets that life can bring... animals, people, history and music.

Harriet's prints are a collection of strange, quirky and bizarre dialogues. They create a sense of nostalgia that has two sides. One is a childhood playful silliness; the other is a sense of recreating a feeling of the past through her drawings of places.

To get a real sense of Harriet's highly detailed illustrative prints, they can be found on permanent display at Bellis Gallery (see page 132) on Kings Road, just off East Street.

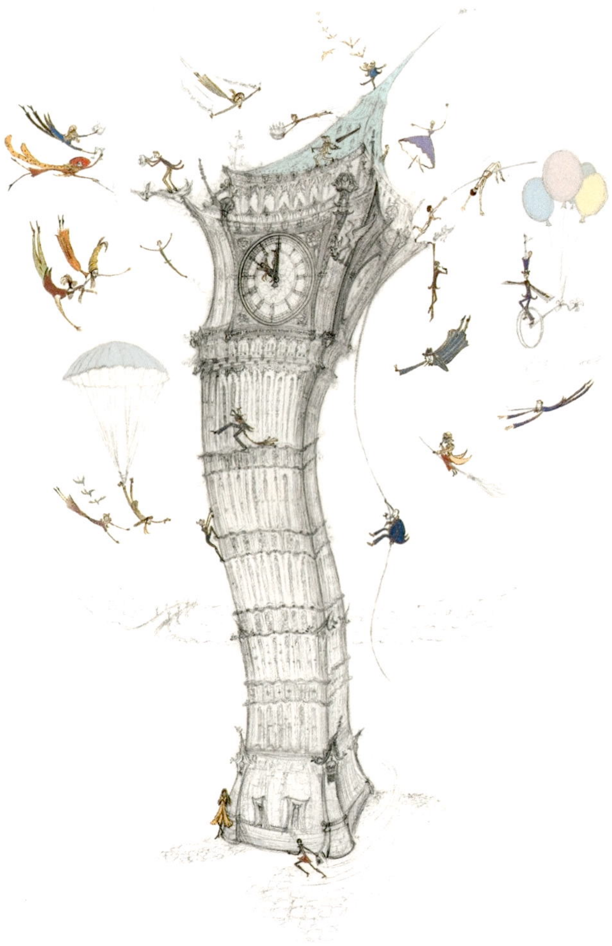

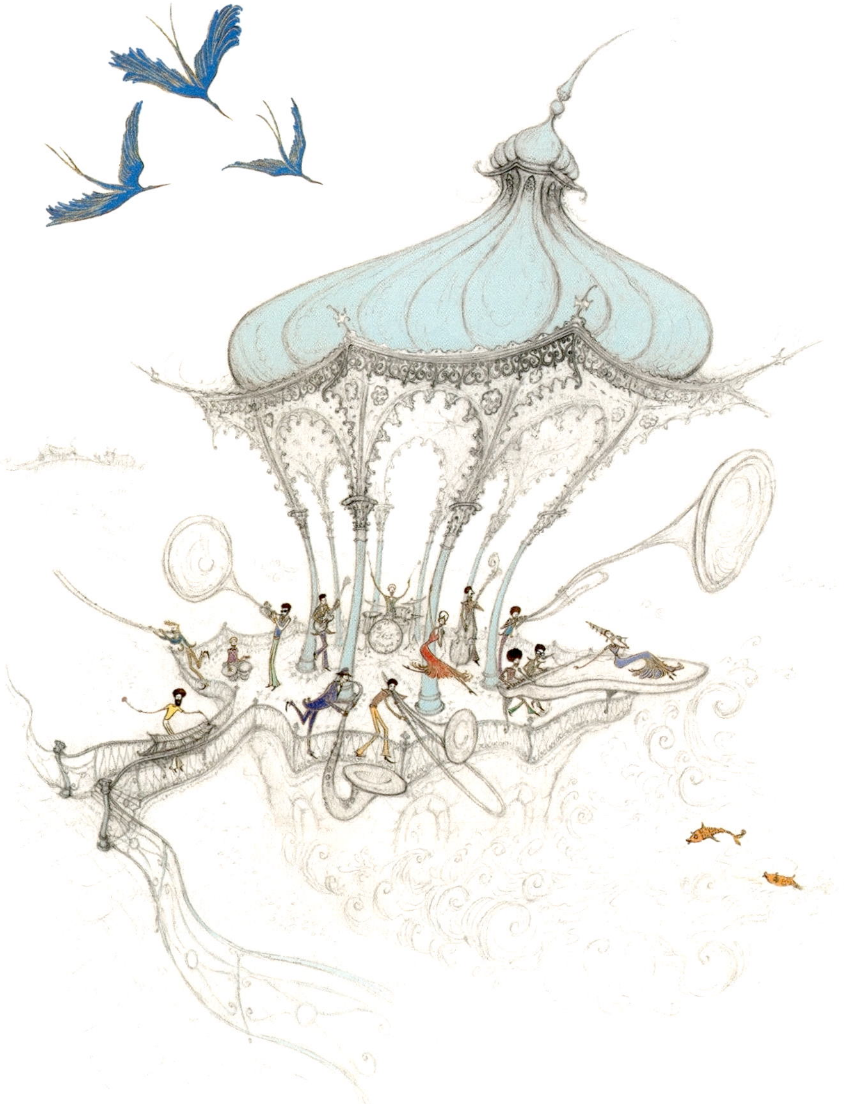

Christina Fedyk

Artist

Clockwise from top left:
Acoustic; Black Skew;
Grid 1; Friend to Bird

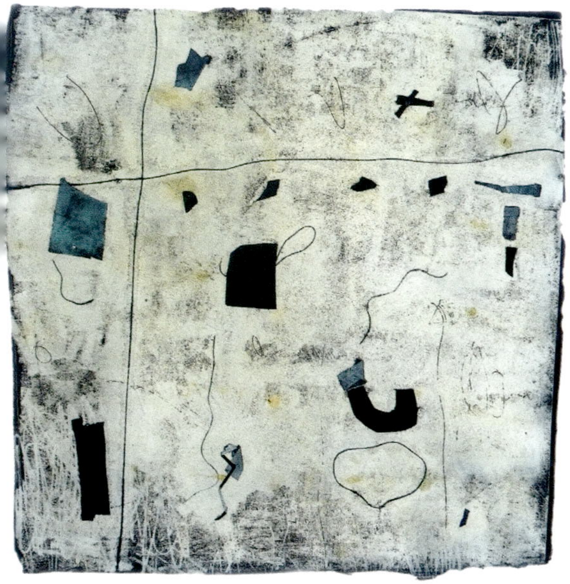

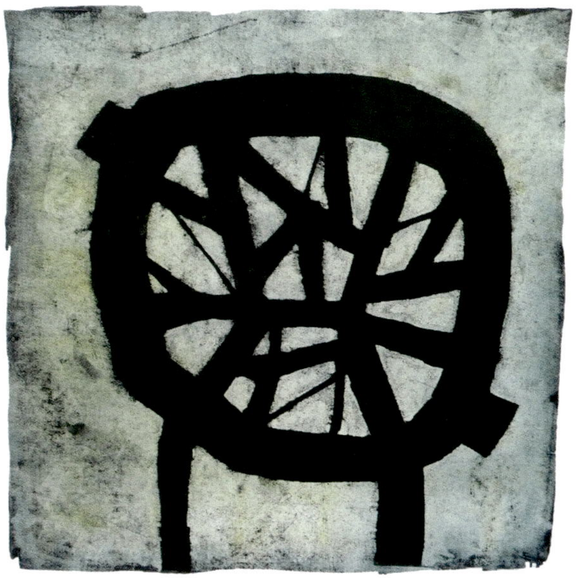

Christina Fedyk graduated from Leicester De Montfort University with a Fine Art Degree. She expresses her creative ideas through painting, print making and 3D work.

In observing the details of daily life, she collects a wealth of imagery that then informs a process of mark-making and abstraction. This dialogue shifts and changes until the overall image begins to convey an energy, emotion or a sense of its own.

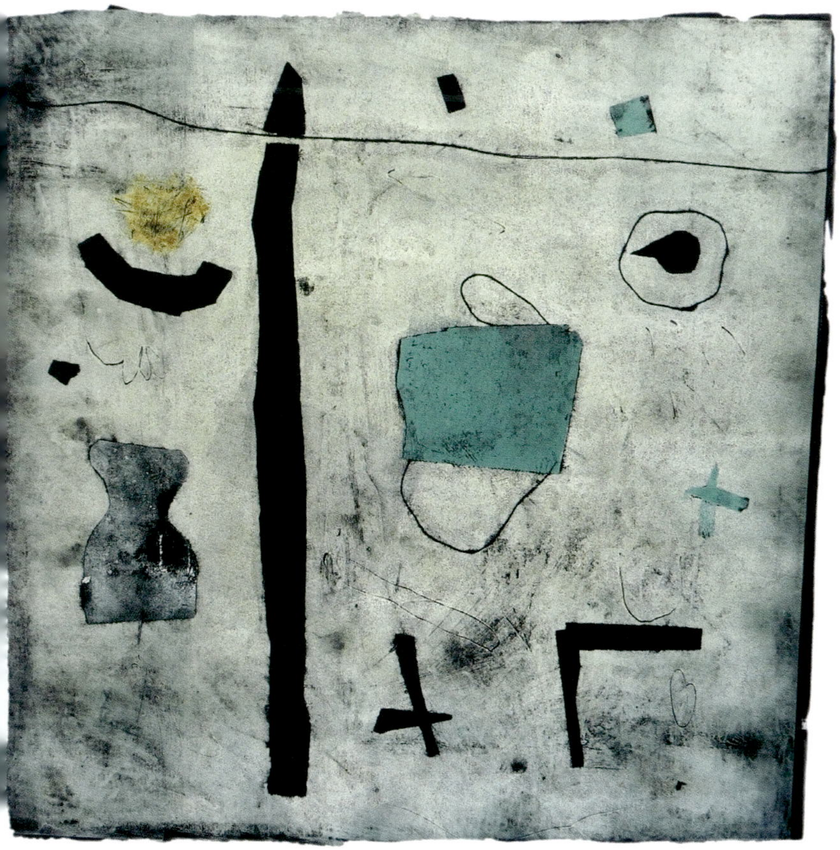

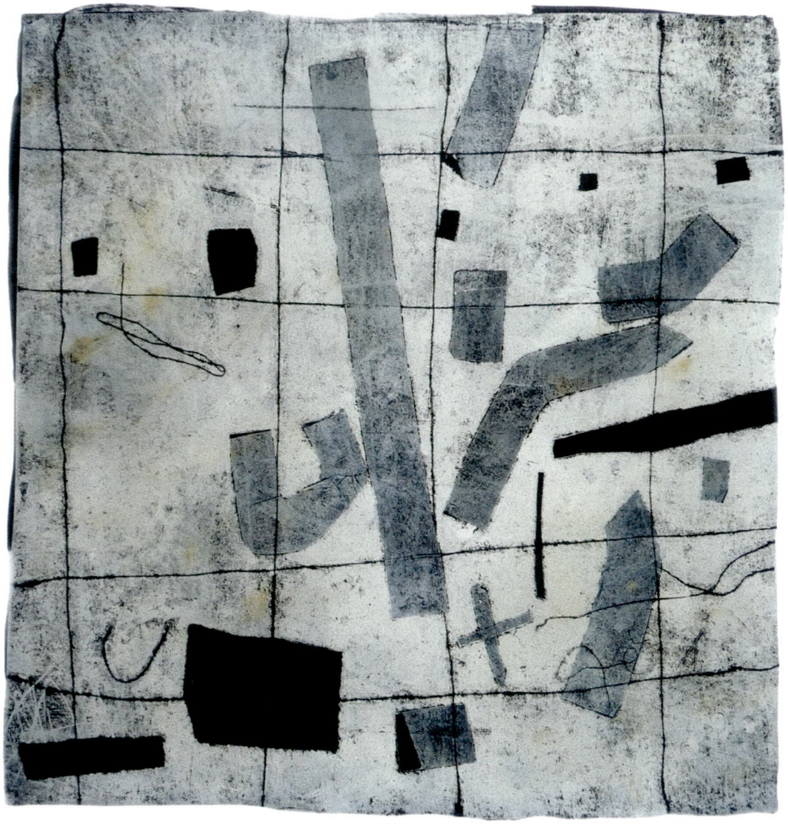

Amanda Davidson

Artist & Author

This page, (clockwise from top left): Sawyer & Co; Dolly the Cat; Madame Butterfly Theatre in a Suitcase

Amanda Davidson is a published children's book illustrator and author. She works mainly in pen and ink, watercolour and acrylics, but also in oils. Her recent commissions include the challenge of creating a puppet theatre in a suitcase for a theatrical prop, which she worked on with a fellow puppet theatre enthusiast.

As well as creating her own artworks, Amanda is the art gallery organiser for The Grange Art Gallery and Museum in Rottingdean. Previous exhibition themes include 'Ballet and theatre'. This October visitors can look forward to an exhibition on Tudor Close – once a famous hotel in the 1930s – which explores Amanda's love of architectural drawing and storytelling.

Charleston farmhouse and the paintings of the Bloomsbury Set have also been a strong influence on Amanda's skills as a furniture painter and mural artist.

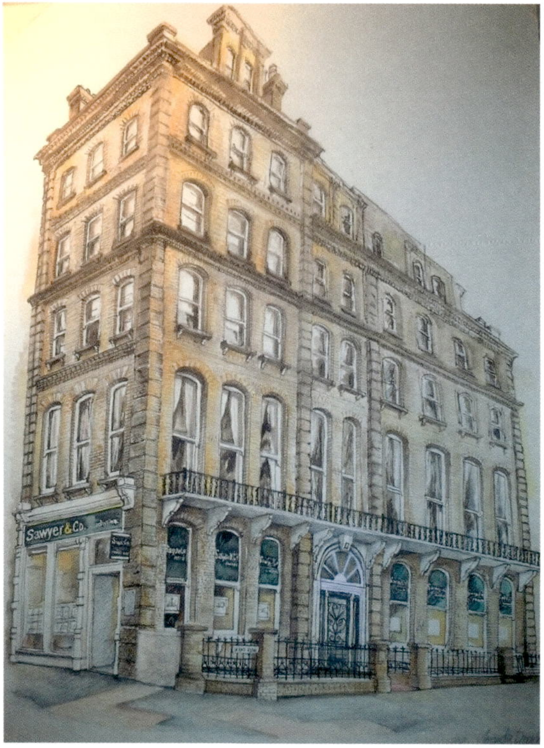

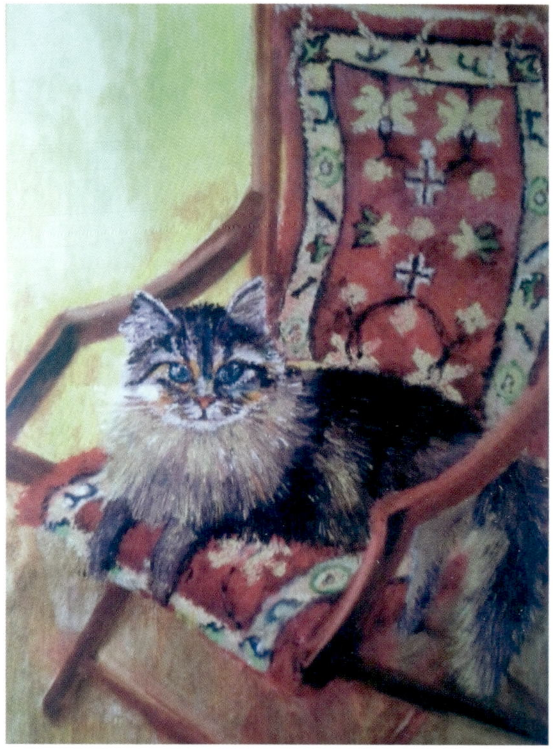

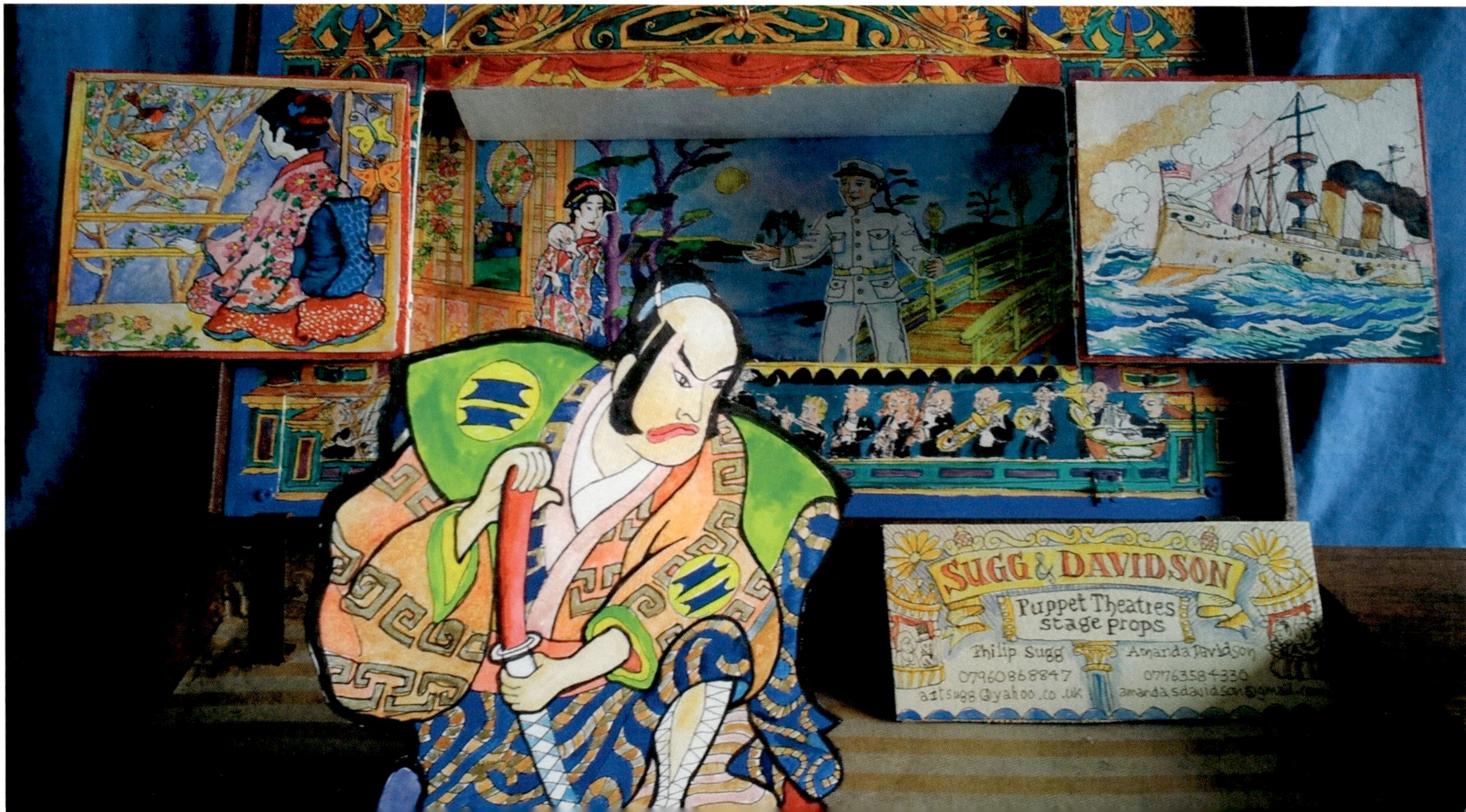

This page: (clockwise from top left):
Charleston-style table; Swan Lake;
Petrouchka; Klimt Collage

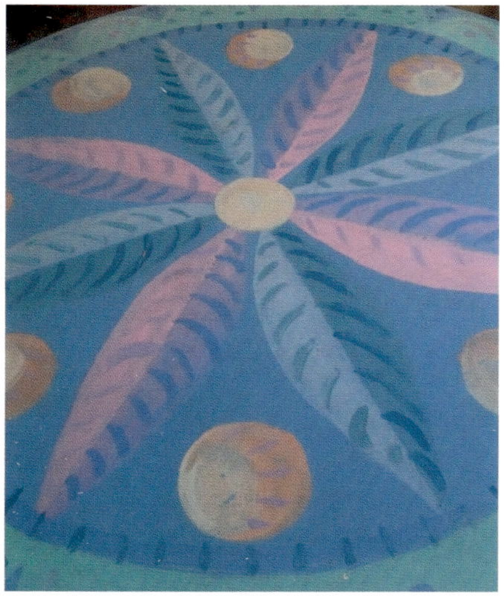

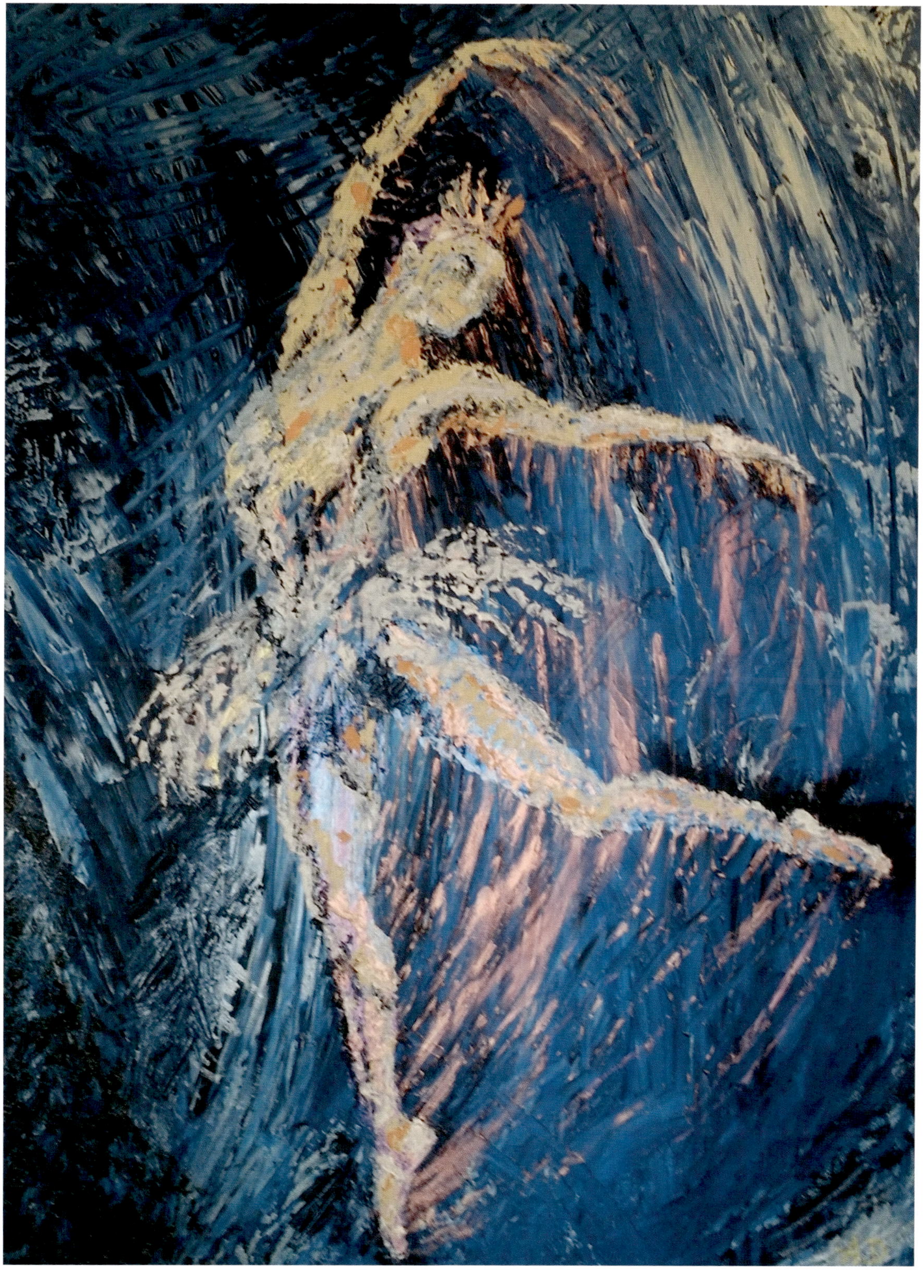

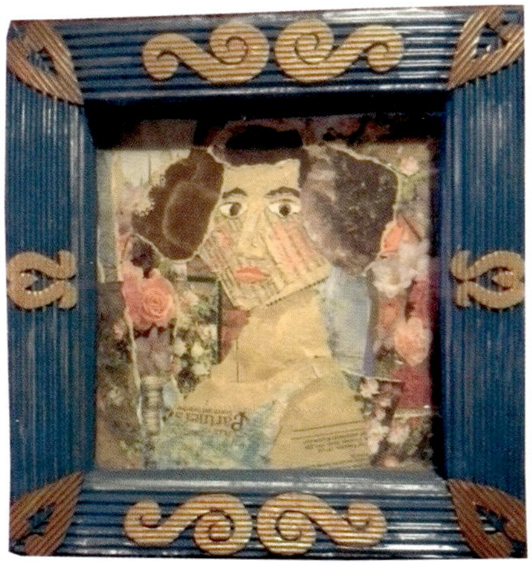

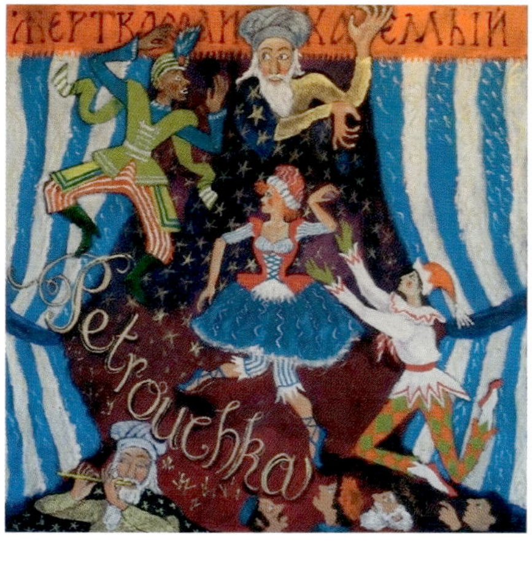

Francesca Grace McLeod

Artist

This page (clockwise from top left): James; Spyglass; Incoming!; Adam
Opposite page: Beret

From her earlier works of dark sensuality to her latest celebrations of life in bright hyper-colour, Francesca continues to explore surveillance and ambiguity in her painted works. Her interest in photo-journalism and pop culture helps to produce work that is often confrontational and forces her audience to decide where they sit with their own voyeuristic impulses.

The striking, very warm and generous use of colour and texture is playful to the extreme; and, whether they portray intense coital moments, visceral street life or alarming portraits, McLeod's works are always very pleasing to the eye and teeming with vitality.

Her latest works, a series of hyper-expressive portraits, feature a host of gloriously entertaining gurning and perplexed profiles. Here, in this Instagrammed age of the 'selfie', McLeod turns the indulgent focus of 'the self' back onto the audience as perversely as she's ever done. We, the audience, are almost attacked by the sheer bloody-minded expression on her subjects' faces. We, the audience, seem to be the focus of their lives, their reason for such exaggerated expressions as they often lock uncomfortable eye contact with us, peer at us through a magnifying glass (that theme of surveillance again) or even seem to be making fun of us. How dare they?! Yet you cannot help but fall in love with the characters of McLeod's world; whether they pull faces at us, intentionally make us feel awkward with their alarming stare, or are maybe caught off-guard in a private moment of their own, there's so much seductive life and emotion on show here.

One perfect question is left forever unanswered whenever one looks at McLeod's work: who is actually looking at whom? For it seems that we, the audience, are just as much the focus of Francesca's world as her beautifully painted models and scenes. They are forever staring back at us, confronting us, forcing us into becoming part of their private or intimate moments. Could it be that we are the reason for their playful antics? Our focus on them becomes a focus on ourselves in some kind of perpetuating cycle of voyeurism.

Francesca's work is a sensual and painterly celebration of the moment that leaves your senses tingling; you feel as alive and vital as her vibrant subjects.

Follow Francesca's work at facebook.com/Artist.Francesca.Grace.McLeod

Text: Phil Barrington, artist and curator, 2013

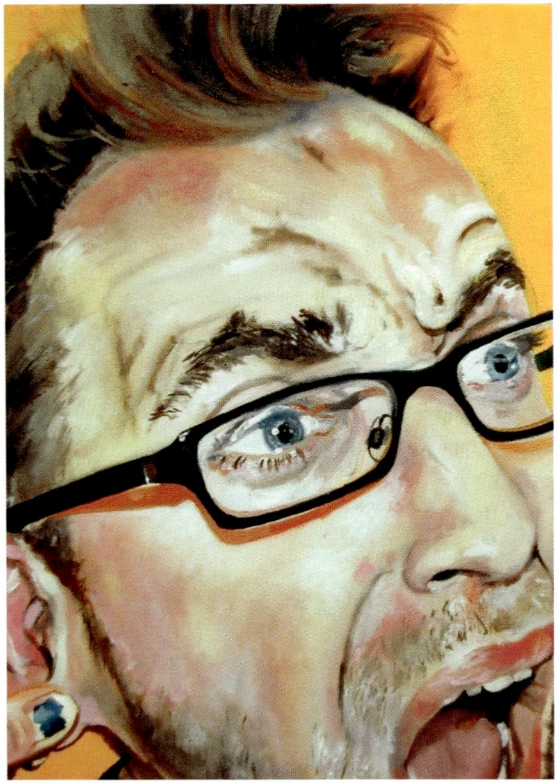

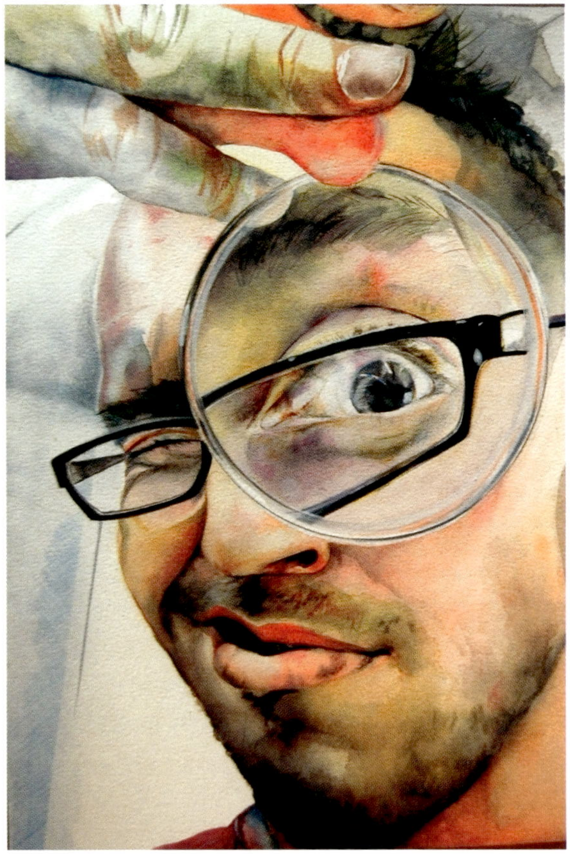

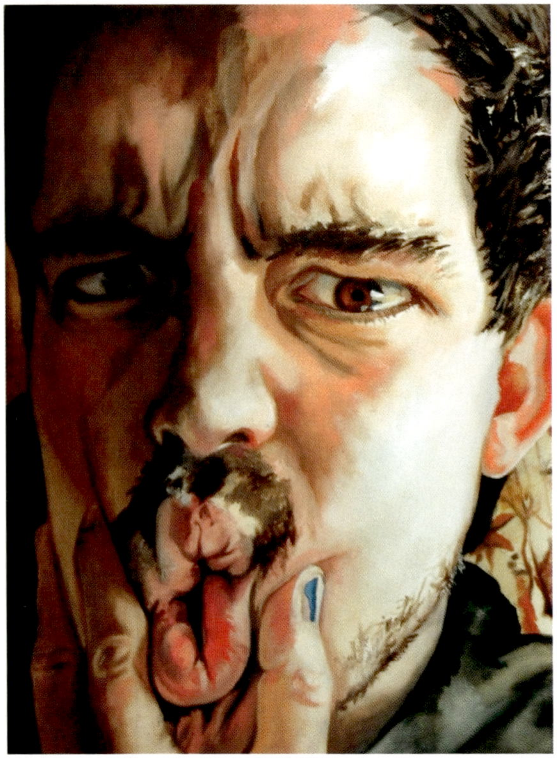

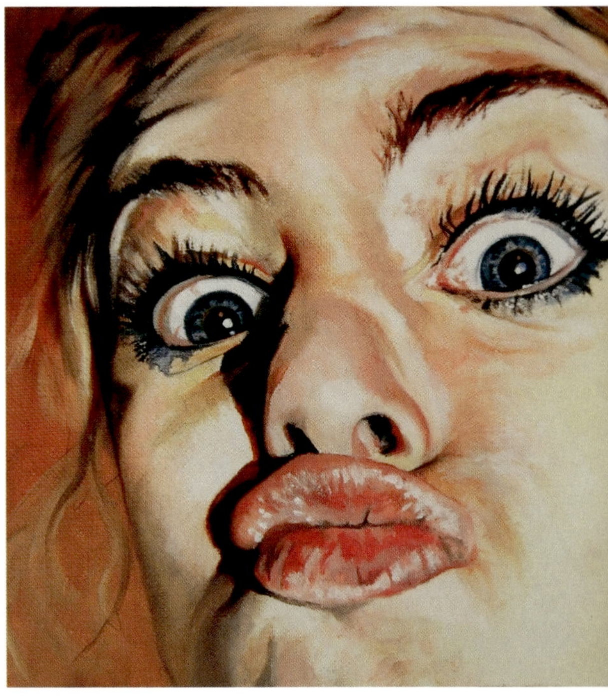

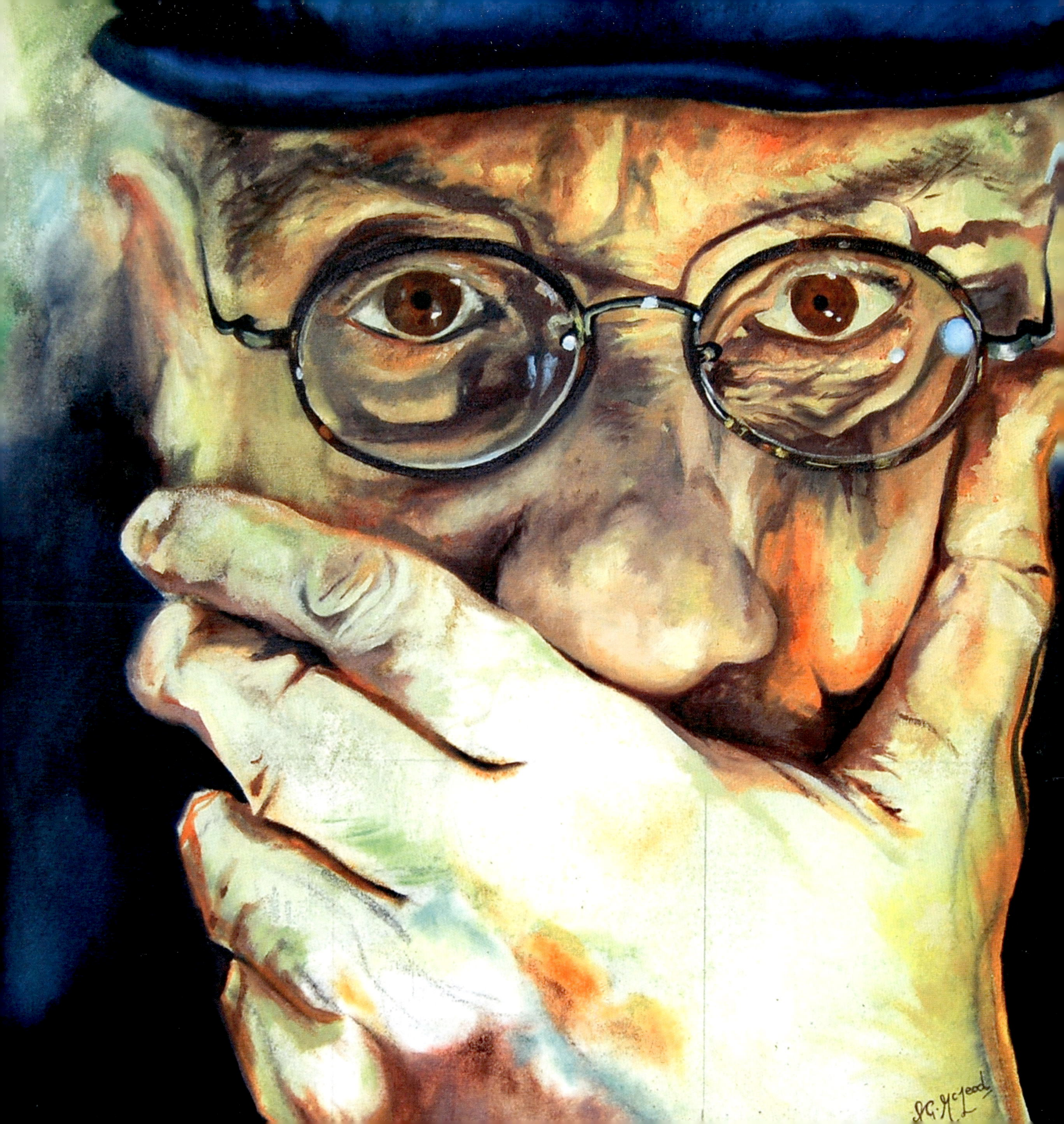

Richard Denne

Artist

This page: (clockwise from top) But for the Grace...; Butterfly Collector; Hi-lite; Find Your Way Home
Opposite page: To the Beach...

Richard Denne's work is both graphic and bold. Working within the Collage tradition he integrates emerging digital print process, such as photopolymer etching (21st-centrury Photogravure) with traditional processes to create mixed media work. Recently he has been working with other artists in collaborative projects and sharing his expertise as a printmaker to realise and edition their work.

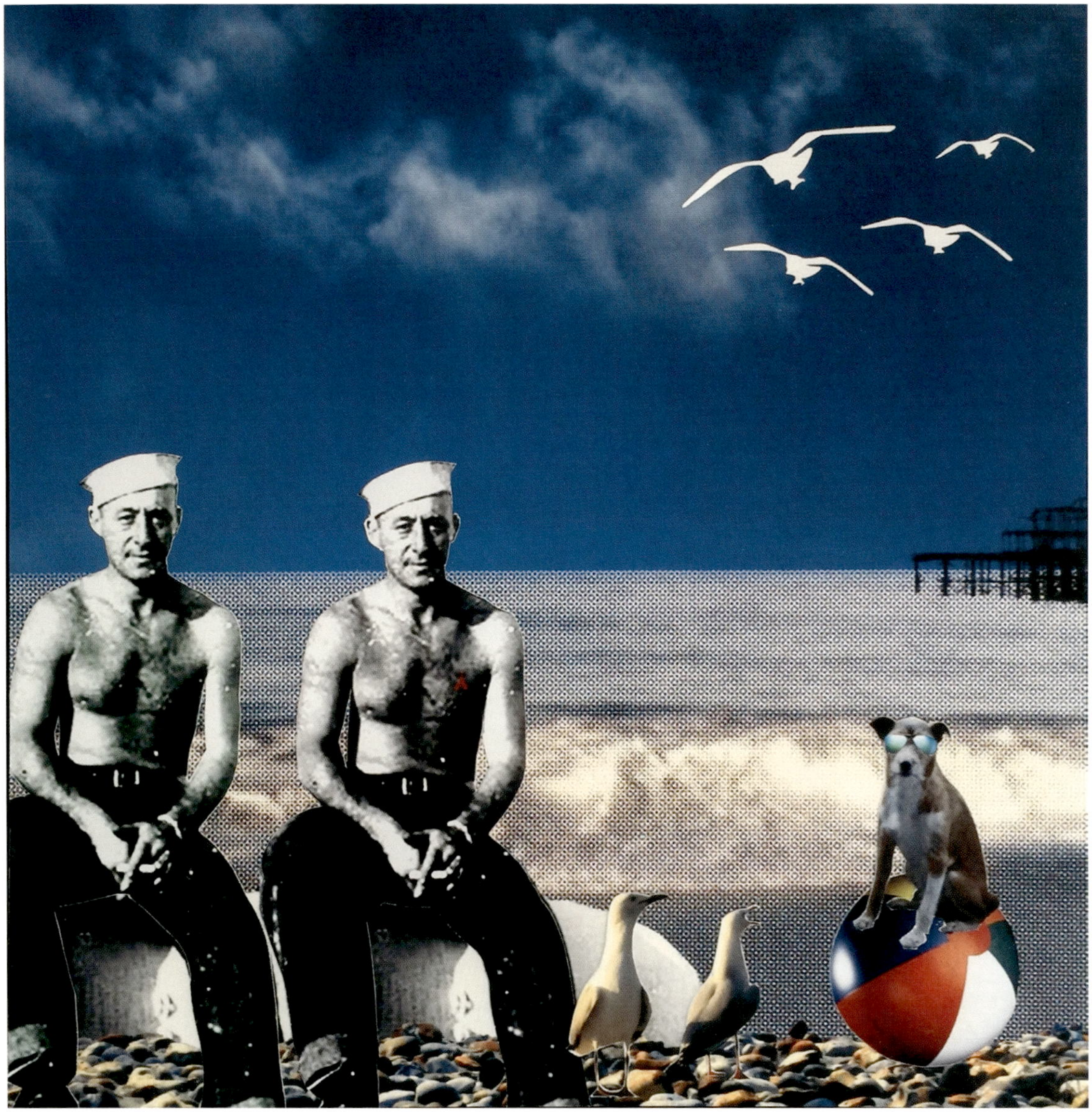

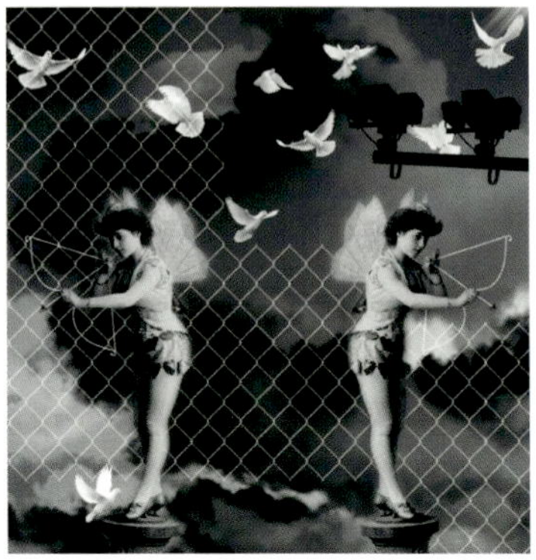

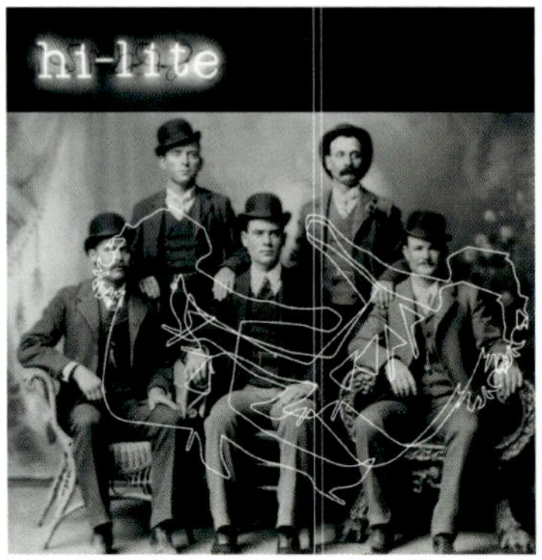

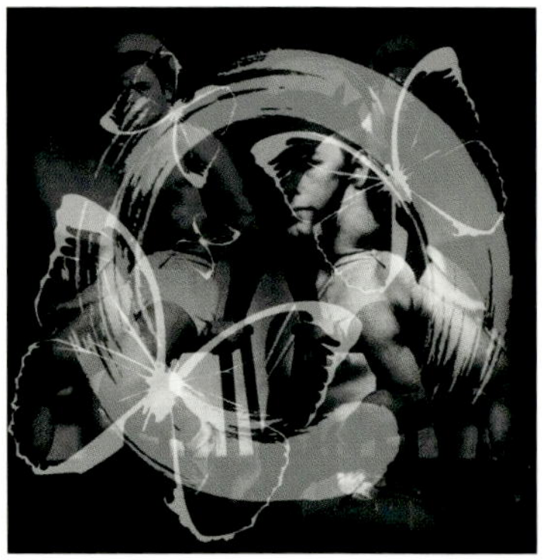

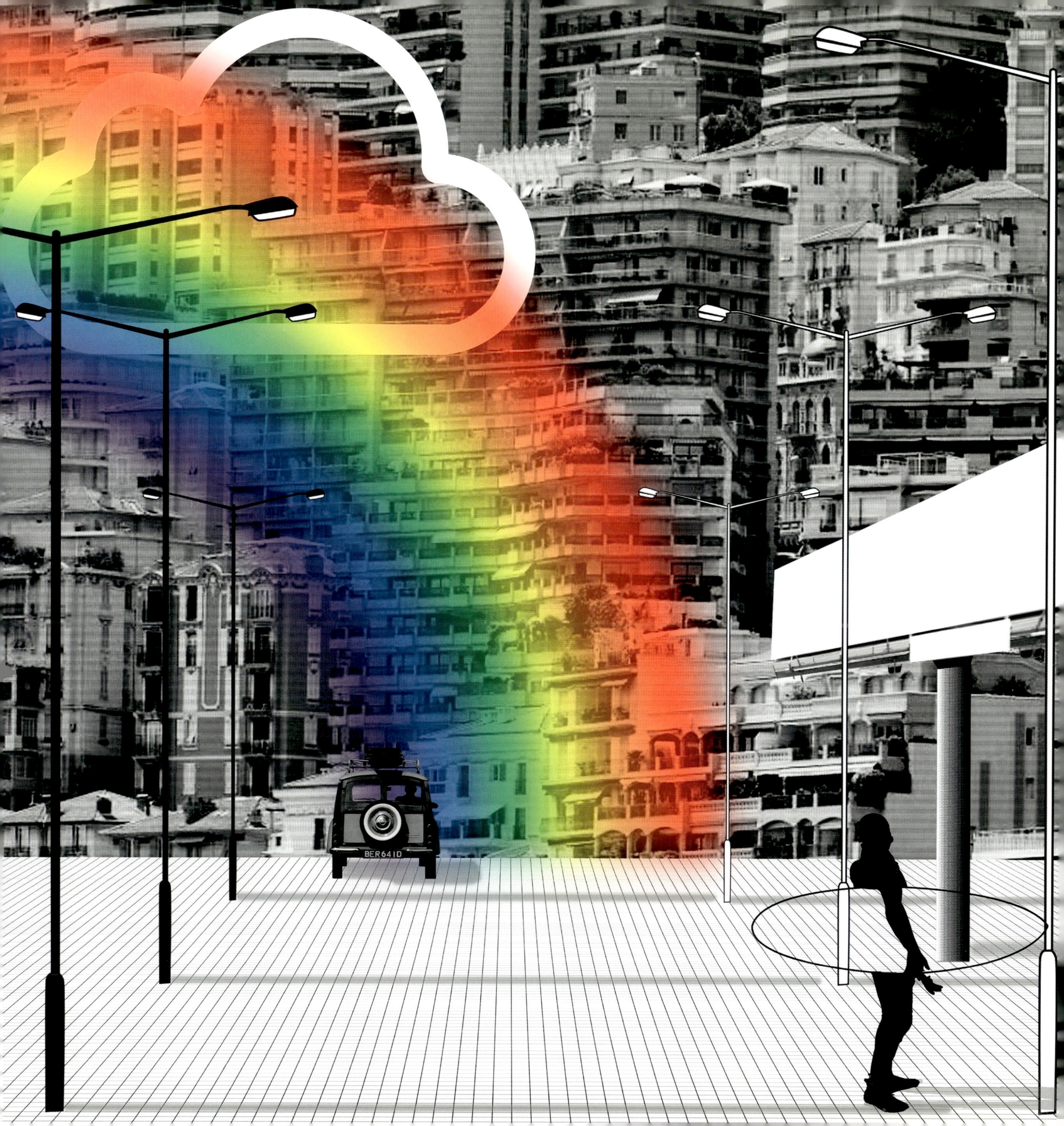
BER641D

Diane Rogers

Textile Artist, Designer & Painter

Clockwise from top left:
Entrada para Los Torros;
Sandy Rock Pool; Wall; Purple Craze

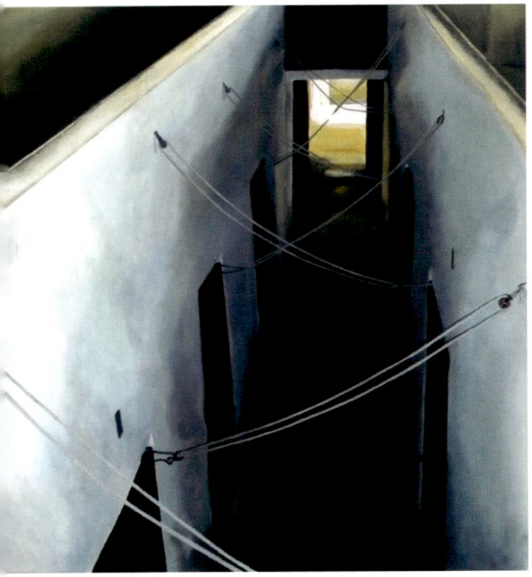

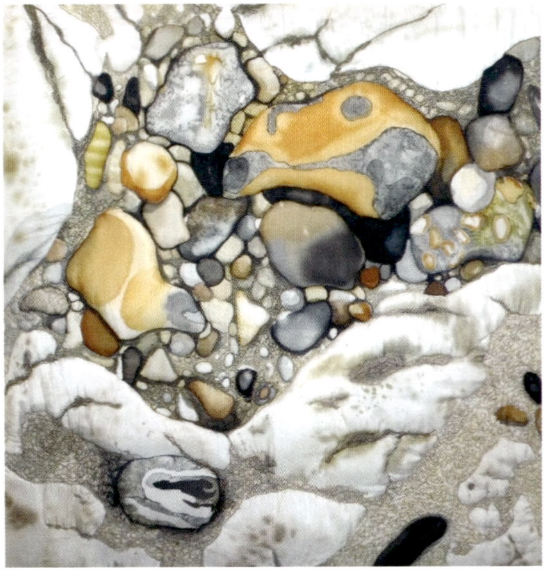

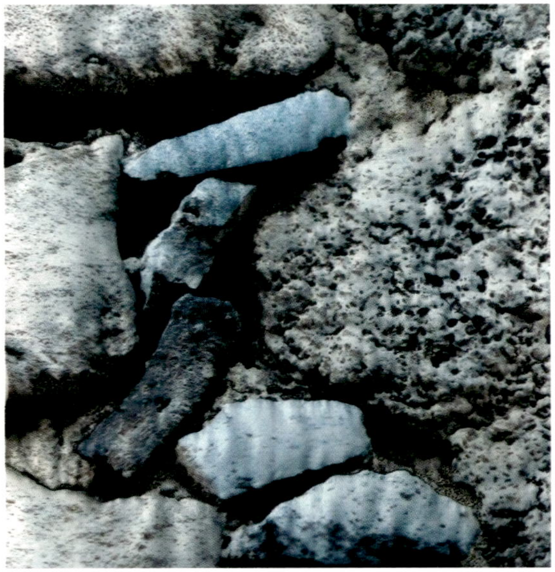

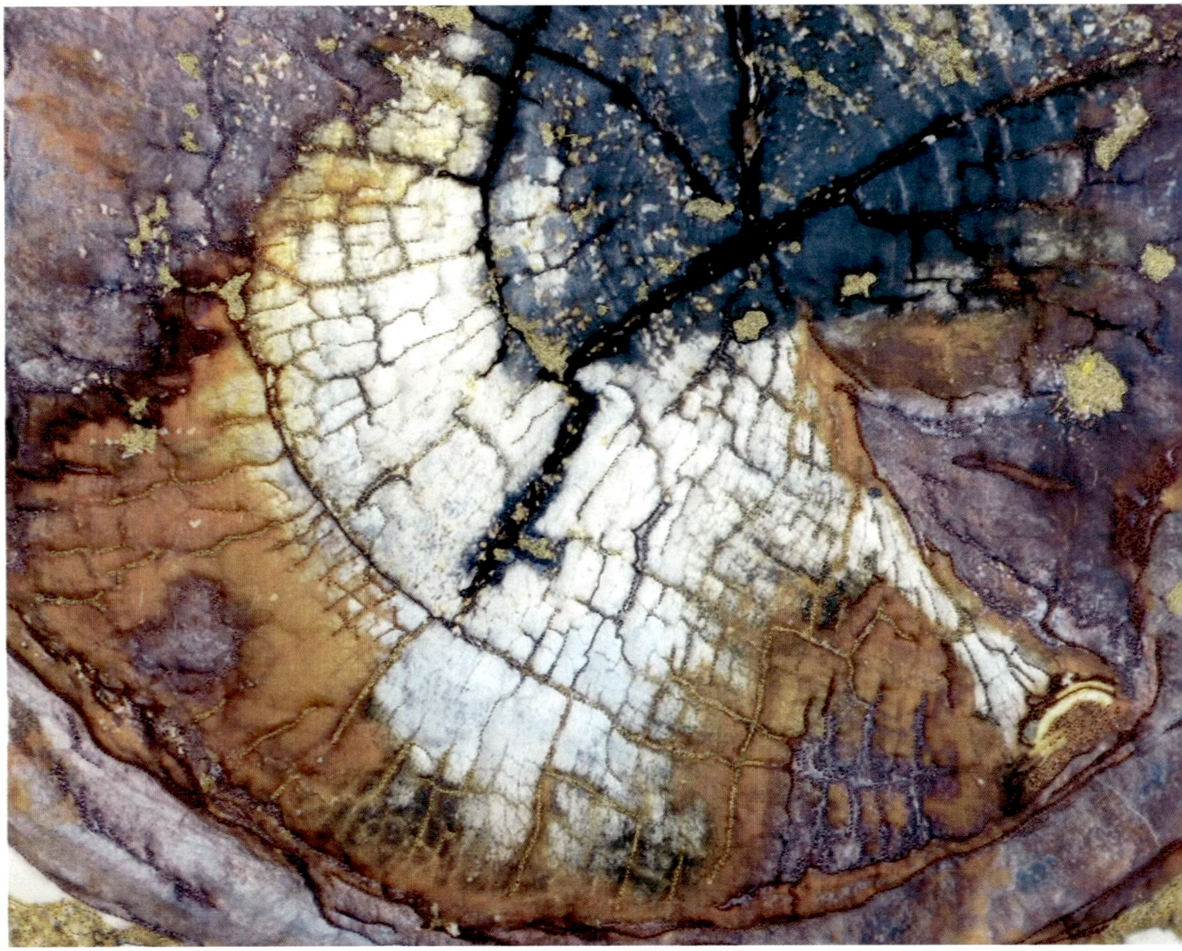

Diane Rogers is a textile artist, designer and painter. The inspiration for her textile art comes from nature and the environment.

Main themes are rich carpets of leaves, the gnarled, grainy texture of tree bark, the beach and its weathered structures, pebbles and rock pools. Images are hand-painted or printed onto silk, then quilted, embroidered and embellished by hand and free machine stitching. This creates texture and raised areas in relief, and gives a compelling, irresistible tactile quality to each piece. There is a fascinating discord between the smooth, lustrous qualities of silk as a medium and the subject matter.

Diane's acrylic paintings are inspired by neglected, decayed structures and facias of buildings. Exposure to the natural elements, can often reveal interesting surfaces, shapes, colours, textures and patterns.

Diane exhibits at art fairs and galleries in London and the South East. As a member of the Fiveways Artists Group, she holds an Open House exhibition during the Brighton Festival in May.

Sarah Jane Whittaker

Jewellery Designer-Maker

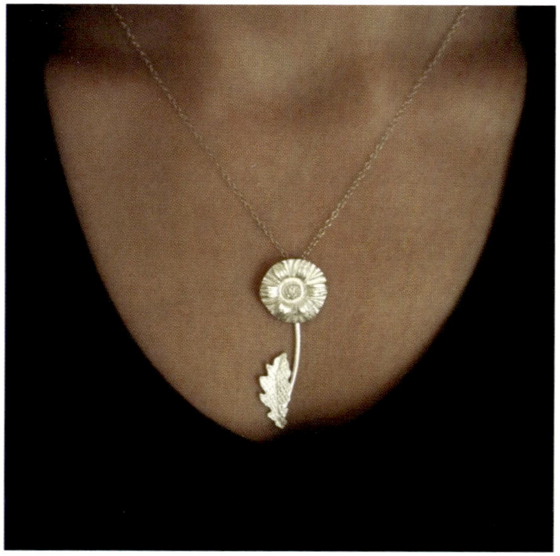

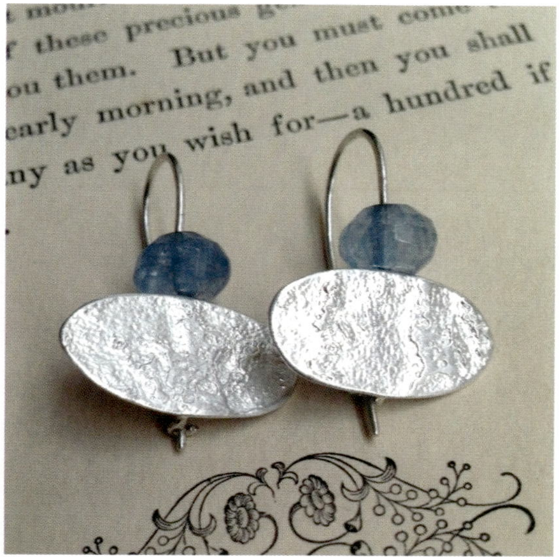

Sarah Jane Whittaker is a jewellery designer-maker and a silverwork tutor at the Sussex Jewellery School in Eastbourne. Combining traditional silver jewellery bench skills with casting and moulding, she seeks to interpret the plant-life, creatures and geology of the Sussex Downs in the form of affordable and beautiful wearable treasures.

Sarah Jane's studio jewellery is available to buy via carefully selected galleries including Cuckoo Cuckoo Contemporary Art & Craft Gallery in Hastings Old Town and The Green Tree Gallery in Haywards Heath. Her work is also available online via her website (www.sjwjewellery.com), or direct from her studio. Sarah Jane's newest jewellery ranges, for online retailer Not on the High Street, are being launched during 2014.

Reader offer: During 2014, *Brighton's Arty* readers can claim 15% off any purchase made in person at Sarah Jane's studio. Call or email for a no-obligation appointment, quoting code BrightonArty15.

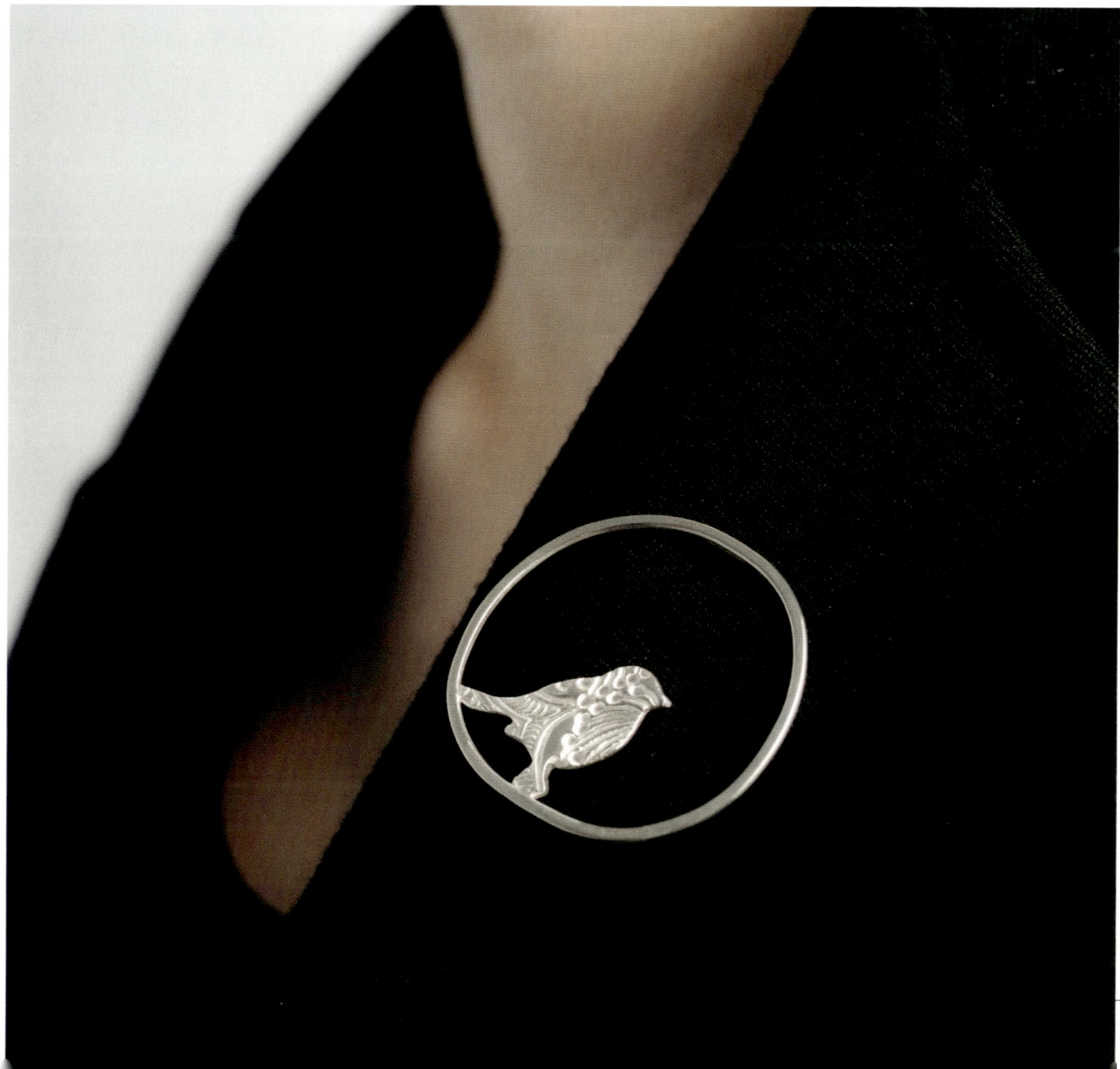

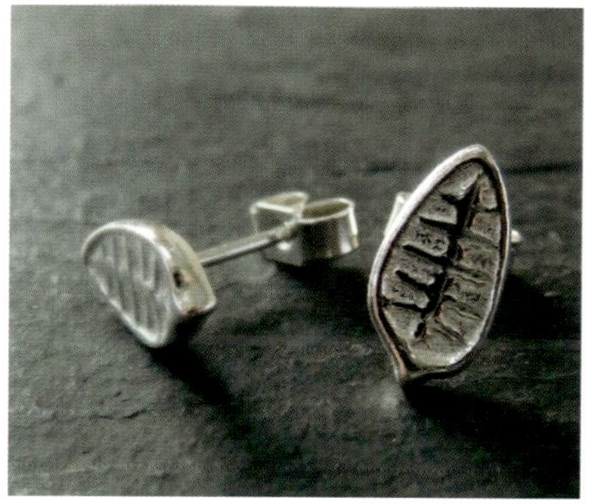

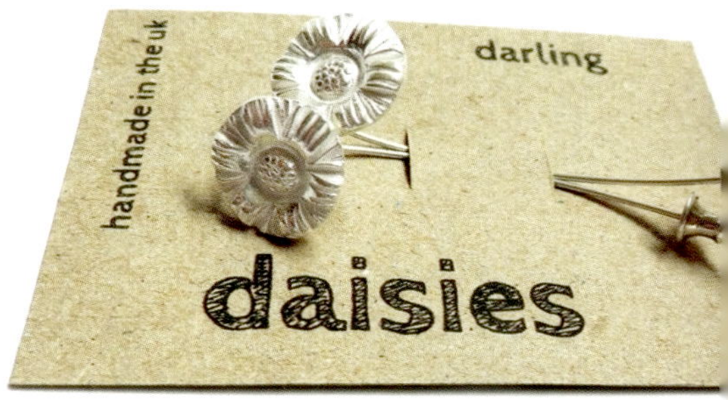

Simon Royer

Artist

Close Encounter (top); Gulls and Chip (bottom)

Simon Royer has exhibited work in both the Royal Society of Marine Artists (RSMA) and the Royal Society of Oil Painters (ROI) Annual Exhibitions at the Mall Galleries in London. He was a finalist in the prestigious 2013 BBC Wildlife art competition.

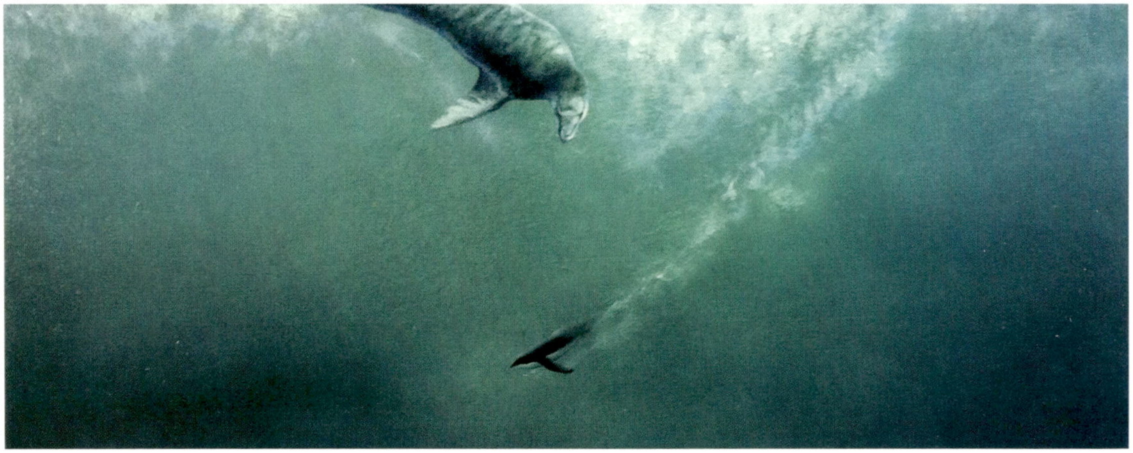

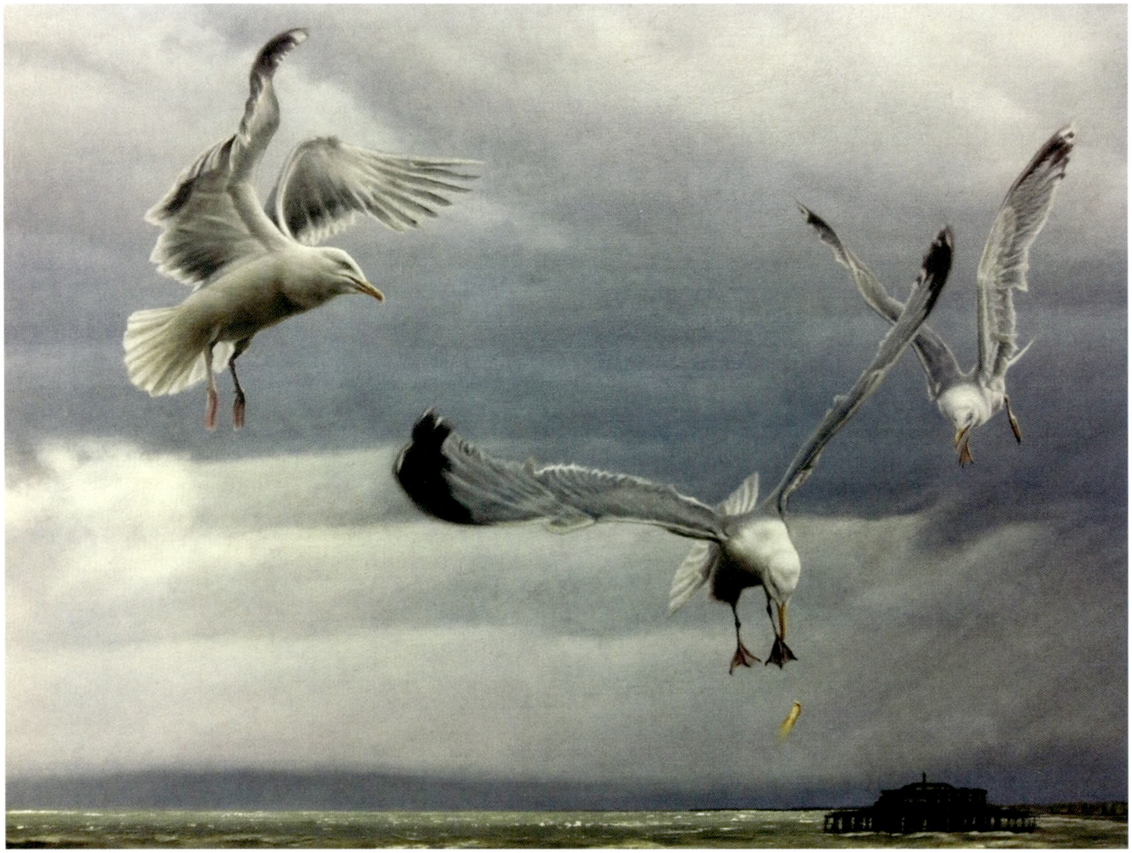

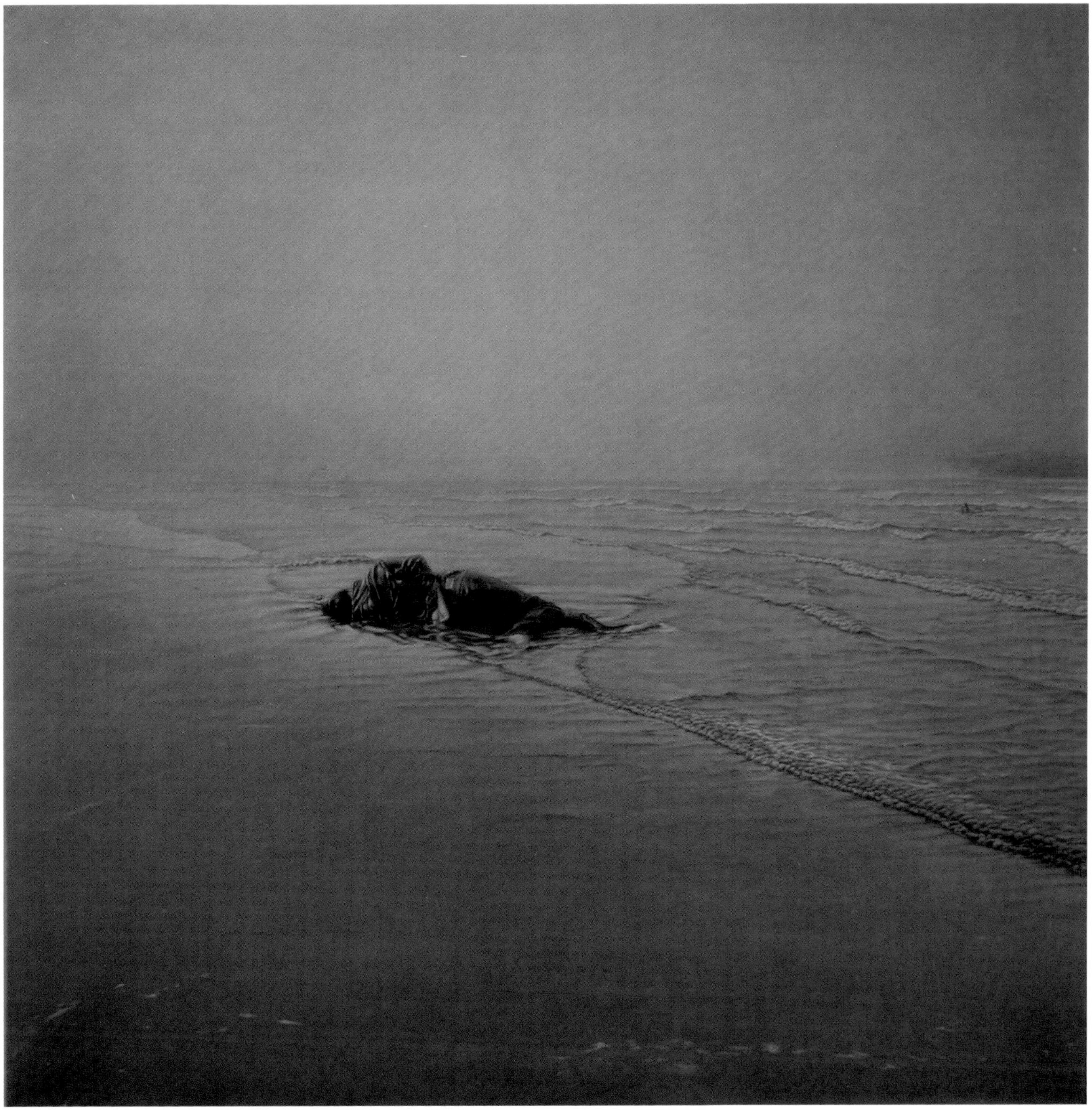

"The ghost of pleasures past captured in an iron skeleton that withstands the tides of time"

Louise Dear

Artist

Clockwise from top left:
YumYum; Alpha Romeo Commission;
Ooh My Daisy!; YumYum Too; True Romance

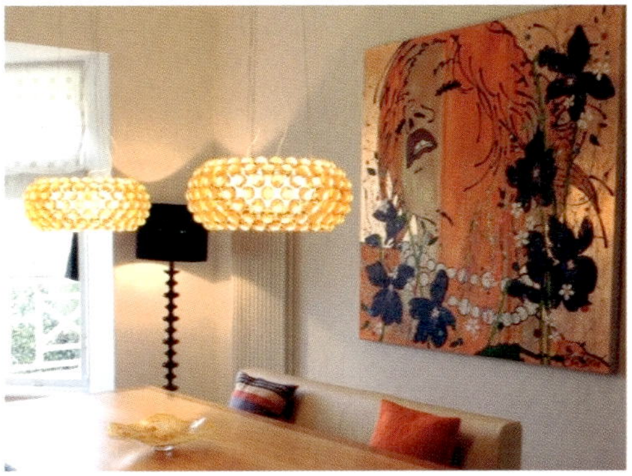

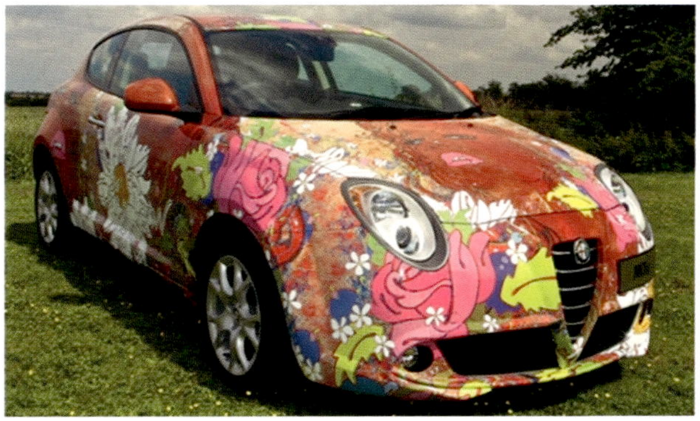

Louise Dear's paintings are a sumptuous feast. Seduction is her aim, and her works skillfully demand that the audience experiences the delight with which they were created. These neo-pop infused works are expertly fashioned using a multitude of media: golds, glitters and glosses layered on large panels of distressed aluminum. Lavish, richly textured figures are sensually erotic, luminous and powerful, overlaid with flowers and frivolity that entice and seduce. In some, elements of nostalgic kitsch emerge and storybook-beautiful children – their unique spirits captured – secure tender moments; snatches of childhood memory.

Louise's works are addictive, and many of her collectors become obsessed with surrounding themselves with the pure pleasure they portray. Having been exhibited extensively, these vibrant paintings have sparked the interest of several major museums and are held in numerous collections including those of Rick Stein, Qatar Holdings (the owners of Harrods) and Sir Elton John.

After a decade in Devon, Louise has recently returned to Brighton and set up her workshop at Vine Street Studios in the North Laine.

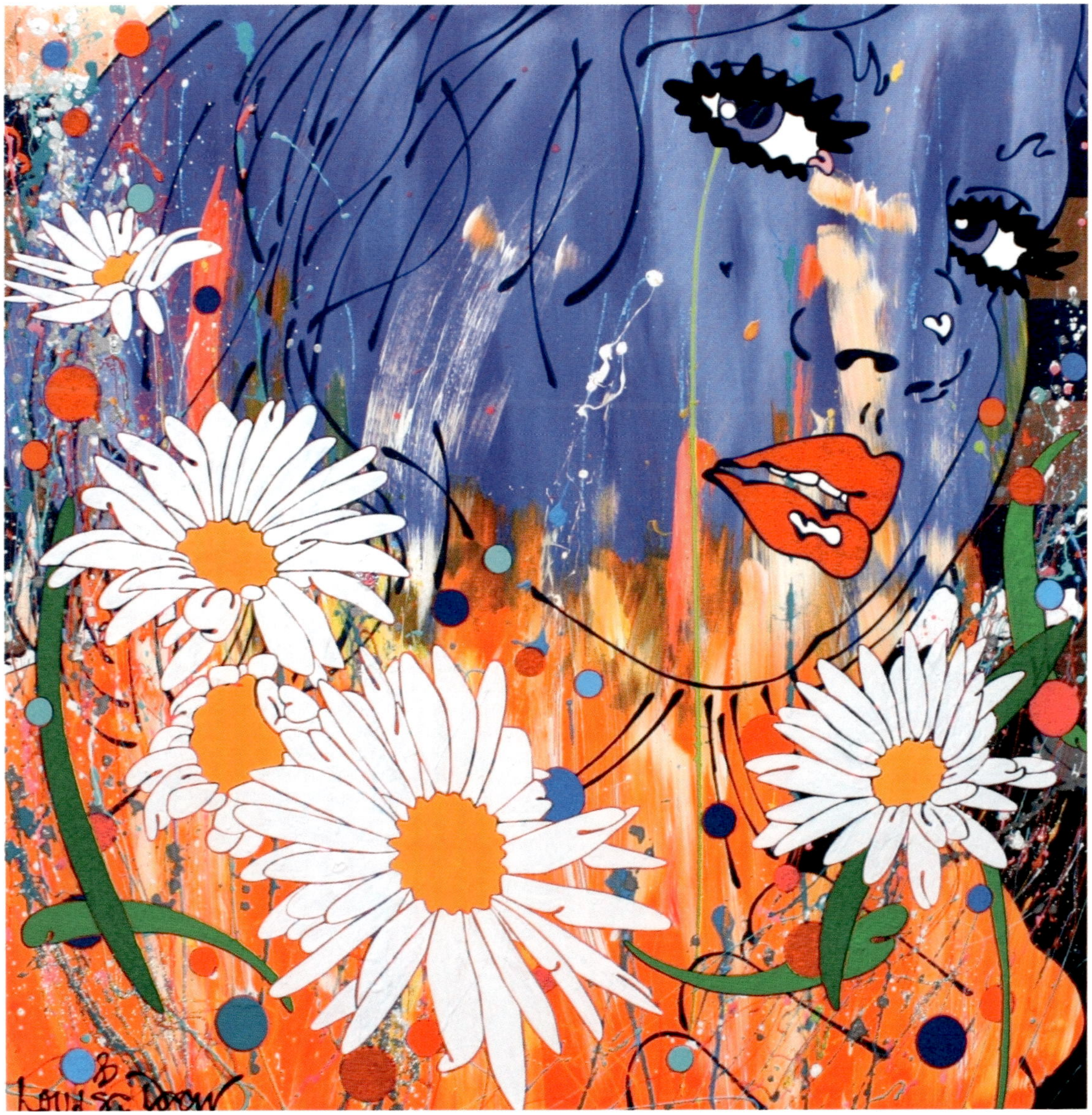

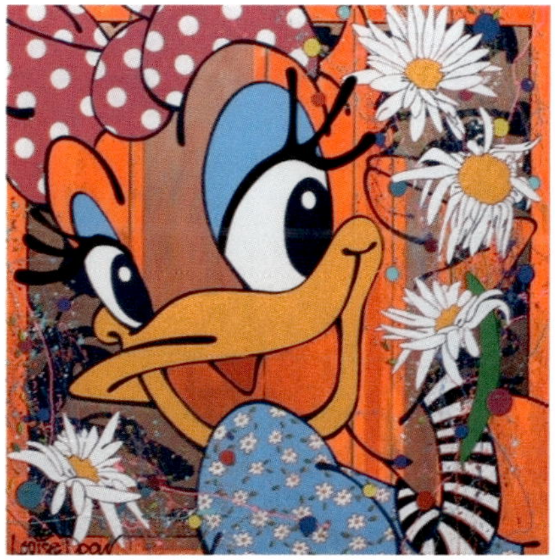

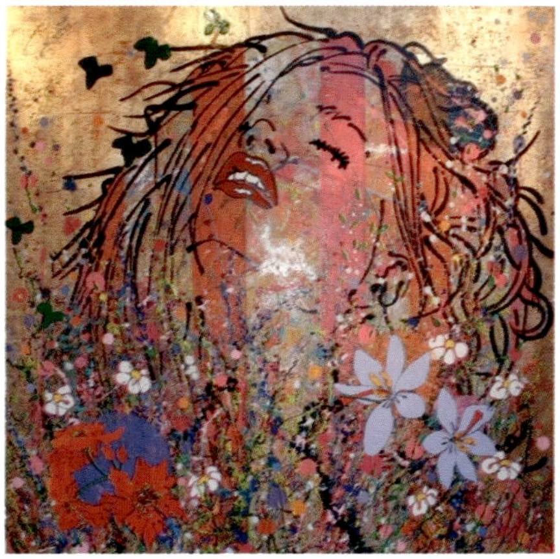

Galleries

The pleasure of buying art is enhanced by the warm welcome you'll experience when you step into any of Brighton's galleries or art spaces.

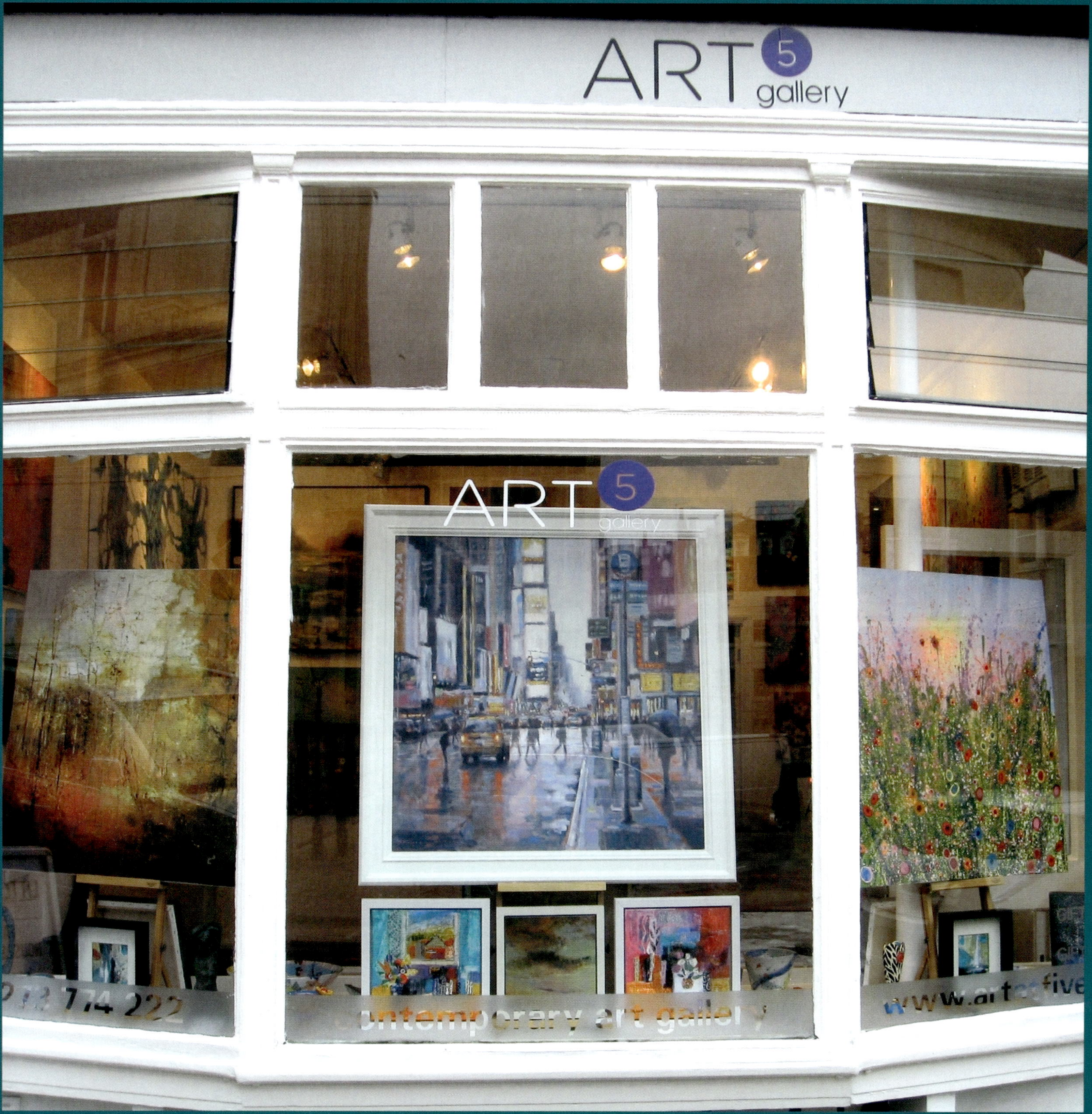

Art5 Gallery

Brighton's Arty Gallery Guide

Brighton's wonderful variety of independent galleries defies all preconceptions of intimidating spaces where only the serious collector is welcome. Warm and friendly – and in all shapes and sizes – many are also artist-run, which makes the experience of your visit all the more rewarding. Here's a tour of some of our favourites.

Off Western Road

Tucked away in Farm Mews, *Naked Eye* provides the blank canvas for a variety of shows throughout the year and is a staunch supporter of local artists such as Ian Hodgson (page 19), James Fenner and James Hunter. Owner David Donno also offers a bespoke framing service here.

For a very different visual experience, head towards the town centre along Upper North Street and down into the basement at *Magnum Opus* where Phil Kyle and the MOT crew host some astounding examples of the world's greatest tattoo art.

Along the seafront

Down on King's Road Arches *Two Kats and a Cow* is one of the city's oldest and most successful galleries, now run by Katty McMurray and Kathryn Matthews, and featuring the work of John Marshall. Kathryn's vibrant coastal scenes, the clean lines and gentle palette of Katty's everyday scenes and John's remarkable, idiosyncratic cows complement the space perfectly.

Towards Brighton Pier, opposite the merry-go-round, a much newer entrant on the gallery scene is *Naughty Pirates*, with a whimsical selection of images, mounts and hand-enhanced prints by Heidi Jane Rhodes (page 55), Katja Dell (page 100) and manager Stephen J Connett.

Carry on under the Pier to *Simon Royer's Art Gallery* (page 116), where his remarkable seascapes are just some of the artwork inspired by natural history. Then further along you'll find a vibrant collection of eclectic talents at *JAG Open Studios & Gallery* on Madeira Drive. You can watch work being created or commission something from resident artists who include founder Julie Anne Gilbert, Jacqueline Hammond (page 13), Eve Poland (page 59) and Susan Taylor (page 42).

South Lanes and city centre

Bellis (page 132) is Latin for daisy and perfectly captures the simple elegance of this light, airy gallery on Kings Road. The sense of harmony created by the keen curatorial eye of owner Sema Ugur is all the more remarkable considering the variety of textiles, ceramics, jewellery and artwork on show. And if you love our cover artwork by Harriet Butler (page 106), you'll find her prints on permanent display here.

Just moments away on Bartholomews, *Art5 Gallery* (page 127) represents a diverse selection of national and international artists ranging from the evocative oil paintings of Lisa Ridgers (page 84) to the sparkling flowerscapes of Yvonne Coomber. Owner Paola Calise also offers a free home and business art consultancy.

North Laine

At *artrepublic* on Bond Street, indulge in one of the UK's largest collections of cutting-edge, signed, limited-edition art by legendary British artists such as Sir Peter Blake, Banksy, Damien Hirst plus artists rapidly building their reputations including Dave White, Pure Evil and Magnus Gjoen.

There's more challenging and exciting contemporary art in the quirky and intimate artspace that's *ink_d Gallery* on North Road. Ink_d curates eight exhibitions a year, and upstairs its permanent gallery shop is packed with unusual artist-made products, books and artzines.

On Church Street you'll find *Unlimited* (page 134), an independent design shop and gallery that is run alongside their graphic design studio. It showcases unique and affordable artwork, textiles, jewellery and homeware from a wide range of talented contemporary illustrators, designers and makers.

On Sydney Street at *iO Gallery* (page 124), the eclectic mix of over 100 local designer-makers and artists, such as Heike Roesel (page 38), is carefully curated and with its fortnightly mini-exhibitions there is always a new reason to visit.

Then round at Gloucester Road, there's a hub of creative activity emerging thanks to Peter Leafe's pop-up initiative *Gallery40* (page 126), hosting a programme of temporary shows on the corner of Foundry Street. Opposite, *White Rabbit Gallery* shows the work of glass-blower John King, while the recently established *Art Schism* co-operative and collective has transformed the corner of Kemp Street into an ever-changing work of graffiti art in itself.

Hove

If you're looking to get plastered, over in Hove's hottest artist studios, just by the station, sculptor Jamie McCartney is waiting to immortalise your body parts at *Brighton Body Casting*. Faces, hands, boobs, bums, torsos or complete body moulds can be cast into unique personal sculptures in anything from plaster to bronze or glass.

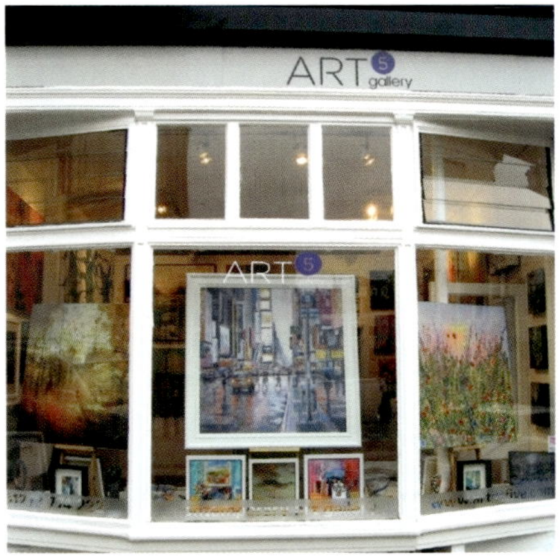

Art5, Bartholomews

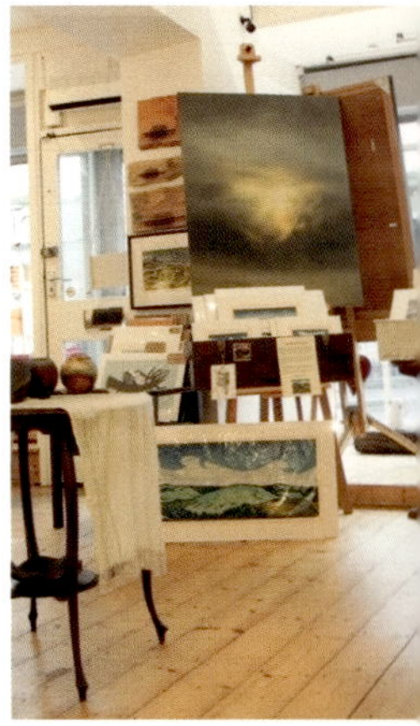
Bellis, Kings Road

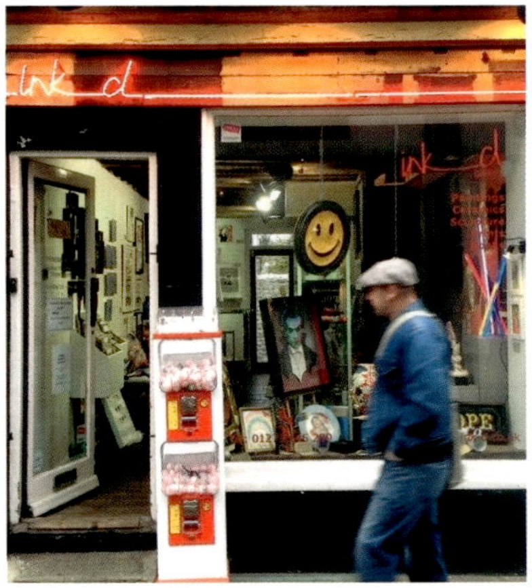
Ink_d, North Road

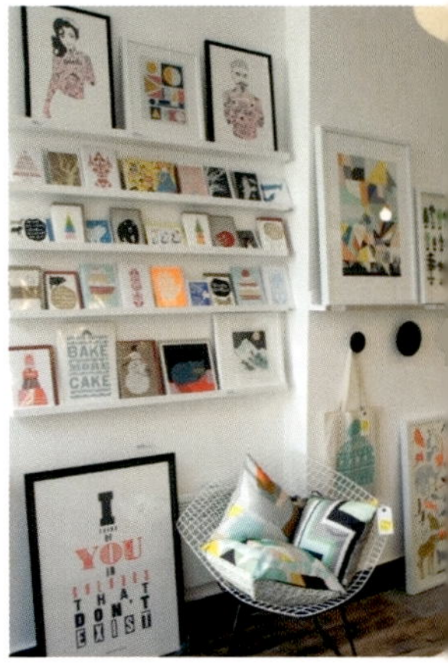
Unlimited, Church Street

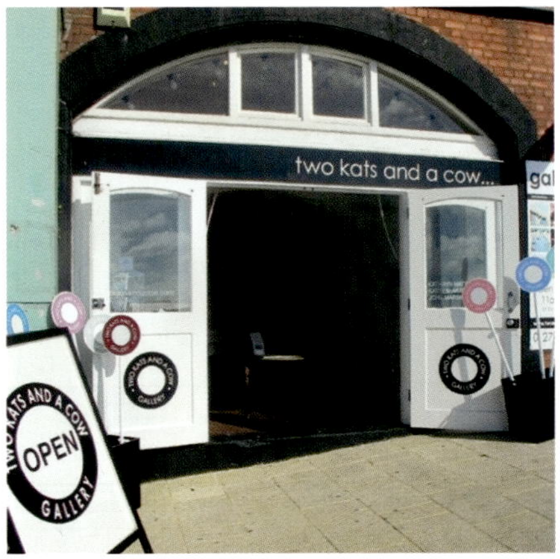

Two Kats & a Cow, King's Road Arches

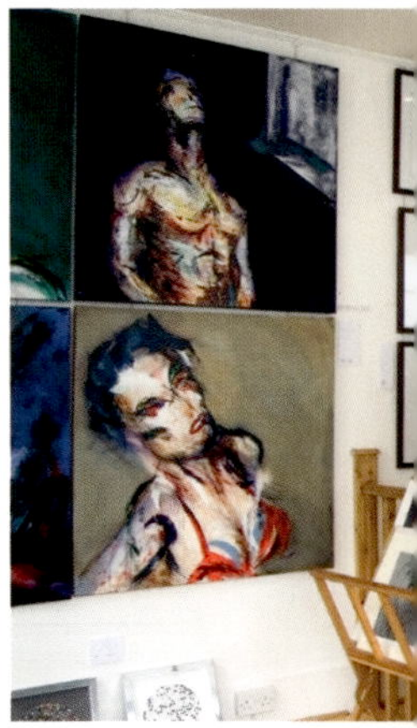
Gallery40, Goucester Road

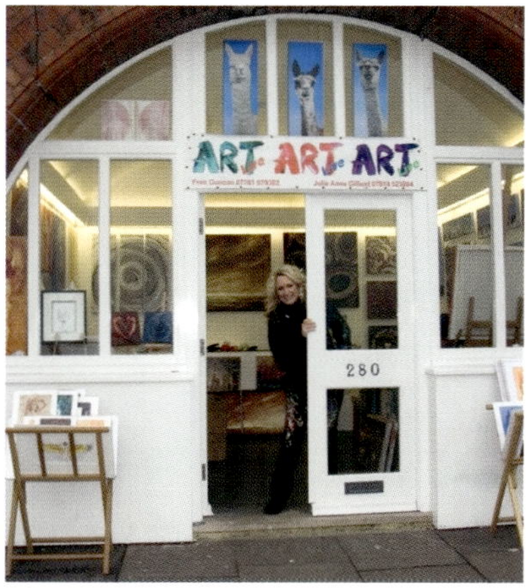

JAG, Madeira Drive

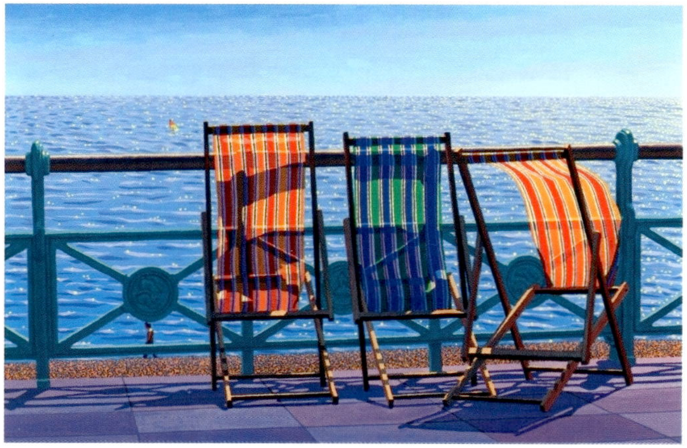
The Window Gallery, Ditchling

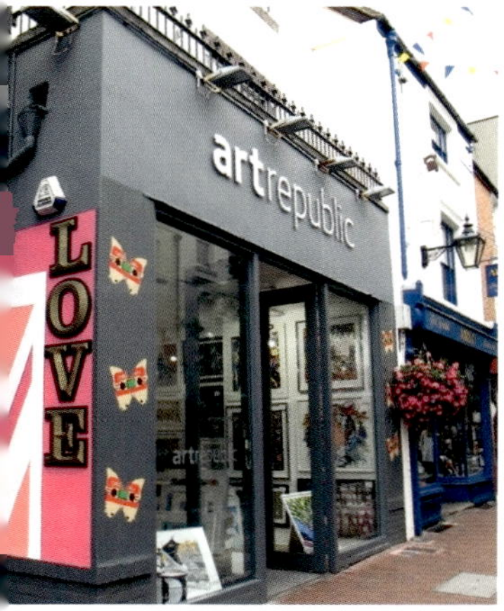

artrepublic, Bond Street

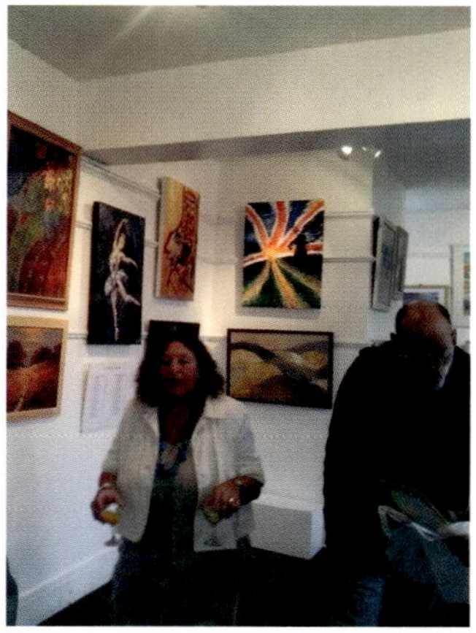
The Grange, Rottingdean

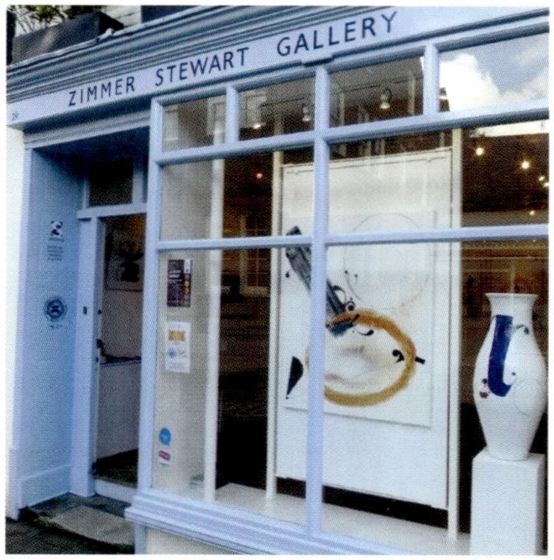

Zimmer Stewart Gallery, Arundel

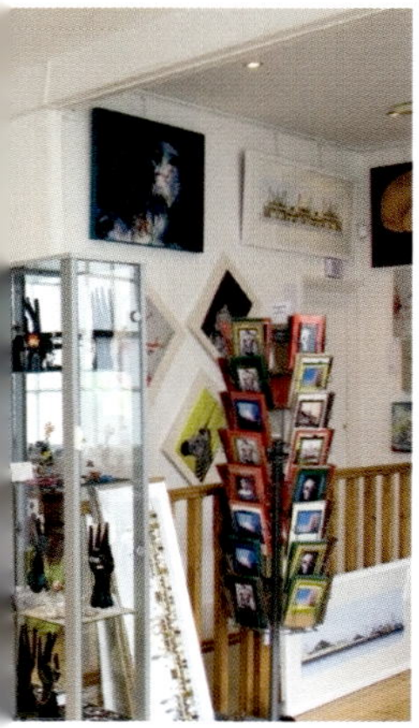

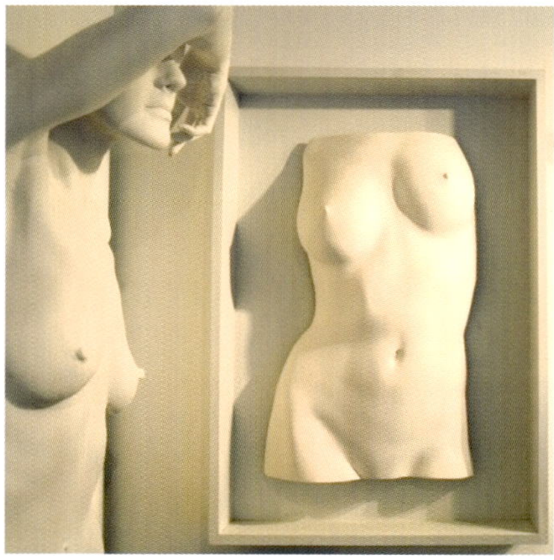
Brighton Body Casting, Hove

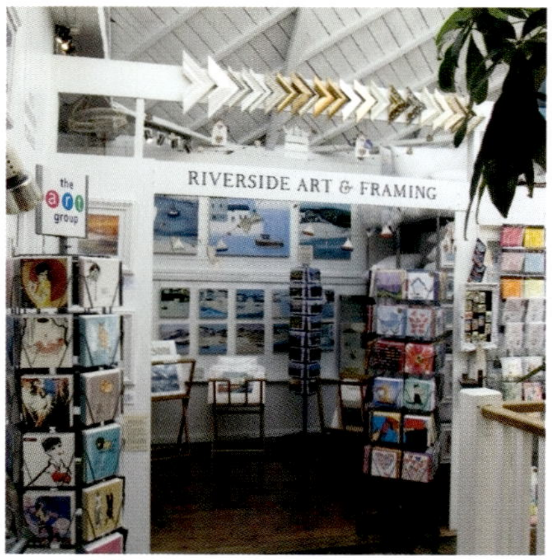

Riverside Art & Framing, Lewes

Arundel

Zimmer Stewart Gallery (page 128)

James Stewart and John Zimmer believe artists want their work to be seen by as many people as possible, so browsers are always welcome to this delightful, welcoming gallery on Tarrant Street exhibiting paintings, original prints, ceramics, sculpture and mixed media works.

Ditchling

The Window Gallery

Home to one of Brighton's best-loved artists, Philip Dunn, and his evocative and vibrant paintings, prints, and giclee reproductions – with and without the deckchairs for which he is renowned. Plus an eclectic exhibition of other works of art and craft.

Lewes

Chalk Gallery (page 136)

This friendly gallery in North Street is run by a collective of artists, so you can expect a warm welcome and well-informed advice. A featured artist is showcased every three weeks with a re-hanging of approximately 80 works every six weeks.

Hop Gallery (page 130)

In the 18th-century Star Brewery in Castle Ditch Lane, Hop runs an exciting programme of visual art exhibtions. The Mohamed Hamid Pottery is also housed in the brewery building, where you can watch the artists at work.

Riverside Art & Framing

Located upstairs in the Riverside Shopping Hall on Cliffe Street, here you'll find key pieces by local artist Liz Jameson, known for her 'Turneresque' painting style; the distinctive woodcut prints of Helen Brown depicting Downs scenes; and a quirky range of gifts.

Rottingdean

The Grange Art Gallery & Museum

Once the home of artists Sir William Nicholson and his son Ben Nicholson, this elegant Georgian house by the village green, has a bright and spacious gallery for contemporary artists to hire. Contact The Rottingdean Preservation Society.

Shoreham-by-Sea

Shoreham Gallery

Run by a collective of talented local artists, Shoreham Gallery promises 'art from the heart' on Brunswick Road. The diverse selection on display includes oil paintings, watercolours, photography, sculptures, jewellery, ceramics, wood, glass, textiles and mosaics.

iO Gallery

Brighton Designers & Makers Ltd, 39 Sydney Street, BN1 4EP

iO Gallery was established in 1997 and is situated in the heart of Brighton's vibrant North Laine. The majority of its eclectic and contemporary range of art and craft is produced by local designer-makers. iO collaborates with artists across a wide spectrum of practices, and exhibits a fine selection of ceramics, glassworks, mirrors and lighting, and a gorgeous array of both silver and mixed-media jewellery. The gallery also has an inspiring mixture of limited-edition prints, paintings and other wall-mounted pieces in its downstairs space.

Hundreds of commissions have been arranged over the years, and iO Gallery will happily organise special one-off pieces of artwork for customers wherever possible. Fresh new work is regularly displayed in the window – as a series of fortnightly mini exhibitions – and iO delights in allocating some of the gallery space to a variety of new and guest artists. Full details of new exhibits are regularly updated on the gallery's new Facebook page.

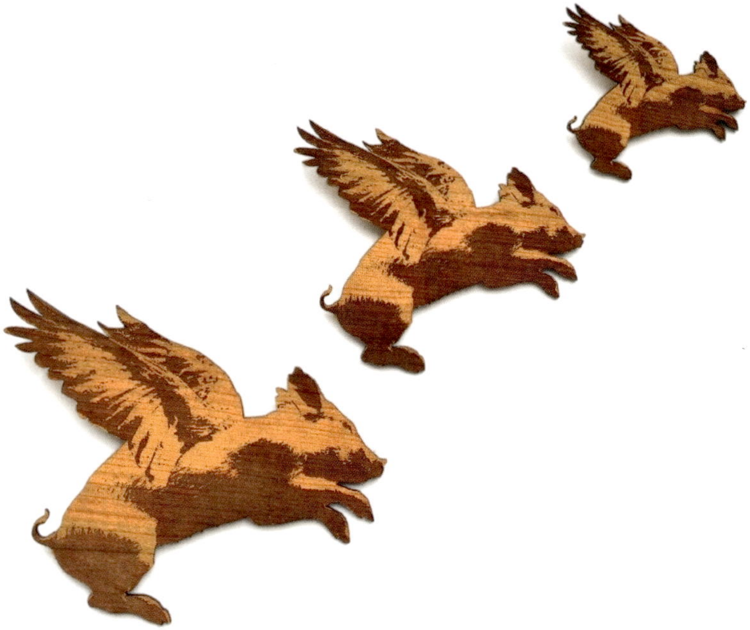

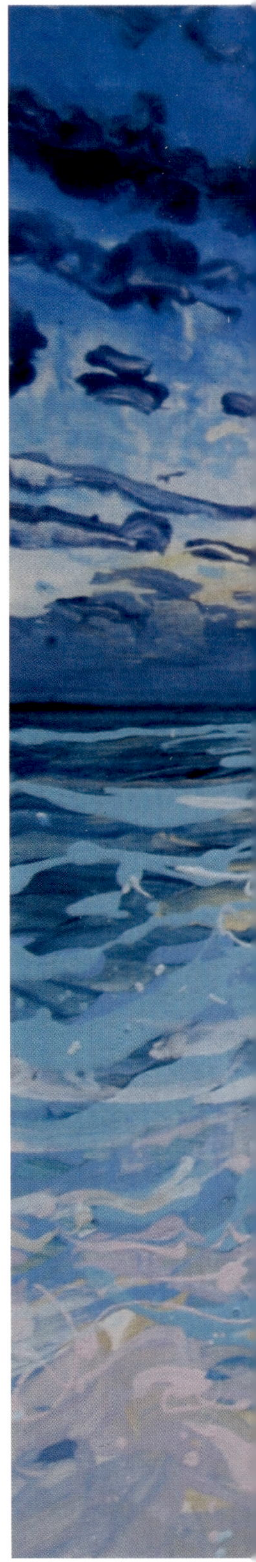

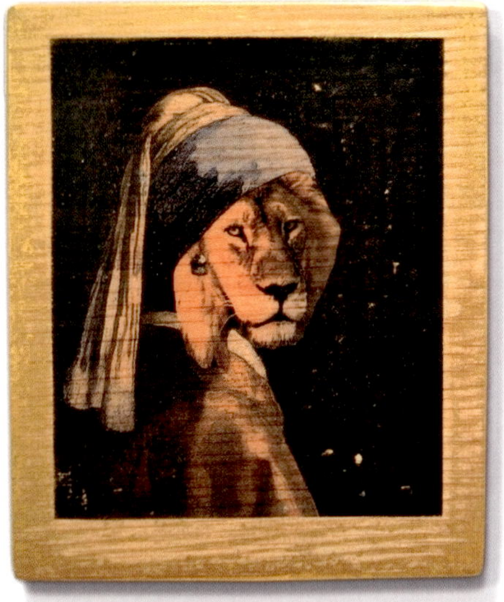

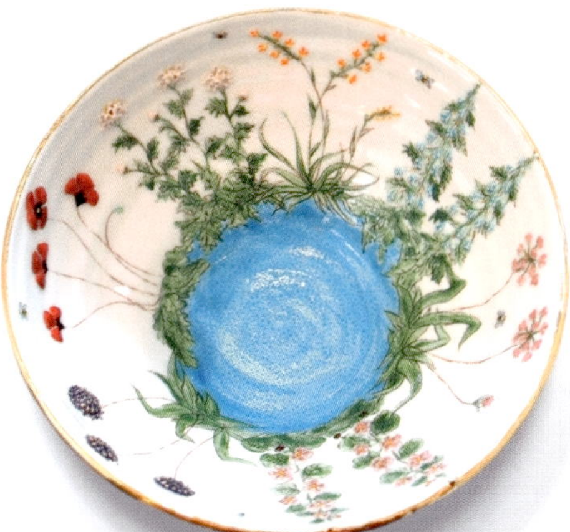

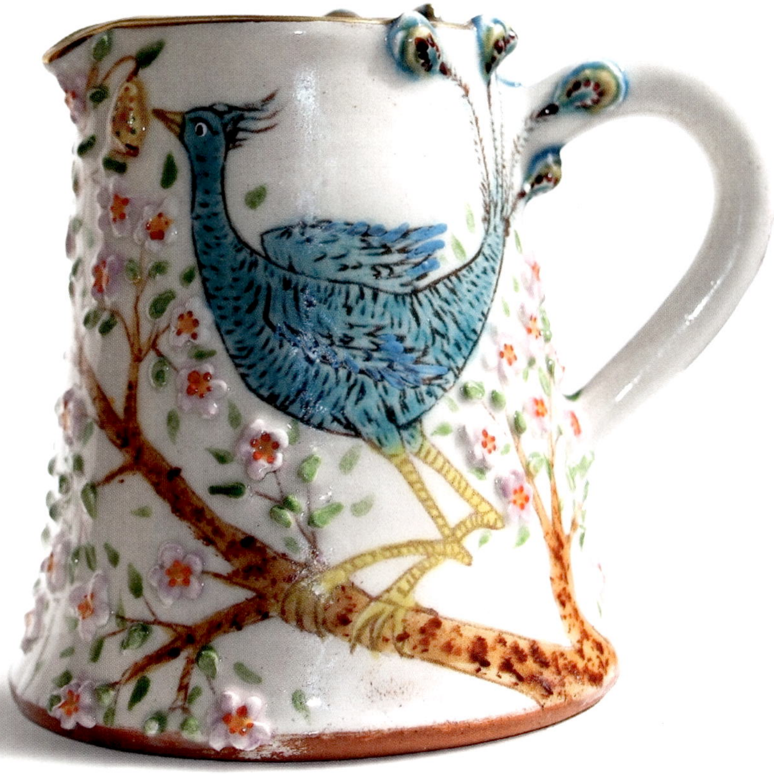

This page: Beautiful Morning, Tania Corbett
Opposite page (clockwise from top): Flying Pigs, Cath Laffan; Big Bird jug, Stacey Manser Knight; In the Garden ceramic dish, Stacey Manser Knight; Lion with a Pearl Earring, Cath Laffan

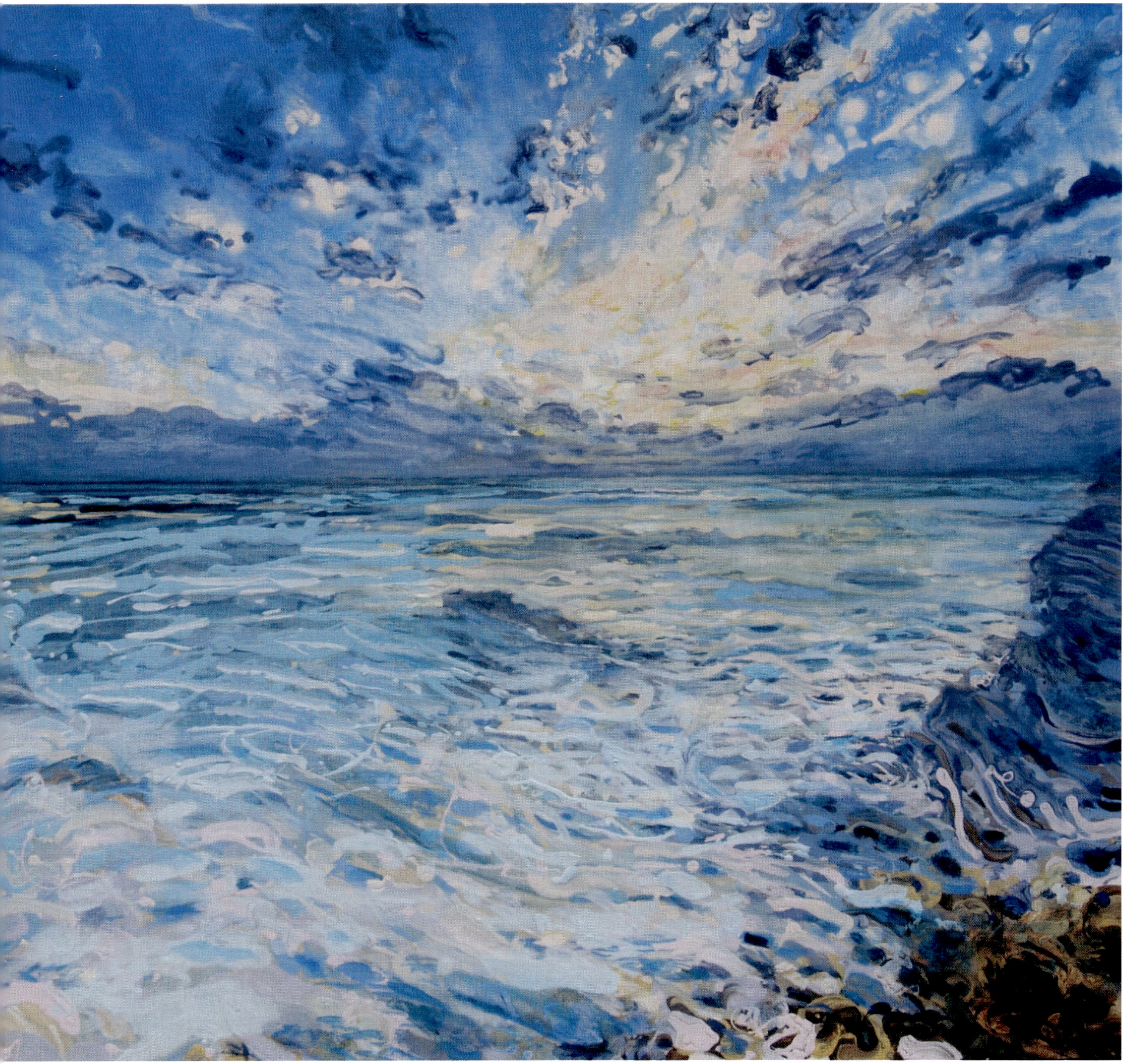

Gallery40

40 Gloucester Road, Brighton BN1 4AQ

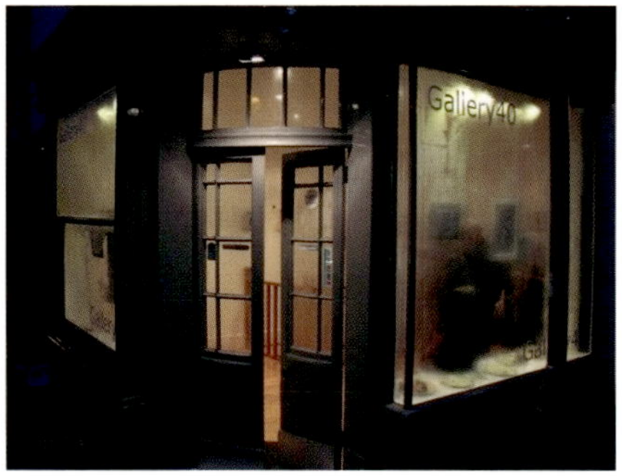

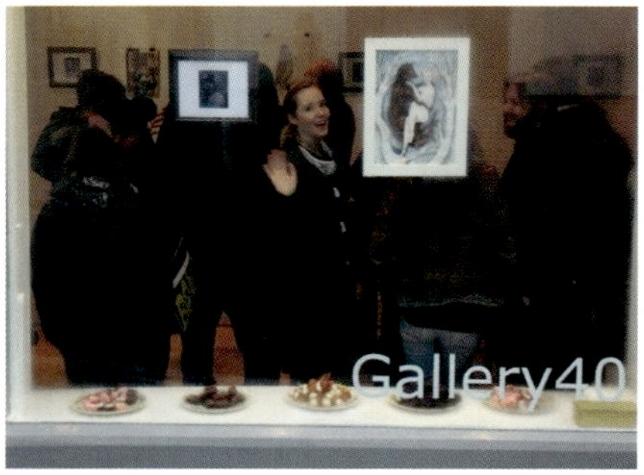

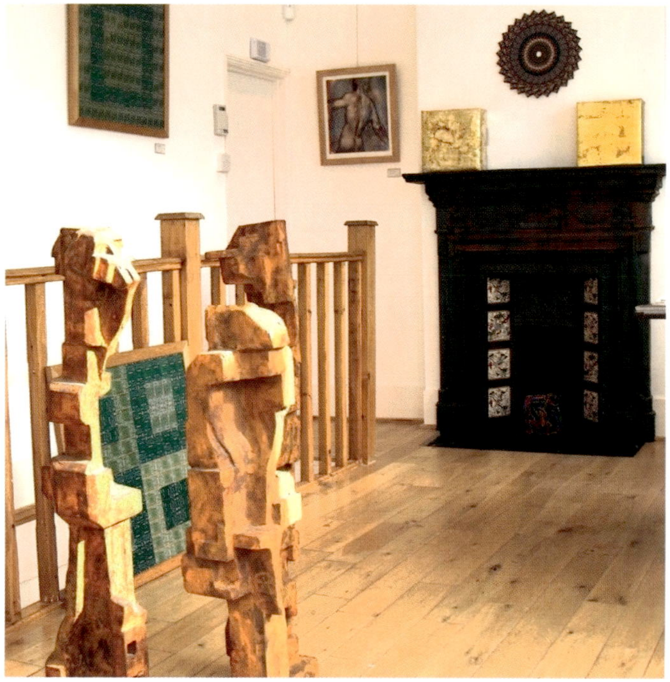

In the popular North Laine, Gloucester Road continues to rise as a vibrant destination for art lovers thanks to its eclectic mix of galleries and shops. If you're in the area, a 'must visit' is Gallery40, which provides two floors in a well-lit space with plenty of natural light – and is looking even better for 2014 thanks to its recent exterior refurbishment and redecoration with new branding and illuminated signage.

Providing a space to showcase local East Sussex artists is extremely important to Gallery40, and throughout its annual pop-up programme, work in disciplines as varied as painting, photography, sculpture, stone carving, performance art and installations add to its unique feel. Owners Pete and Rich are also keen to continue their relationship with new and emerging artists from Brighton University (check Gallery40's website for more details).

As Gallery40 enters its third successful year, Pete and Rich would like to thank the exhibitors and returning artists who give so much support to making this unique pop-up art and event space what it is.

In June, Tim Patrick returned to showcase new works in another successful summer exhibition '*Something, Elsewhere*'. It was great to experience his new work and for visitors to meet the artist and discuss his work. Also returning to Gallery40 were Jake Spicer and the DRAW team who exhibit regularly and whose students have the opportunity to showcase their work in an end-of-year '*Atelier*' exhibition.

This year Gallery40 is looking forward to the Brighton Festival and Artists Open Houses, with five different exhibitors during this period. Another highlight will be the autumn Photo Biennial, which is booking up fast.

At the time of going to press, 11 artists new to Gallery40 are booked to exhibit this year, as well as returning artists who have held pop-up shows here before.

Keep up to date with what's happening at this unique space on Twitter @gallery40. You'll find information about hiring and availability on its website (see index page 150).

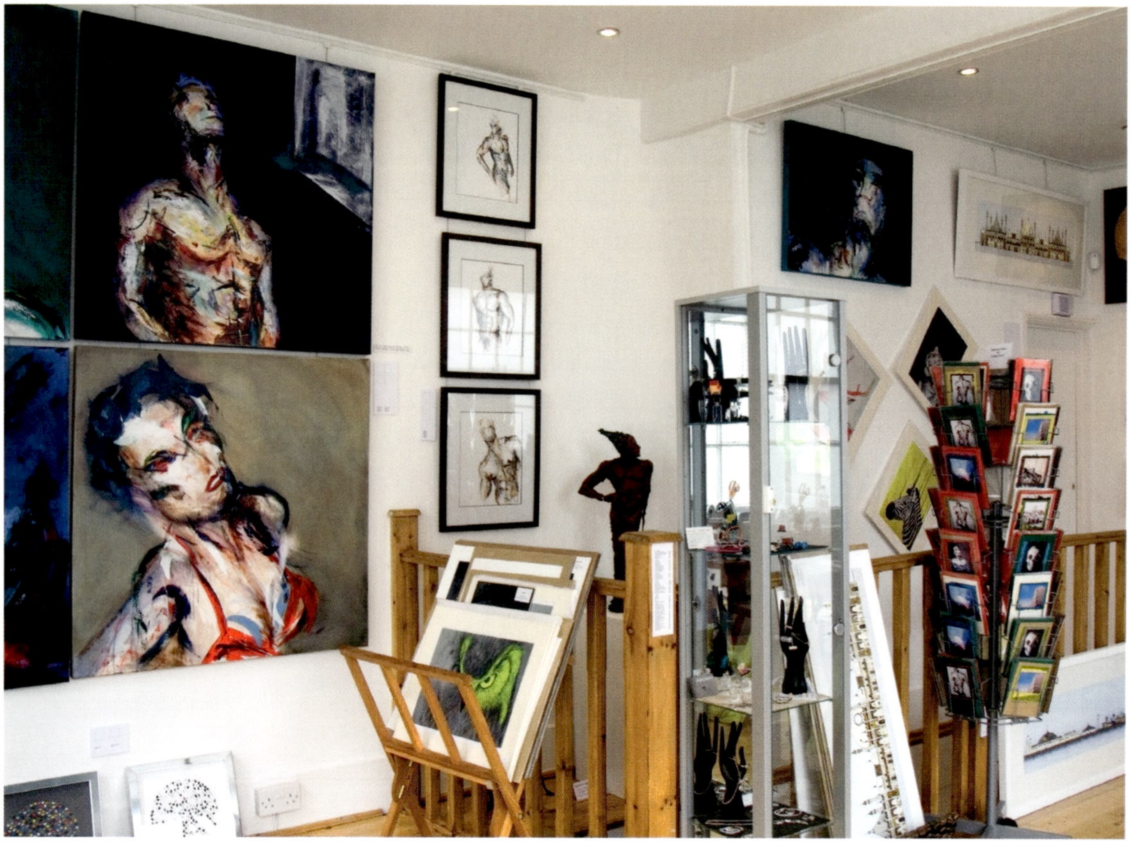

Clockwise from top left:
Rose Quartz Bay, My Sweetest Darling, Sidewalk Reflections towards Times Square, Forest Clearing, Art5 Gallery (from outside and inside), Let's go to the Beach-Kefalonia, Flowing into the Wild and Wonderful

Art5 Gallery

5 Bartholomews, Brighton BN1 1HG

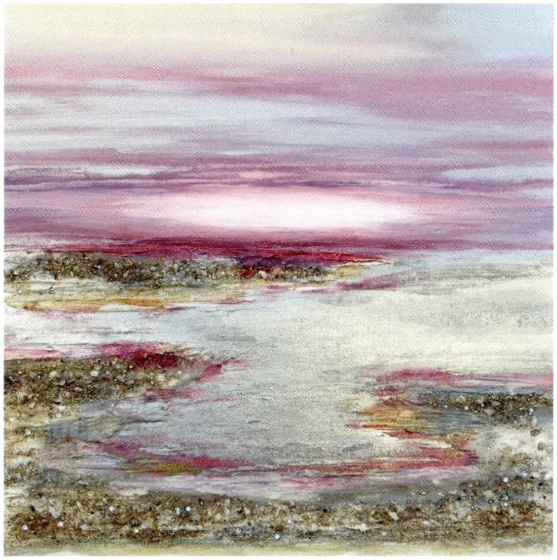

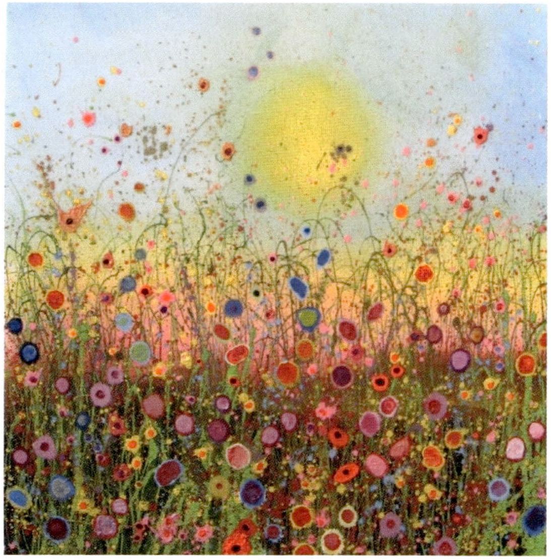

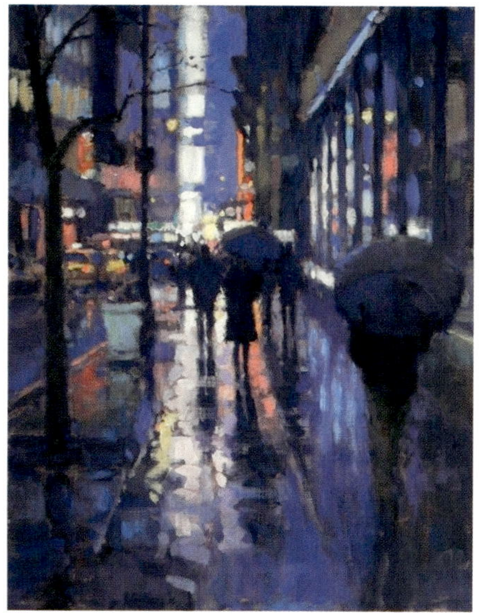

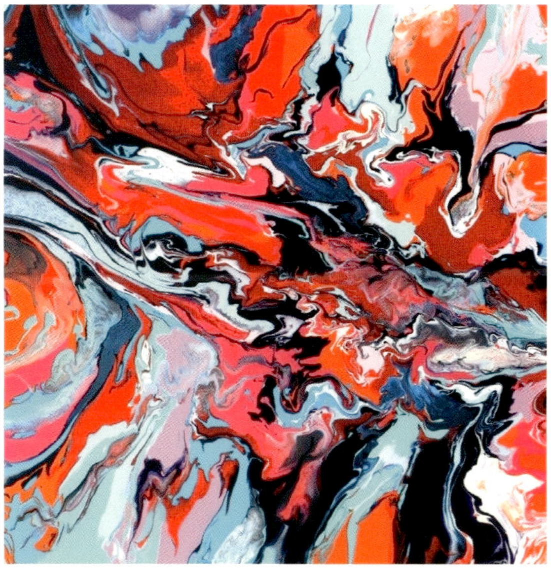

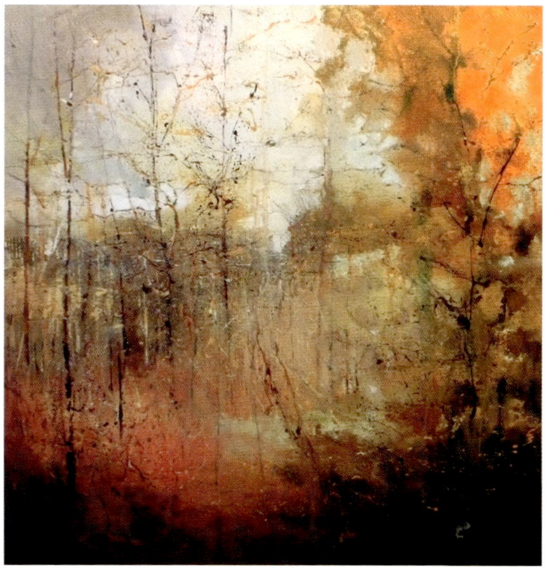

Art5 Gallery is situated in the heart of Brighton, in the fashionable Lanes, and over the past 10 years has established itself as one of Sussex's leading contemporary galleries. The gallery represents a diverse selection of national and international artists, showcasing an extensive range of quality art at affordable prices, from original paintings to unique ceramics and sculptures.

Art5 Gallery offers a free home and business consultancy service, which gives you the opportunity to view the artwork in situ. The gallery's art consultants can provide practical and creative advice on choosing artwork that reflects personal style and taste, while complementing and enhancing your space.

Art5 Gallery is an established member of Own Art, the Arts Council's interest-free loan scheme, which is designed to make it easy and affordable to acquire contemporary works of art. Visit the gallery and enjoy browsing its fantastic art collection in a friendly and informal environment.

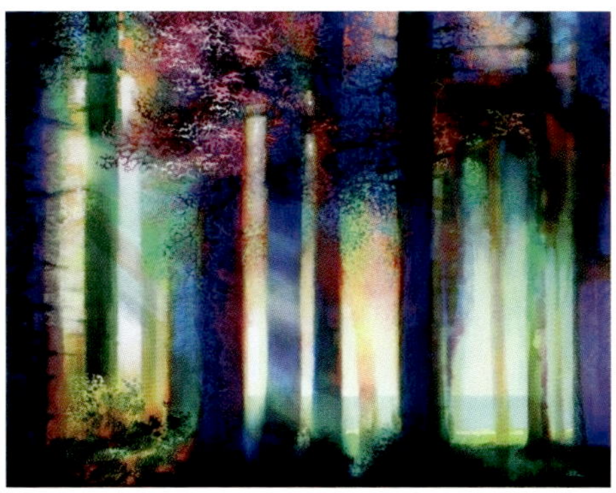

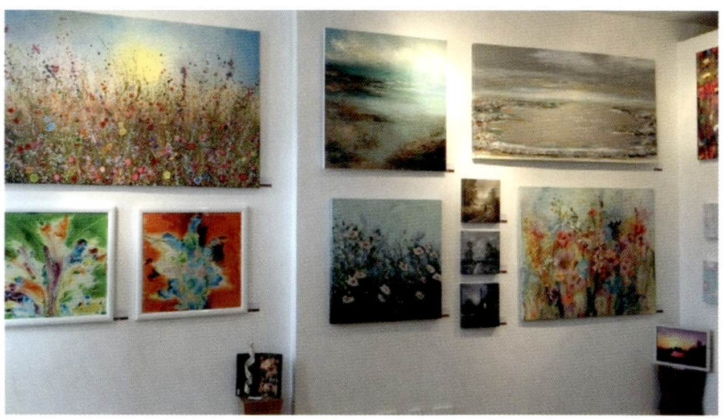

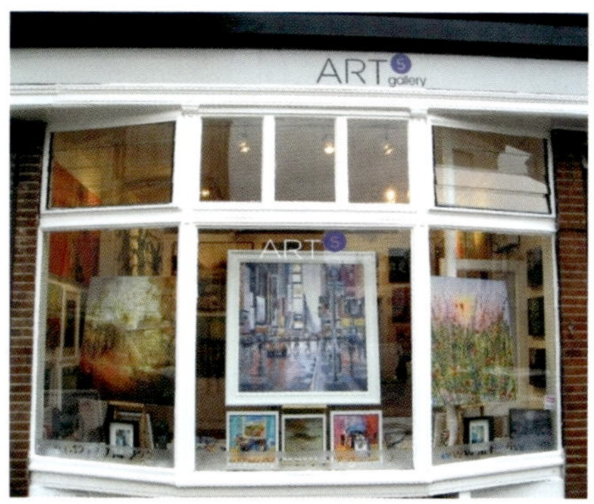

Zimmer Stewart Gallery

29 Tarrant Street, Arundel, BN18 9DG

Clockwise from top left: The Kiss, Gary Goodman; Enter The Son – The Blind Poet, Jonathan Joubert; Glider, Anthony Frost

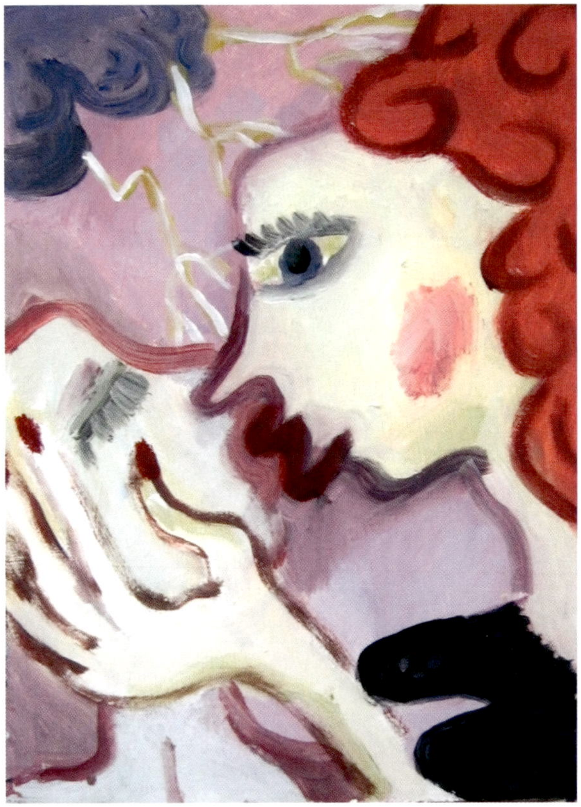

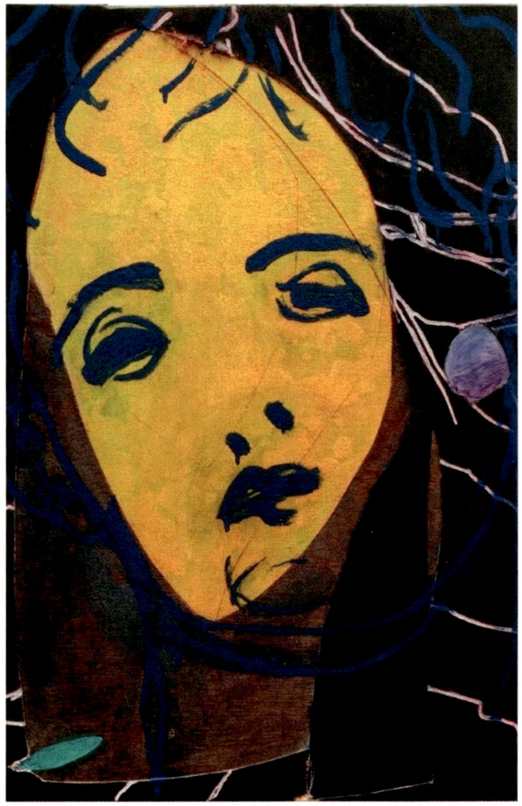

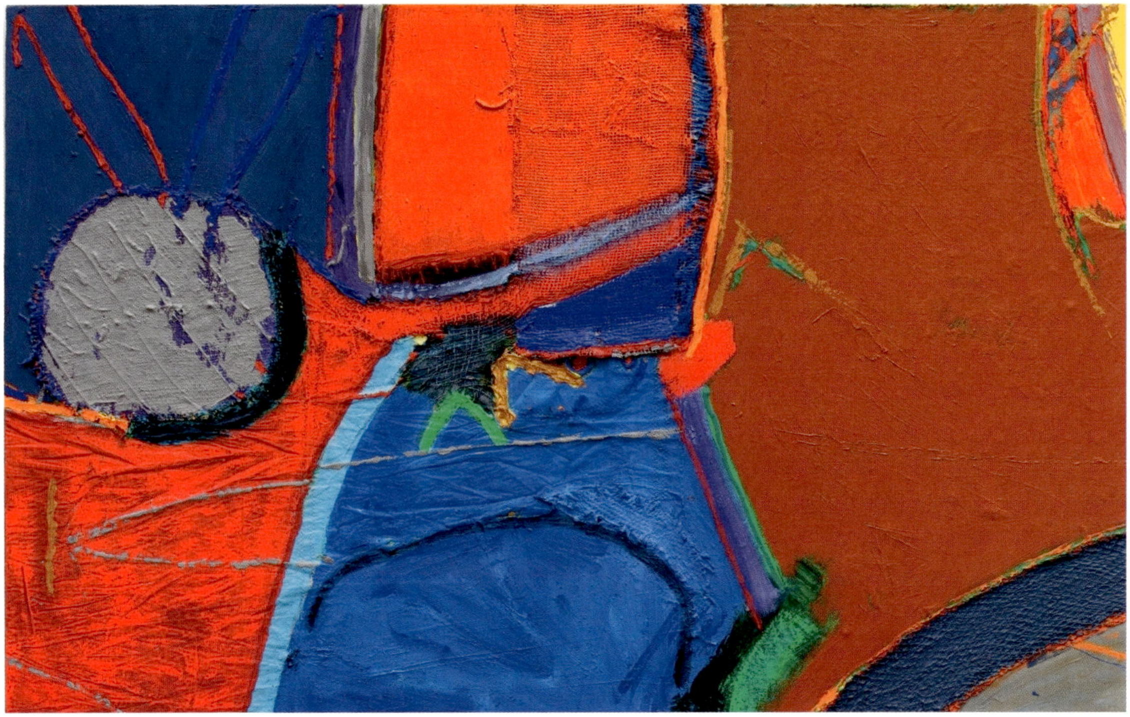

James Stewart and John Zimmer established Zimmer Stewart Gallery back in 2003, and continue to surprise and delight visitors with the breadth of work they show both in terms of the mediums and artists represented.

They exhibit paintings, original prints, ceramics, sculpture as well as mixed-media works through a rolling programme of 8-10 solo and group exhibitions each year. In July and December the gallery holds regular mixed group shows.

Many of the artists have exhibited in this Arundel gallery for a number of years, showing a new body of work every 18 months to two years, but new and emerging artists are also introduced from time to time. 2014 will be no different.

The programme starts with 'Love Stories' in February, an exhibition of paintings and constructions by Gary Goodman. This is followed by the first of three generations of Frost exhibiting: Anthony Frost in March, Luke Frost in June and Terry Frost in August. The latter covering paintings and works on paper as well as prints.

During May 2014, the gallery is excited to welcome back Jonathan Joubert. After a four-year break from exhibiting – during which he completed an MA at the Royal College of Art – Joubert's exhibition will include some new works in mixed media.

The year will end with minimalist conceptual artist Andrea Schulewitz (October) and landscape painter Matt Bodimeade (November).

These pages give a taste of the work that can be seen at Zimmer Stewart Gallery. You will find the full exhibition programme and list of artists at the gallery's website (see index page 151).

Browsers at the gallery are welcome, as James and John believe artists want their work to be seen by as many people as possible – and they enjoy showing it.

'Own Art Loans' are available.

You can follow Zimmer Stewart Gallery on Facebook and Twitter: #zimmerstewart

Clockwise from top left:
Tangerine Volts, Luke Frost; Offham Barn, Matt Bodimeade;
Yellow Sunburst Collage, Terry Frost; Cross, Andrea Schulewitz

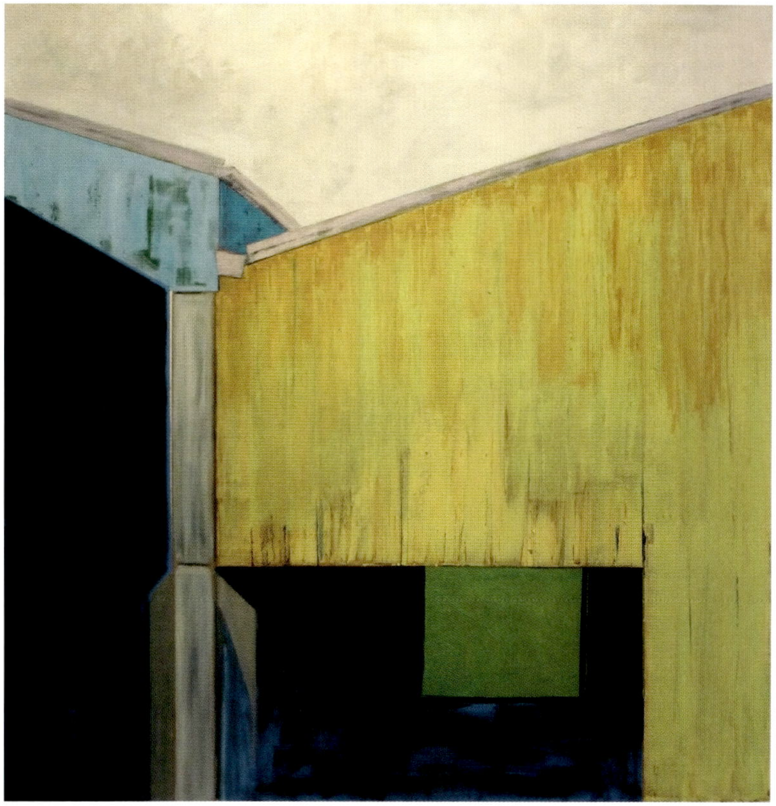

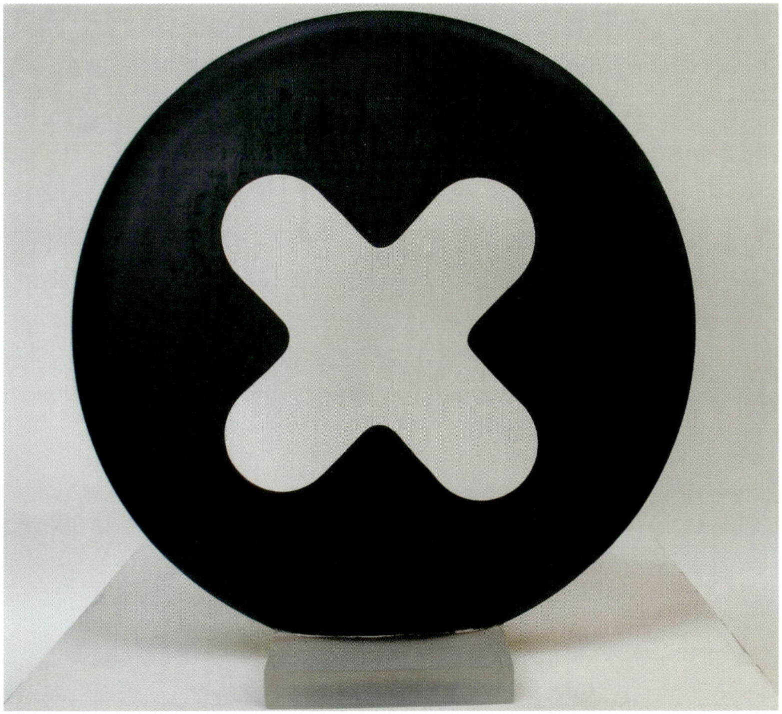

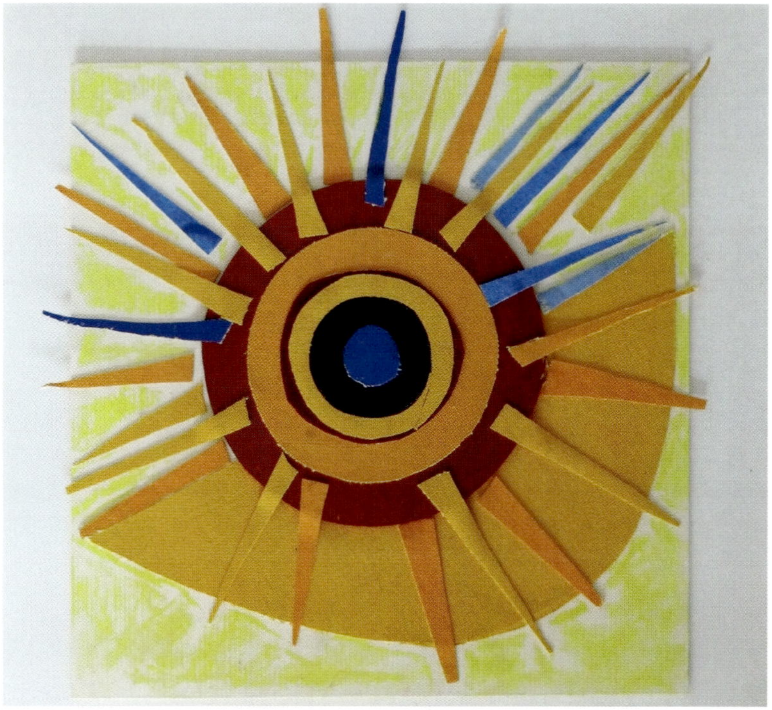

Hop Gallery

Star Brewery, Castle Ditch Lane (off Fisher Street), Lewes BN7 1YJ

Top of this page: (clockwise from top left) A tout va Bien, 2013; The Fearsome Holly; Earthworks; Sculpture; St Michel de Chavaignes 2
Below: Hop Gallery, Exhibition Body

Hop Gallery is a delightful, light and calming visual arts exhibition space situated in the 18th-century Star Brewery building, with its ancient brickwork, massive beams and echoes of a fascinating industrial past in Lewes, the vibrant county town of Sussex.

Considered to be one of the most significant and prestigious visual arts venues in the South East, Hop Gallery is multifunctional and complements traditional and contemporary art, sculpture and installation work equally well.

The Gallery is proud to host exhibitions by regional, national and international artists, and showcase accomplished as well as up-and-coming artists and makers, enabling it to offer a diverse programme of exhibitions.

Within the Star Brewery building, visitors will also discover a variety of studios, including the renowned Mohamed Hamid Pottery Studio. Through the higgledy piggledy streets between the Gallery, the Castle and the River Ouse, enjoy exploring a huge array of atmospheric coffee bars and eating houses along with unique shops all less than five minutes' walking distance from the Gallery.

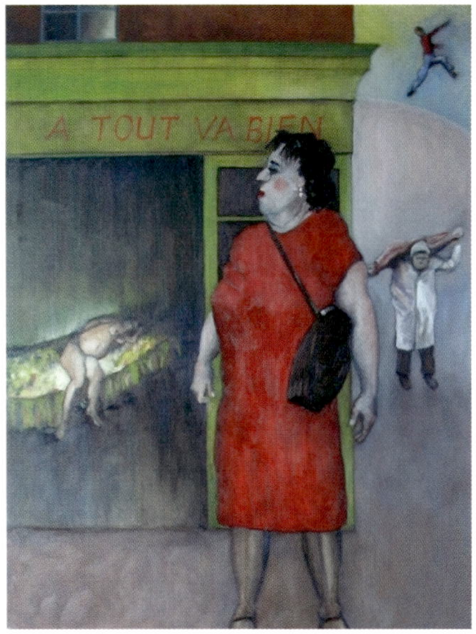

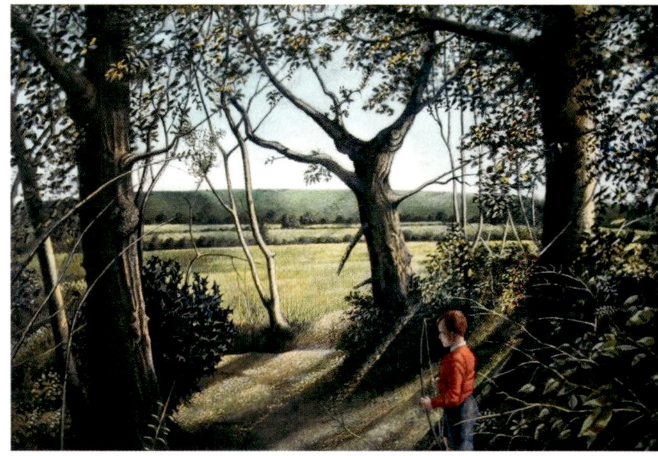

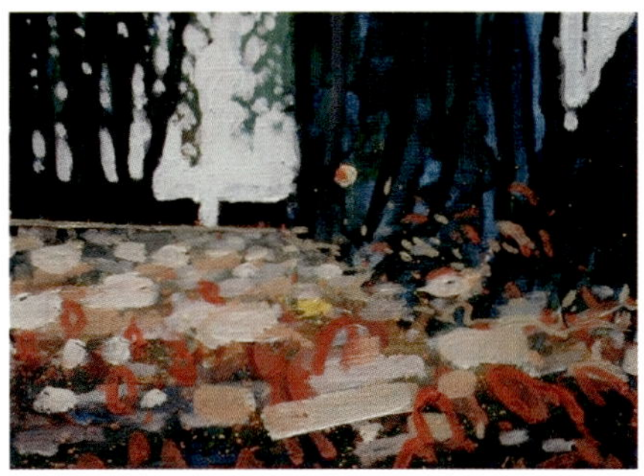

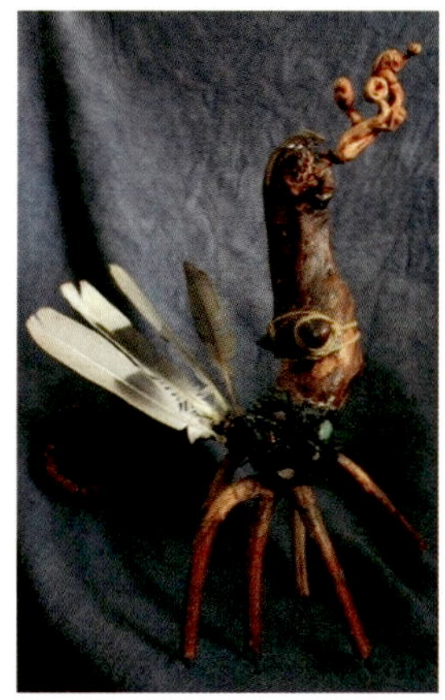

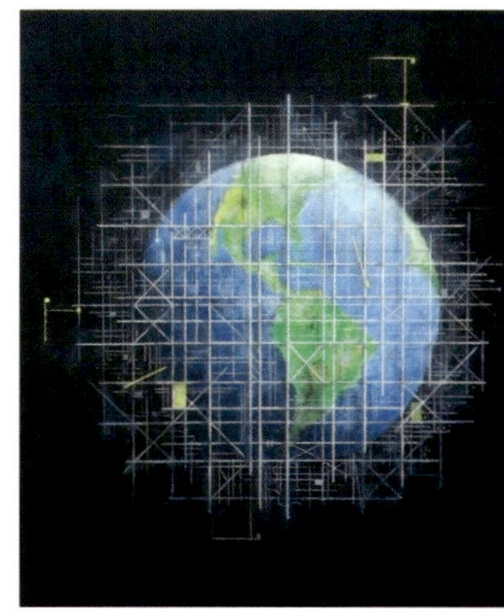

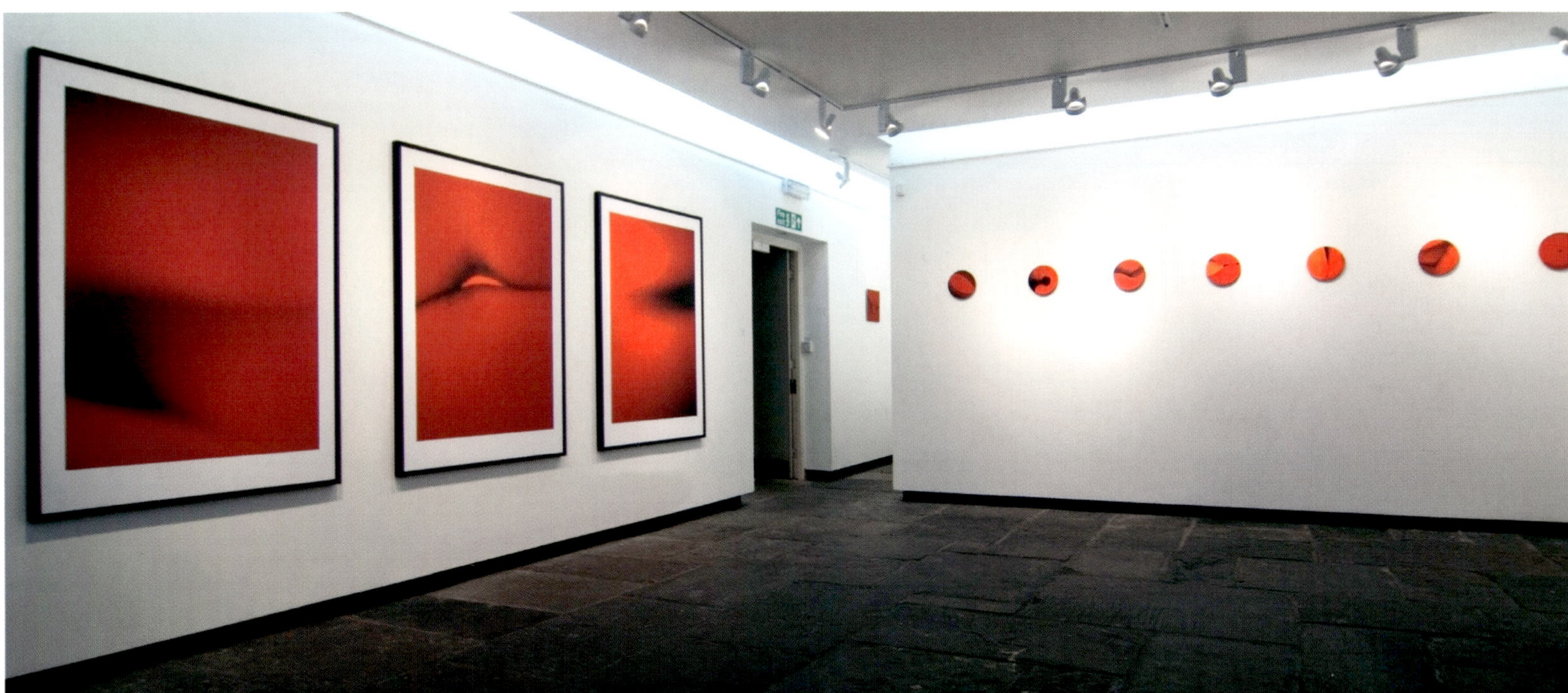

HOP
ART GALLERY

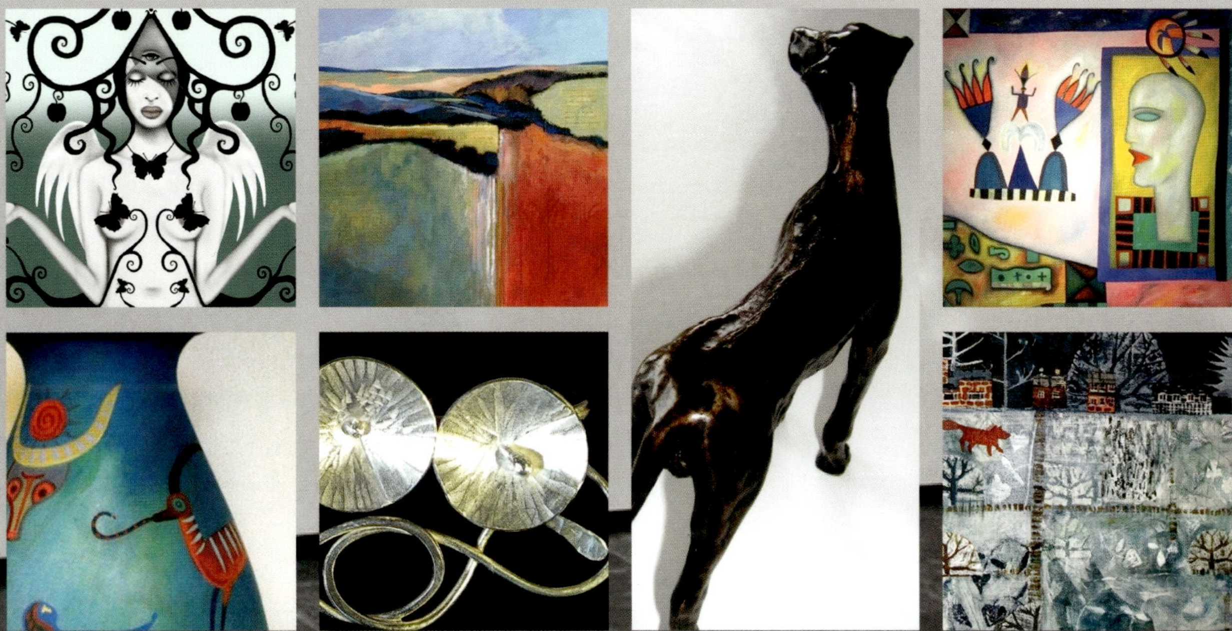

EXHIBITIONS
THROUGHOUT 2014

Bellis Gallery

8-9 Kings Road, Brighton BN1 1NE

In this spacious and lovingly restored Victorian building just off East Street, Sema Ugur curates one of Brighton's most elegant and enticing gallery spaces. She brings together a fabulous mix of overseas, Fairtrade and local artists' work to ensure there truly is something for everyone – and surprisingly affordable prices.

The variety of individually sourced artwork, textiles, ceramics, jewellery and accessories is astounding. And the sense of harmony and calm the gallery exudes is a tribute to Sema's curatorial skill, ensuring everything takes its place beautifully. On permanent show, expect to see fantastical illustration by our cover artist Harriet Butler (page 106) and Heike Roesel's (page 38) extraordinary etchings.

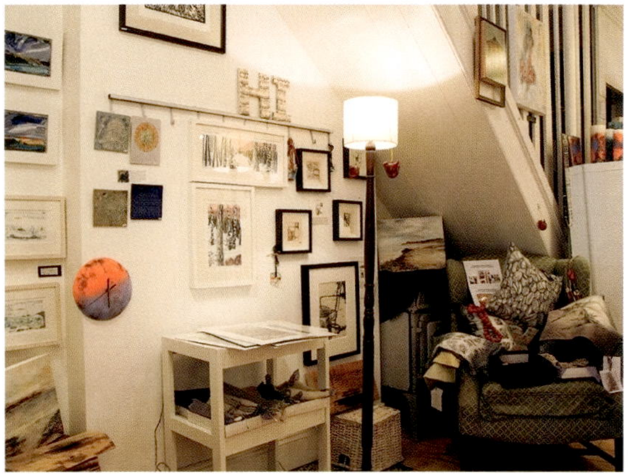

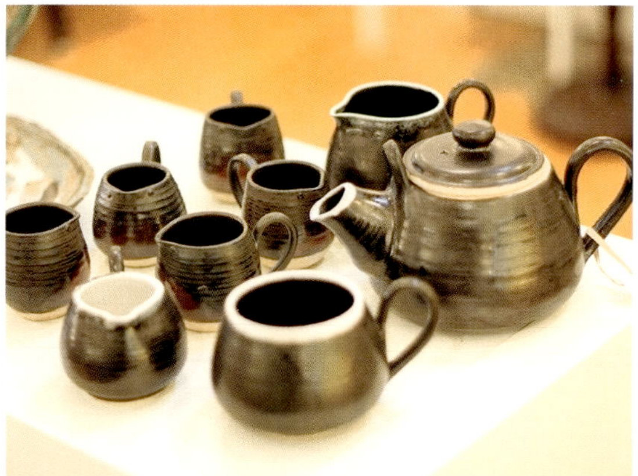

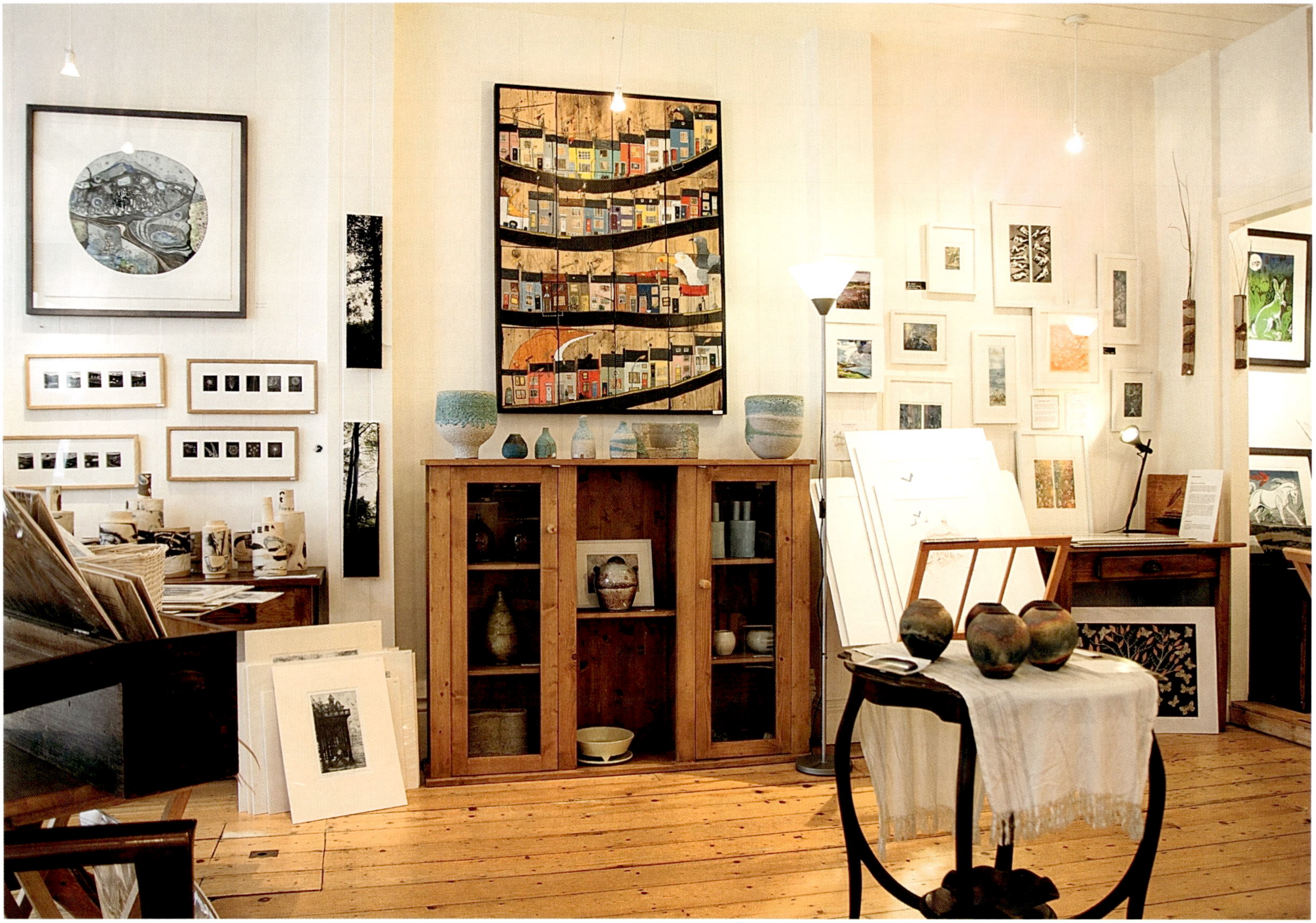

Clockwise from left:
Dog Head Henry II; Bistro area with gallery, Bedroom; French-style cuisine

New Steine Hotel

The New Steine Hotel, Bar and Bistro & Gullivers Hotel, 10, 11 & 12a New Steine, BN2 1PB

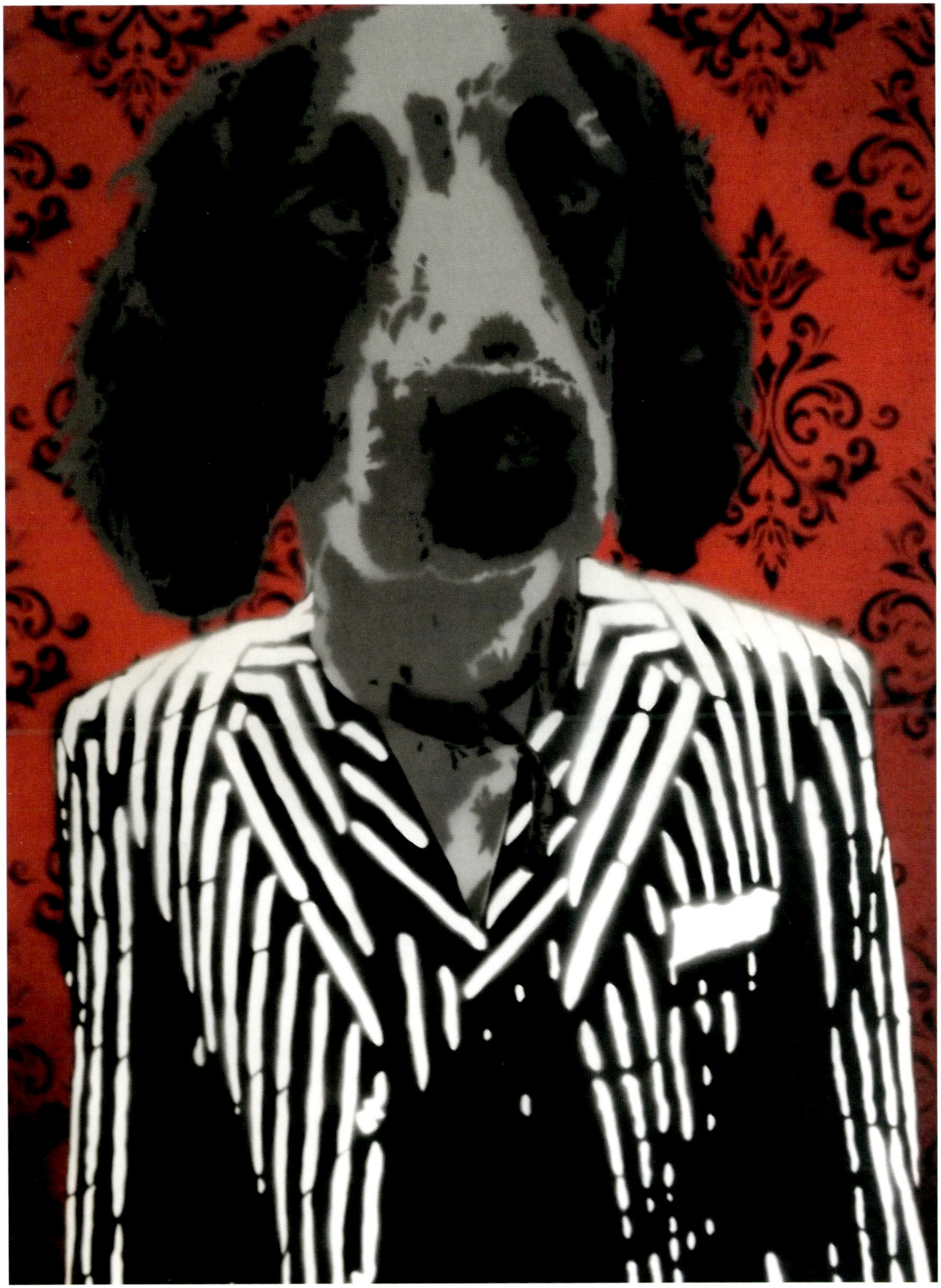

New Steine Hotel is an elegant and fashionable Georgian Townhouse located in the centre of Brighton. This boutique hotel exudes warmth and style, with a hint of French influence.

New Steine has two passions: food and art. Its bistro is famous for mixing local produce with traditional French recipes. The atmosphere is cosy and continental with contemporary design, ideal for a romantic dinner or a night out with friends.

But while you are visiting, look up at the walls. The New Steine holds regular art exhibitions and will be showing 'Dog Heads' – a solo show by the Funky Red Dog – as part of the Brighton Fringe Festival in May 2014.

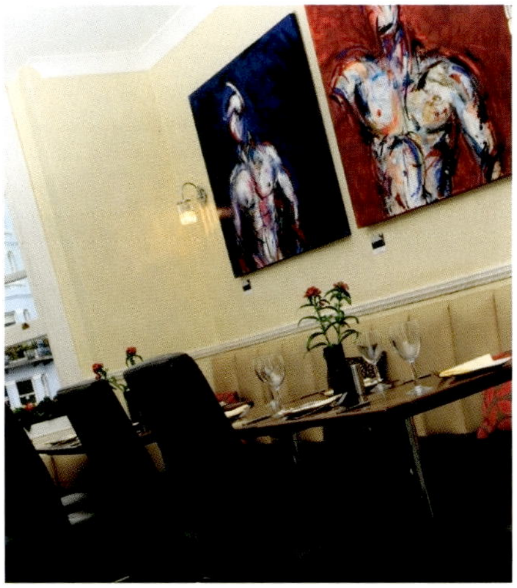

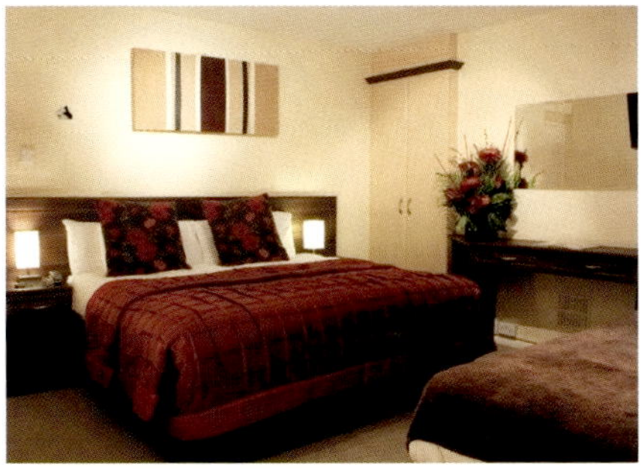

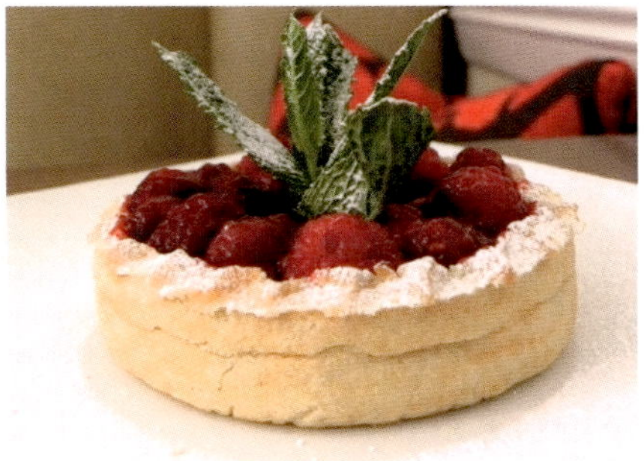

Unlimited

10 Church Street, Brighton BN1 1US

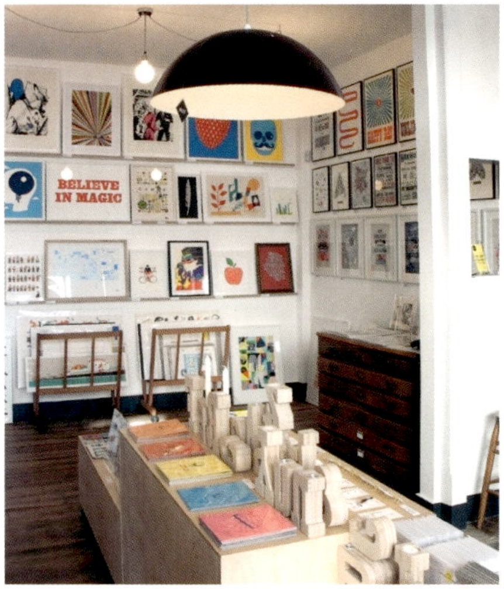

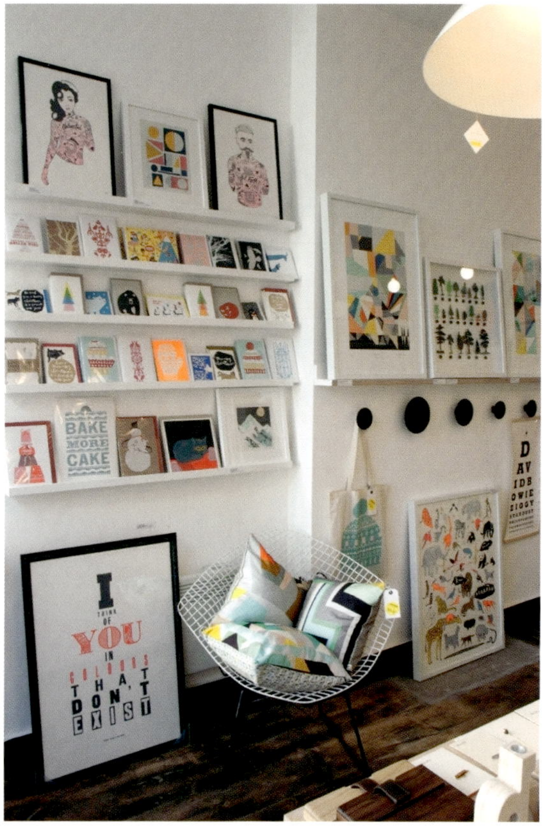

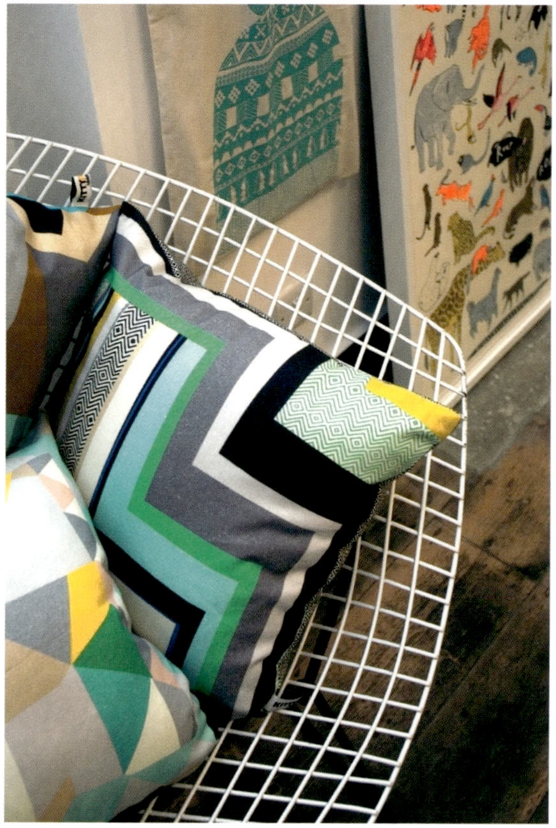

Unlimited is an independent design shop, gallery and studio in Brighton. The design studio was founded in 2008 by husband-and-wife team Patrick and Sara Morrissey. In 2010 they also started showcasing the work of a collective of like-minded contemporary illustrators, designers and printmakers from their weekly 'pop-up' studio shop. They participated in three years of Artists Open House exhibitions, and have held a number of their own exhibitions showcasing new and exclusive bodies of work from a number of local designers including Will Scobie, Imeus, Box 2 and Julia Trigg.

In spring 2013, Unlimited exhibited at Pick Me Up (the UK's most prestigious annual Graphic Arts event, held at Somerset House, London), which was a huge success. Then over the summer they moved to their brand spanking new space in the heart of Brighton's North Laine, opening their design gallery and shop to the public last September.

Continuing to work closely alongside each other, Patrick runs the Unlimited design studio, while Sara focuses her energies on the shop and gallery – where they continue to curate, showcase and sell prints and design-led products by an exciting and ever expanding collective.

The feedback over the last few years has been amazingly positive, and the gallery and shop has grown organically as a reaction to this. Sara hopes it feels more 'honest' than engineered – filling a need rather than foisting another venture onto the market! Their aim is to keep forging new connections with other skilled creatives, keep evolving as a business and be inspired by what's going on around them. The new studio and gallery space making them a more visible and pro-active part of the Brighton creative and retail scene. Their main drive at Unlimited is to continue to source, provide and promote a great selection of concept-led, unique, affordable and innovative work.

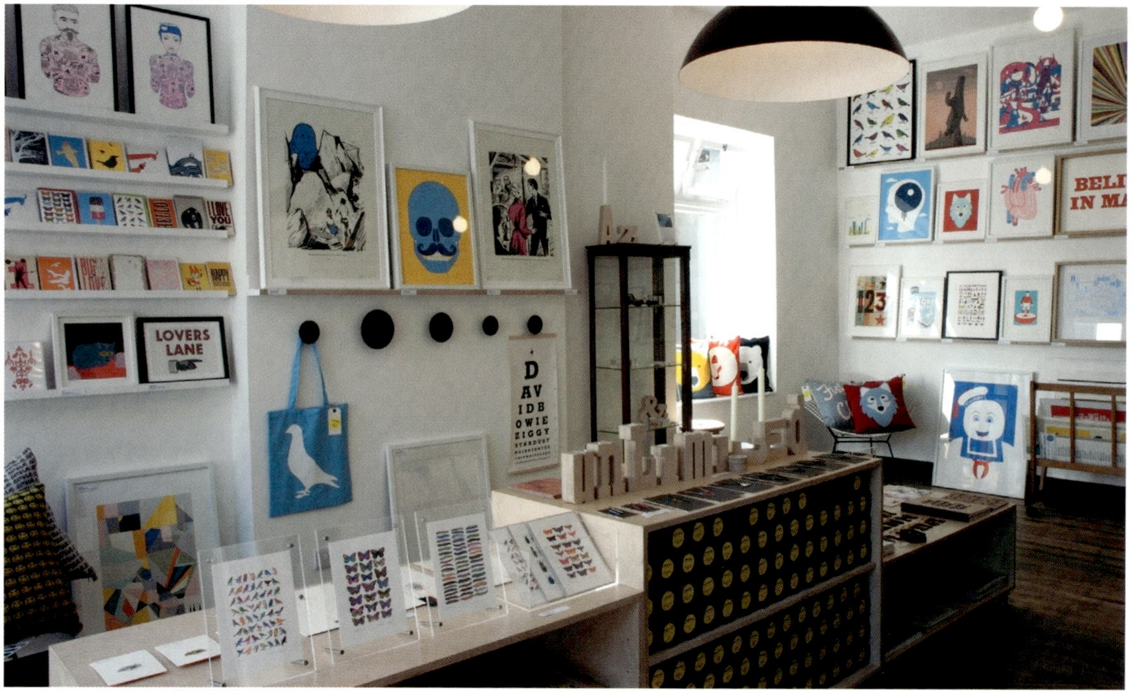

Main image: Mike Page
Additional images: Unlimited

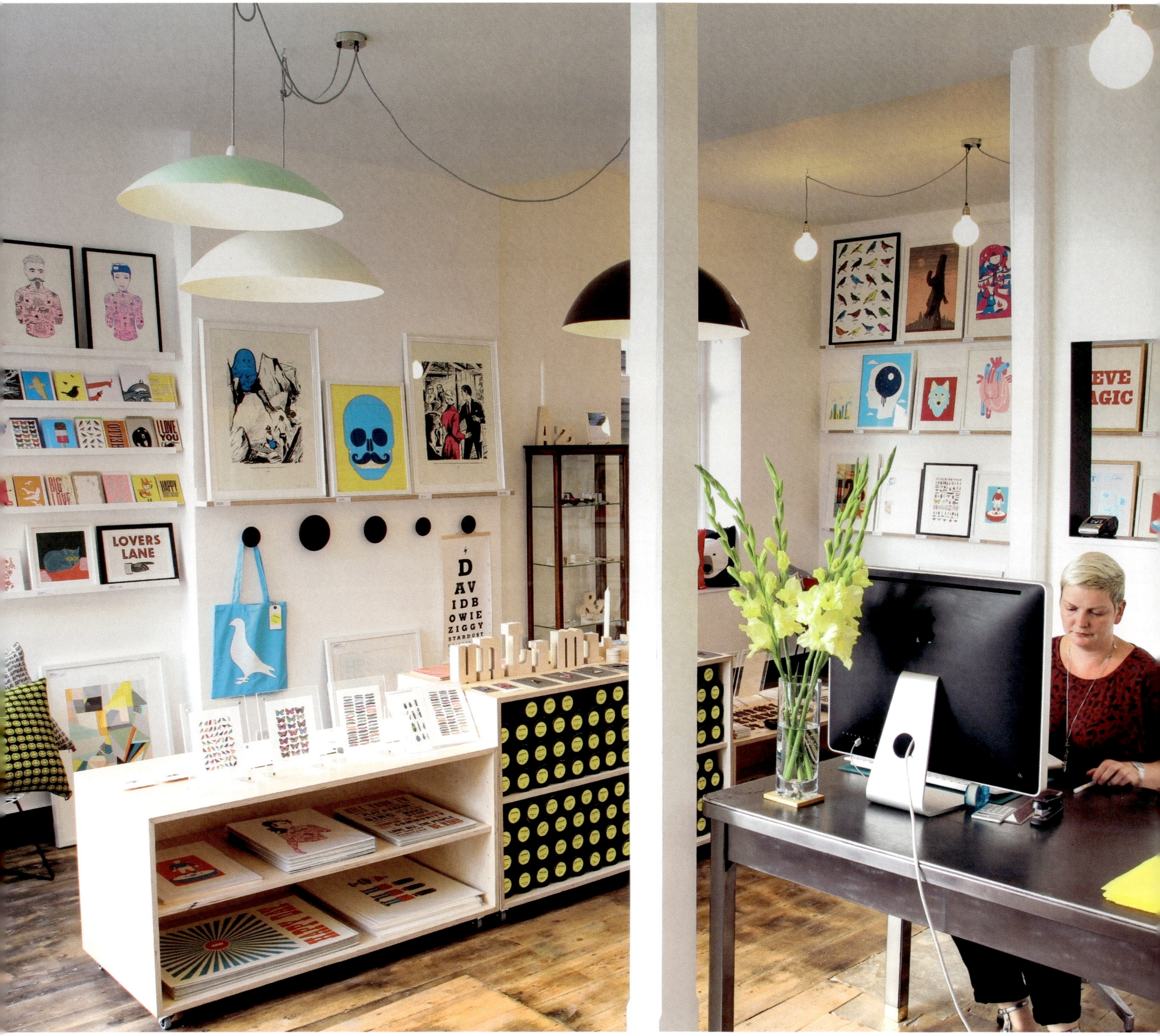

Chalk Gallery

4 North Street, Lewes BN7 2PA

Clockwise from top left:
Eastbourne Sunset, by Chris Liddiard; Egbert and his Hens, by Veronica van Eijk;
Last Light, by Caroline Gold; Seed Heads, by Sonya Tatham

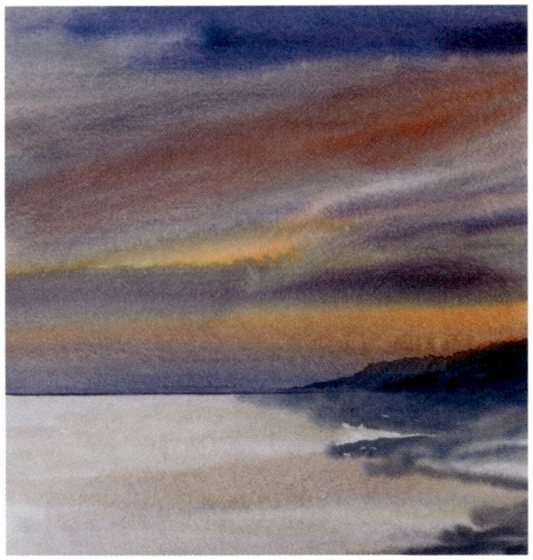

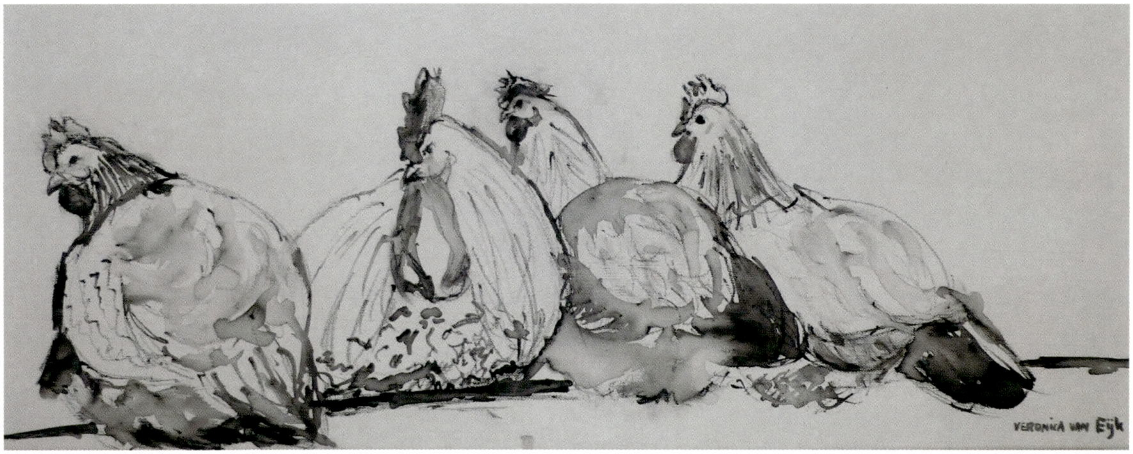

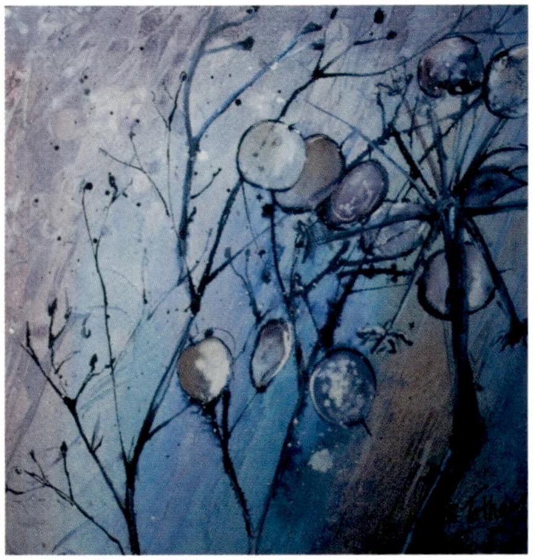

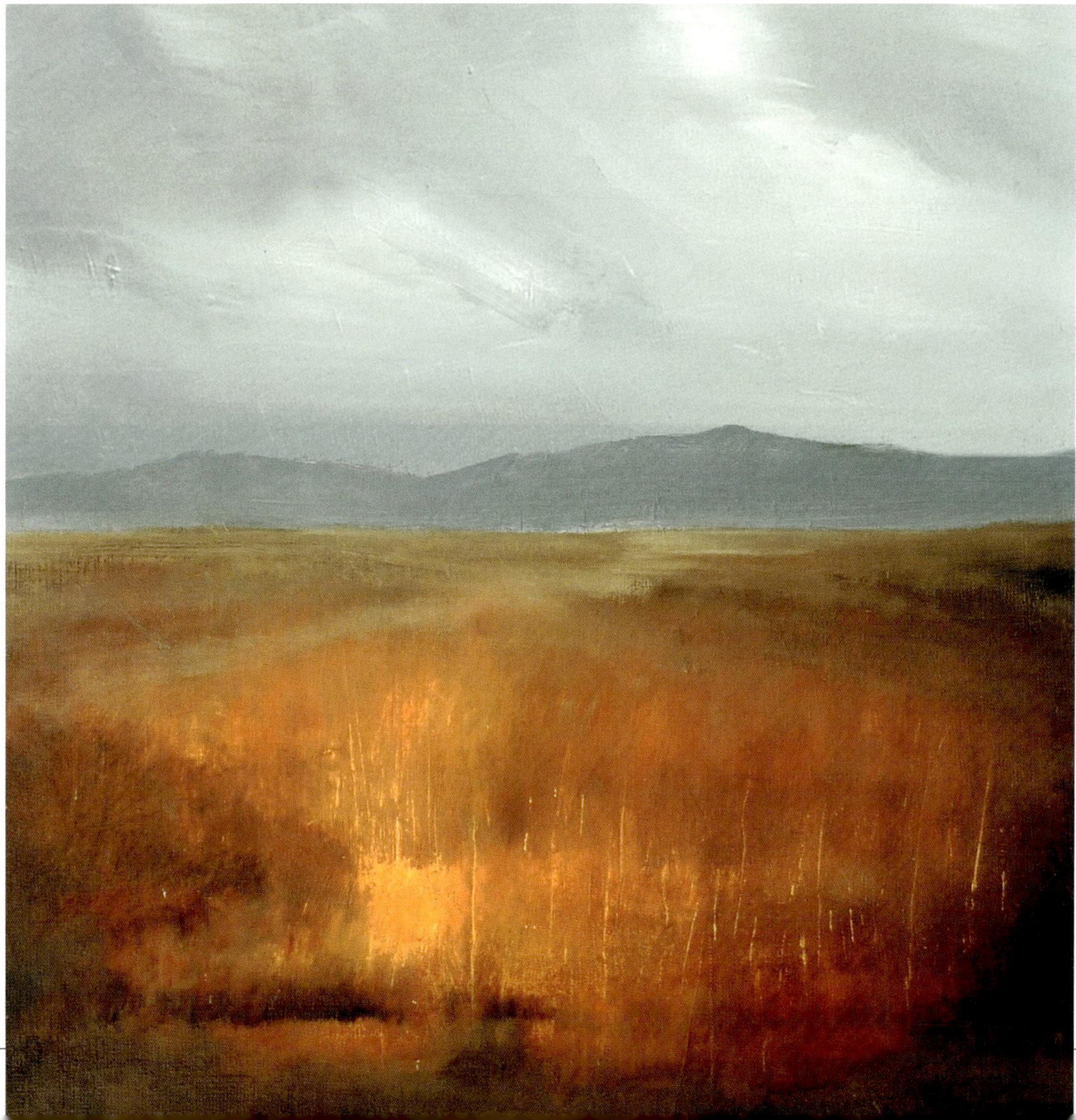

Formed nine years ago by a group of like-minded Sussex artists in the heart of historic Lewes, Chalk Gallery has developed a workable concept giving 21 artists a venue to display their work and share every aspect of running the gallery. The aim is to provide high standard art at affordable prices and a friendly welcome to customers.

Visiting regularly pays dividends as a new hang takes place every six weeks, including featured and guest artist slots. This maintains a constant level of change and interest in this small but perfectly formed exhibition space.

The gallery offers paintings, prints, ceramics, sculpture and art jewellery. Its survival and success depends upon getting the right artists. The selection criteria are high, and both the work and artist need to be compatible with the Chalk ethos.

2014 will be another exciting year with plenty of innovative, affordable art by local artists for Chalk's customers to enjoy. The gallery is open 10am-5pm, Monday to Sunday.

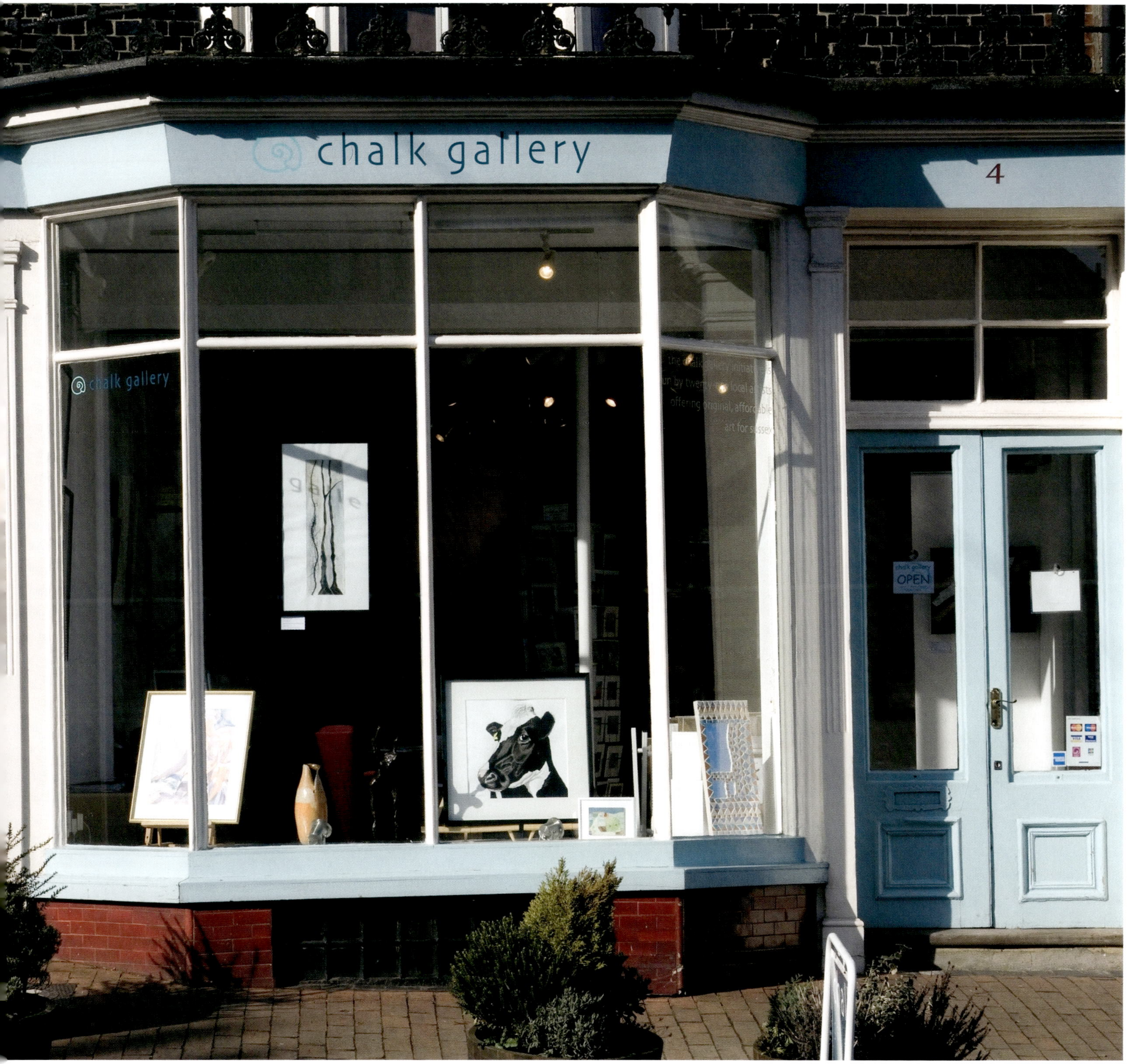
chalk gallery
4
chalk gallery
offering original, affordable
art for sussex
OPEN

Shops

If you're looking for an unusual gift or something beautiful for your home – or perhaps you just want to spoil yourself – Brighton boasts some of the best independent shops you'll find.

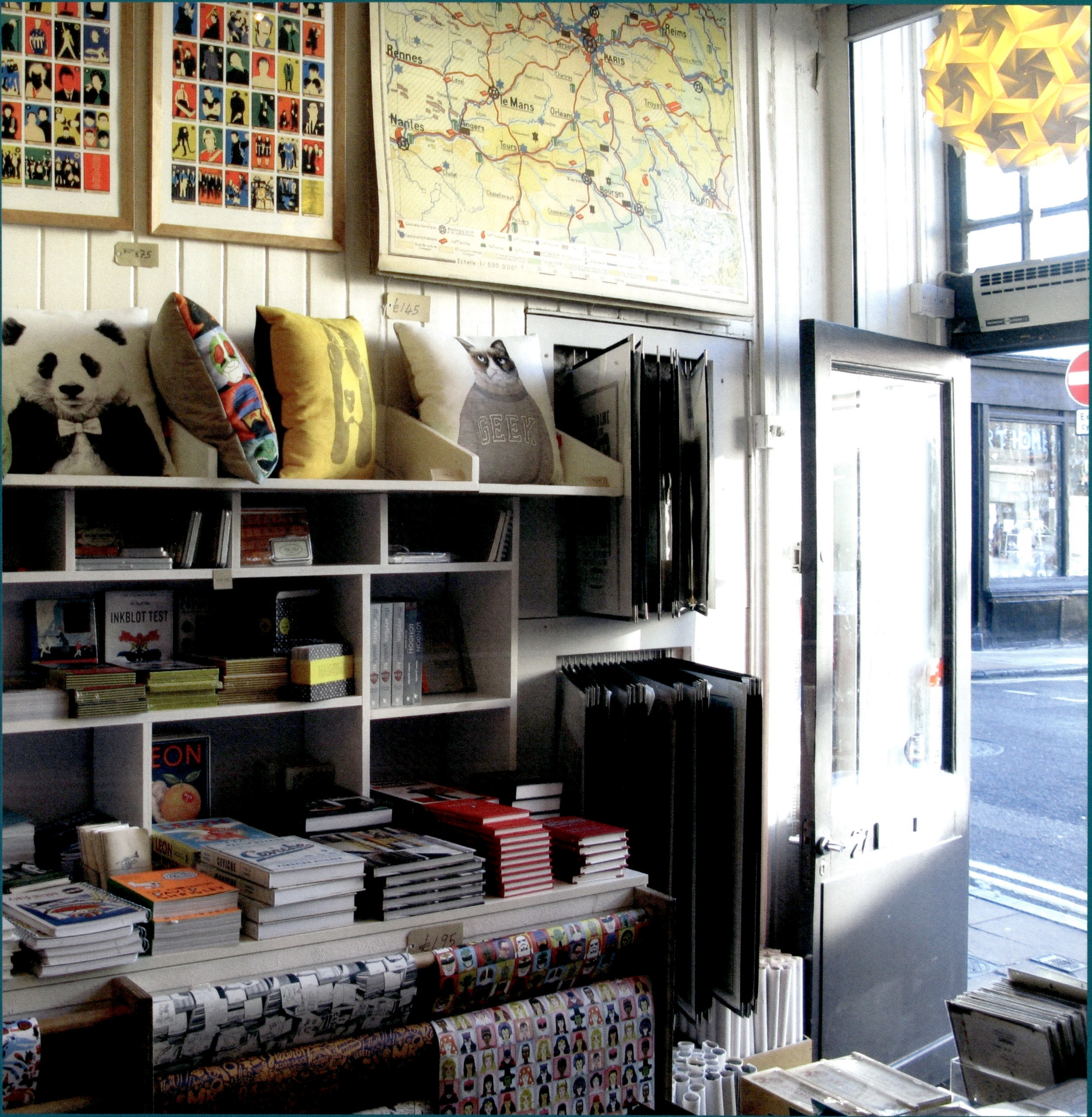

Rennes
Reims
PARIS
le Mans
Nantes
Angers
Orleans
Tours
Troyes
Bourges
INKBLOT TEST
GEEK
LONDON

Junkfunk

Perhaps it's because we live here that we're such fans of the North Laine. The streets that weave between Trafalgar Street to North Street are abuzz with the creative vibe that comes from so many innovative independent enterprises. Whether you're shopping for contemporary, vintage or just plain quirky – for your home or for yourself – I defy you not to find something perfect here. And when you've shopped till you're ready to drop, there are loads of great pubs and cafés where you can rest and revive.

Trafalgar Street

A stone's throw from Brighton Station down Trafalgar Street, *One in the House* showcases a veritable Tardis of treasures for your home. And the building – a diminutive former pub – is as intriguing as the enticing collection of furniture, lighting, glassware, accessories and jewellery sourced with flair by owner and interior designer Terri Prior.

Over the road at *GAFF (Great Art For Floors)*, you can express your creativity underfoot in Brighton's quirkiest rug shop. You can even bring in your own design and have it made up in your own choice of colours. From children's scribbles to modernist masterpieces, the only limit is your imagination.

Before you turn right into Sydney Street, a special mention to *Mad Hatters* for its irresistible and irrepressible supply of headgear for men and women. Cosy colourful berets, soft sculptural designs, amazing occasionwear... a great many of which find their way back round the corner and into my cupboard.

Sydney Street

At number 10, *KerrieBerrie* offers more than just the dazzling display of beads, findings and exclusive handmade jewellery that lures you in. You can drop in and join one of its daily workshops (no need to book), or sign up for specialised evening and weekend classes.

Gloucester Road

You've spotted someone wearing a T-shirt proclaiming 'No Pasaran' (They shall not pass) and you want one too? There's only one place to go. At *Junkfunk* (page 142) you'll find one of the coolest collections of statement T-shirts in the city – some limited editions – alongside affordable designer clothes, and truly unusual gifts, books and stationery.

Next door, *InHouse Space* is a must-stop for contemporary home accessories sourced from around the world. Then pop over and say hello to Sebastian at *Scent* – the tiny, tucked-away florist shop whose imaginative window displays delight the neighbourhood all year round. (The flowers are hard to beat too!)

Heading upwards, prepare yourself for the surprise that's *In My Room*, where mid-century design classics sit alongside contemporary furniture and whatever has recently captured owner Ollie Learmouth's eye. It could be an original piece of Eames or Ercol. It could be a tribute to space-age technology or a retro toy. The collection is ever changing, utterly unpredictable and guaranteed to provide a talking point for your home.

Continue up a step or two and you'll find the home of *Mr Magpie*. Two amazing floors stacked with all manner of collectables plus superb letterpress printing woodtype letters, numerals and picture blocks. (The Victorian dust is included for free.) Then towards the corner of Kemp Street opposite Gallery40 (page 126), a great new addition to the area is *TeePony*, an innovative, original T-shirt company. Go in to discover what's 'tee of the week'. All the designs are limited-editions so get one before they go.

Kensington Gardens

Now backtrack a bit, because you don't want to miss this narrow pedestrianised thoroughfare. Time for a rummage? Then push your way through the turnstiles at *Snoopers Paradise* and immerse yourself in its maze of stalls offering antiques, bric-a-brac, some hidden treasures – and perhaps the odd bit of tat.

Further along, a far more serene experience awaits at *Rose Hill Boutique*. Its light, bright interior is the perfect backdrop for a carefully selected mix of handmade, vintage, beautiful one-off pieces of furniture and accessories ranging from soaps and candles to cushions and purses. A few steps away, *Appendage* puts a strong emphasis on colour and creative use of pattern and materials, stocking innovative work by British makers.

North Road

Before you head along the main Gardner/Bond Street drag, don't pass by one the North Laine's best-kept secrets. A collectors' paradise, *Rin-Tin-Tin* offers a spectacular selection of mainly original advertising and ephemera including adverts, labels, posters, showcards, promotional items, tins, packaging and playing cards. There are vintage robots too. And if you're tempted by the vintage glamour and pin-up magazine section, owner Rick Irvine is also a skilled framer with a workspace at the back of the shop. He'll show any artwork at its best.

Bond Street

Last but not least, *This is Not a Butchers* is an emporium of all the stuff you never knew about, but now you've seen you can't live without. A massive hit since it opened in spring 2013, go and gaze in awe. It's packed to the rafters with covetables we know you won't be able to resist. Cat lamp anyone?

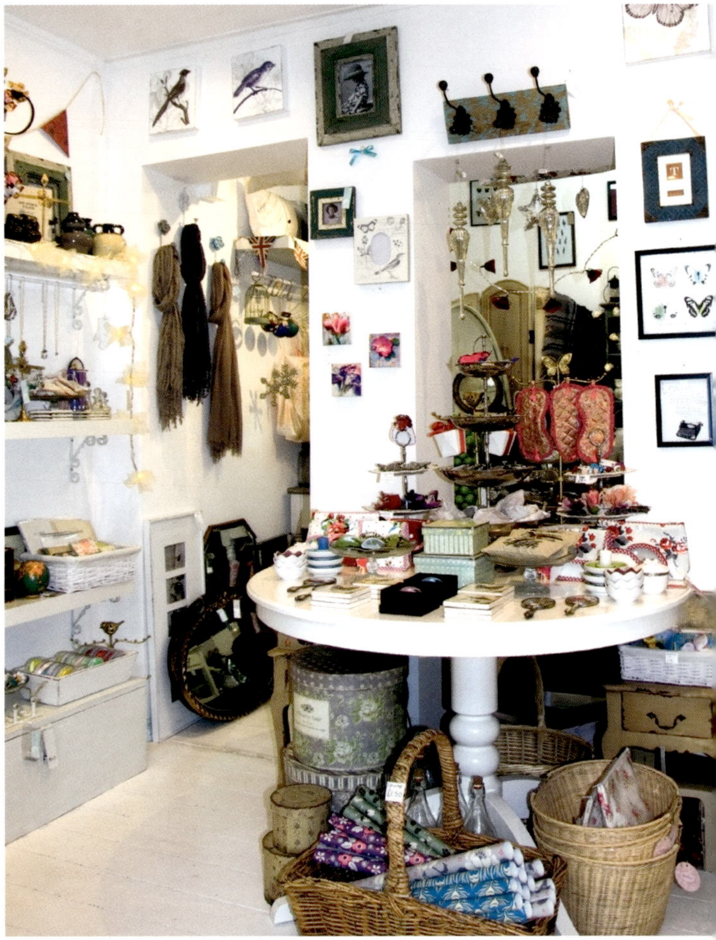

Rose Hill Boutique

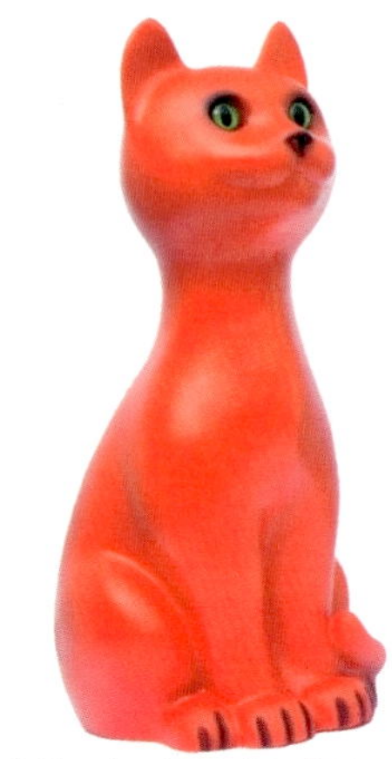

Cat lamp from This is Not a Butchers

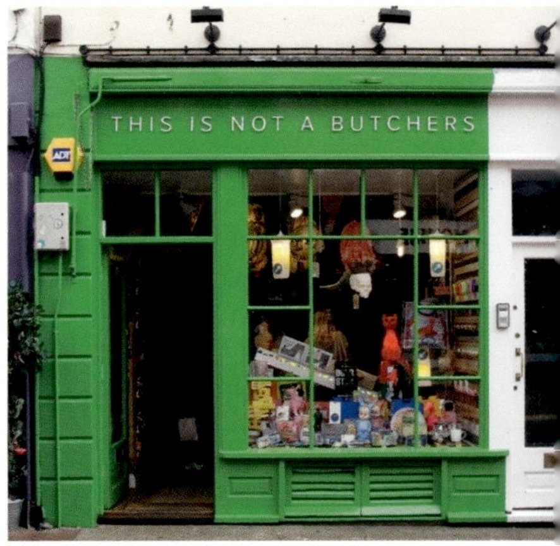

This is Not a Butchers

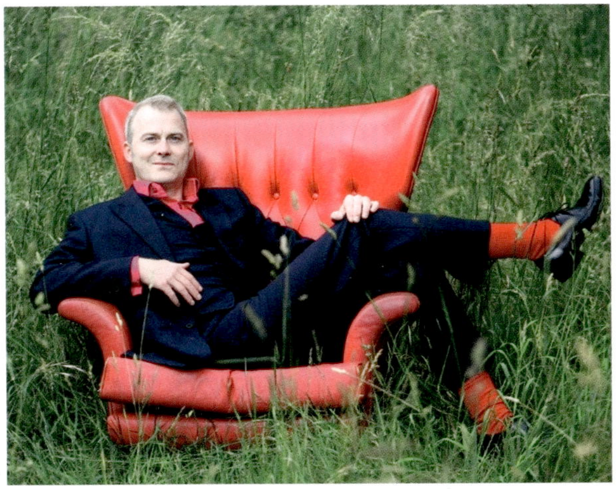

In My Room

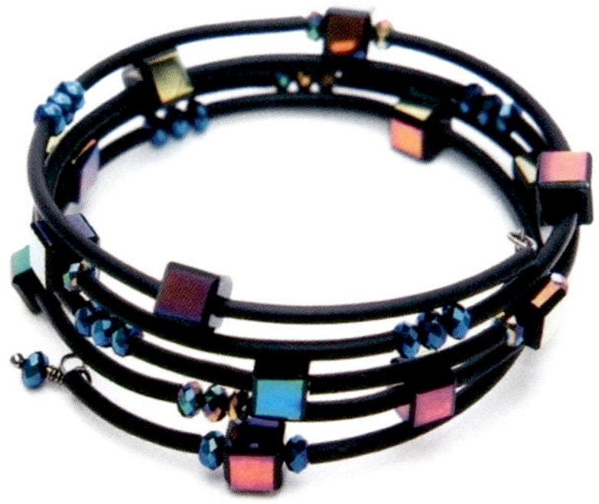

KerrieBerrie

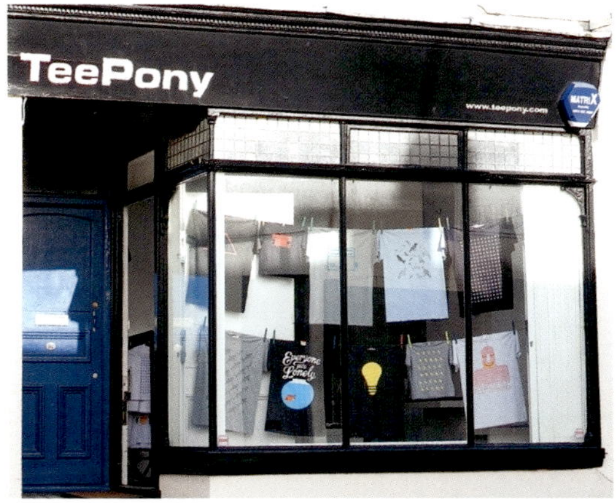

TeePony

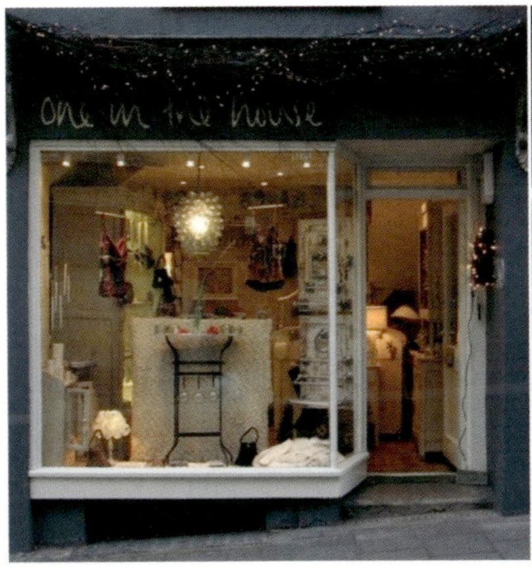

One in the House

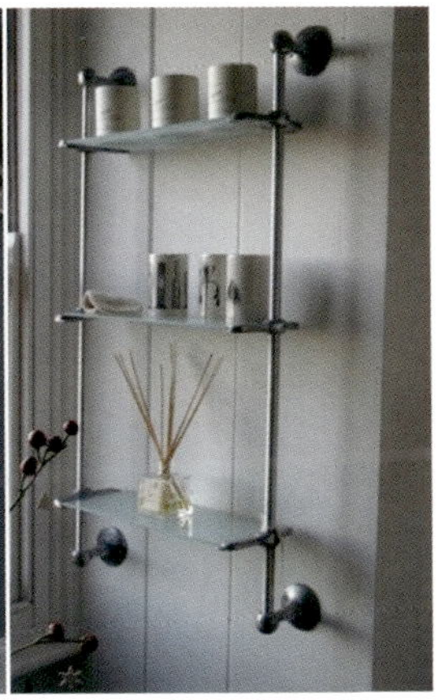

Inside One in the House

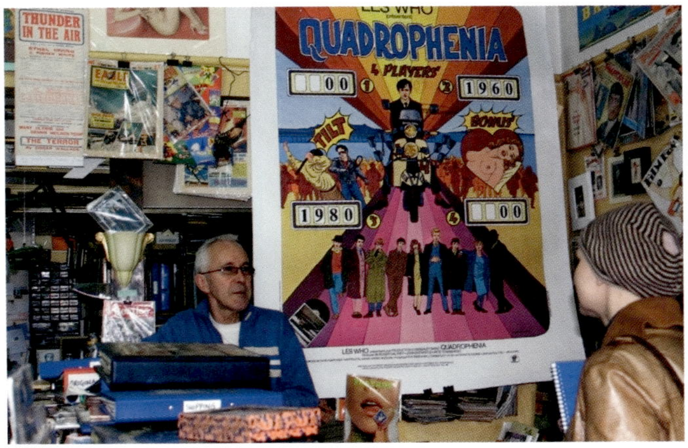

Rin Tin Tin

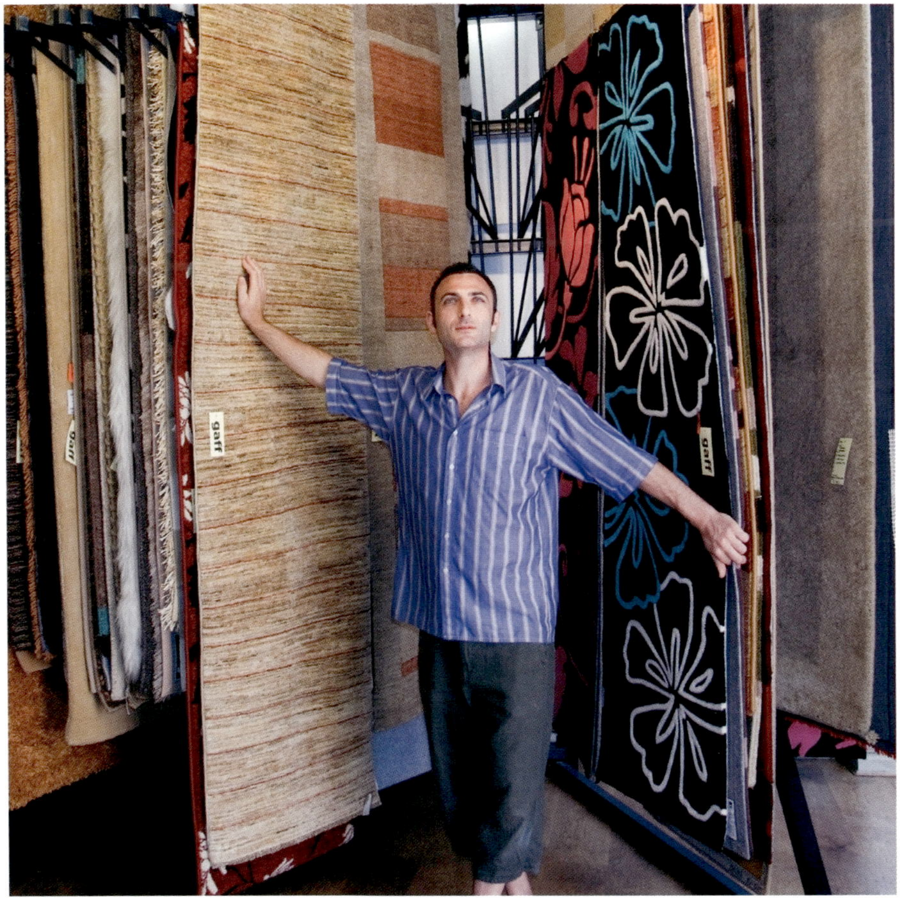

GAFF (Great Art For Floors)

Junkfunk

27 Gloucester Road, BN1 4AQ

Junkfunk is an independent design gift shop in the heart of Brighton's North Laine. The shop started life as a stall in London's Spitalfields market in 2003 selling its own-designed T-shirts, which are still available to buy in store and online. The T-shirts are the shop's main product selling all over the world with one NO PASARÁN (They Shall Not Pass) recently worn by 'Pussy Riot' Punk activist Nadezhda Tolokonnikova at her trial in a Moscow court room in 2012.

Alongside the Tees, there is an ecclectic mix of products from an exciting mix of designers and illustrators and makers. Prints by James Brown, cards by illustrators, Freya, 67Inc, Tom Frost and David Shrigley, with stationery, books, dresses and homeware also.

The unpretentious and quirky nature of the shop appeals to Brighton's creative community and is a great place to find something interesting at an affordable price. Open seven days a week, 10am-6pm Monday to Saturday and 11am-5pm on Sunday.

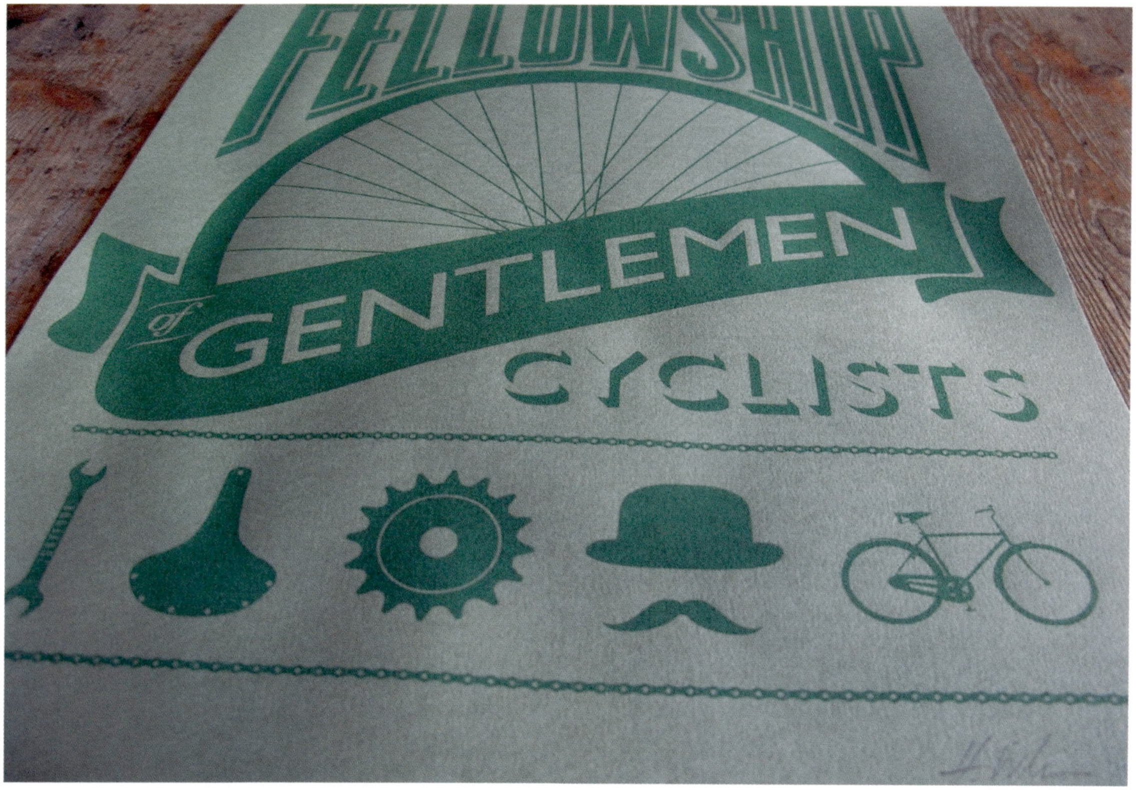

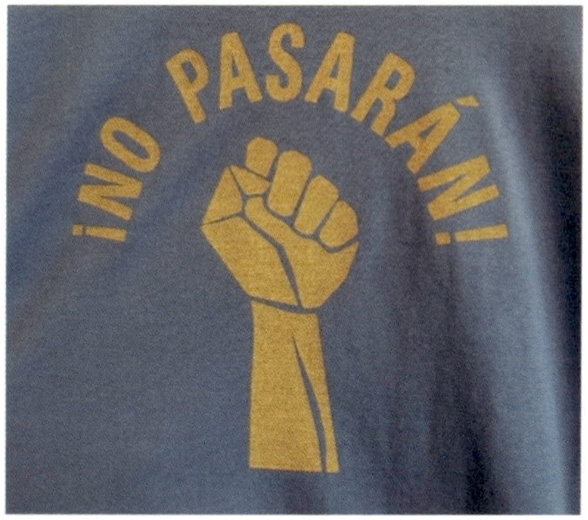

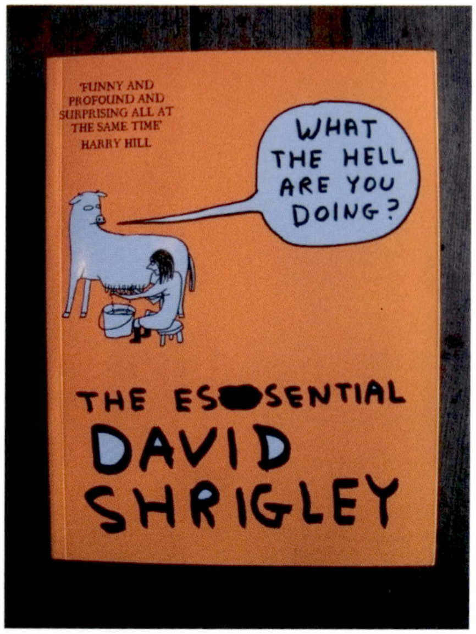

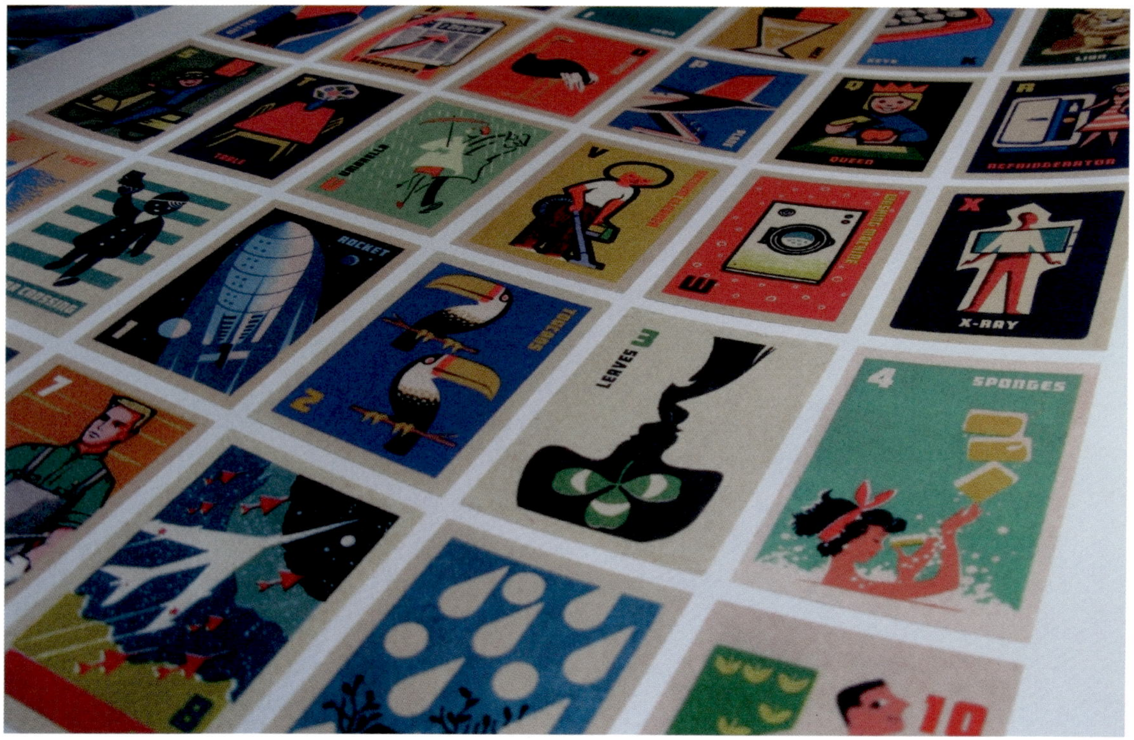

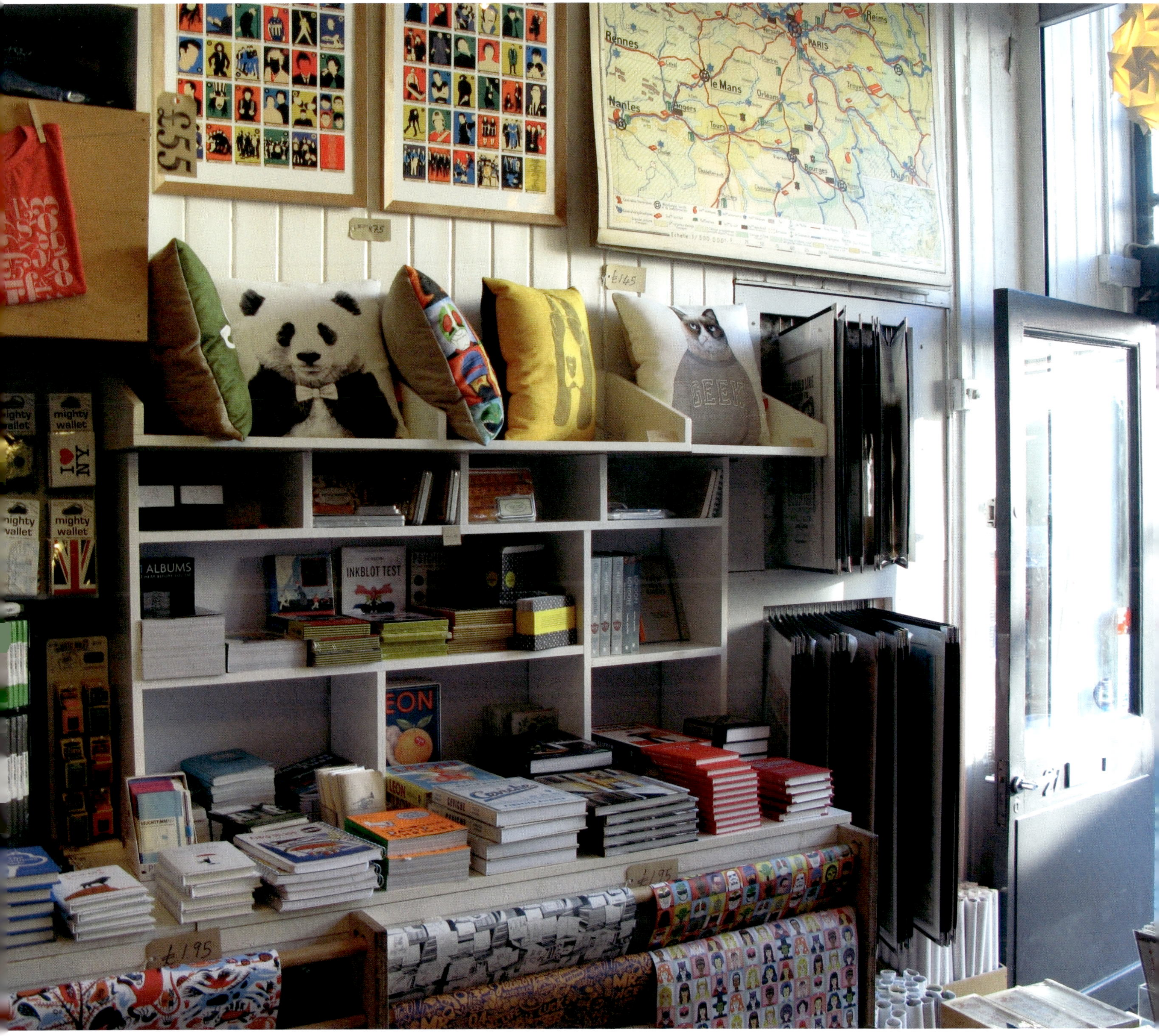

£55
£75
£145
Rennes
PARIS
Reims
le Mans
Orléans
Nantes
Angers
Tours
Bourges
mighty wallet
mighty wallet
mighty wallet
mighty wallet
I ♥ NY
GEEK
ALBUMS
INKBLOT TEST
LEON
£1.95
£1.95

Events

There's always something arty to do in Brighton. Don't miss the chance to meet and buy from artists and makers during May's Artists Open Houses, then later in the year at the Brighton Art Fair and MADE.

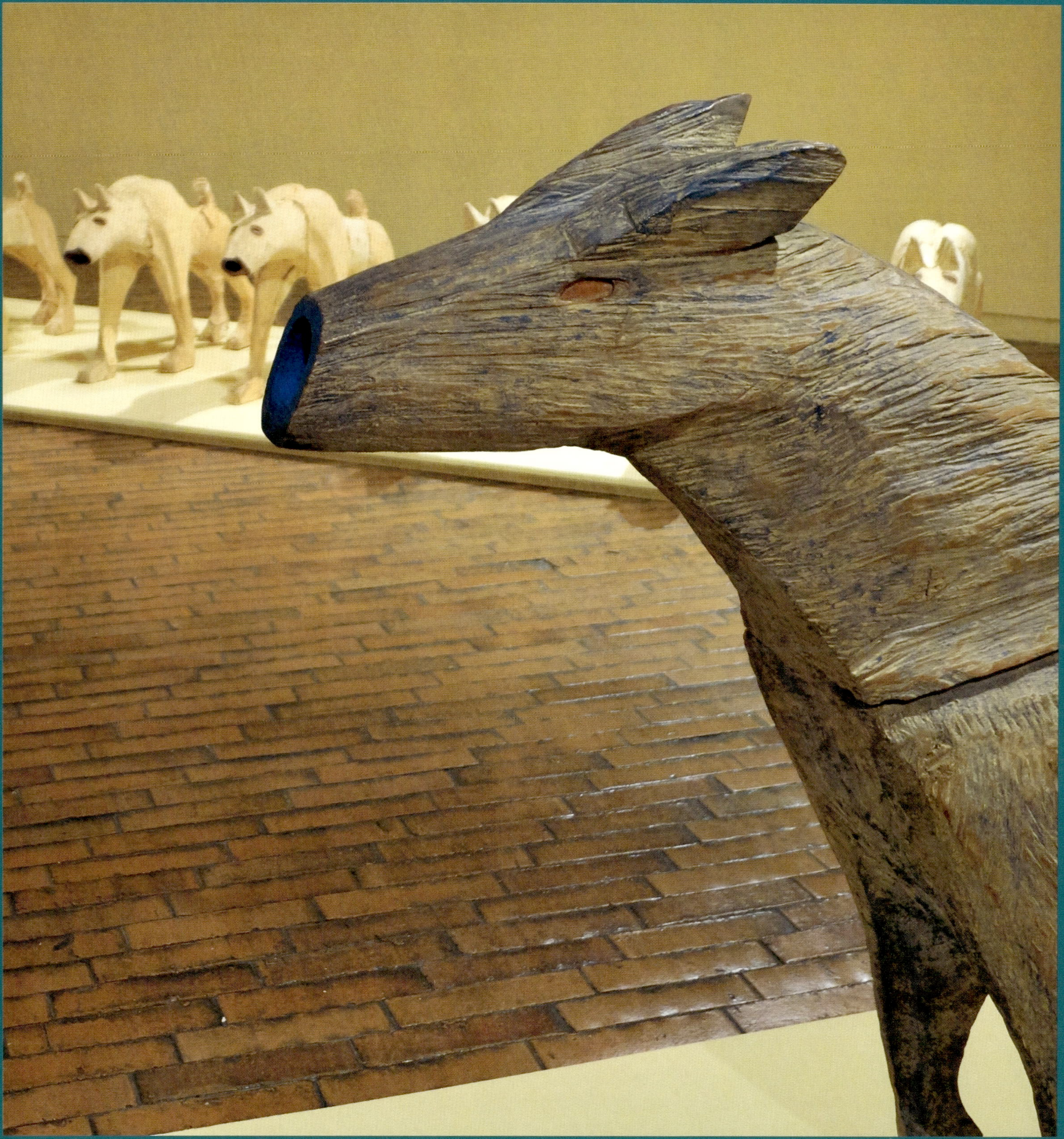

Encounters

Brighton leads the way as a top destination for affordable artworks bought directly from the creators and makers themselves.

Artists Open Houses

If you love art – and meeting artists face to face – then cancel all other activities in May because Brighton is the only place to be. Every weekend during the Brighton Festival month, artists and makers open up their houses and studios for the annual Artists Open Houses (AOH) event.

It's a phenomenon that started back in 1982, when RCA-trained artist Ned Hoskins filled his Hollingbury Road home with an exhibition of like-minded artists working in a wide range of media, originally stimulated by an interest in natural forms. The attention the originality of his enterprise attracted was astounding. Year by year his fellow artists and neighbours joined in until by 1989 four other houses had opened and Five at Fiveways was born.

In an era when the only art most people had access to were Athena posters or a framed print from Boots, the Fiveways artists revolutionised the way people could view and acquire art. People who might never set foot in a gallery could suddenly become critics, buyers and hopefully collectors.

More than three decades later, there are now 14 trails covering most of the city as well as a variety of independent venues. A brochure and map are produced by AOH, to guide you through the amazing range of art that's on show – jewellery, ceramics, textiles, paintings, sculpture, printmaking, photography and many other media – with the opportunity to chat directly with the artists. There's also now a second AOH event in the run up to Christmas.

Brighton Art Fair & MADE

Local artists Jon Tutton and Sarah Young became 'accidental event organisers' when – frustrated by the lack of opportunities for showing and selling work in Brighton – they launched the Brighton Art Fair (page 149) in 2003. This first show at the Corn Exchange was a sell-out, with visitors round the corner queuing in the sleet to come in... And since then the city's annual September art fest has gone from strength to strength.

The show doesn't adhere to any particular selection criteria. Jon and Sarah just look for honesty, enjoyment, skill, enthusiasm and originality – and not necessarily all at once. They maintain a balance between artists who have shown many times, and whose work has changed and developed over the years (or not), and new artists exhibiting for the first time. There is usually about a third of new artists each year and many who have only exhibited once or twice before.

The success of the Brighton Art Fair led to Jon and Sarah organising a second annual creative showcase for the city. Also at the Corn Exchange, MADE Design and Craft Fair (page 148) brings together more than 100 contemporary designer makers across all media. From colourful glassware to the softest knitted textiles, elegant ceramics to dazzling jewellery, and luxurious leather to quirky accessories, there is something for everyone. It's held in November – so the perfect place to find truly unique Christmas presents too.

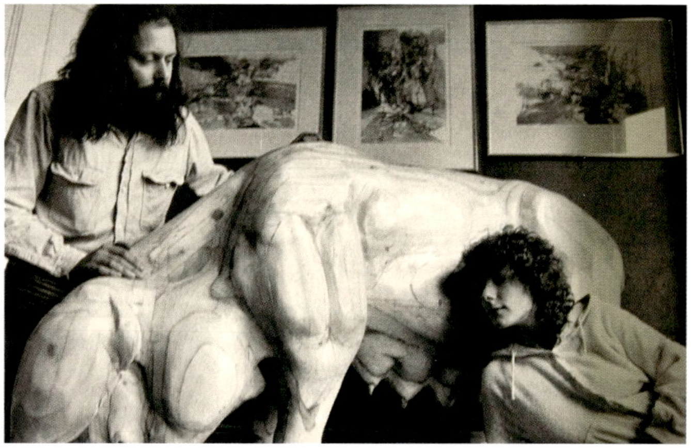

Nicholas Johnson's 'Pig' featured in the first exhibition organised by Ned Hoskins

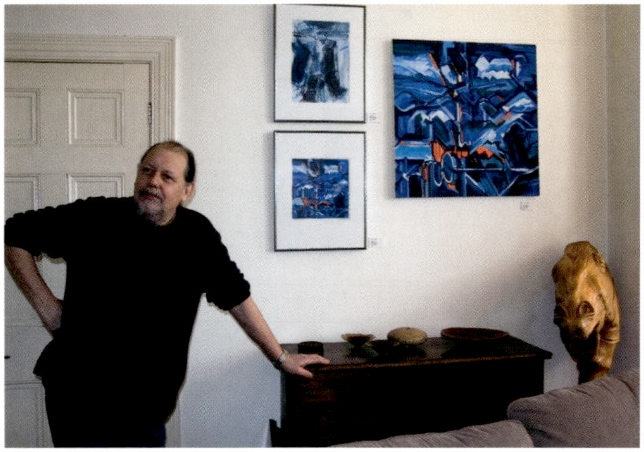

Ned Hoskins

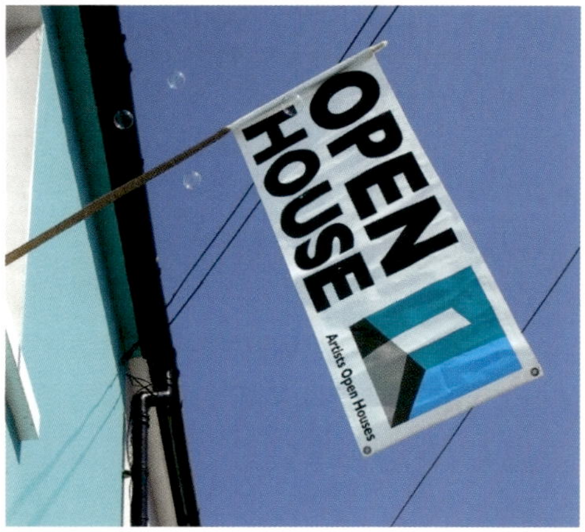

Artists Open Houses

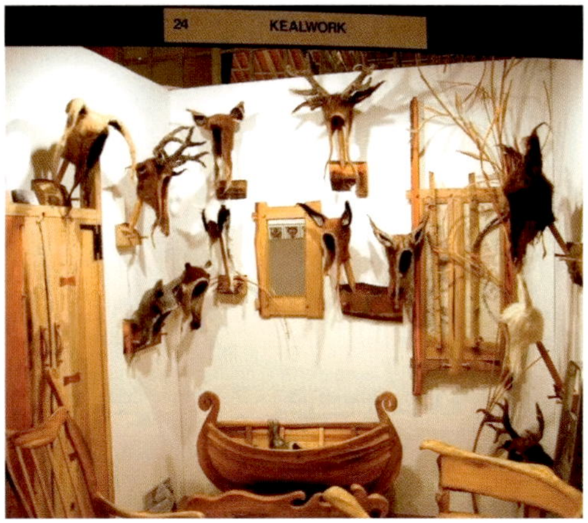

MADE Design & Craft Fair

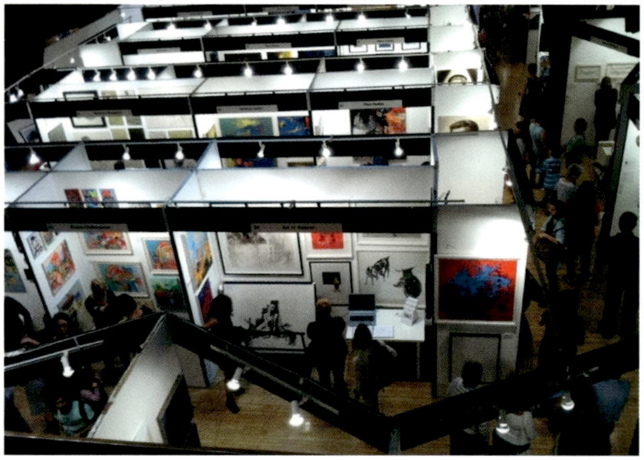

Brighton Art Fair

Clockwise from top left: Ruben Dario Monsalve; Gaudi Este; Stefan Mildenberger; Installation by Miladys Parejo; Cristobal Ochoa; Lior Hod; Jewellery by Carlos Sanchez

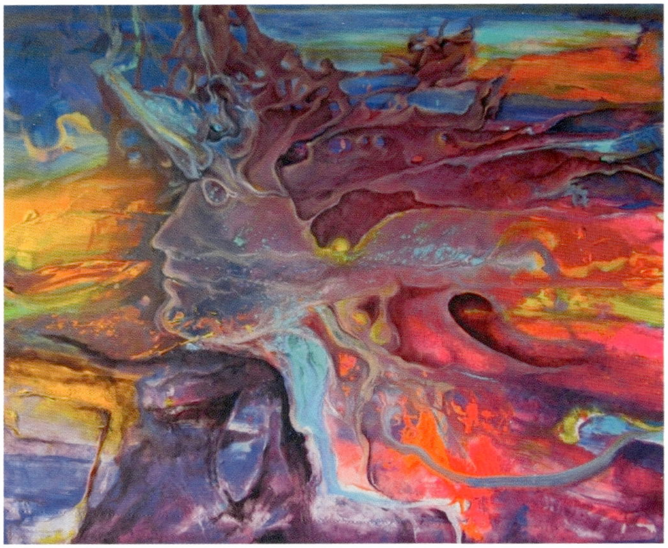

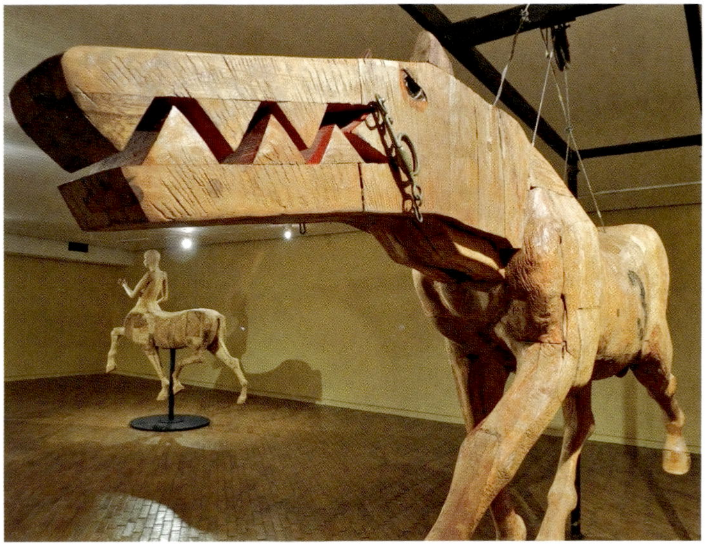

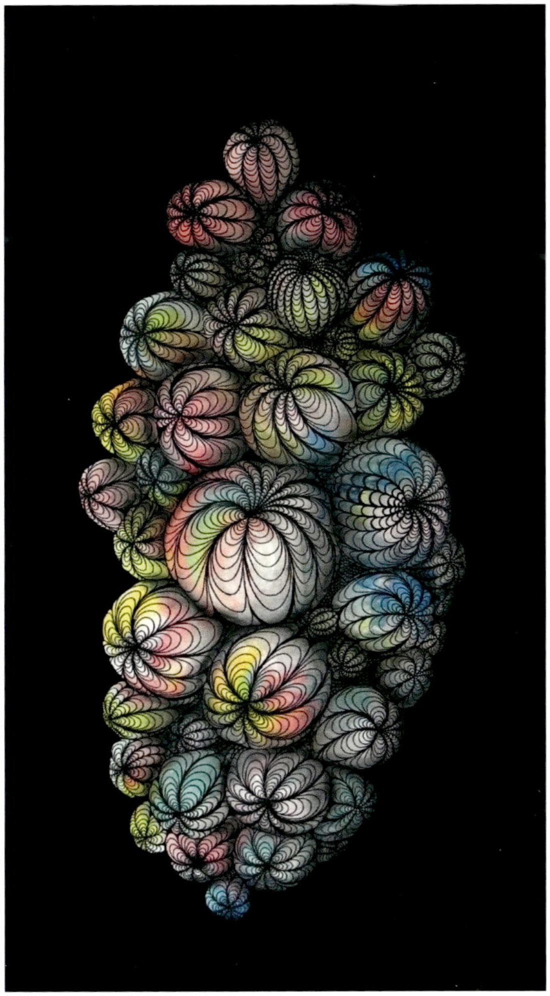

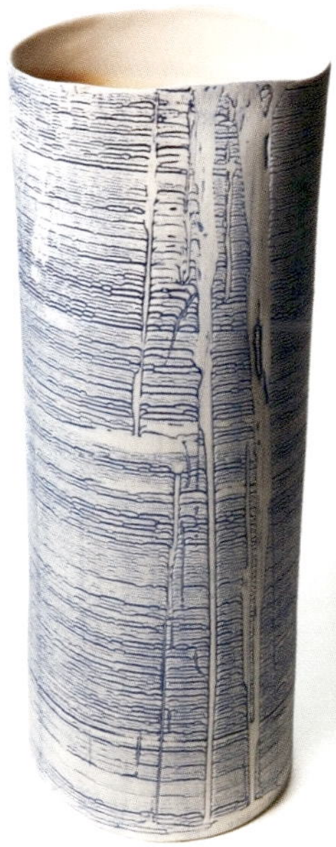

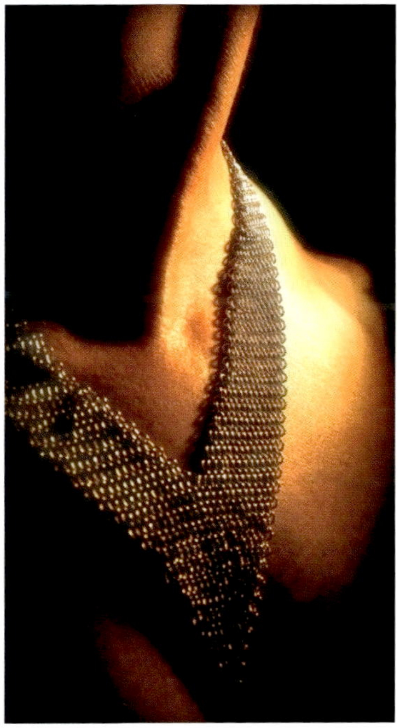

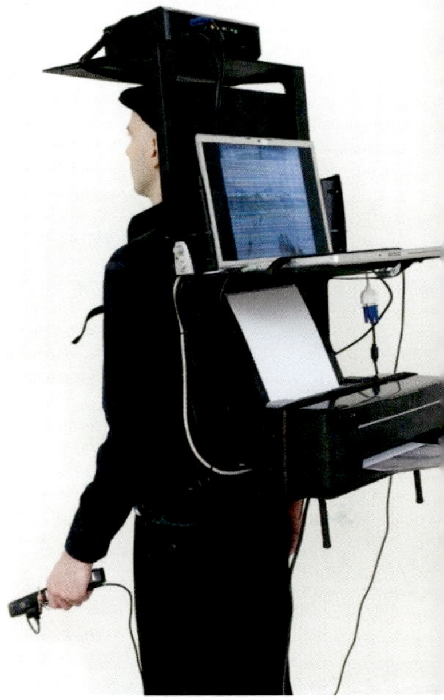

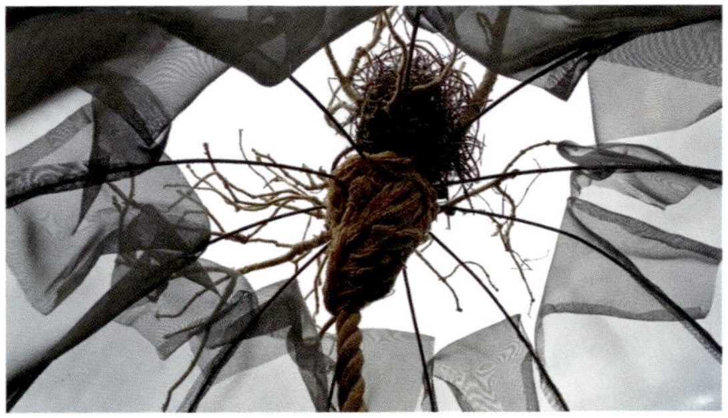

Encounters' combination of dynamic exhibitions, exciting new work, diverse media and interactive shows is a not-to-be-missed destination during Brighton's Festival season.

This year Encounters celebrates five years of success.
2012 Awarded prize as Best Open House
2013 In the top three Open Houses
2014 Celebrating its fifth anniversary with a retrospective show

Encounters opens each May and promotes its artists internationally throughout the year.

MADE BRIGHTON

21-23 November 2014, The Corn Exchange at The Dome, Church Street, BN1 1UG

Clockwise from top left: Mercury Table, Justin O'Brien; Willow Neck Bag, Tammy Child; MADE 2013

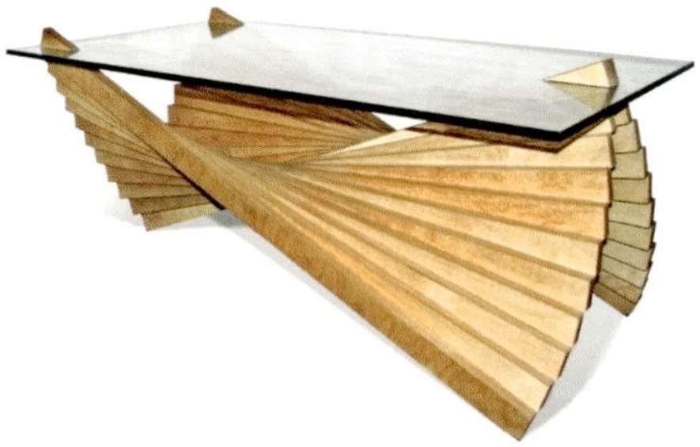

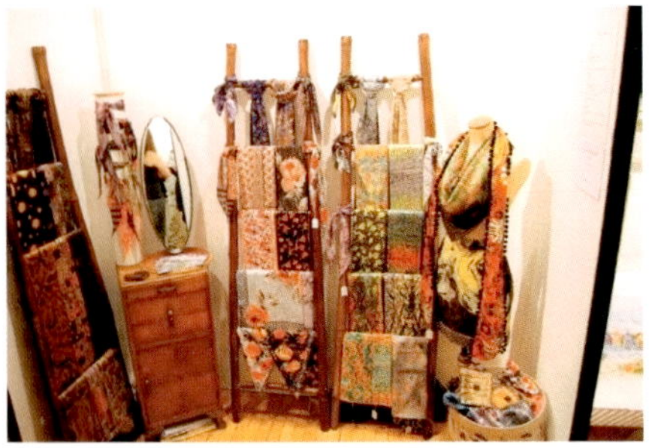

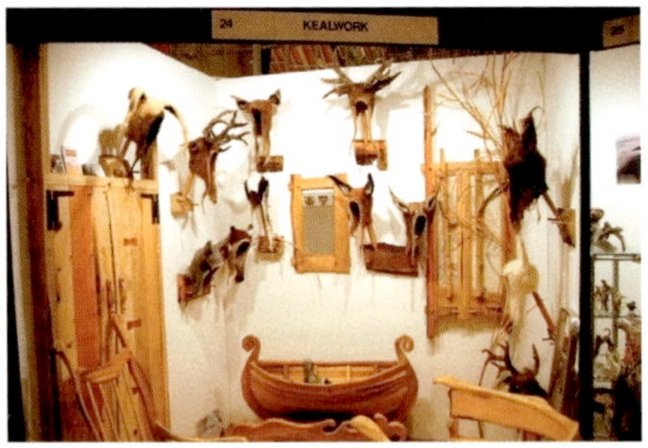

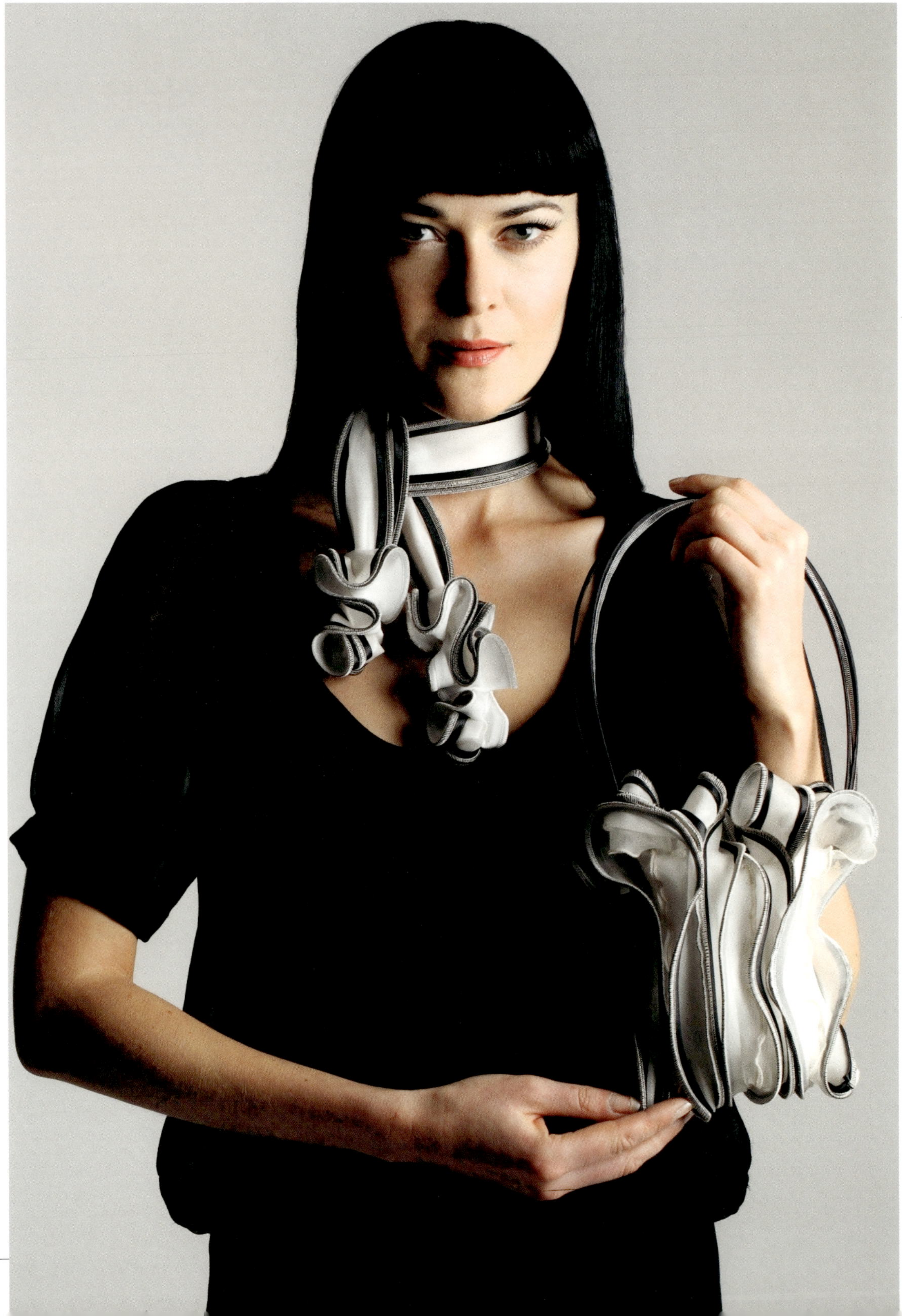

MADE BRIGHTON is the city's annual contemporary craft and design fair, which takes place in the beautiful Corn Exchange at The Dome. Now in its 9th year, the fair offers the public the opportunity to buy original and exceptional pieces of craft and design direct from the best local and national makers, and has become firmly established as a friendly, accessible and top quality event. More than 5,500 visitors attend – the majority of whom return year on year knowing that the work on show won't disappoint.

MADE BRIGHTON showcases jewellery, textiles, ceramics, basketry, glassware, furniture, home accessories, fashion and much more. All the work is hand-crafted, unique and often quirky.

A café provides a place for visitors to relax and take refreshment. With so much work to see, many people like to make a day of it, spending the morning viewing work, stopping for a bite to eat, then returning to continue shopping. It's wonderful!

Clockwise from top left: Brighton Art Fair 2013; Yellow Birds, Maddy McClellan; Main Square, Sam Hewitt

Brighton Art Fair

26-28 September 2014, The Corn Exchange at the Dome, Church Street, Brighton BN1 1UG

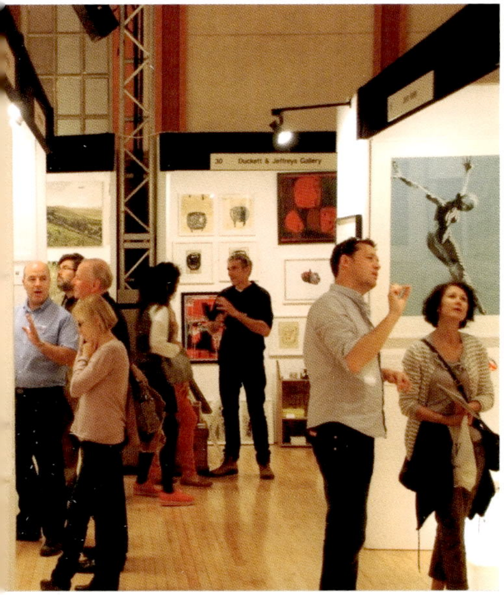

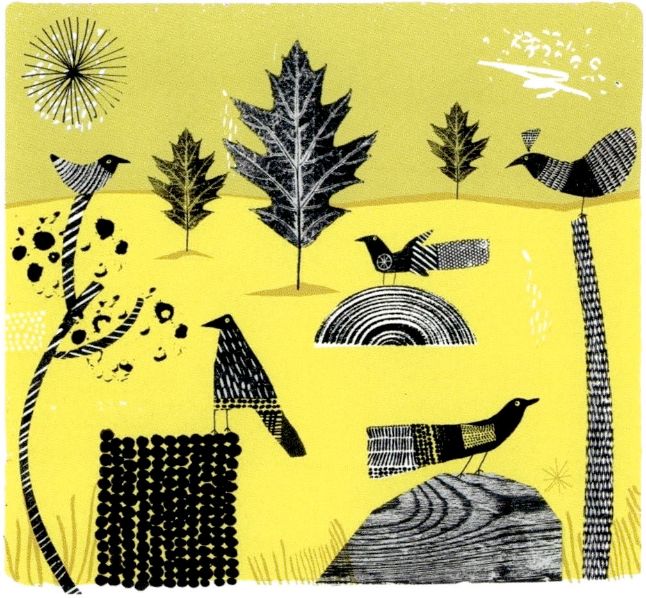

Brighton Art Fair brings together more than 100 of the best contemporary artists from the UK and abroad, some of whom have exhibited before, some of whom are brand new to the event. The Fair always promotes a good balance of established and emerging artists, and insists that all work is exciting, fresh and exceptional. This is what keeps Brighton Art Fair's strong reputation as one of the must-see visual arts events on the south coast.

Painters, printmakers, ceramicists, photographers and sculptors exhibit, with the most original and eclectic work across as wide a variety of methods and subjects as possible. Artists themselves sell their work direct to the public, bringing a personal feel to viewing and to the buying process. The show welcomes more than 5,000 visitors each year: buyers, collectors, galleries and curators – many of whom return year on year. Artworks are shown in the majestic and historic Corn Exchange in the heart of the city, in a relaxed, informal and friendly environment. A café provides space to take refreshment and contemplate work.

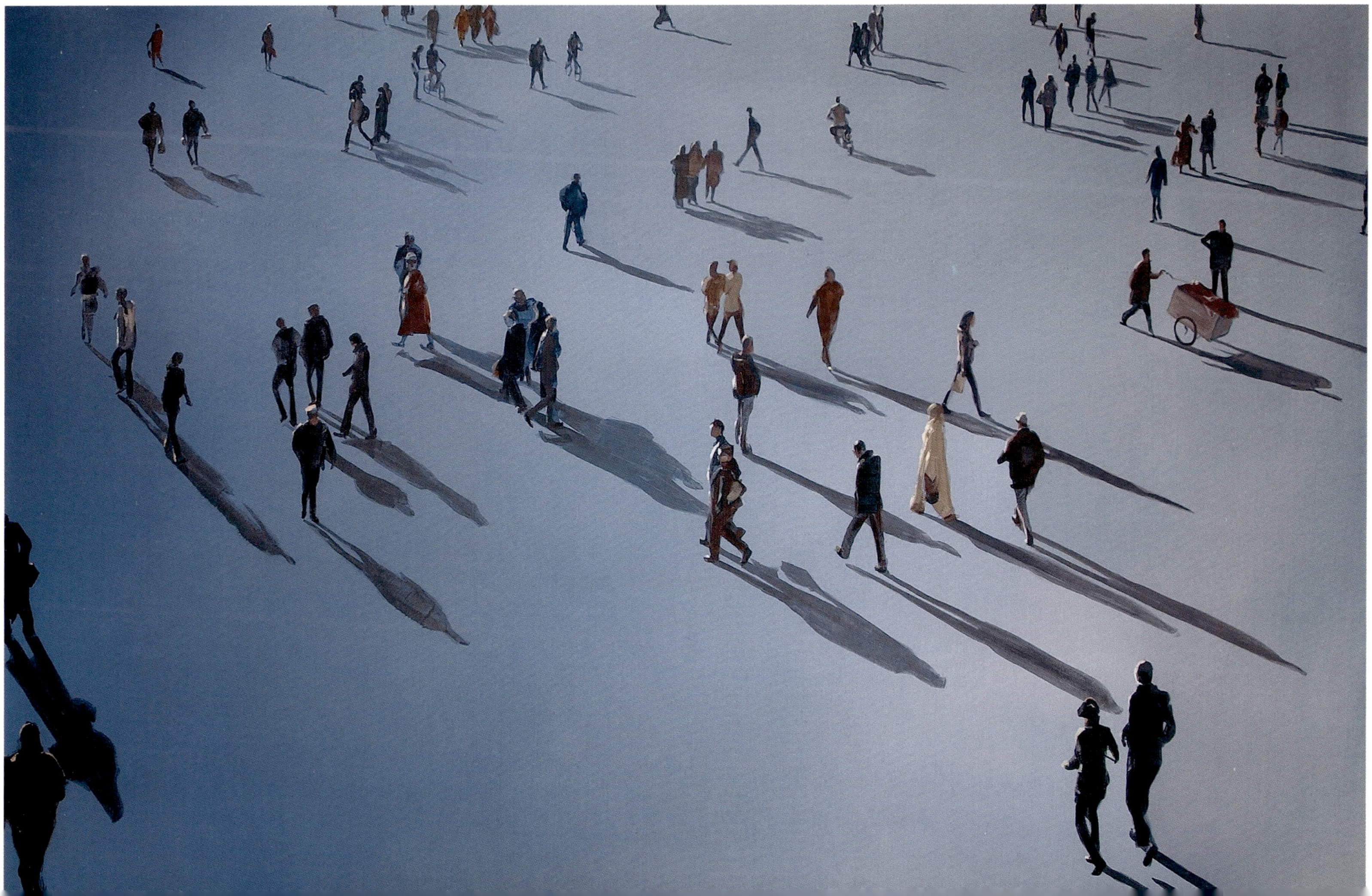

Index

Please get in contact with us

Adam Regester 007
www.adamregester.com
adamregester@gmail.com
07775 432016

Alexander Johnson 062
www.alexander-johnson.com
alexart63@yahoo.co.uk
07913 540323

Alison McGechie 094
www.alisonmcgechie.com
alettedarcy@hotmail.com
Brighton Open Market Studios

Amanda Davidson 108
amandasdavidson@gmail.com
07763 584330

Angela Collier 044
www.angelacollier.com
angelacollier1@sky.com
07801 017490

Angela Newman 077
www.missnewman.com
missnewman.art@hotmail.com
07971 225184

Angie Meaden-Bonnel 089
www.artymagazines.com
angiemeadenbonnel@icloud.com
07756 946281

Art5 Gallery 127
www.art5gallery.com
info@art5gallery.com
01273 774222

Auricula 102
www.auricula.co.uk
natasha@auricula.co.uk
01273 845582

Bellis Gallery 132
8-9 Kings Road, BN1 1NE
Open 10.30am - 6.30pm
01273 747429

Betty Shek 054
www.facebook.com/
BettyAndFriendsArtistsOpenHouse
bettywcshek@yahoo.co.uk

Brighton Art Fair 149
www.brightonartfair.co.uk
info@brightonartfair.co.uk
01903 608757

Caia Matheson 065
www.caia.co.uk
www.saatchiart.com/caia
twitter.com/CaiaMatheson

Chalk Gallery 136
www.chalkgallerylewes.co.uk
chalkgallery@btconnect.com
01273 474477

Chanchala Ariyaratne 064
www.chanchala.co.uk
chanchala@hotmail.co.uk
www.facebook.com/ByChanchala

Chris Hawkins 020
www.chrishawkinsjewellery.com
chris@chrishawkinsjewellery.com
01273 554632

Chris MacDonald 045
www.chrismacdonald.eu
art@chrismacdonald.eu
07941 445470

Christina Fedyk 107
www.christinafedyk.com
christina.fedyk@ntlworld.com
07806 806577

Claire Fearon 056
www.clairefearon.com
claire@clairefearon.com
07872 530 598

David Moore 069
www.phoenixbrighton.org
davidscottmoore.wordpress.com
davemoore99@hotmail.co.uk

Dawn Stacey 090
www.dawnstacey.co.uk
dstacey50@btopenworld.com
01273 483460

Diane Rogers 114
www.dianerogers.co.uk
dianerogers@email.com
07901 898727

Dinah Dufton 082
www.dinahspace.com
dinahspace@gmail.com

Emma Troy 066
www.emmatroy.net
hello@emmatroy.net
07788 412389

Encounters Open House 147
www.encounters.org.uk
Twitter @encountersAOH
01273 734311

Eve Poland 059
www.evepoland.com
mail@evepoland.com
07818 417 935

Firb 097
www.wolfandpigeon.co.uk
mikey@wolfandpigeon.co.uk
07888 731100

Firefly Studios 021
www.chrishawkinsjewellery.com
chris@chrishawkinsjewellery.com
01273 554632

FOX 071
www.salutehq.com
www.raphaelfox.com
salutehq@gmail.com

Frances Bloomfield 022
www.francesbloomfield.com
f.bloomfield@btinternet.com
07515 122860

Francesca Grace McLeod 110
www.francescamcleod.co.uk
mcleodfrancesca@gmail.com
07756 250333

Gallery40 126
www.gallery40.co.uk
info@gallery40.co.uk
07810 204663

Geoff Hands 052
www.geoffhands.co.uk
geoff.hands@btopenworld.com
01273 502451

The Gilded Cage Tattoo Studio 070
www.gildedcagetattoostudio.com
gildedcagetattoostudio@gmail.com
01273 933420

Graeme Richardson-Locke 058
www.eye4colourprints.com
info@eye4colourprints.com
01273 732301

Harriet Butler 106
www.harrietbutler.com
harriet@butlerarts.co.uk
07966 399650

Heidi Jane Rhodes 055
www.heidirhodestextiles.com
heidi.jane@tiscali.co.uk
07979 960807

Heike Roesel 038
www.heikeroesel.co.uk
info@heikeroesel.co.uk
@HeikeB5 on twitter

Hiroko Lewis 011
www.hirokoart.co.uk
happyhiroko@gmail.com

Hop Gallery 130
www.hopgallery.com
info@hopgallery.com
01273 487744

Ian Hodgson 019
www.ian-hodgson.co.uk
ian@ian-hodgson.co.uk
07796 331764

Ilana Richardson 072
www.ilana-richardson.com
art@ilana-richardson.com
01273 726464 / 07947 327690

Ink Spot Press 017
www.inkspotpress.co.uk
info@inkspotpress.co.uk
01273 691496

iO Gallery 124
www.iogallery.co.uk
www.facebook.com/iogallery
info@iogallery.co.uk

Jacqueline Hammond 013
www.jacquelinehammond.co.uk
jaxxhammond@aol.com
07977 486603

Jan Irvine 051
www.janirvine.com
info@janirvine.com
01273 748058 / 07748 046847

Jane Sampson 016
www.janesampson.com
www.inkspotpress.co.uk
info@inkspotpress.co.uk

Janet Brooke 039
www.janetbrooke.com
mail@janetbrooke.com
07943 577271

Jay Collins 023
www.kemptownartistsgallery.com
j.collins759@btinternet.com
01273 604141

Jessica Barrah 036
www.jessicabarrah.com
jessicabarrah@yahoo.co.uk
01273417215 / 07967477618

Jessica Zoob 074
www.jessicazoob.com
jessica@jessicazoob.com
07966 572204

Jill Tattersall 014
www.jilltattersall.co.uk
jill@jilltattersall.co.uk
www.facebook.com/JillTattersallartist

Jo Riddell 010
www. joriddell.net
cjriddell50@gmail.com
07990 510380

Jo Watters-Pawlowski 101
www.jowatterspawlowski.com
jowp.ditchling@hotmail.co.uk
07926 082354

Junkfunk 142
www.junkfunk.com
info@junkfunk.com
01273 680555

Karl Smith 076
www.carvedoak.co.uk
karl@carvedoak.co.uk
07717 740206

Kate Osborne 028
www.kateosborneart.com
kate@kateosborneart.com
01273 875126 / 07787 515714

Katja Dell 100
www.katjadell.com
katjadell@hotmail.com
07776 094267

Kellie Miller 060
www.kelliemiller.com
info@kelliemiller.com
07803 589059

Leila Godden 018
www.leilagodden.com
leila.godden@btinternet.com
07837 965887

Linsay Oliver 086
www.LinsayOliver.com
linsay@email.com
07970 140484

Lisa Ridgers 084
www.lisaridgers.com
www.lisaridgers.co.uk
07427 668700

Lizzie Thomas 068
www.lizziethomas.co.uk
lizzie@lizziethomas.co.uk
07535 558700

Louisa Crispin 088
www.louisacrispinart.co.uk
louisacrispin@btinternet.com
07708 148413

Louise Dear 119
www.louisedear.com
louise@louisedear.com
07900 117430

Luella Martin 046
www.luellamartin.co.uk
mail@luemartin.co.uk
07986 938751

MADE BRIGHTON 148
www.brighton-made.co.uk
info@brighton-made.co.uk
01903 608757

Marga Beuth 103
www.sepalia.com
Facebook & Twitter: Sepalia Symbols
07570 771197

Mark Charlton 008
www.markcharltonart.com
mark@markcharltonart.com
07791 260765

Mark Glassman 048
www.markglassman.org.uk
glassmarky19@gmail.com
01323 899296

Mark Oliver 087
www.TheLitterBug.com
mark@olly.net
07804 193 541

Min Cooper 093
www.mincooperprints.co.uk
info@mincooperprints.co.uk
07904 801528

Monika Jakimauskaite 037
www.moniusia.eu
moniusia@ymail.com
07540 648108

New Steine Hotel 133
www.newsteinehotel.com
reservation@newsteinehotel.com
01273 681546

Nicole Carman 083
www.brightonandhovephotos.com
nicolecarman@gmail.com
07545 271677

The Omnia Scroll Exhibitions 081
www.omniascroll.com
omniascroll@gmail.com
01323 423627

Paul Martin 040
www.martinstudios.co.uk
paul@martinstudios.co.uk
01903 248121

Penelope Oakley 080
www.penelopeoakley.org
oakleypenelope@gmail.com
07887 670785

The Private Press 050
theprivatepress.org
hello@theprivatepress.org
07973 140202

Richard Denne 112
www.richarddenne.com
info@richarddenne.com
07976 708075

Rick Fullwood 024
www.rickfullwood.com
info@rickfullwood.com
07761 953263

Rob Ollerenshaw 012
www.artymagazines.com
rob.ollerenshaw@btopenworld.com
01273 748338

Robin Cooper-Hannan 079
www.robincooperhannan.com
r.cooperhannan@btinternet.com
07910 153517

Romany Mark Bruce 033
www.romanymarkbruce.com
romanymb@mac.com
07799 600908

rubandagar 078
www.rubandagarart.com
rubandagar@gmail.com
Facebook.com/Rubandagarart

Sarah Jane Whittaker 115
www.sjwjewellery.com
sjwjewellery@gmail.com
07939 696465

Sarah Shaw 104
www.sarahshaw.co.uk
www.ink-d.co.uk
info@sarahshaw.co.uk

Sheila Marlborough 006
www.sheilamarlborough.co.uk
spmarlborough@aol.com
01444 246605

Simon Royer 116
www.simonroyerpaintings.com
royerpaintings@hotmail.com
07970 881848

Sophie Abbott 027
www.sophieabbott.net
sophieartist@hotmail.co.uk
07745 834066

Stephanie Else 026
www.glassinfusion.co.uk
info@glassinfusion.co.uk
07887 975818

Steve Carroll 092
www.stevecarrollssussex.com
stevecarroll3@me.com
07786 034580

Stuart Dodman 030
www.stuartdodman.com
stuartdodman@gmail.com

Sue Collins 096
www.suecollinsart.com
suecollins9@hotmail.com
07756 420794

Susan Taylor 042
www.susan-taylor.co.uk
info@susan-taylor.co.uk
07530 672888

Suzanne Breakwell 047
www.suzannebreakwell.com
info@suzannebreakwell.com
07881 957056

Torben Krog 118
www.artymagazines.com
torben@artymagazines.com
07768 638115

Unlimited 134
www.unlimitedshop.co.uk
facebook.com/weareunlimited
01273 204423

Veronica van Eijk 029
www.vaneijkarts.com
vaneijkarts@gmail.com
07740 104501

Vincent Donlin 034
www.vincentdonlin.co.uk
vincent1311@btinternet.com
07738 981805

Viv Martin 098
www.martinstudios.co.uk
viv@martinstudios.co.uk
01903 248121

Wendy Standen 043
www.wendystanden.co.uk
wstandenart@gmail.com
01273 504588

Xavi Dom Buendia 032
www.xdbphotography.com
xdbphotography@gmail.com
Facebook/Twitter@XDBPhotography

Zimmer Stewart Gallery 128
www.zimmerstewart.co.uk
james@zimmerstewart.co.uk
01903 882063

*"There is a phrase: 'the sweet smell of success'.
And I can only tell you, I've had two experiences of that
and it just smells like Brighton and oyster bars and things like that."*

Laurence Olivier